GOSSIP MEN

GOSSIP MEN

J. EDGAR HOOVER,
JOE MCCARTHY,
ROY COHN, AND
THE POLITICS
OF INSINUATION

CHRISTOPHER M. ELIAS

The University of Chicago Press
Chicago and London

The University of Chicago Press, Chicago 60637
The University of Chicago Press, Ltd., London
© 2021 by The University of Chicago
Published 2021
Printed in the United States of America

30 29 28 27 26 25 24 23 22 21   1 2 3 4 5

ISBN-13: 978-0-226-62482-2 (cloth)
ISBN-13: 978-0-226-75152-8 (e-book)
DOI: https://doi.org/10.7208/chicago/9780226751528.001.0001

Library of Congress Cataloging-in-Publication Data

Names: Elias, Christopher M., author.
Title: Gossip men : J. Edgar Hoover, Joe McCarthy,
Roy Cohn, and the politics of insinuation /
Christopher M. Elias.
Other titles: J. Edgar Hoover, Joe McCarthy, Roy
Cohn, and the politics of insinuation
Description: Chicago ; London : The University
of Chicago Press, 2021. | Includes bibliographical
references and index.
Identifiers: LCCN 2020037898 | ISBN 9780226624822
(cloth) | ISBN 9780226751528 (ebook)
Subjects: LCSH: Hoover, J. Edgar (John Edgar), 1895–
1972. | McCarthy, Joseph, 1908–1957. | Cohn, Roy M. |
Politics and culture—United States. | Gossip—United
States—History—20th century. | Gossip—Political
aspects—United States. | Masculinity—United States—
History—20th century. | Masculinity—Political
aspects—United States. | United States—Biography. |
United States—Civilization—20th century.
Classification: LCC E747 .E43 2021 |
DDC 306.20973/0904—dc23
LC record available at https://lccn.loc
.gov/2020037898

♾ This paper meets the requirements of ANSI/NISO
Z39.48-1992 (Permanence of Paper).

For my mother.

There is gossip and, in perhaps its most elevated form, there is history. The distinction between the two may not be so hard and fast as we might suppose.

ROBERT WERNICK

CONTENTS

INTRODUCTION

The hearing room was sweating. Though the weather was mild—partly cloudy with a high of seventy-four degrees—the temperature inside the Senate Caucus Room kept climbing steadily. An ornate space designed for three hundred occupants, on this day it was packed with eight hundred; even congressmen were sometimes escorted out by apologetic Capitol policemen who cited fire codes. Klieg lights and television cameras cramped the chamber even further, and the heat from the bulbs pushed the temperature higher. But any discomfort felt by those in attendance was secondary to the need to broadcast the hearings to the twenty million people watching on television.[1]

The hearings became the most-watched live event in television's infant history, offering a clear look at the phenomenon already known as "McCarthyism," referring both to Wisconsin Senator Joseph R. McCarthy's campaign against communist subversives in the federal government and his controversial tactics.[2] For over four years McCarthy had mesmerized the nation and attracted millions of fawning supporters. He had created a serial drama that promised glimpses into the clandestine operations and backroom dealings of the era's most pressing geopolitical concern, the fight against communism. Since the end of World War II the United States

FIGURE 1. Television cameras stand at the ready during the Army-McCarthy hearings.
Credit: Erich Hartmann, Magnum Photos.

had been gripped by fears that the Soviet Union and the global communist movement were conspiring to destroy Western-style capitalism and democracy. That threat required constant vigilance against domestic subversion, and McCarthy's rapid rise to power had largely been fueled by his promise to protect the nation.

But McCarthy and his crusade were deeply controversial. Critics accused him of trampling individual liberties, attacking innocent federal employees, flouting civil discourse, and fabricating evidence. Even members of his own party spoke out against McCarthy, charging him with promoting "a national feeling of fear and frustration that could result in national suicide and the end of everything that we Americans hold dear."[3]

Now McCarthyism faced its most substantial test. The US Army had accused McCarthy and his top aide Roy M. Cohn of seeking preferential treatment for G. David Schine, a recently drafted private who was both a McCarthy staffer and Cohn's close friend. In turn, McCarthy and Cohn charged that the Army was using Schine's draft status to thwart McCarthy's investigation of both communists and homosexuals in its ranks. The former were cast as sworn enemies of the American experiment, the latter as deviant fellow travelers who were inherently subversive.

As the Caucus Room filled on the afternoon of April 30, questioning turned to a photograph McCarthy had presented to support his case. Special Counsel for the Army Joseph Nye Welch noted that the image had been cropped, and he wondered aloud where the photograph had originated and who had ordered the doctoring. On the stand sat a perspiring Jim Juliana, the McCarthy assistant who had prepared the print, pudgy-faced and dressed in a baggy suit. After Juliana repeatedly pled ignorance, Welch asked whether he thought the photograph "came from a pixie."

Welch's sarcasm was characteristic. But this comment cut more deeply than previous barbs, and the audience's light laughter at it was mixed with guffaws of deeper understanding. For many months both McCarthy and Cohn had been hounded by rumors that they themselves were homosexuals, and were perhaps intent on securing preferential treatment for Schine because one (or both) of them was having an affair with him. Keenly aware of the large audience and hoping to parry Welch's attack, McCarthy asked Welch to define the term "pixie," suggesting that Welch was possibly an expert on the subject. Welch replied that a "pixie is a close relative of a fairy" and asked if that "enlightened" McCarthy.[4] As the audience burst into even greater laughter, the television feed cut from a view of the entire Caucus Room to tighter shots of Welch, McCarthy, and those seated with them. Viewers could see the senator chuckle and roll his eyes knowingly. Next to him Cohn, just twenty-seven but with heavy bags under his eyes, tried to smile, but a look of frustration washed over him. He shifted nervously, his shoulders slumped, and he dropped his gaze to the table, or possibly to his hands.

*

The Army-McCarthy hearings have long been seen as a critical juncture in postwar American politics, a moment when McCarthy and his strident, often baseless accusations were cut down in an instant of national conscience epitomized by the famous rhetorical question Welch asked McCarthy toward the end of the hearings: "Have you no sense of decency, sir?" But that story can obscure another, equally striking one that is visible in the homoerotic language of the pixie-fairy exchange. Since the end of World War I, American politics had been deeply influenced by a new political identity, which I call "surveillance state masculinity." It emerged from three dynamics that had been percolating since the late nineteenth century: a revolution in how male identities were developed and expressed, a shift in the way Americans thought about media and information, and a transformation in how the federal government approached national security. Those changes deeply altered the relationship between the public and its leaders, influencing how political figures are measured, the values they

FIGURE 2. McCarthy and Cohn cover microphones to ensure their private communications are not broadcast during the Army-McCarthy hearings. Credit: Getty Images.

espouse, and the way they communicate with the American people. In defining and exploring this political identity, this book examines how issues of gender, sexuality, gossip, and the national surveillance and security states intersected between approximately 1885 and 1954, with a particular focus on the first decade of the Cold War.[5]

Though McCarthy and Cohn came to embody and perfect surveillance state masculinity, the godfather of that political identity was FBI Director J. Edgar Hoover. Arguably the most influential American bureaucrat of the twentieth century, Hoover was essential to the creation of the national surveillance and security states, as well as the first major political figure to fully realize the possibilities of modern mass media. He used masculinity—both his own and that of his agents—as a vehicle to achieve his personal, professional, and ideological goals. McCarthy, combining roughneck masculinity and fervent anticommunism, built on Hoover's foundation as he seized the national spotlight. Cohn took Hoover and McCarthy's masculinist strategies to their logical ends, using secrecy, manipulation, and misinformation to secure influence—and inspire a new generation of leaders to do the same.

Hoover, McCarthy, and Cohn all rose to power by taking advantage of political anxieties over changing gender roles, communist infiltration, shifting social mores, and perceived increases in criminality. Each conspicuously performed his masculinity, even while being hounded by rumors and insinuations that he was "queer" or a "sissy," and thus insufficiently manly to guard the country's moral well-being and ensure its security.[6] These rumors spread through a growing industry in political gossip, which purported to traffic in "national intelligence." Indeed, gossip—spread through syndicated newspaper columns, wildly popular magazines, and word of mouth—became a means to express, discuss, and negotiate concerns about national security, gender roles, and sexual identity.

Those overlapping anxieties fostered a specific form of masculine identity that came to dominate American politics by the middle of the twentieth century. Its hallmarks can be seen in the maneuvers individuals made in navigating its expectations. For instance, why did Hoover continually mislead the press about his physical attributes? Why did McCarthy stress his roughneck manliness while on the campaign trail? Why did Cohn actively seek to have his name associated with starlets in gossip columns? The answers to these questions help illuminate how individuals negotiated the gendered valences of political culture during—and ultimately in relationship to—the founding, expansion, and codification of the emerging national surveillance and security states.

That context gave rise to a collection of characteristics that observers used to determine a man's fitness for leading and defending the national security state. Such a man had to be aggressive, in control, unapologetic, informed, professional, competitive, deliberate, and unquestionably heterosexual. It was a political identity born at the intersection of two sets of anxieties: those about national security and those about the rise of "consumerist masculinity."[7] More a style than an ideology, this kind of masculinity was embodied by a variety of bureaucrats and politicians.[8] Hoover, McCarthy, Cohn, and others sought to project its central components—including "hard masculine toughness"—to demonstrate their fitness for protecting America.[9]

Studying these three men can help us understand long-term developments in politics, gender, and sexuality.[10] Examining how Hoover, McCarthy, and Cohn—both as national figures and private individuals—negotiated the expectations of their times can illuminate those expectations and the institutions that gave them force.[11] Gossip—the public circulation of information that interested parties would prefer remain private—played a particularly central role in this process, binding security state politics and gendered identity. Gossip and innuendo have influenced American politics since the nation's founding, but the 1885–1954 era (especially 1945–54) was transformative for a number of reasons. First, it featured a growing gossip industry (tabloids, magazines, and columnists) with increased social and political influence—ironically a product of the Progressive-era professionalization of journalism. Until around the turn of the twentieth century, many news outlets explicitly tied themselves to one political party or faction; afterward, they became purportedly objective enterprises dedicated to exposing hidden "truths" about society, politics, and culture. Rumors became more powerful partially because they could not be immediately dismissed as the productions of biased parties. Second, gossip's influence grew alongside the birth of "celebrity." In the first half of the twentieth century, Americans came to think differently about public personalities, becoming more deeply interested in the private lives of movie stars, popular musicians, sports heroes, and politicians and coming to believe that private actions would determine public ones.[12] Finally, gossip's expansion was fueled by the Cold War and the Second Red Scare, which popularized narratives of "secrecy" and "national intelligence." Information once derided as idle talk became a matter of national security: a man having sex with other men was not merely perverted but also someone who was both exposing himself to blackmail and undermining the nation's moral fabric.

Thus, Hoover's, McCarthy's, and Cohn's use of gossip in national security was intertwined with a revolution in the content, accuracy, prevalence, and dissemination of gossip generally. Columnists such as Walter Winchell and magazines like *Confidential* used rumor and insinuation to combine the personal and the political, defining bureaucrats and politicians as much by their changeable personalities as by their seemingly fixed character. Fueled by the building up and tearing down of reputations and personalities, the gossip industry resonated with deeper trends in how Americans were thinking about what identities were and how they came to be.[13]

Surveillance state masculinity shaped both the national security and surveillance states, as well as American political culture more broadly. It arose amid anxieties accompanying America's emergence on the global stage, a new emphasis on the significance of "intelligence," and a shifting media landscape featuring pervasive gossip, tabloid journalism, national radio personalities, and, ultimately, live television coverage. And it became dominant because it helped pacify those worries.

But Hoover, McCarthy, and Cohn did not embody surveillance state masculinity merely because it answered the questions dominating American politics at the moment they sought power. They also needed to hide what were seen as their masculine deficiencies. In a time of deep anxiety, they too were driven by fear.

*

This story emerges at the crossroads of three historical developments: the creation of the national surveillance and security states; a revolution in gender and sexual politics; and the emergence of gossip as a key element of American politics and society. Understanding the history of all three is essential to appreciating the revolutionary nature of what Hoover, McCarthy, and Cohn did.

The advent of "the national security state" was a watershed moment in the foreign policy of the United States and the expansion of its federal government. It includes all the governmental agencies, laws, regulations, and initiatives that ensure the United States' safety against threats foreign and domestic. Its origins are typically traced to the National Security Act of 1947, which reorganized the nation's defense establishment and led to the founding of the Department of Defense, the National Security Council, the Joint Chiefs of Staff, and the Central Intelligence Agency.[14] Though the national security state was ostensibly born of a need to combat international threats, its focus on intelligence gathering deeply influenced domestic operations. When President Truman sought to insert language into the National Security Act limiting the surveillance powers of the FBI, his efforts were thwarted by a Republican-controlled Congress that included freshman senator Joseph McCarthy.[15]

But the roots of the national security state actually penetrate much deeper than the Cold War. The US government used concerns about national security to collect information decades before the Soviet Union was even founded. The American colonial administration of the Philippines in the late nineteenth century has been called the "world's first surveillance state" and was a testing ground for policies later used in the United States.[16] American leaders there employed new technologies such as commercial typewriters, the Dewey decimal system, punch cards, and a telegraphic communications system to collect, organize, and manage data about possible enemies of the state, resulting in what one historian termed "an integrated system of information-based police controls."[17] That approach to counterintelligence would inspire later American officials—including J. Edgar Hoover—in their own efforts to make the nation more "secure."

Many of the same concerns that helped forge the intertwined national surveillance and security states—the obsessive collection of information on potential threats, the constant fear of attack, the blurring of the line between the personal and the political—also shaped the masculine identities adopted by Hoover, McCarthy, and Cohn. In part, those three men were products of their time. But those issues were particularly important to them because of their desire to join and even master the nation's power elite. Moreover, those concerns informed a sea change in how Americans thought about gender and sexuality, particularly male behavior, between the Victorian era and the Cold War. Terms like "masculinity" and its cousins "manhood" and "manliness" underwent significant shifts at the turn of the twentieth century. According to gender historian Michael Kimmel, in the late nineteenth century

> *manhood* had been understood to define an inner quality, the capacity for autonomy and responsibility, and had historically been seen as the opposite of *childhood*. Becoming a man was not taken for granted; at some point the grown-up boy would demonstrate that he had become a man and had put away childish things. At the turn of the [twentieth] century, *manhood* was replaced gradually by the term *masculinity*, which referred to a set of behavioral traits and attitudes that were contrasted now with a new opposite, *femininity*.[18]

The impetus for this change was closely related to the remaking of the American economy between the end of the Civil War and the beginning of World War I. The transition from a primarily agrarian economy to one focused on industrial production was transformative, with "the movement from farm to factory and office, and from physical labor outdoors to sedentary work indoors" inspiring quests for political, spiritual, and physical rebirth unseen since the nation's earliest days.[19]

That restructuring of the economy influenced nearly every aspect of American life.[20] It recast not only how people worked, but where and with whom they lived, how they traveled (as well as how often and how far), how they communicated, what they ate, how they were educated, when they married, when and how often they procreated, how they worshiped, and how they thought about their place in the world.

At the same time, that revolution gave Americans the opportunity to craft identities around consumer goods and leisure activities. Americans' relationship to consumer products changed as a result of new distribution models, advertising, marketing, and branding. Though people were still constrained by largely immutable associations such as ethnicity, familial ties, race, and sex, consumerism partially loosened those restraints.[21]

These sweeping social and economic changes, which evolved episodically over many decades, abetted fundamental shifts in gender. Women's gradually increasing social and economic independence began to challenge, if not dissolve, the doctrine of "separate spheres," which assigned distinct realms of life to men and women. Between the end of the Victorian era and World War I, middle-class women expanded the boundaries of their social and economic worlds by deemphasizing traditional community ties, participating in the marketplace, forming new social connections, and becoming increasingly involved in politics. For their part, working-class women were drawn out of the household and into paid labor in rapidly increasing numbers.[22]

In this context, American men, particularly middle-class men, lost many of the cultural touchstones that had previously defined manhood. Most men could no longer claim to be independent producers. Many who worked with their hands did so for wages, and increasingly found that how they consumed—which is to say how they lived—was more important than what they made. As the ideals of a "producerist" economy gave way to those of a "consumerist" one, what did it mean to be a man? The resulting anxieties lasted well into the twentieth century. As late as 1931, the novelist Sherwood Anderson remarked that "modern man is losing his ability to retain his manhood in the face of the modern way of utilizing the machine," and argued that man had been left with "no definite connection with the things with which he is surrounded, no relations with the clothes he wears, the house he lives in. He lives in a house but he did not build it. He sits in a chair but he did not make it. He drives a car but he did not build it. He sleeps in a bed but he does not know where it came from."[23]

As a result, historian Martin Summers notes, "masculinity" supplanted "manliness" more rapidly among middle-class men than among working-class ones.[24] "Manhood" had meant production and patriarchy; "masculinity" was social, consumerist, and constantly under pressure to be proven and reproven, "lest the man be undone by a perception of being too feminine."[25] This continual process saddled men with endless anxiety over their gender identity.

Such a conception of masculinity chimes with the feminist idea that gender conventions are, to a significant degree, socially constructed—meaning that what is considered to be "masculine" or "feminine" is not preordained by biology but defined by ever-shifting social standards constructed through social processes.[26] For individuals, this framework means that gendered identities can shift depending on situations. This process is, of course, a messy one: the degree of control people have over their gendered persona fluctuates, and it also depends on a variety of factors including—but not limited to—age, location, social space they inhabit, and other social relations.[27] That said, the fact that masculinity is socially constructed does not mean that all forms of masculinity are regarded as equal. As Kimmel has argued, "What it means to be a man in America depends heavily on one's class, race, ethnicity, age, sexuality, [and] region of the country . . . At the same time, though, all American men must also contend with a singular vision of masculinity . . . the model against which we all measure ourselves."[28] Scholars use the term "hegemonic masculinity" to refer to this socially constructed "model."[29]

Prevailing notions of American masculinity as marked by a series of sporadic crises have lost favor among historians, who now typically hold that American men (and women) have faced a constantly shifting gender terrain.[30] Yet one must also recognize that there were specific, contingent moments—the 1890s and 1950s being two—when the gender identities of American men appeared to be under unprecedented strain. The concept of "manliness" experienced a significant period of upheaval following World War II. A shift to middle-management careers among American workingmen during the 1950s, coupled with a postwar emphasis on consumerism and consumption, fostered a moment during which American culture made room for multiple versions of masculinity, from John Wayne to Hugh Hefner, from James Dean to Liberace.[31] This shift allowed men to continue to lay claim to masculinity even if they were unable to prove their manhood in more "traditional" ways like physical exertion. As a result, just as McCarthy and Cohn stepped into the national consciousness, a social debate was raging over the elasticity of masculinity. Both men would ultimately be participants in and subjects of that debate.

Social prejudice held that masculine characteristics were found in Anglo-Saxon, Protestant, prep-school and Ivy League graduates with clear-cut membership in the East Coast establishment. Hoover, McCarthy, and Cohn did not fit this prescribed background in a variety of ways: Hoover and McCarthy did not attend elite schools; Cohn and McCarthy were not Protestant; McCarthy was from the Midwest; Cohn and Hoover never married; none of the three ever fathered children. As a result, all three men had to work to present themselves as worthy of the mantle of masculine leadership. Hoover, McCarthy, and Cohn were social outsiders who reshaped themselves in efforts to become essential parts of the national surveillance and security states.

At the same time, Hoover, McCarthy, and Cohn did not share a standardized masculine identity—each found his own way to demonstrate that he possessed hard masculine toughness. Their variations can be attributed to their differences in age, class, wealth, religion, geographic origin, occupation, and personality. A conservative Protestant raised in a family of federal bureaucrats, Hoover crafted a white-collar version of masculinity rooted in propriety, organization, and institutional loyalty. To amplify his claims to machismo, Hoover adopted elements of the muscular manhood which had gained traction in the late nineteenth century. In so doing, Hoover helped create a new approach to professional manhood that governed both his public image and that of the FBI agents he led. McCarthy's hardscrabble upbringing in Wisconsin, including a stint as a farmer, meant that his masculine identity was more aligned with the working-class values of thrift and self-sufficiency. Relying on those characteristics as he crafted his public masculine persona, McCarthy embraced a form of masculinity which sought to alight memories of producerist manhood while embracing modern means of demonstrating his masculine faculties. As the son of an influential Democratic judge and an ambitious social climber, Cohn built his masculine identity atop a foundation of status-based power. Because Cohn could not rely on his ethnic background, religious affiliation, or physical attributes to project manliness, he emphasized social rank, professional success, and access to power. Throughout his life, Cohn's claims to manhood were based more on what he could accomplish than on intrinsic identity markers.

These efforts at gendered performance were complicated by the fact that the Victorian-to-modern shift in gender was accompanied by a concurrent, related revolution in sexuality. The forces of modernization and urbanization enabled Americans—especially young ones—to push the boundaries of socially acceptable sexual behavior.[32] That process was accelerated by transformative events such as World War I, the Great Depression, and World War II, each of which promoted social upheaval by prompting Americans to migrate away from their home communities and the often conservative sexual regulations governing them.[33] The population density, cultural exchange, and social vivacity found in the urban areas to which Americans flocked between 1890 and 1950 fostered experimentation in sexual relationships and with gender identities, including the formation of recognizable gay and lesbian subcultures. Questions promoted by these changes would weigh heavily on Hoover, McCarthy, and Cohn as they too left home and sought to define their own masculinities. When all three men began fighting the Cold War, the new public visibility of women and homosexuals—especially in Washington, D.C., where transplanted workers attracted by the expansion of the federal government during the New Deal and World War II had promoted a comparatively cosmopolitan ethos—

helped fuel fears that bureaucrats lacked the strength to successfully defeat communism. Thus, Hoover, McCarthy, and Cohn had to continually prove their heterosexuality as they came to embody surveillance state masculinity.

The third leg of the tripod upon which my argument rests is perhaps the most difficult idea to define. What is gossip? The answer is not as obvious as it might seem. Must it be titillating or uncouth? Is it necessarily frivolous? Is it an explicitly private form of communication, or can gossip enter public discourse? Is gossip still gossip if its information is verifiably accurate? How is gossip different from related concepts such as rumor, insinuation, libel, slander, and deliberate disinformation? Most importantly, can something as seemingly insubstantial as gossip be said to carry any political or historical weight? Put more simply: does gossip matter?

Any definition should begin with the origins of the term. "Gossip" is a knotty concept that has shifted in meaning throughout its existence in regard to both the kind of information it communicates and the form that communication takes. It grew from *godsibb*, a word for the attendants at a child's baptism with roots dating back to the eleventh century ("godparent" shares the same derivation). Over time, *godsibb* was uncoupled from its religious origins and called to mind the more festive aspects of a child's arrival, including drinking and general neighborliness. By the sixteenth century *godsibb* had become *gossip*, a noun used to refer to the "close female friends whom a woman invited to attend her at childbirth."[34] Men—who were explicitly barred from the birthing room—came to fear what was being said in their absence. Would women together in an intimate space be prompted to speak frankly about their husbands and other male relatives? If so, what embarrassing details would be shared? As a result, the term came to embody the two interrelated meanings that are most common today. By the early seventeenth century, English writers were using it to refer to what the *Oxford English Dictionary* defines as "a person, mostly a woman, of light and trifling character, especially one who delights in idle talk." As that definition suggests, gossip was understood to be a feminine form of communication; a 1755 British dictionary defined it as "one who runs about tattling like women at a lying-in." But as early as the seventeenth century, American and British writers were referring to gossip as a form of communication rather than the person who expressed it, deriding it as "women's idle chatter and rumormongering."[35] The *Oxford English Dictionary* reports that by 1811 the definition had expanded to include its second modern meaning, "the conversation of such a person; trifling or groundless rumor."

I am interested in two forms of gossip, both of which fall under one critic's definition of it as "private talk" that exhibits "intense interest in the personal."[36] The first is "distilled malice," that is, information circulated in an attempt to negatively color an individual or group.[37] Examples of distilled malice are not difficult to locate, and their ubiquity in everyday life extends from a neighbor's discussion of the misbehaving teenager to a tabloid magazine's report on the latest philandering movie star. The second form can be thought of as "positive rumor," an insinuation that is spread—often at the urging of the subject—to construct an identity. Examples of this form of gossip might be trickier to identify, but they might take the form of an office worker subtly lobbying for a friend's promotion, or a news story hinting that a congressional candidate has spent years anonymously donating money to a local foster home. Together, these two qualities suggest another essential component: while gossip traffics in private information, it is definitionally intended to be shared. In fact, I hold that gossip cannot be called gossip *until it is shared*—its raison d'être is to convey information. In practice, gossip actually necessitates three parties: a transmitter, the individual who shares the gossip; a receiver, who absorbs the gossip; and a subject, whom the gossip concerns.

Gossip is distinguished from rumor in two primary ways. First, while gossip often conveys unconfirmed information, even a verified report can be considered gossip. News of the dissolution of an acquaintance's marriage can be gossip even after the divorce is confirmed. This possibility of veracity increases gossip's believability while amplifying its value. Second, gossip always revolves around human subjects. A city planning office's decision to zone a lot as suitable for an adult video store might have the salaciousness necessary for gossip, but its lack of a specific human subject places it more firmly in the realm of rumor. Humanity is central to gossip because, at base, gossip is about social relationships. Gossip's social function means that it is never frivolous, regardless of its content. It defines and redefines values, sets the parameters of group identity, can be used to challenge the social hierarchy, and—centrally—reflects larger sociocultural anxieties.

Social critics have long held that the primary role of gossip—irrespective of its content, subject, and purveyors—is to assist in community formation, specifically through publicizing and reaffirming societal values, standards, and customs.[38] Journalist Neal Gabler notes that the governing power of gossip became even more important when "communities" composed of individuals who "knew one another and were bound by ties of kinship and neighborhood" transformed into "societies," formations "where secondary relationships increasingly supplanted primary ones."[39] Building off the work of sociologist Louis Wirth, Gabler presents gossip as essential to helping determine an individual's status in societies where most people know each other only by reputation.

Despite gossip's history of feminine and sinful associations, it has been used by Americans of all genders to serve a variety of purposes. Yes, gossip is a means of circulating information.[40] But it is also evaluative; the mere sharing of information through gossip means that the sharer is passing judgment—positive or negative—about the subject. For example, historians have identified gossip as key to "fomenting and shaping the social and political disorder that resulted in witchcraft accusations and trials in colonial New England" and shown that gossip was a way for women from all social classes to make their voices heard in colonial Virginia.[41] Others have demonstrated that gossip was a cudgel wielded by elite men in colonial America and the Early Republic to maintain social order.[42]

Innuendo has played a role in American politics since the nation's founding, as epitomized by the way Thomas Jefferson and Alexander Hamilton used media allies to accuse each other of moral impropriety. (The early newspaperman James T. Callender spread nefarious rumors on behalf of both men.) Gossip also helped convey information in the diplomatic corps, with "US Foreign Service professionals [recognizing] gossip's potential as an internal mode of communication within the professional diplomatic community, fostering relationships, fomenting professional competition, and providing much-needed information about job security, promotion, and transfers."[43] In that system, gossip became an essential source of reliable information during crises, with Presidents Theodore Roosevelt and Woodrow Wilson regarding gossip as more trustworthy than official reports from politically interested diplomats.[44]

Just as modernity transformed gossip, so too did it allow personality to overtake character as the primary determiner of identity. In *Self-Exposure*, historian Charles Ponce de Leon shows how the obsession with public personalities ("celebrity culture") emerged. "Celebrity is intimately related to modernity," he writes, in that it is a "unique way of thinking about public figures . . . [that] is a direct outgrowth of developments that most of us regard as progressive: the spread of a market economy and the rise of democratic, individualistic values. The culture of celebrity is not some grotesque mutation afflicting an otherwise healthy organism, but one of its central features, a condition arising directly from the encouragement that modern societies provide for social mobility and self-invention."[45]

Gossip also provided an awareness of and glimpse into the shadow worlds behind the headlines, those darkened corners populated by Hollywood fixers, mafia bosses, corrupt lawyers, and scheming politicians. In addition, the availability of gossip in national media helped introduce topics of public discussion that were previously considered impolitic, including reports of homosexuality, adultery, "transsexuality," various forms of vice, and mental illness. While in some ways the arrival of such subjects seemed to vulgarize public debate, it also increased public awareness of gender and sexual identities that otherwise stayed underground. The rapid growth of gossip magazines after World War II occurred alongside an increased concern about national intelligence and "state secrets" in the light of the Cold War; as newsstand sales of the gossip magazine *Confidential* surpassed those of *The Saturday Evening Post* and *Look*, rumor and speculation were finding their way into FBI files and being forwarded as legitimate evidence during congressional inquiries (including those led by Joseph McCarthy). Gossip had become a form of surveillance, with word-of-mouth rumors and tabloid reports enabling society to police behavior and identities.[46]

The historian of gossip faces two distinct challenges. First is tracing the distribution and reception of gossip. Much gossip is, of course, spread by word-of-mouth and thus represents an archive lost to the winds of time. Circulation figures for historical gossip magazines are difficult to locate, as are back issues. This fact is particularly true for publications from the early Cold War, all of which have long since ceased publication and were produced by companies that have shuttered. Gossip magazines were often shared among friends, so each copy of *Confidential* and its imitators was probably read by numerous people.[47] When gossip did appear in more mainstream news outlets, it was often communicated in oblique language reliant on slang and innuendo. Thus, it is nearly impossible to determine the number of people who came into contact with a specific piece of gossip, whether they understood the suggestion that was being made, and the degree to which they believed the charge.

The second challenge is in determining the "truth" of gossip. Distilled malice specifically concerns information that its subjects would typically prefer remain hidden, and the acknowledgment of a rumor is often accompanied by a denial. The accuracy of any piece of gossip is also colored by the self-interest of those sharing it. Partially as a result of these challenges, this book focuses on the *impact* of gossip more than its *accuracy*.

Hoover, McCarthy, and Cohn used gossip in two key ways. For all three men, it was an important means of gathering information that might prove useful in achieving their political and professional ends. They employed more conventional sources in constructing dossiers on their political allies and rivals, but also placed a significant weight on hearsay. Their other central use for gossip was to communicate information—both about them-

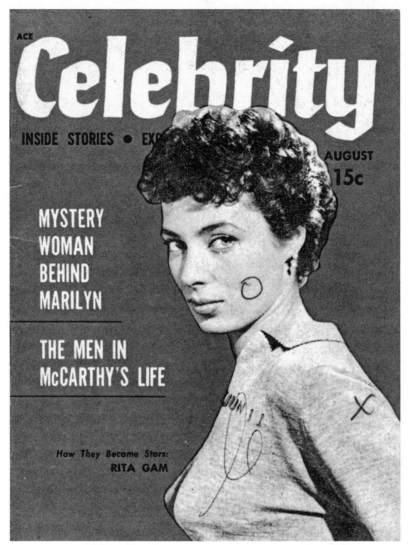

FIGURE 3. The August 1954 issue of the gossip magazine *Celebrity* featured an article with the suggestive title "The Men in McCarthy's Life." Credit: Private collection.

selves and others. They all adeptly wielded the tools of gossip journalists, including hyperbole, insinuation, and guilt by association. Hoover, McCarthy, and Cohn used the media to enhance their own public images while concurrently employing distilled malice to paint their opponents in a negative light, including with the broad brush of effeminacy that they themselves so feared. By projecting their own "deficiencies" onto others they deflected criticism and lambasted their enemies in one sweeping motion.

But there was a danger in that process. The precise tactics that Hoover, McCarthy, and Cohn used to build their own political identities and pillory their enemies were ultimately turned against them, and all three men became targets of distilled malice. This targeting occurred precisely because of the apparent paradoxes they embodied. The central contradiction was the fact that while all three men came to wield considerable power both prior to and especially during the Cold War, they did so in spite of their failure to display many of the traits demanded of surveillance state bureaucrats. Often, those critiques took the form of questions about their own gender and sexual identities, and, to varying degrees, each man was ultimately hoist with his own petard. That blowback profoundly altered their careers, even as the political identity they had helped shape maintained its outsized influence in American politics.

THE TOPOGRAPHY OF MODERNITY

In their 1929 book *Middletown: A Study in Modern American Culture*, sociologists Robert and Helen Lynd explored how modernization had affected a small Midwestern city between 1890 and 1925. The Lynds concluded that "Middletown"—later revealed to be Muncie, Indiana—had undergone transformative changes largely as a result of new technologies such as automatic machinery, electrical devices, automobiles, and motion pictures. Those technological developments led to economic and social ones, affecting nearly every aspect of life for Middletown's residents: how they earned a living, how they ran their home, how they raised their children, how they spent their leisure time, how they practiced their religion, how they participated in their community.

Among other cultural changes, modernization allowed Middletowners to fully participate in a thriving national print culture. Popular publications like *The American Magazine, The Saturday Evening Post, McCall's,* and *Ladies' Home Journal* instructed their readers in both cultural trends and social propriety.[1] But as some national magazines largely reaffirmed Victorian-era moral values, others helped question them. In addition to those middle-brow titles, the postal workers of Middletown were delivering a new type of periodical in high numbers, what the Lynds called "sex adventure magazines." Focused on presenting first-person, purportedly factual stories of romantic relationships, sex adventure magazines included articles such as "The Primitive Lover (She Wanted a Caveman Husband)," "How to Keep the Thrill in Marriage," and "Can a Wife Win with the Other Woman's Weapons?"[2] Approximately one of every ten Middletown residents subscribed to a sex adventure magazine like *True Story, True Confessions, True Detective, True Stories,* and *Live Stories.* Those publications pledged to provide their readers with "a knowledge of the rules of life." This promise to reveal hidden truths about how the modern world operates was also a key element to the gossip magazines that were then being produced in major American cities. In the eyes of one Middletown mother, the new, salacious periodicals were impacting the actions of her town's youngsters: "Children weren't bold like they are today when we were young!"[3]

She was not alone in her unease. Though the citizens of Middletown were quick to embrace "new ways of behaving toward material things," similar shifts in personal relationships and toward "non-material institutions" prompted anxiety.[4] Modernization had promised simplicity and efficiency, but the Lynds discovered that those changes had also caused the people of Middletown to feel an "increasing sense of strain and perplexity in [their] rapidly changing world."[5] They worried about ill-defined "social problems," which encapsulated anything from the actions of "the young generation" and "corrupt politics" to issues with "housing" and "street traffic."[6]

In nearly every corner of the country, Americans struggled to find their place in a brave new world. Some, like the young J. Edgar Hoover, reaffirmed their ties to institutions—including churches, schools, and the government—even as those stabilizing organizations were changing to keep up with the times. Others embraced the new social and cultural landscape that modernization had wrought, looking to novel resources such as sex adventure magazines and the emerging gossip press as a way to understand modern life. These varied, sometimes paradoxical navigations were motivated by many of the same anxieties and ambitions that built surveillance state masculinity.

*

The house that once stood at 413 Seward Square in Washington, D.C., was unremarkable. It was a two-story frame home with large, dark shutters. In one of the few nods to decoration, the small porch was crowned with dentil molding. It was almost exactly a half mile southeast of the US Capitol building, in a neighborhood replete with government workers, most of whom were Protestant, all of whom were white. It was in this simple dwelling near the corridors of power that J. Edgar Hoover lived for his first forty-three years. That home witnessed the Hoover family's youngest child become a successful leader in high school, a law student, a government clerk, and finally the leader of the first federal bureau of investigation. It was a path that fostered in Hoover the characteristics that came to dominate his personality (and that of the bureaucracy he built): boundless ambition, a desire for respectability, moral absolutism, and an unshakable fidelity to order. But Hoover's early life and young adulthood concurrently imbued him with many of the anxieties that would also mark his path and that of the nation, most notably the need for acceptance coupled with the paralyzing fear of being considered unfit for membership in the power elite.[7]

Hoover was deeply influenced by the anxieties of the Protestant middle-class that were born of Progressive Era modernization and its accompanying harbingers of social upheaval, including immigration and urbanization. This crucible of uncertainty forged the values that would so deeply impress themselves on Hoover's character. In some ways he can be seen as a nineteenth-century relic attempting to guide the twentieth, seeking to promote an ethical code unsuited for the nation's social realities. At the same time, the values imparted to Hoover during his childhood and adolescence would help him manage human and informational capital so deftly as to become arguably the most powerful American of the twentieth century.[8]

John Edgar Hoover entered the world on January 1, 1895, at the outset of what Henry Luce would come to christen "the American century." His mother called him "Edgar," while the rest of the family referred to him as "J.E." His parents, both Washington natives, had married fifteen years earlier. Edgar was their fourth child, though the couple's second daughter, Sadie, had died at age three of diphtheria—sixteen months before Edgar was born. As the baby of a family so recently touched by tragedy, Edgar would receive fawning treatment from his parents and older siblings, Dickerson Jr., and Lillian.[9]

Like many of his neighbors, Dickerson Hoover Sr. worked for the government, serving as the director of the printing office at the US Coast and Geodetic Survey. Government service was the family business: Edgar's paternal grandfather also worked for the Coast and Geodetic Survey, his mother's grandfather and uncle both served as the ranking Swiss diplomat in the United States, and his older brother would eventually work for the US Steamboat Inspection Service. In short, Hoover was born into bureaucracy.[10]

Though he was quiet around the home, the letters of Dickerson Sr. reveal an emotional attachment to his family. In a 1904 missive to his youngest son, from the St. Louis World's Fair, Dickerson Sr. adopted the tone of a sentimental roughhouse:

> I wish you were here so that I could fight you in the morning. Mama might think you aint strong but just let her try to fight you and she will find out . . . Take good care of Mama . . . Be a good boy. With a good big kiss. From Papa.[11]

Thought of as a "replacement" for his deceased older sister, Edgar was deeply loved by the rest of his family. In the words of one biographer, "Edgar was the adored and achieving son of doting parents . . . the cherished brother of an older sister and brother . . . the pet of the Hoover household, protected by its care and love."[12]

Yet this tenderness did not mean that Edgar was spoiled or enjoyed unchecked freedom. His mother instilled a sense of order. The daughter of a mining engineer, Annie was a strict disciplinarian who "encouraged Edgar with rewards and punishments."[13] Her sense of control permeated the domestic space; she was particularly tough on the family's servants, who were often relieved of their duties at the slightest provocation.

Whatever scolding Annie directed at her youngest son did not seem to strain her relationship with him. According to political operative (and friend of Hoover's) George E. Allen, Edgar was "very much a mother's boy."[14] Annie was the greatest influence in Edgar's life and his loyalty to her was unshakeable. Edgar only moved out of the Seward Square house following Annie's death in 1938.

As a child, Edgar stuttered. He researched the problem extensively and learned of a theory that the trick to surmounting the verbal speed bumps of stuttering was to speak as rapidly as possible. The technique largely worked and is partially responsible for Edgar's childhood nickname "Speed." He would speak rapidly throughout his life and the stutter would plague him only during moments of great stress.

The other root of the Speed nickname was Edgar's nimbleness at his first job, delivering groceries. Hot for tips, Edgar made his deliveries at a breakneck pace, quickly weaving in and out of pedestrian traffic in Southeast Washington. In an effort to bolster his image, Hoover would later claim that the nickname had been bestowed on him on the football field, or would at least not correct those who said so.[15] In reality, Edgar's small size meant he was cut from Central High School's football squad early in his freshman season. In a similar massaging of the facts, members of the FBI's public relations team were directed to say that "the Director is just a shade under six feet tall," even though that added at least a couple of inches.[16] In the words of one biographer, "A raised dais under [Hoover's] desk, the avoidance of tall people at parties, and the rare promotion of tall agents to headquarters positions helped maintain the illusion."[17]

While Washington was not quite a sleepy Southern town (after all, it was the fifteenth-largest city in the country in 1900), it did enjoy a certain level of stability during Hoover's boyhood.[18] Such constancy was particularly apparent in the Hoovers' neighborhood. In the words of Richard Gid Powers, "Seward Square was a microcosm of white, Protestant, middle-class America. There were within its borders few rich and no poor; except for the servants who came each day to do the cooking and cleaning, it was all white. The only religious differences were friendly rivalries among the Lutherans, Presbyterians, and Methodists. A child of Seward Square would have grown up knowing no one who was, in any essential respect, different from himself."[19] The neighborhood's homogeneity fostered in Edgar a lifelong awareness and distrust of the "other," whether that difference manifested itself racially, ethnically, religiously, politically, or sexually.

This demographic sameness extended to Edgar's schooling. He always attended public schools, first Brent Elementary (which stood only a block from his house) and then Central High. Living south of the Mason-Dixon line in the age of Jim Crow, Edgar was enrolled only at all-white institutions. In those years, Washington's public schools "stressed citizenship and discipline (corporal punishment was not abolished until 1913). Dress was formal: boys wore jackets and ties, knickers in the lower grades, trousers by the eighth grade; girls wore dresses or skirts with middie blouses."[20] Edgar's decision—his, not his parents'—to attend Central High is illuminating; though Eastern High was closer to the Hoover house, Central was thought to provide a more challenging and rigorous education. There was likely little surprise in the Hoover household when the ambitious Edgar made his selection.

At Central, Hoover earned a reputation for enrolling in the most demanding elective courses and was eventually named class valedictorian—an elected position that demonstrates his popularity.[21] His junior year report card shows that he earned "excellent" marks in all his subjects: English, French, geometry, history, trigonometry, and drawing. He also earned perfect marks for "neatness," never missed a day of school, and was always on time for class.[22]

Following his freshman year, his extracurricular energies were expended on two pursuits that played to his strengths: debate and drill. The Central High School Debate Society dominated the city's circuit so completely that it often held meets against the debate teams of regional colleges as a challenge. By his senior year, Hoover was considered the society's best speaker, displaying a "cool, relentless logic" in debates about women's suffrage, the presidential primary system, and the governance of public utilities. His arguments often relied on a higher sense of justice; in a debate over capital punishment, Hoover defended the practice as both biblically sound and supported by "all Christian Nations."[23] This appeal to Christian morality foretold Hoover's fidelity to an ethical and masculine standard to which he would aspire throughout his career.

Hoover's other focus outside of class was the drill team, the Central High School Brigade of Cadets. Though not popular nationwide, military-style drill teams were an important part of public school life in Washington. Each of the public high schools fielded a cadet corps of approximately 180 students organized into three companies, and each spring saw a drill competition on the White House Ellipse. In 1913, Hoover led Central's cadet corps down Pennsylvania Avenue as part of the four-hour parade celebrating Woodrow Wilson's inauguration. Hoover's rise through the ranks was capped by his elevation to the command of Company A during his senior year. He implemented policies that he believed would make the corps more orderly and efficient, including mandatory weekly meetings of all cadets. At the end of the school year, Company A placed second in the citywide drill meet, losing to a larger company that executed more challenging maneuvers. Still, Hoover's leadership earned him the admiration of his peers and placed him in the upper echelons of popularity in school, second only to the leaders of Central's athletic squads. So proud was Hoover of his association with the Brigade of Cadets that he even wore his freshly pressed uniform to church on Sundays.[24] Cadets would often gift ribbons featuring the insignia of their company to their girlfriends, and the citywide Cadets' Ball was considered the most important dance on the teenage Washingtonian's social calendar.[25] Yet when asked about Hoover's romantic life during high school, his classmates replied that though they were sure he went on dates, he never went steady with any one girl because his focus was elsewhere; Hoover was "in love with Company A."[26]

It was a relationship that became essential in molding numerous aspects of his character, personality, and value system. It taught him the joy of commanding others, the sense of self-worth and empowerment that results from leading a group of individuals toward a common goal. It also instilled a belief in the value of a tiered organizational structure, both in the sense of operational layout and adherence to a chain of command. The way Hoover later configured the FBI used principles from the cadet corps. Hoover's time as a cadet also schooled him in institutional fidelity, and he found that giving the entirety of oneself to an organization would pay dividends. It forecast a lifetime of using the power of institutions to forward his personal and professional goals. This belief in organizational power does not mean Hoover always worked within the constraints of those organizations, but rather that he understood how being a part of a larger organization could help promote his own agenda.

Thus, though Hoover never served in the armed forces, the cadet corps instilled in him a belief in the virtue of martial discipline. This fidelity to order governed both Hoover's own personal code and his approach to the men under his command. He was a man of consistency and precision; every day, he rose at the same time, ate the same breakfast, and lunched at the same restaurant. Hoover placed an exaggerated emphasis on ensuring that the special agents who made up the heart of the FBI were well-dressed, courteous, presentable, and punctual. This militaristic sensibility would extend to Hoover's approach to fighting crime, exemplified in his insistence that the FBI adopt "scientific methods" such as a national fingerprint database. The Bureau was truly made in his image.

*

Hoover's early years illuminate how social concerns about masculinity influenced his development. The building blocks of Hoover's gender identity can be traced to two overlapping movements from the turn of the century: first, anxieties about boyhood born of dramatic shifts in both the character of work and the ideology of separate spheres for men and women; and second, the way those secular anxieties came to be expressed through a more masculine iteration of Protestant Christianity. In his efforts to fulfill the ideals of white Christian manhood, young Edgar was attempting to embody the expectations his class had for a boy while concurrently establishing an identity that would afford him entry into the highest tier of society.

The transformations in America during Hoover's youth were profound and unprecedented. Between 1880 and 1920 the population of the United States doubled, from 50 million to 106 million. Population density also doubled during that period as Americans redistributed themselves between urban and rural areas.[27] At the same time, huge shifts marked the country's demographics (ethnic and racial makeup, the number of single young people living in cities, family size, etc.), its transportation system, its economic organization and wealth distribution, its international standing, and its ways of entertaining itself.

Perhaps the most visible of these developments was the extraordinary spike in immigration between the 1880s and 1920s, particularly from non–Western European nations. During that period approximately 28 million immigrants arrived.[28] By 1900, 37.8 percent of US residents were either foreign born or the children of immigrants.[29] That influx contributed to a significant increase in the overall population, which was already on the rise as a consequence of an increase in birth rates and life expectancy. Immigration and population growth joined with an increasingly industrial economy to foster the rapid expansion of cities.

Another development was the physical, social, economic, and cultural domination of American Indians and African Americans (through the Indian Wars and racist legal policies). Simultaneously, the United States expanded its global reach, using new imperialist policies to influence or control areas of South America, Southeast Asia, and the Pacific Islands. This expansion was buttressed by the emergence of an American economic juggernaut through the development of corporations, the advent of the managerial class, the instillation of scientific management principles (and consequential downfall of the skilled worker), and an increase in the availability of business capital.

Equally revolutionary changes transformed the culture. Intensified urbanization connected Americans to each other in novel ways, promoting cultural exchange. Advances in the media saw newspaper and magazine readership grow to unprecedented levels, the development of "new" (or tabloid) journalism, an expansion of book publishing into the more popular realms of pulp fiction and dime novels, and the dawn of advertising as a significant source of income. With this expanded news industry came the promotion of new cultural heroes, including athletes (particularly boxers and college football players) and the stars of radio and the vaudeville stage. The popularization of such stars was supported by new forms of mass media, including photography and, later, film. In the domestic sphere, the average age men first married increased as they resisted the responsibilities of family and community and partook in new entertainments, resulting in what one historian has dubbed "the age of the bachelor."[30]

The seismic shifts in nearly every corner of society drove cultural fears that American men had become too civilized, particularly as they adopted white-collar middle-management positions and eschewed physical work. Between 1870 and 1910, the number of white-collar jobs increased more than sevenfold.[31] Furthermore, the economic panics of 1873–79, 1884, and

1893 had fomented domestic upheaval and emasculated men who could not adequately provide for their families.

Those concerns profoundly influenced the way boys of the era were raised. Guidebooks such as Kate Upson Clark's *Bringing Up Boys: A Study* (1899) and Frank Orman Beck's *Marching Manward: A Study of the Boy* (1913) purported to teach parents how to promote masculine growth in their sons. In general, they advised that young men should be energetic, pious, disciplined, and moral, while assiduously avoiding any type of abnormality—sexual or otherwise.

Clark's work was directed at families in the upper middle class or ones that aspired to that level of respectability, a group that included the Hoovers. Her central advice held that boys should be vigorous and industrious, and that outward appearance and manners indicated internal character. These positive traits could be honed through play and organized athletic pursuits, which were "a crucial test of moral nature."[32] Baseball was particularly helpful in imbuing desirable qualities such as honesty and resilience. At the same time, sports did present moral dangers. Clark lamented the gambling often associated with them, such as the 1877 scandal in which players for the Louisville Greys threw games in exchange for bribes from gamblers. She also disapproved of more violent sports, particularly football, because of the chance of injury.[33] While *Bringing Up Boys* stressed neatness in dress and bearing, Clark did not want that refinement to undermine a more manly comportment. Like others, Clark bemoaned that the urbanization of boys undermined their work ethic, worrying that nonphysical jobs would erode the association of labor with success. As evidence, Clark pointed to numerous examples of "country boys" becoming great men as a result of their childhood industriousness, including Daniel Webster, David Livingstone, Nathaniel Bowditch, Benjamin Franklin, Henry Clay, Abraham Lincoln, and William Lloyd Garrison.[34]

Along similar lines, and building off the work of noted psychologist G. Stanley Hall, Frank Orman Beck constructed an image of the ideal ten-year-old boy as energetic, athletic, organized, curious, loyal, and thrifty. A boy who acts out through "outbursts of lawlessness" was simply not receiving proper outlets for the expression of "pent-up instincts." Beck advocated play as beneficial to both physical and mental development; it could serve as an outlet for the energies of the restless and as a means of keeping up boys' vitality.[35]

There was also a change in the way manhood was depicted in works aimed at boys. Jeffrey Hantover notes that "popular magazine biographies of male heroes in the period 1894 to 1913 shifted from an earlier idealization of passive traits such as piety, thrift, and industry to an emphasis on vigor, forcefulness, and mastery."[36] A similar series of characteristics were valued by the Boy Scouts of America, an organization that had become the most popular boys' group in the United States within a decade of its founding. According to its executive secretary, James E. West,

> the REAL Boy Scout is not a "sissy." He is not a hothouse plant, like little lord Fauntleroy. There is nothing "milk and water" about him; he is not afraid of the dark. He does not do bad things because he is afraid of being decent. Instead of being a puny, dull, or bookish lad, who dreams and does nothing, he is full of life, energy, enthusiasm, bubbling over with fun, full of ideas as to what he wants to do and knows how he wants to do it. He has many ideals and many heroes. He is not hitched to his mother's apronstrings. While he adores his mother, and would do anything to save her from suffering or discomfort, he is self-reliant, sturdy and full of vim.[37]

West's dismissive reference to the "sissy" was more than a critique of a boy who lacked athleticism and vigor. Guidebooks noted that masculine growth could be easily undermined by sexual deviance. In Beck's view, "sexual vice" was "the greatest foe which the family has to face," quoting a Protestant bishop who opined that "the most serious and pernicious question in the present social life is the increase of impurity, which is physically disastrous to the individual and to the people."[38] Such strong language left little doubt as to how society would receive young men who engaged in deviant behavior.

In *Middletown*, the Lynds argued that the rise of the automobile and increased high school attendance had helped change the landscape of adolescent relationships, particularly by distancing young people from their parents and helping to erode the separate spheres that had defined preindustrial gender relations. Those developments allowed unsupervised contact between the sexes and new forms of sexual expression. Anxiety over these social shifts abounded in Middletown, and many of its citizens appealed to traditional advocates of order (including religious organizations and the state) to manage what they viewed as dangerous social developments.

The perceived increase in immoral acts had already been targeted by the Catholic Church, various Protestant leaders, and a number of private organizations dedicated to promoting public morality, including the New England Watch and Ward Society, the Committee of Fifteen, and the Committee of Fourteen, all founded between 1878 and 1905.[39] Immorality was also a concern of a number of women's and temperance organizations that wielded political influence beginning in the latter half of the nineteenth century: the Women's Christian Temperance Union, the National Purity Congress, the Young Women's Christian Association, the General Federation of Women's Clubs, and the National Vigilance Association. Significantly, the fight against social vice earned support from influential voices across the political spectrum. The powerful American Social Hygiene Association, founded in 1914 to combat the spread of venereal disease through education and the promotion of high morals, was led by progressives including Hull House founder Jane Addams and former Harvard University president Charles William Eliot.

Perhaps the foremost advocate for public morality was the New York Society for the Suppression of Vice (NYSSV), which had been established by Civil War veteran and devout Christian Anthony Comstock in 1873. With support from the Young Men's Christian Association, Comstock and his allies tipped off police to dens of prostitution, sought to block the sale of liquor on Sundays, convinced authorities to indict birth control advocates, and successfully lobbied Congress to pass legislation prohibiting the distribution of "obscene literature and articles of immoral use" through the US Postal Service. Partially as a result of such pressure, authorities in New York City began to more actively monitor and prosecute "immoral" acts; according to historian George Chauncey, "the number of men convicted in Manhattan for homosexual solicitation leapt from 92 in 1916 to 238 in 1918 to more than 750 in 1920—an eightfold increase in four years."[40] Though Comstock was a controversial figure, he and the NYSSV enjoyed significant public support, particularly from the upper class. When Comstock died in 1915, his handpicked successor, John Saxton Sumner, carried on the fight against sexual liberalism.[41]

The primary ways in which Hoover encountered these anxieties about sexuality, promiscuity, and masculinity was through his church and its attempt to promote a new version of Christian manhood. In the face of rampant concerns about shifting gender roles and a more general crisis in masculinity, church leaders sought to reaffirm their view that men were the primary builders of God's kingdom on earth. At least part of this agenda was expressed in the way the church approached boyhood, with proponents holding that "boys now at the age of twelve or fifteen will, in a score of years, manage the affairs of the world."[42] Central to this new approach was the emergence of "muscular Christianity," a movement that emphasized the role of male virility in mainline Protestantism.[43]

Imparting a strong sense of Christian ethics would pay dividends as those boys grew into men of influence. In *The Minister and the Boy*, his 1912 guidebook for clergymen, Allan Hoben contended that churchmen should advocate for their young male followers to enter government work (rather than the ministry), claiming that "because of the influx of foreign peoples, the unsolved race problem, political corruption, and official mediocrity, America stands more in need of good citizenship than of generosity, more in need of statesmen than of clergymen."[44] According to Hoben and his allies, America was facing a sociopolitical crisis, and the most promising route to redemption was to influence young men to adhere to a more righteous set of moral, professional, and personal standards.

The first task of advocates of the new Christian manhood was to convince the public that Christianity and virile masculinity were not incompatible. Christian virtue and the glorification of God were recast as manly acts. The language Christian commentators used to describe piousness became imbued with a certain toughness. In his 1915 guidebook *The Boy Problem in the Home*, William Byron Forbush advised parents to encourage their adolescent sons to be "young gladiators" with a "manly fear of God."[45] This sword-over-ploughshare representation of Christianity was specifically designed to appeal to corners of the populace that felt modernization had promoted a general weakness in American society. Another tactic associated Christianity with historic models of leadership and success; Ohio minister Jason Noble Pierce opined in a 1912 pamphlet that "the greatest men of the world were mostly Christian men."[46] Thus, Christianity was the route to greatness.

Ministers were taught that they could attract young men to their congregation by engaging boys on their own turf, the schoolyard and the athletic field. Hoben advises pastors to try to earn the loyalty of young men "through association in the boys' club, at play, in camp."[47] In a 1909 tome titled *The Boy and the Church*, Eugene C. Foster issued a similar recommendation, noting that ministers could use sports to foster connections with young men. Foster also advised church leaders to focus on biblical lessons that would appeal to young men, warning that boys feel "so often the Sunday-school emphasizes the 'sissy' variety of goodness."[48]

Sissydom appeared to be a concern for a number of ministers, both in the way their churches were perceived and the actual content of teachings. Foster seemed to want more realism throughout the church curriculum, lamenting Sunday school libraries that include "supposedly boys' books in which 'sissy' boys lived angelic lives, and girls' books which were nauseating in the over-sweetness of the characters."[49] He also opined that churches should not be silent when it came to sexual education, advocating that pastors discuss "the physical facts of life" with boys whose parents had shirked that duty.[50] This approach can be seen as both an attempt to address the social reality of evolving gender relations as well as an effort to portray the church as attuned to the challenges of the modern world.

As further evidence of Christianity's masculine credentials, religious thinkers provided a reassessment of Christ that emphasized the Son of God's identity as the ideal human male, instead of simply a heavenly being sent to earth. In such a light, Christ's earthly virility became the standard toward which all men should strive. In his 1912 pamphlet *The Masculine Power of Christ: or, Christ Measured as a Man*, Jason Noble Pierce presented Christ as the epitome of manliness, arguing that "the life of Jesus is at every point suggestive of strength."[51] As evidence, Pierce pointed to Christ's ability to resist temptation, his incorruptible morality, and his penchant for leading other men. He also presents Christ's challenges on earth in more adversarial language, constantly speaking of Christ's "enemies" and comparing him to military leaders such as Caesar, Napoleon, and Alexander.[52] This reassessment did not saddle Christ with the same personality as the God of the Old Testament; he is still portrayed as loving his neighbor and caring for society's weakest members. But it is noteworthy that Pierce argues that the affection for which Christ advocates is explicitly not "soft or foolish love." It is hard, it is energetic, it is efficient; it is the kind of love a man can be proud to demonstrate.

Robert Warren Conant's 1915 treatise *The Virility of Christ: A New View* echoed and expanded upon Pierce's vision, emphasizing that *"Christ stands for the highest type of a strong, virile man, and there was nothing effeminate about him."*[53] Defining Christ as the ultimate man also meant presenting him as the antithesis of femininity. This approach was more than aesthetic posturing. In Conant's view, the "feminization of Christianity" had played a central role in undermining the virility of society as a whole, particularly in weakening the citizenry's moral character. But the source of the disease could also provide the cure, wrote Conant, "for it is the duty and should be the privilege of religion to furnish the needful antidote to weakening tendencies of all kinds, and the virile psychology of Christ . . . should have supplied the inspiration and pointed out the way."[54]

Christ's manliness was so profound that it was even credited with granting Christ the ability to fulfill his ultimate destiny; according to Pierce, Christ "possessed virile power which every man may share, which makes every man great, which will save the world."[55] This same redemptive power could be harnessed to promote the moral well-being of Christians and humanity generally. As Conant rhetorically asked, "Will not the teaching of a manly Christ and virile Christianity promote righteousness by promoting manly strength of character?"[56] Here was the key point underlying Christian manhood: the characteristics that created a complete man were the same as those that could provide moral leadership to the world. Manhood was morality.

In their own lives, Christian men could echo the virility of Christ in ways physical as well as moral. Part of this new Christian manhood was influenced by "muscular Christianity," a Victorian-era movement that endeavored to link religious devotion and physical virility. Originating in mid nineteenth century England, "muscular Christianity" enjoyed its broadest influence between approximately 1880 and 1920, when "droves of Protestant ministers in England and America concluded that men were not truly Christians unless they were healthy and 'manly' (a term used to connote strength, endurance, and other stereotypically male attributes)."[57] According to historian Clifford Putney, the "high-water mark of muscular Christianity" in America occurred in 1919 at the Columbus Exhibition in Ohio, during which the fairgrounds were patrolled by the Centenary Cadets, one thousand of the healthiest, most physically fit young men that the Methodist Church could locate, charged with demonstrating "that religion was 'manly, muscular, and attractive to boy life.'"[58]

This interest in conjoining Christianity and young male physicality naturally found a home in athletics. Church leaders began to rethink the Victorian hierarchy of sport, which held that some pursuits promoted gentlemanly development while others were too likely to foster more animalistic behavior. Now, even those more physical, aggressive sports (including football) could help cultivate desirable characteristics in young men. Hoben presented team sports as "the most effective means of developing, through expression, the boy's sense of justice or fair play," noting that "under proper leadership, the boy soon learns that the true spirit of manly sport is the farthest removed from that of the footpad and the blackguard."[59] Properly supervised athletic competitions could now play an essential role in imparting the values of civilized manhood.

In the United States, baseball and football were viewed as the most effective organized sports for instilling a desirable system of values. Hoben thought baseball could impart a number of virtues, including teamwork, loyalty (through acts such as the wearing of uniforms and the "sacrifice hit"), and placing the success of the team above individual achievement.[60] Football was seen as a more intense version of the national pastime:

All of the virtue that attaches to baseball will be found in football, only in accentuated form. Physical bravery is, of course, more emphasized; while team loyalty, with all that it implies, is more intense. The relation of the members to one another in a well-organized team amounts to an affection which is never forgotten. The words of cheer when the team is hard bushed and has to take a "brace"; the fighting spirit that plays the game to a finish, no matter what the odds; the hand extended to help to his feet the man who has just advanced the ball; the pat on the back; the impulsive embrace; the very tears shed in common after a lost game—all of this is a social and moral experience of no small value.[61]

The physicality of football was robust enough that it could excuse the more effete acts "impulsively" undertaken by participants, including weeping and physical displays of affection. Emotionality was acceptable as long as it appeared in a muscular context and was deployed in an effort to achieve a greater goal.

The clearest manifestation of the Christian advocacy of male physicality was the rapid growth of the Young Men's Christian Association. The YMCA had been founded in London in 1844 for the purpose of improving the "spiritual, mental, social, and physical condition of young men" and established its first American outpost in 1851.[62] On both sides of the Atlantic, it became a space where young Christian men were encouraged to undertake physical and athletic activities to glorify God through bodily perfection. Such physical activity also helped distract from less wholesome pursuits in two ways: it occupied their time and it provided an outlet for masculine energies. Hoben heartily supported the organization, noting that "the Young Men's Christian Associations, with their reproduction of the Greek ideal of physical well-being, have served to temper the otherworldly type of Christianity with the idea of a well-rounded and physically competent life as being consonant with the will of God."[63] To many contemporary observers, the YMCA was attempting to produce precisely what American society was most lacking: male leaders whose moral strength was matched only by their physical vigor.

The rules of Christian manhood were first imparted to Hoover at home. Hoover's parents—and, more importantly, his older brother—were insistent that the youngest member of the family be schooled in the ways of the Lord. Hoover recalled, "I strongly believe the molding of character begins at home . . . In my own home, I never remember having a meal that wasn't opened by someone saying grace. I just grew up that way."[64] Edgar first belonged to the Lutheran Church of the Reformation, which stood around the corner from his house. Following the lead of Dickerson Jr., Edgar became heavily involved in the church at a young age; he once was awarded a copy of the New Testament for having arrived on time for Sunday school every week for a year.[65] He eventually began teaching Sunday school at Reformation and was appointed the church's corresponding secretary at the age of fourteen.[66]

In his mid-teens, Edgar transferred both churches and sects, joining the First Presbyterian Church of Washington. The switch went against both geographic convenience and domestic tranquility: "Old First" was farther away from home, and Annie Hoover was vocally opposed to her youngest son leaving Lutheranism. But First Presbyterian was where Dickerson Jr. had recently started bringing his young family, and the church enjoyed a position of prominence in Washington society. The congregation was one of the city's oldest and most respected, established in 1812 with monetary gifts from city luminaries such as James Madison and James Monroe. Membership in the church assured contact with influential members of society and a certain air of respectability.

Most importantly, attending First Presbyterian meant that Edgar could spend his Sundays listening to the preaching of the church's charismatic leader, Donald Campbell MacLeod. Originally a resident of Meadville, Pennsylvania, MacLeod had been installed as pastor of "Old First" in 1899. Only twenty-six years old, he enjoyed broad popularity among his parishioners, particularly the younger ones. Though some biographers have claimed that Edgar was merely following his older brother's lead when he transferred to Old First, Hoover himself claimed that the most important factor in his decision was Reverend MacLeod's cult of personality, going so far as to refer to the reverend as "my hero."[67]

It was from Reverend MacLeod that Edgar would receive his clearest lessons in the responsibilities of Christian men. In a 1954 interview, Hoover remembered MacLeod as "a virile, wide-awake man with a lot of punch. He'd come out and referee our ball games. If a 'damn' popped out he'd ignore it. He was interested in us and he wasn't sanctimonious. He almost induced me to go into the ministry. He was the kind of man I wanted to be."[68]

MacLeod's focus on preventing sexual perversion can also be seen in his endorsement of *Damaged Goods*, a moralistic play written by Eugène Brieux that told the story of a young man whose premarital trysts result in him contracting syphilis, passing it onto his wife, and fathering a sterile child as a result. Before the play's 1912 performance in Washington, MacLeod "mounted the rostrum usually occupied by the leader of the orchestra, and announced that the nature of the performance, the sacredness of the play, and the character of the audience gave to the play the significance of a tremendous sermon in behalf of mankind, and that as such it was eminently fitting that a divine blessing be invoked."[69] In making such public pronouncements, MacLeod modeled moral leadership for his young charges, including Edgar. This application of religiously based moral principles to civic responsibilities certainly made an impact on young Hoover. He joined the Anti-Saloon League, the YMCA, and the Student Volunteer Movement, and he held an honorary membership in the Women's Christian Temperance Union. Hoover biographer Richard Powers has read this roster of organizations as "all part of Protestant America's defense against the immigrant threat."[70] And indeed, these public demonstrations of faith expose the roots of how Hoover came to view Christian morality and justice as the best way to manage a rapidly transforming American society. Later, Hoover would demonstrate his belief that the federal government was the ideal institution to serve as a moral regulator.

But an equally compelling explanation for Edgar's interest in organizations invested in moral instruction can be found in those groups' commitment to molding gentlemen of high moral character. Excepting the Student Volunteer Movement (which was focused on promoting international missionary service), a central interest—if not *the* central interest—of all these groups was the regulation of male morality. The Women's Christian Temperance Union and the Anti-Saloon League portrayed their missions as they related to *men*. They believed the most significant action that could be taken to improve the well-being of women and children was to curb the drinking of men. A reduction in male drunkenness provided a variety of moral improvements, including more consistent and present fathers, fewer rapes, less domestic violence, fewer women driven to prostitution, and fewer johns. Overall, temperance promised to return men to the home and thus reaffirm patriarchal order within the family. Hoover was thus constantly reminded of how central responsible Christian manhood was to the development of moral society. Thus, though the government may be the ideal institution to regulate societal adherence to Christian morality, male leadership—in the home, at the office, in Washington—had to be the primary vehicle for communicating that value system.

The tranquil domestic space that had nurtured Edgar during his childhood crumbled in the months before he graduated high school. In early 1913, Dickerson Sr. was hospitalized after a nervous breakdown. Suffering from "alternating moods of irritability and inconsolable sadness," he remained at the Laurel Sanitarium in Maryland for several months.[71]

No record exists as to whether (or how often) Edgar visited his father at that time. Dickerson struggled with mental illness in the subsequent years, and a relapse caused him to lose his job with the Coast and Geodetic Survey in April 1917. Shortly thereafter, he returned to the Laurel Sanitarium as a permanent resident. He would remain there until his death in 1921.

In addition to the emotional stress, Dickerson's institutionalization was a significant financial hardship for the Hoovers. The family lost his $2,000 annual income, and though he had worked for the government for forty-two years he was not entitled to a pension. Since Dickerson Jr. had his own family to support, the role of primary breadwinner fell to the family's youngest member. Though offered a scholarship to the University of Virginia, Hoover decided to remain close to home and attend George Washington University. College became an extension of his home life. When Edgar joined the Kappa Alpha fraternity, Annie Hoover became the brotherhood's "unofficial housemother." Edgar never seemed to quite shake the moralistic aspects of his upbringing; though he "seemed to enjoy masculine camaraderie, and loved playing practical jokes, one member [of Kappa Alpha] later recalled that Hoover 'took a dim view of such antics as crap games, poker, and drinking bouts.'"[72]

In July 1917, three months after his father's firing and shortly after receiving his master's degree in law from George Washington, Hoover accepted a clerkship with the United States Department of Justice. He would be employed there for the remainder of his life.

*

As Hoover negotiated the challenges of modernity by embracing a Christian-influenced version of masculinity and morality, a different discussion of those topics was taking shape in the pages of America's tabloids and gossip magazines. In many ways, the gossip industry of the early twentieth century was driven by many of the same anxieties—urbanization, immigration, industrialization, corporatization, changing gender roles—that animated the more conservative institutions to which Hoover pleaded fidelity. But the issues that kept social reformers awake at night were commercialized in the gossip press, which sought to entertain readers rather than frighten them. Most significantly, tabloids and gossip magazines provided Americans of all backgrounds a glimpse of the excitements of the modern city as well as a framework for making sense of the changing social landscape.

Though American gossip magazines have a deep, hazy lineage, their modern iteration can be traced to *Town Topics, the Journal of Society*. The magazine was founded in 1879 as *Andrews' American Queen: A National Society Journal* and primarily focused on publishing lists of attendees at society events. This formula did not lead to commercial success, and though retitled *Town Topics* in an effort at profitability, the enterprise was forced to declare bankruptcy in 1885. It was then acquired for bottom dollar by twenty-nine-year-old Eugene Mann, a lawyer with no publishing experience. Mann's retooled magazine adopted a livelier tone and modestly advertised itself as "the newsiest, brightest, wittiest, wisest, cleverest, most original, and most entertaining paper ever published."[73] Key to the redesign was "Saunterings," a breezy, gossip-filled column that reported stories too risqué for other publications. Over the next six years, "Saunterings" helped increase the magazine's circulation from 5,000 to 63,000 and justified a sevenfold increase in the publication's advertising rate.[74]

The magazine's new direction also attracted unwanted attention, particularly from the subjects of its unflattering reports. Aggrieved parties would present themselves at the *Town Topics* offices, demanding to see the author or editor of the offending piece. Those visits became so frequent that the editorial room instituted a new policy of telling angered visitors that whomever they sought had "died yesterday," and tearfully report that the offending article contained "the last words he ever wrote." No records exist as to whether this ruse was successful. Subjects' anger also took the form of an increasing number of lawsuits, both for libel and on the basis of sending vulgar materials through the mail. Mann was convicted on an obscenity charge in 1887 but only served a suspended sentence. He was arrested on the same charges in 1891, probably as a result of a "Saunterings" entry about the increasing popularity of abortion among young society women.[75]

Recognizing that a second conviction would likely lead to significant jail time, Mann faked an illness and skipped town, passing the editorship of *Town Topics* to his older brother, Colonel William d'Alton Mann. After being discharged from the Army in 1864, Colonel Mann had spent the next twenty-five years engaged in various entrepreneurial schemes—patenting a balancing mechanism for cavalrymen's rifles, prospecting for oil in western Pennsylvania, designing railroad cars—all of which met with varying degrees of failure.

Before inheriting *Town Topics*, Colonel Mann's one foray into media was as owner of the *Mobile Register*, a venture he had formed by combining three smaller newspapers in coastal Alabama. Using the newspaper to espouse Democratic Party positions and boost the politics of the newly founded Ku Klux Klan, Colonel Mann established a loyal network of supporters—no small feat for a Union veteran at the height of Reconstruction.

In the 1869 special election held after Alabama's readmittance to the Union, Colonel Mann ran for Congress as a Democrat, but lost primarily on account of the Black vote. He remained in Mobile for nearly three more years before leaving for New York and London, by then focused on his railroad car manufacture.[76]

Nearly two decades later, Colonel Mann returned to the editor's chair. He had probably owned a third of *Town Topics* since his brother bought it in 1885, but only undertook a significant role there upon the 1889 collapse of his railroad car business. It was likely Colonel Mann who had suggested that his brother lead *Town Topics* toward indecency after witnessing the success of salacious London tabloids such as the *World* and *Truth*.

Larger than life in every sense of the phrase—his prodigious gut was partially the result of daily meals at the Delmonico's Restaurant in Madison Square Park—Colonel Mann expanded on his brother's approach and turned *Town Topics* into a weekly treasury of rumors and innuendo about New York's elite, including the Astors and Vanderbilts.[77] He is credited with creating the "blind item," a now-ubiquitous feature of gossip publications that prints a rumor without identifying the subject. Never one for subtlety, Colonel Mann would place the subject's name in a nearby paragraph (often on the facing page), making the item much less opaque. He also pioneered the tactic of keeping on retainer various informants, including hotel clerks, theater stagehands, and restaurant maître-des.

"Saunterings" was filled with topics that were regarded as off-limits for other society magazines: alcoholism, premarital sex, venereal disease, adultery, children born out of wedlock, homosexuality, divorce. "New York society," Colonel Mann once claimed, "cannot become more worthless, meaningless, and theatrical than it is today. It is inhabited by jackasses, libertines, and parvenus."[78] His ambition, reported an interviewer in the *New York Times*, was to reform socialites "by making them too deeply disgusted with themselves to continue their silly, empty way of life." In Colonel Mann's own words, he was "teaching the great American public not to pay any attention to these silly fools," noting that if he did not publish *Town Topics* then a rival "without any sense of moral responsibility" would do so. "I do this work," he concluded, "for the sake of the community and for the sake of the great American Nation."[79]

There was not much that Colonel Mann's "sense of moral responsibility" prevented him from publishing. "Saunterings" was a tour de force of judgment, insult, and scorn. "Mrs. Belmont dyes her hair," one issue cattily reported, "[and] though covered with diamond rings, her hands are wrinkled like a washerwoman's." Another column described a Miss Van Alen who "suffers from some kind of throat trouble—she cannot go more than half an hour without a drink."[80] The magazine also charged subjects with homosexuality and effeminacy, such as when it described the socialite "Harry Lehr's proud parade of his many sissy qualities," including "his pink complexion and golden hair, his thin voice, his peculiar gestures, [and] the feminine prettiness of his general make-up," which had "gone beyond the limits of tolerance by decent society."[81] In using gender to allude to well-known rumors of Lehr's homosexuality, *Town Topics* pioneered a classic gossip magazine tactic. Furthermore, *Town Topics*' suggestion that there was *any* level of tolerance for "sissy qualities" in a male socialite speaks to an evolving, class-contingent definition of hegemonic masculinity in late Victorian America.

At the same time, "Saunterings" presented gossip with a knowing wink. Regardless of how serious the accusations may have been, the overall affect was largely one of levity. As Colonel Mann had claimed, "Saunterings" sought to poke fun at the self-seriousness of New York's upper crust; he was intent on playing the court jester whose jokes cut a bit too deeply. Embracing a lighter approach, the column included brief, topical jokes in between its longer news items: *"May—'I hear you are very charitably inclined'; Merit—'Yes; I always give my cast-off suitors to my younger sisters.'"*[82] That breezy, knowing tone would be adopted by most subsequent American gossip magazines. But "Saunterings" largely avoided explicitly political gossip, preferring to focus on domestic and social intrigues.

Most importantly for *Town Topics*, "Saunterings" attracted readers. By 1893 the magazine's cover included the proud declaration, "Guaranteed Circulation, Over 75,000."[83] A New York socialite later recalled that *Town Topics* "found its way into almost every cottage in [Tuxedo] Park, as it did into the cottages, villas, and mansions at Newport. It was read upstairs, downstairs, and backstairs."[84] The magazine's appeal to readers from across the socioeconomic spectrum is apparent in both its content and the types of advertisers it attracted. A recurring section called "Other People's Money" used energetic prose to identify "hints for both bulls and bears." The shallowness of that advice—and the fact that it appeared in the back pages of a gossip magazine—suggests that it was aimed at casual investors, or those looking to the stock market as a way to improve their middling class position. "The spring season is never propitious for a bull movement," the February 16, 1893, issue cautioned, "but it offers opportunities to the capitalist and gives even the investor with a comparatively small margin to pick up, on weak days, securities which, if held a certain time, will return very handsome profits." The same column also referred to terms that were popular in "Wall Street parlance," suggesting that the imagined audience was not Wall Street insiders.[85]

Advertisements typically appeared in the final two or three pages of the magazine (like the classifieds section of a newspaper) or as one-line reminders at the bottom of each column. Notices for railroad lines and investment opportunities were popular and suggest a more monied readership.[86] But the most common advertisements were those promising routes to aesthetic improvement. In January 1893, Mrs. M. A. Potter (the "only lady practitioner in the city") advertised "ELECTROLYSES: The only known permanent method for removing superfluous hair and blemishes without pain and without leaving the slightest scar." Immediately below Mrs. Potter's notice appeared advertisements for Packer's Tar Soap ("For Chapping, Chafing, Itching, Bad Complexion and Odors from Perspiration"); a mystery cure offering "Superb Form, Lovely Complexion, and Perfect Health," by Mrs. Ella M. Dent of San Francisco; and "Lilacine" sold by the Ladies Elite Club of South Bend, Indiana ("Ladies use Lilacine for Beautifying and Developing their features. Used by all leading Society Ladies").[87] The surfeit of listings related to self-improvement can be read as bringing together the national focus on social improvement with the anxieties born of the instability of "personality."

The advertisements also trace the development of national name brands, which were both indicative of and enabled by modernization. The Smith-Dunkley Company of Kalamazoo, Michigan, promised to mail its Famous Kalamazoo Canned Celery to any American address for free, and the Chicago-based Pozzoni Company hawked its Complexion Powder as being available "at all druggists and fancy stores."[88] At the bottom of an "Other People's Money" column, a beverage company advised readers to remain brand loyal: "Ask at your club or at the café for 'JOHANNIS.' It mixes perfectly with all liquors and wines. Don't accept any other water as a substitute."[89] At the same time, advertising took up a very small portion of the magazine and the majority of *Town Topics'* income was derived from subscriptions and newsstand sales.

The magazine's widespread popularity faltered only as a result of a sensational trial. In 1905, Mann and *Town Topics* were charged with blackmail after an employee was caught extorting Edwin Post, the cheating husband of future etiquette expert Emily. Reenacting a common scene, Colonel Mann's representative approached Post with evidence of his misdeeds, including the address of a cottage at which Post had installed his mistress. If Post wanted to avoid seeing the details of his affair in *Town Topics*, he would have to pony up $500. Frightened—and possibly not liquid enough—

Post confessed to his wife, who then suggested they involve the police department. A sting operation resulted in the arrest of Charles Ahle, Colonel Mann's assistant. *Town Topics'* extortion schemes had been the bane of the city's misbehaving elite; when Post arrived for work at the New York Stock Exchange the day after the sting, his fellow stockbrokers paused trading to give him a standing ovation.[90]

The Posts also filed a civil lawsuit. Colonel Mann was able to successfully fend it off; in fact, he never lost a libel case. But *Town Topics* was changed forever. Though the magazine continued to cover gossip—especially via the "not-so-blind items"—it became relatively gun-shy and adopted a more conservative tone. That moderation ultimately led to a dip in its circulation numbers and it never regained the status it had once held.[91]

Though relatively brief, *Town Topics'* reign coincided with a key moment in the development of surveillance state masculinity. The magazine was a product not only of the Manns' combination of entrepreneurship, boldness, and social acumen, but of larger forces that were transforming American society at the end of the nineteenth century. In a way, *Town Topics* was an attempt to respond to a variety of social challenges posed by the ongoing developments wrought by modernity, including the desire for social connection in an increasingly complex and anonymizing public sphere, the opportunity to craft a new identity in the context of burgeoning consumer capitalism, the anxiety surrounding shifting gender and sexual politics, and the resulting need to redefine social mores.

A decade after Edwin Post effectively sterilized *Town Topics*, the magazine *Broadway Brevities and Society Gossip* emerged as the nation's most notorious gossip periodical. Published in New York City between 1916 and 1925 by the Canadian-born provocateur Stephen G. Clow, *Broadway Brevities* featured both society and theater gossip, and was a master class on using innuendo to suggest scandal. Years after the magazine's downfall, the syndicated columnist Westbrook Pegler would dub Clow "the originator of Saloon journalism."[92] Notably, *Broadway Brevities* identified the subjects of its gossip by name. In the words of media historian Will Straw, "the targets of its gossip were often social types who had assumed a new notoriety in the postwar economic boom: newly rich entrepreneurs, manufacturers of faddish products (like facial regeneration creams), and Manhattanites newly arrived from the Midwest."[93] But like Colonel Mann, Clow used *Broadway Brevities* to fuel a blackmail operation, promising glowing coverage of wealthy targets such as the producer Tex Rickard so long as they advertised in the magazine.[94] Other men—including yeast magnate Julius Fleischmann, New York Yankees owner Jacob Ruppert, and banker

W. Averell Harriman—paid Clow to keep unflattering items about them out of *Broadway Brevities*.

Perhaps the most noteworthy element of *Broadway Brevities* was its homophobic sensationalism, an aspect most visible in the recurring feature "Nights in Fairyland." That series of articles, which purported to be a behind-the-scenes look at the city's gay nightlife, ran to at least thirteen entries. The series promised readers access to the secret world of "androgynes," which *Broadway Brevities* defined as "those psychopathic hybrids we today are pleased to call fairies."[95] The articles' unidentified writers adopted the tone of knowing tour guides, wittily guiding readers through the horrors that lurked in various Manhattan neighborhoods. "Fairydom has its 'quarters,'" one dispatch reported. "In the Bowery poor and shabby fags of every breed may be seen; in the Bronx, fags of Jewish descent; in Mulberry street inverts Italiano; in Chinatown the comical oriental urning. Not less may be observed in the colored neighborhood of Lenox Avenue, on that long reach from 110th Street to 160th Street, hordes of 'big boys,' flamboyantly arrayed, plying the oldest and most noxious of all trades . . . And so throughout the city—throughout the nation—throughout the world."[96] In this tour a reader could identify not only the sexual perversity wrought by urbanization but the troubling amalgamation created by immigration (and the great, ongoing internal migration of Black Americans). Though the series sometimes mentioned lesbianism, the vast majority of its coverage—and its most palpable anxieties—centered on gay men: they were the foot soldiers in this queer world invasion.

In addition to demonstrating that stories about homosexuality could improve sales, "Nights in Fairyland" helped introduce the reading public to terminology referring to homosexuals, including "camp," "fairy," "punk," "fag," and "invert." The series also identified famous theater actors, directors, and producers who attended parties where same-sex liaisons were said to occur; full names were sometimes reported, but more often the authors only provided a subject's initials—a tactic that expanded the umbrella of suspicion. Despite the series' playful tone, the nefarious implications of the subculture it revealed were clear. The series' eleventh entry, from November 1924, closed with a "Warning to Fagdom!":

What a dirty mess! Yet it's but a hint of "things present and things to come." Verily, in this year of our Lord, 1924, the question is—as a brilliant psychiatrist remarked to us the other day—not of "who is" but of "who isn't." Into the very warp and woof of our modern social fabric has eaten devastatingly this cancer of sexual inversion, wiping out manhood and womanhood, making a mockery of natural love, of normal behavior, wrecking homes and lives untold. The sickening stench of homosexuality is in the nostrils of all of us, and for all of us its menace is stupendous. It is, indeed, the pestilence that stalks alike at noonday and night, enfeebling and degrading our civilization, making a by-word of all that is clean and sweet and of good repute. If, in these articles, *Brevities* has been able to abate by one jot this epidemic of shameless lechery, then we feel that our efforts have not been in vain. And to such noble purpose are dedicated the still more relentless exposures to come![97]

In such a cultural milieu, any man who did not actively affirm and reaffirm his masculinity and accompanying heterosexuality was open to constant suspicion.

THE PROFESSIONAL BUREAUCRAT
IN THE PUBLIC EYE

As J. Edgar Hoover strode toward the parked car, the driver turned and lunged for a rifle in the back seat. Before Alvin "Creepy" Karpis could reach the weapon, Hoover grabbed him by the collar. Karpis raised his hands in surrender. "Put the cuffs on him, boys," Hoover directed his associates. The twenty-eight-year-old criminal known to newspaper readers as the current "Public Enemy No. 1" had been captured.[1]

At least, that is how Hoover recounted the events of May 1, 1936, when he spoke to the news media later that day. "Karpis Captured in New Orleans by Hoover Himself," announced a front-page headline in the *New York Times*; "Hoover Leads 20 Agents in Arresting Nation's No. 1 Outlaw," the *Washington Post* echoed.[2] Once again, J. Edgar Hoover had secured the top target in his "War on Crime."

It is unclear what actually transpired when Hoover and a group of agents from the Federal Bureau of Investigation captured Karpis outside a small apartment building on the 3300 block of New Orleans's Canal Street. FBI records largely support Hoover's retelling: Hoover was in the raiding party; Karpis was visibly frightened upon arrest; there were weapons—including a rifle—found in the Plymouth. But those same records include no mention of Hoover literally "collaring" Karpis or even approaching the car.[3] In his

1971 autobiography, Karpis argued that Hoover was not the hero, emerging only after his underlings had cornered Karpis and made sure the area was secure. "He didn't lead the attack on me," Karpis wrote. "He waited until he was told the coast was clear. Then he came out to reap the glory."[4] Karpis also noted that it would have been impossible for him to reach for a gun in the back seat because his Plymouth was a coupe—there was no back seat.

Nevertheless, contemporary reports of Karpis's capture illuminate much about the FBI's early years and Hoover's role in them. Hoover's presence at Karpis's arrest was part of a public-relations push by the agency's forty-one-year-old leader, whom a senator had recently accused of falsely burnishing his own reputation as a crime fighter. During an April meeting of a subcommittee of the Senate Appropriations Committee, Tennessee Democrat Kenneth McKellar had suggested that Hoover and his FBI were taking credit for investigative successes that should have been attributed to local and state police forces. McKellar even insinuated that Hoover was not the stellar policeman the Bureau's public relations arm had made him out to be. "How many arrests have you made," McKellar asked Hoover, "and who were they?"[5] Though Hoover cited successful cases that he had led, an honest answer would have been "none." To reclaim lost face, Hoover vowed to be present for the Bureau's next major arrest. Upon hearing that agents had traced Karpis to New Orleans, he hopped a plane to be present for the raid.

In his public comments after Karpis was apprehended, Hoover drew reporters' attention to details that portrayed the Bureau as a force that married traditionally hard-nosed law enforcement with modern police tactics. Echoing the Bureau, the United Press dispatch praised the agents' boldness and efficiency. "Out to avenge the murder of four fellow agents, of which Karpis was suspected," the report said, "the Federal men struck with such dramatic suddenness that people in the neighborhood thought it was only a minor police case disturbance." The UPI also noted that the Bureau agents were "so sure of their prey that they had chartered a special airplane to take Karpis to St. Paul even before they sprung their trap."[6] When reports emerged that the Bureau's success had been the by-product of a random tip from a car salesman, Hoover sought to reaffirm the investigation's scientific nature, telling reporters that the real break in the case was a fingerprint pulled off a beer bottle spotted by eagle-eyed FBI agents at a former Karpis gang hideout.[7]

Media reports portrayed the dynamic between Karpis and his Bureau pursuers as a classic black hat vs. white hat narrative familiar to readers of Western pulps. Numerous articles identified Karpis as a "desperado"—

a canned reference to outlaws of an imagined Wild West—and his captors to legendary lawmen like Wyatt Earp.[8] Like those sheriffs of yore, the Bureau agents were motivated by more than merely a sense of duty, they were also "out to avenge the murder of four fellow agents." Hoover continually stressed that once Karpis was captured, the criminal's true colors were promptly revealed. He emphasized Karpis's fear, recalling that "immediately after his arrest he begged me to order him killed immediately. I never saw a man more afraid. His knees were actually knocking together when we closed in on him in his automobile."[9] Karpis was "so damned scared he couldn't talk," recounted Hoover to another reporter, concluding that criminals "are all yellow rats to us."[10]

Karpis was the last celebrity criminal captured during the so-called War on Crime to be deemed worthy of the front page. Though the phrase "war on crime" predated J. Edgar Hoover's use of it—American newspapers had employed it for authorities' concerted efforts to combat lawbreaking since at least the mid-1920s—it was Hoover who turned the term into an advertising slogan during a three-year period in which Bureau agents battled a rotating cast of bandits, bank robbers, and gangsters. To celebrate the Bureau's successes, the *Chicago Daily Tribune*'s coverage of Karpis's arrest featured a yearbook-like spread of photographs documenting the criminals Hoover and his men had captured or killed, including John Dillinger, "Machine Gun" Kelly, "Pretty Boy" Floyd, Bonnie Parker and Clyde Barrow, "Baby Face" Nelson, and members of the Barker family ("Ma" and her son Fred).[11] The "war" cemented Hoover in public consciousness as the nation's foremost bulwark against encroaching criminal activity. But in a deeper sense, Hoover had situated himself and the Bureau in a way that allowed each to take advantage of a changing economic landscape, concerns over a perceived decline in national morality, the corporatization of the federal bureaucracy (particularly in relation to its law and order responsibilities), and the emergence of the mass media. In all these areas, Hoover used public perceptions of gender to position both himself and the Bureau as a masculine bulwark against threats to the nation.

Between the time Hoover joined the Department of Justice in 1917 and the end of World War II, the Bureau of Investigation (BOI, rechristened the Federal Bureau of Investigation in 1935) became a crucible in which many of the central elements of surveillance state masculinity were forged. Even before Hoover's arrival, the Bureau had sought and embraced a role not just as a federal police force but as the nation's moral arbiter, a position that allowed it to increase its stature relative to other law enforcement arms of the federal government and supersede local and state authorities. But the early Bureau also experienced organizational disarray and its leaders fell victim to accusations of malfeasance; the 1924 Teapot Dome scandal created the leadership vacuum that enabled Hoover to exert such complete control over the BOI when he assumed the role of its director that same year. As director, Hoover continued the BOI's interest in policing morality, arguing that domestic security was directly related to the nation's moral character. But he also remade the Bureau by instituting a set of sweeping personal, professional, and moral standards. The introduction of scientific policing tactics, instillation of a corporate organizational philosophy, and the repositioning of Bureau agents as a new kind of American hero (the "G-Man") turned the Bureau into one of the government's most powerful agencies and Hoover into one of the nation's most culturally significant figures. In his quest to remake the Bureau and create a cult of personality around himself, Hoover was both aided and impeded by the nation's mass media; Hollywood movies, radio serials, and comic books sang the praises of the G-Man and friendly journalists treated Hoover as a celebrity, but gossip columnists and reporters suspicious of Hoover's growing power printed rumors questioning Hoover's self-styled machismo. Overall, Hoover relied on a gender-based understanding of identity that blended white-collar concepts of morality and respectability, emerging notions of modern epistemology suggesting scientific certainty, and classic masculine tropes like the frontier lawman.

It is tempting to argue that the intended beneficiary of Hoover's approach was Hoover himself, particularly since many portrayals of the man depict him as possessing a Macbethian obsession with power and control. But Hoover's actions were predicated on more than a personal quest for power. They were the expression of a worldview centered on the interests of heterosexual, pious, law-abiding, white men dedicated to preserving "true Americanism," that is, men who fit the mold that Hoover himself had sought to fill. In a way, Hoover did not pursue policies that would benefit himself personally; he forwarded ones that ensured America would become a nation in his own image.

*

Hoover began working for the federal government while he was an undergraduate at George Washington University, serving as a messenger and clerk for the Library of Congress. In the spring of 1917, Hoover used family connections to secure a job as a clerk at the War Emergency Division of the Department of Justice.[12] Although the United States had recently declared war on Germany, Hoover's status as a government employee meant that he was granted a deferment from the draft. Some commentators have seen cowardice in this avoidance of military service, but Hoover's motivation was most likely to support his mother in the wake of his father's institutionalization. The more telling aspect of Hoover's first full-time employment is that the job owed its existence to an expanding wartime government, an expansion that would become the institutional basis for the creation of an unprecedented national security apparatus.

Wartime manpower demands in the Department of Justice led Hoover to be promoted twice within his first six months of employment. By all accounts, this rapid rise was deserved. A 1937 *New Yorker* profile described Hoover in those days: "He dressed better than most, and a bit on the dandyish side. He had an exceptional capacity for detail work, and he handled small chores with enthusiasm and thoroughness. He constantly sought new responsibilities to shoulder and welcomed chances to work overtime. When he was in conference with an official of his department, his manner was that of a young man who confidently expected to rise."[13] He was constantly in the office, working twelve hours a day, seven days a week. That notorious work ethic remained with Hoover throughout his professional life.[14]

Hoover was soon named the head of the War Emergency Division's Alien Enemy Bureau, and at the conclusion of the war in November 1918, he was made an assistant to the attorney general. Less than a year later, Attorney General A. Mitchell Palmer placed Hoover in charge of the General Intelligence Division (GID, sometimes known as the "radicals section"). Two years after that promotion, when the GID was assigned to the Bureau of Investigation as part of a reorganization, Hoover was named the Bureau's assistant director. On May 10, 1924, after a series of scandals in the Warren G. Harding administration had decimated the upper ranks of the Department of Justice, new attorney general Harlan Fiske Stone appointed Hoover acting director of the Bureau. The position was made permanent later that year—effectively, Hoover would hold the job for the rest of his life.

Hoover's rapid ascent from Department of Justice clerk to director of the Bureau of Investigation coincided with a fundamental shift in the role of those two institutions in American law enforcement. In addition to protecting citizen safety, guarding personal property, and promoting civil order, in the first decades of the twentieth century the Bureau of Investigation became a vehicle for the Department of Justice to enforce a conservative code of sexual morality, exerting control over activities such as prostitution, miscegenation, adultery, and bigamy. The primary reason for the Bureau's investment in policing sexual morality was apparent public demand. The forces of industrialization, including economic modernization, urbanization, immigration, and the resulting shifts in social relationships, combined to make a substantial sector of the public fear a fracturing of the nation's moral structure.[15] The Bureau was also motivated to police sexual morality because it presented an opportunity to improve its standing in the federal bureaucratic hierarchy. The circumstances surrounding the Bureau's 1908 founding had left it without a clear operational directive, and thus it was constantly competing with other agencies—local, state, and federal—for jurisdiction. Policing morality allowed the Bureau to increase its power, relative both to other federal agencies and local and state institutions. The legal device enabling that oversight was the White-Slave Traffic Act—popularly known as the Mann Act. That legislation outlawed the interstate or foreign transportation of "any woman or girl for the purpose of prostitution or debauchers, or for any immoral purpose."[16] The act's broad, nonspecific language—particularly the "any immoral purpose" clause—left its exact limitations open to interpretation. Was the act merely an antikidnapping and antiprostitution bill? Or was it intended to also allow the state to police sexual immorality more generally, including cases of adultery and bigamy?

By and large, the Bureau embraced the broader interpretation. It was particularly aggressive in targeting "nontraditional" relationships, especially unmarried couples and pairings in which the marriage seemed to be one of convenience (i.e., founded on a business relationship rather than a procreative one). The Bureau believed that in policing sexual vice it was ultimately protecting American families by promoting marital fidelity and combating the transmission of venereal disease. This focus only expanded under J. Edgar Hoover's leadership. From 1921 until 1936, the Bureau investigated approximately 47,500 Mann Act cases. In a 1930 appearance before Congress, Hoover estimated that Bureau agents spent nearly a third of their time investigating Mann Act violations.[17] A decade later, Hoover bragged that Bureau investigations had led to 476 Mann Act convictions during the 1940 fiscal year.[18]

Perhaps Hoover's most significant early contribution to the Bureau's morality policing was his creation of the Obscene File. The sense that the nation's moral sentries were in retreat had only been exacerbated by developments in the late 1910s and early 1920s. The mass mobilization of citizens to urban areas as a result of World War I provided newly independent individuals the opportunity to push the limits of conservative value systems, and the nearly two million American soldiers and sailors deployed to Europe during the war had come into contact with more sexually permissive societies there.[19] The economic growth facilitated by the United States' subsequent emergence as a true global power fostered libertine excess during what history has come to call the Roaring Twenties. These anxieties led a number of social reform organizations to advocate for more stringent limitations on the distribution of obscene materials. The high-water mark of this effort came in 1923–25, when a series of moral reformers banded together to begin the Clean Books Crusade, a series of campaigns to eradicate works branded as literary smut from libraries and booksellers.[20]

In March 1925, Hoover established a formal policy for dealing with any material that Bureau special agents deemed obscene: it was to be placed in a sealed envelope or box with the word "OBSCENE" printed in bold on the exterior. It appears that the agents initially had their choice of housing the materials at their regional field office or forwarding them to Bureau headquarters in Washington. The process of collecting and organizing these materials began slowly, but Bureau officials noted that by 1932 they possessed a "substantial collection of obscene materials."[21] Though an official, centralized Obscene File was not formally indexed until 1942, Hoover's decision to institute a process for managing obscene materials so soon after becoming director signifies a number of key aspects of his leadership style, including his concern with issues of morality, his penchant for organization, and his focus on building archives that could be used in future investigations and anticrime initiatives.

Those final two emphases—organization and archive building—contributed to Hoover's establishment of the Bureau's crime laboratory in 1932. It was intended to bring the Bureau into the twentieth century through the application of what Hoover described as "scientific policing tactics." These new methods included the recovery and matching of fingerprints (relying on the Fingerprint Division that Hoover had established as a nationwide clearinghouse in 1924), handwriting analysis, moulage (the study of physical injuries), fiber analysis, and firearms ballistics. In 1938, Hoover proudly claimed that the Bureau's Identification Division "annually aids in the capture of nearly 6,500 fugitives from justice."[22] The 1935 establishment of the National Police Academy helped cement the Bureau's reputation for investigative expertise in the minds of the general public by serving as a kind of graduate program at which local and state police officers were schooled in the Bureau's purportedly advanced investigative methods.

In Hoover's self-serving words, academy graduates were "equipped to return to their communities as well versed in the latest methods of apprehension and detection as the G-Men themselves."[23]

Hoover sought to present the Bureau as a thoroughly modern policing unit that used a logical, scientific approach to solving crimes too complex for other investigative forces. Hoover wanted to foster in the public a certain awe for the Bureau, thus rendering unimpeachable the agency's investigative approach—especially its more problematic aspects. As Hoover's later actions demonstrated, emphasizing these characteristics also helped establish G-Men as the personification of a new kind of white-collar, professional masculinity. More fundamentally, the institution of those "scientific policing tactics" enabled the Bureau to more closely monitor American bodies, meaning that the actual physicality of a person could be regarded as criminal. In so doing, Hoover's Bureau was not only helping to define which actions were illegal, but projecting criminality onto bodies themselves and thereby embracing a biologically based notion of how identity traits like race, class, gender, and sexuality indicated an individual's morality.

Other strategies instituted or reintroduced by Hoover brought the Bureau into citizens' private spaces, including the use of listening devices such as bugs and wiretaps, and a reliance on confidential informants.[24] The adoption of those tools infused domestic policing with surveillance tactics that the US military had originally used to counter the Filipino insurgency during the first decades of the twentieth century.[25] Paired with the concurrent criminalization of bodies, that incursion into private space would fundamentally influence how Americans perceived the linkages among criminality, sexuality, and political identity.

From a bureaucratic standpoint, policing sexual morality through the Mann Act and the collection of obscene materials offered the Bureau the opportunity to carve out a niche for itself in the national law enforcement apparatus. At the time, many of the tasks that might be delegated to a national police force were already performed by state and local authorities. The fledgling Bureau was able to use obscenity and Mann Act cases as routes to increased jurisdiction precisely because those issues both necessitated the involvement of a federal agency and enjoyed broad public support.[26] By witnessing these developments firsthand, Hoover learned that public opinion could bestow upon a public servant the ability to cut through bureaucratic red tape and even circumvent constitutional limitations.

*

Upon being named its director, J. Edgar Hoover set out to rebrand the Bureau and cast off the corrupt reputation it had developed during its first thirteen years of existence. Because Hoover's promotion had been so closely tied to the bureaucratic impropriety of the Harding administration, he was insistent on instilling a strict organizational code of ethics, noting that "the Bureau cannot afford to have a public scandal visited upon it in the view of the all too numerous attacks made . . . during the past few years. I do not want this Bureau to be referred to in terms I have frequently heard used against other government agencies."[27] In order to effectively regulate morality, the Bureau itself had to be a model of integrity.

Hoover ultimately wanted to refashion the Bureau into the nation's most elite, efficient, and respected police force. To do so he relied on a two-pronged strategy, both aspects of which grew out of the moralistic masculinity he had learned in the pews of "Old First" Presbyterian and the hallways of Central High School. Hoover endeavored to make the Bureau skilled, resourceful, methodical, moral, and just, embodying a series of masculine-aligned characteristics that it had lacked. Concurrently, he also sought to ensconce himself in the public imagination as the personification of those masculine hallmarks. He would be the Bureau, and the Bureau would be him.

Imbuing the agency with Hoover's sense of masculine propriety and tough-mindedness served multiple purposes. First, it reassured a skeptical public that the Bureau would place morality at the center of its mission. Second, it spoke to that public in a common language, aligning the Bureau's value system and hierarchy with a familiar, readable patriarchal order; Hoover was the father figure of an organization committed to keeping the national "family" safe. Finally, it placed Hoover himself in a stronger position, associating him with the characteristics the nation valued in its heroes while concurrently cloaking him in a protective garment that deflected attacks on his own sexuality and gender identity.

But Hoover's efforts to redefine the Bureau's institutional culture were born of more than a personal fidelity to neatness, discipline, and order. They also represented an attempt to mold the Bureau into an embodiment of a masculine ideal. In presenting the Bureau of Investigation as the product of masculine ideals applied to a modern police force, Hoover created a new class of law-enforcement officer, the G-Man. The origins of the term—short for "Government Man"—are unclear. The FBI itself likes to point to a (likely apocryphal) tale surrounding the arrest of kidnapper and bank robber George "Machine Gun" Kelly in September 1933. Realizing that Bureau agents had surrounded the small Memphis home in which he was hiding, Kelly relinquished his namesake weapon and emerged from the house with his hands in the air, pleading, "Don't shoot, G-Men! Don't shoot!"[28] A more likely explanation is that the term began as slang for any government agent before being specifically attached to Bureau agents during the 1930s War on Crime.

Though the nickname would not enter the popular lexicon until the mid-1930s, Hoover began to create the G-Man as soon as he was appointed director. The G-Men who roamed Bureau headquarters and its field offices were constructed as professional guardians of American domesticity and security, the living embodiment of a masculine, Christian approach to law and order. With the cultural G-Man—the men who populated the public imagination—Hoover created a modern super-sleuth, combining elements of comic book heroes, matinee cowboys, and pulp fiction detectives.

The origins of Hoover's masculine vision can be seen in a fundamental shift in manhood that developed as a result of the corporate and managerial revolutions of the late nineteenth century. Those economic changes prompted structural transformations in the American labor market, ultimately divorcing men from the fruits of their labor and promoting the growth of a middle class of white-collar middle managers. No longer able to prove their masculinity through physical labor or artisanal creation, men sought to change sociocultural notions of office work. As historian Angel Kwolek-Folland notes, "The evolving nature of managerial capitalism in the late nineteenth century demanded new notions of manhood . . . The popular definition linking manhood with business attempted to reconcile the sedentary, acquisitive, and consumer-oriented pursuits of business with new physical notions of manhood, and older mercantilist ideas of economic structure and the place of men in society."[29]

To reclaim their manhood, white-collar men employed a variety of tactics. One was to embrace an aggressive form of masculinity constructed around the idea that—in the words of historian John Pettegrew—men had inherited "pugnacity from their savage progenitors and prehistory's violent demands of heterosexual competition, hunting, and war."[30] This "primitivism" was regarded as one way to counter the effeminizing impulses of "overcivilization." An interrelated tactic was for men to embrace individualism, which, alongside virility, was regarded as the most likely quality to be lost to modernization.[31]

In seeking to resuscitate the manhood of white-collar government employees, Hoover was negotiating not only changing notions of white-collar manhood generally, but longstanding stereotypes that regarded government bureaucrats as powerless paper pushers. In 1873, one commentator wrote that a government clerk had "no independence while in office, no manhood . . . he must openly avow his implicit faith in all his superiors, on pain of dismissal, and must cringe and fawn upon them."[32] This impotence might have been put to rest by adopting a primitivist, individualist outlook, but the bureaucratic imperatives of Hoover's position meant that he had to redefine obedience and fidelity as masculine attributes. To accomplish this delicate task, Hoover sought to combine the impulse for masculinist individualism with Protestant-influenced ideals of manhood that emphasized what one historian describes as "self-control, the stabilizing effect of property ownership, a responsible paternalistic relationship to family and society, altruism, charity, and the religious virtue inherent in fulfilling one's 'calling' in life."[33] Of course, this understanding of masculinity fit well with the lessons a younger Hoover had learned.

Looking to begin with as blank a slate as possible and impress his congressional overseers, upon taking the reins of the agency Hoover immediately cut its workforce and returned 12.5 percent of its annual budget appropriation.[34] To both ensure and measure his success, Hoover turned to the theory of scientific management, an approach that "posed business operations as mechanical, automatic, impersonal, and measurable."[35] Hoover understood that the adoption of such principles would attract the approval of a Congress and public that had been offended by the agency's recent scandals.

He then redesigned the Bureau's hiring practices. Hoover wanted to ensure that most successful applicants to the position of special agent fit a narrow profile: white men from "high class" backgrounds who had achieved graduate degrees in the law or accounting and who demonstrated neatness in their physical appearance. Ideal candidates had often demonstrated their fidelity to Christian virtue and community building through their memberships in national fraternal organizations such as the Masons. Hoover preferred to hire single men, arguing that they were less encumbered by familial obligations and could privilege the job above all else.[36]

Clyde Tolson, who would become Hoover's top assistant at the Bureau and lifelong companion, fit this profile almost perfectly when he applied to the Bureau in 1928. When asked about Tolson's desirability as an employee, a former supervisor gave a positive report, noting that Tolson "has shown no particular interest in women."[37] Though this remark could be read as revealing Tolson's sexual preferences, it does nothing of the sort.

So inconceivable was it that a young professional man would be anything but heterosexual that the comment was a mark of praise, demonstrating his single-minded dedication to the job. As historian Claire Bond Potter has noted, "By the early 1930s, men at the upper levels of the Bureau would have made annual reports similar to Tolson's: Kappa Alpha, Sigma Nu, the Masons. Youth organizations that promoted masculine value systems, such as cadet corps and the Boy Scouts, also counted in an applicant's favor. Those patterns project[ed] Hoover's belief not only in the correctness of his own career path but also that virtuous men were not born but made as they adopted institutional values and disciplines."[38] Hoover also focused on hiring men in the early stages of their careers, proudly noting in 1939 that "the average age today of the men of the FBI is scarcely 34."[39] While Hoover advertised this focus as emerging from a commitment to youthful energy, it can also be seen as an effort to indoctrinate agents before other corporate cultures influenced them.

New hires had to complete a rigid, comprehensive training program that Hoover devised to shape special agents into professional, efficient investigators who would serve as the most visible and essential parts of the Bureau machine.[40] No single agent was to be regarded as greater than the agency (excepting, of course, Hoover himself). An agent who criticized his superiors or the agency would find himself sentenced to desk duty at a sleepy field office, regardless of how effective he had been in the field. Even Melvin Purvis, perhaps the Bureau's most famous field agent (who led successful manhunts for "Pretty Boy" Floyd and John Dillinger) felt Hoover's wrath following public remarks the director perceived as critical.[41]

All agents were expected to adhere to a strict code of conduct. To assure compliance, the director commonly surprised employees with unannounced inspections of their offices, recordkeeping practices, and personal appearance. Like a drill sergeant (or the drill team captain he had been), Hoover insisted that agents have shined shoes, well-tailored suits, trimmed mustaches, and neat hairstyles. He required that all agents take an annual physical fitness test and promoted athletics by sponsoring a number of interagency sports teams.[42] In a memo to all special agents in charge, Hoover explained his belief that each agent "must so conduct himself, both officially and unofficially, as to eliminate the slightest possibility of criticism as to his conduct or actions . . . What I am trying to do is to protect the force of the Bureau of Investigation from outside criticism and from bringing the Bureau of Investigation into disrepute because of isolated circumstances of misconduct upon the part of employees who are too strongly addicted to their own personal desires and tastes to properly keep in mind at all times and upon all occasions the honor and integrity of the service of which they are a part."[43]

Hoover's demand that Bureau employees manage "their own personal desires and tastes" suggests that he believed all men possessed urges that necessitated conscious management. That belief fit with the understanding of male primitivism that had found acceptance in popular culture and sociology since the late Victorian era.[44] If Hoover did identify in himself "abnormal" sexual proclivities that he needed to control, his directive can also be read as self-referential. There is evidence to suggest that Hoover saw homosexual acts in such a framework; during an investigation into allegations of homosexuality against Undersecretary of State Sumner Welles in the early 1940s, Hoover attributed Welles's misbehavior to a lack of self-control.[45] As Hoover said in 1941, "In the FBI, we demand that the character of our men be unsullied and above suspicion."[46] Personal associations aside, that phrasing also provides insight into Hoover's view that a moral character was something a man could cultivate through self-restraint. The capacity for and necessity of self-control were essential elements that G-Men borrowed from turn-of-the-century notions of professional, white-collar masculinity, particularly in their suggestion that agents were not criminally corruptible and could be trained to serve as moral role models for the general populace.

Ever aware of the import of public opinion, Hoover was determined to manage how his Bureau and its agents were portrayed in the media.[47] The first step in this process was to foster warm relations with journalists. Hoover knew that the press had helped galvanize public support behind the early Bureau's fights against sex trafficking and obscenity, and he instructed agents to act accordingly. "It is my desire that all Bureau employees be courteous at all times in dealing with representatives of the press," Hoover wrote to Melvin Purvis after the agent had been less than gracious to a United Press reporter.[48] Hoover himself sought to foster congenial relationships with powerful newspapermen such as Walter Winchell, Ed Sullivan, and Rex Collier. Attending a boxing match at Yankee Stadium in the fall of 1935, Hoover strategically elected to sit with one group of reporters while Tolson charmed another cluster; the fight itself was clearly not the only reason the G-Men appeared at the event.[49]

Hoover—often via ghostwriters—directly addressed the public through regular contributions to newspapers and magazines. Articles carrying his byline appeared frequently beginning in 1933–34, coinciding with the advent of the War on Crime. In these columns and op-eds, Hoover delivered lectures on numerous topics, including the role of classroom teachers in combating crime, espionage, juvenile delinquency, female criminals, and criminality in the military. Many of these articles appeared in Hoover-authored series such as "For a Better America" and "For a Crime-Free America" that were syndicated in newspapers across the country. Regardless of topic, Hoover's authorial voice was consistently self-assured and paternalistic. He continually emphasized the ability of the Bureau to use its scientific investigative approach to protect America, so long as the agency received the full cooperation of "the average citizen."[50]

These articles also gave Hoover the opportunity to emphasize the manliness of special agents, praising them as brave, tough, prepared, and efficient professionals. He portrayed them as patriotic sons who were willing to make the ultimate sacrifice in their quest to protect the nation, often mentioning Bureau agents who had been killed in the line of duty. The G-Men were also willing and able to violently oppose the criminal threat when necessary. In a 1939 speech on the Bureau's successes under his leadership, Hoover recalled the "16 criminals who, rather than surrender, sought to resist arrest. Facing the guns of gangland, the Special Agents of the FBI had no alternative. They had to meet force with force."[51] Hoover further praised the G-Men's faculty with firearms in *Leatherneck*, the magazine of the Marine Corps Association.[52]

Another key aspect of Hoover's G-Men was their preparedness. Four months before the Japanese attack on Pearl Harbor, Hoover assured readers of his column that the men of the FBI were fully prepared to mobilize against a "fifth column" of enemy spies and saboteurs at a moment's notice.[53] Hoover never missed an opportunity to praise the efficiency of the G-Men and the Bureau as a whole, commonly citing statistics on the high percentage of cases the Bureau had solved and the thousands of dollars it had saved taxpayers by recovering stolen goods.[54] But Hoover also took pains to highlight the honesty of his G-Men, noting that even though the Bureau was proud of its clearance rate, agents were more interested in finding the right man than simply marking the case closed, and that often their work exonerated an innocent party.[55]

The Bureau's public relations arm also underscored the undeniable masculinity of its agents by feeding reporters arrest details that emasculated the Bureau's enemies. One example was George "Machine Gun" Kelly, who was portrayed as a phony man-child controlled by his wife. Hoover (or a ghost-writer) wrote that Mrs. Kelly constantly allowed "longshoreman profanity" to pass her "liquor-loosened lips" in an effort to cow her husband, threatening that she would "take care of" a problem for him, if he was "so damned scared."[56] Portraying the G-Men's adversaries as cowardly and henpecked underscored the more masculine characteristics of the agents themselves.

Most elementally, Hoover presented G-Men as guardians of domesticity. Whether the hearth fires were threatened by illicit sexuality, immoral publications, subversive ideas, or outright robbery and violence, the G-Man was dedicated to protecting them. In the end, perhaps the G-Man's most central responsibility was to ensure that homes were safe spaces in which to nurture the country's youngest citizens. In a 1938 speech to the General Federation of Women's Clubs, Hoover "blamed the apathy of law-abiding citizens for the increase in crime, and said that the ultimate responsibility was in the home where the younger generation acquired its ideas of right and wrong."[57] A decade later, he used a national radio address to advocate for prayer in the home, arguing that "if there is hope for the future of America, if there is to be peace and happiness in our homes—then we, as a nation, must return to God and to the practice of daily family prayer."[58] Speaking about the problem of crime in America, Hoover portrayed criminality as an issue of a "frontier" that needed to be "conquered."[59] In so doing, he constructed G-Men as the modern incarnations of frontier lawmen such as Wyatt Earp and Pat Garrett, using masculine toughness to create spaces protected from those who would subvert law and order.

To Hoover, the safe American home was one in which the values of "Americanism" could be freely practiced and taught. His conception of Americanism combined Christian morality with loosely defined notions of liberty, justice, sacrifice, and freedom. It was also related to the way in which interwar social conservatives used the term to reaffirm a patriarchal approach to sex, gender, and family relationships in the face of encroaching immorality.[60] Rarely did Hoover define Americanism in anything but amorphous platitudes. In a 1940 speech to the American Legion, Hoover outlined what he viewed as the central elements of the national character: a belief in a higher power, particularly in the Judeo-Christian tradition; the ability to practice "intellectual freedom" without resorting to the "un-American" practices of "intellectual license and debauchery"; a dedication to efficiency ("the American way of living will endure only if it is proved to be efficient"); a respect for law enforcement and other government leaders; and an adherence to the "pioneer spirit of [our] Ancestors."[61] All of those elements were clearly visible in the personas Hoover cultivated for both the Bureau and himself.

To promote the growth of such a national identity, Hoover often appealed to his audience's manhood, implicitly aligning his vision of Americanism with his understanding of masculinity. If Americanism and manhood were not precisely the same thing, Hoover presented them as at least symbiotic. Speaking on the theme of citizenship during Boy Scouts Day at the 1939 World's Fair in New York City, Hoover told the assembled "men of tomorrow" that "it is your job to *clean up America!*"[62] He advocated that the boys embrace a "spirit of contest, of ambition, of energetic zeal and desire for the betterment of his fellow man . . . [and to] build Our America ever closer to the clean, wonderful dream of our forefathers." He advised them to "dedicate your thoughts and your energies only to those activities which strengthen character . . . love your home and your church. Keep yourself physically strong, mentally pure, and morally straight . . . Always remain true to the Boy Scout oath, which means, in simple terms, Be a good citizen, Be a good man, and Be a good American—*First, last, and always.*"[63]

In privileging competitiveness, piety, and loyalty, Hoover's definition of manliness was clearly based on the lessons he had learned in the pews and schoolrooms of his childhood. But running through his understanding of masculinity was an emphasis on power as a measuring stick. To merely possess certain masculine characteristics was not enough; real men were also able to marshal those traits in the service of themselves, their community, and their nation.

He struck a similar tone when speaking to a slightly older audience, the (then all-male) Junior Chamber of Commerce. Noting that organization's role in promoting morality, Hoover advised them that "obstacles will beset you, but adversity is the real test of virile manhood."[64] In 1941, Hoover told the all-male graduating class of the University of the South that "we need strong, young blood to strengthen veins which have been weakened by the creeping virtue of apathy, lethargy, deceit and treachery—the rich, red blood of true Americanism!"[65] Along this line, Hoover argued that America's forefathers were successful only "because they possessed an elemental, rugged, uncompromising courage in the face of almost overwhelming difficulties. They never knew the meaning of fear. The word 'surrender' was not in their vocabulary. They were fighters, battlers for their high ideals—martyrs, if necessary. They were ready and eager to sacrifice everything that life holds dear for a cause that to them was greater and more sacred than life itself. They were proud to be Americans!"[66]

In his public statements, Hoover presented manhood and Americanism as fundamentally aligned. He argued that the virtues of manliness—ambition, zeal, physical strength, ruggedness, courage, mental purity, and moral straightness—would ultimately "clean up" and better America. To monumentalize those virtues, Hoover connected them to the Founding Fathers, and thereby the nation's creation. In order to continue that greatness, Hoover argued, America needed to remain committed to those masculine virtues. Though the country is typically referenced using a feminine pronoun, Hoover implicitly personified America as a man, remarking that to protect itself from the "venom" of "foreign ideologies," America "must again become virile and strong."[67] And he expected those characteristics of virility and strength would be clearly displayed by his nation, his Bureau, his special agents, and himself.

Though Hoover's writings and public appearances were plentiful, the public image of the G-Man was most critically shaped by numerous cultural productions. Beginning in the mid-1930s, the G-Man became a cultural icon, chasing criminals across movie screens, over the airwaves, and through the pages of comic books and detective novels. The productions were often directly tied to the Bureau via immediate oversight, the use of Bureau files for source material, or endorsement by Hoover himself.

The earliest noteworthy pop-cultural depiction of Bureau special agents was *G-Men*, a 1935 Hollywood production starring James Cagney which redeployed the hallmarks of the gangster genre with a BOI agent as the protagonist. Though Hoover had to officially claim that "this bureau did not cooperate in the production of *G-Men*, or in any way endorse this motion picture," the Warner Brothers production could scarcely have been more laudatory of the Bureau or its director had Hoover served as executive producer.[68] *G-Men* took the tough, intelligent, loyal, and suave character Cagney had played in popular gangster films such as *The Public Enemy* and gave him a badge, christening him Special Agent Brick Davis. His law practice in shambles as a result of his refusal to take on immoral clients, Davis joins the BOI to avenge the murder of a friend. After proving his investigative acumen in Bureau training—a series of scenes stylized like a documentary depicted agents learning to use machine guns, martial arts, and scientific investigative procedures—Davis sets out to punch and shoot his way to justice. The film's foregrounding of gunplay was particularly noteworthy because agents in Hoover's Bureau had been officially issued firearms only in 1934.[69] The script tiptoed around the Motion Picture Association's ban on depicting the exploits of real-life gangsters by featuring stand-ins for John Dillinger, "Pretty Boy" Floyd, and "Baby Face" Nelson as its main antagonists. The romantic subplot was wholesome, with Davis eschewing his former nightclub girlfriend in favor of a more stable relationship with the sister of his BOI instructor.

The film's primary advertising poster depicted Cagney dressed neatly in a three-piece suit and fedora, pointing a gun straight at the viewer while a frightened Ann Dvorak hid behind him. Promotional materials promised an experience "more sensational than ever—because every word is *true!*," a formulation that nodded at *G-Men's* membership in a lineage of detective thrillers. *G-Men* even included a thinly disguised and flattering Hoover facsimile in the character of Bureau Director Bruce J. Gregory.[70] Perhaps *G-Men's* most significant impact was that it presented the Bureau as an independent organization, divorced from the rest of the federal government generally and the Department of Justice specifically. In so doing, the film also began a relatively rapid process by which Hoover became the public face of the War on Crime, stealing the spotlight from Attorney General Homer Cummings.[71]

In 1935 alone there were seven Hollywood productions featuring a special agent protagonist: *G-Men*; *Public Enemy's Wife*; *Public Hero Number One*; *Mary Burns, Fugitive*; *Let 'Em Have It*; and *Show Them No Mercy*. *Persons in Hiding*, Hoover's 1938 memoir of the War on Crime, inspired no fewer than four B-movie productions by Paramount Productions: *Persons in Hiding* (1939), *Undercover Doctor* (1939), *Parole Fixer* (1940), and *Queen of the Mob* (1940).[72] All constructed the G-Man as an action hero while adhering to the familiar tropes of the detective genre, with the big case being cracked when the G-Man uses innovative thinking and the Bureau's scientific investigative techniques to illuminate a series of clues. The country's newest hero also made numerous appearances in film serials targeted to younger audiences, including *Dick Tracy's G-Men*.[73]

Also in 1935, the Bureau lent the "G-Men" title to a radio serial that purported to dramatize real FBI cases. The show was later renamed *Gang Busters* and became famous under that title, running until 1957. The announcement that opened every show had a distinctive sense of immediacy: "Calling the police! Calling the G-Men! Calling all Americans to war on the underworld!" *Gang Busters* advertised itself as realistic, noting the accuracy of the depicted cases and Hoover's involvement in production. Here, too, Hoover's desired selling points were emphasized, with particular focus on the role of scientific detective work in nabbing suspects. The radio program proved so popular that it entered the national lexicon via the phrase "came on like gangbusters," a reference to the show's cacophonic opening sequence that featured wailing police sirens and bursts of machine gun fire.

The success of *Gang Busters* led to a number of similar radio programs. *The FBI in Peace and War* (1944–58) and *This Is Your FBI* (1945–53) targeted a more adult audience. The latter presented itself as "an official broadcast from the files of the *Federal* Bureau of Investigation" and was explicitly endorsed by Hoover. Its sponsor, the Equitable Life Insurance Society, promoted itself as aligned with the Bureau's mission, telling the listener that "to the FBI you look for national security, and to the Equitable Society for financial security. These two great institutions are dedicated to the protection of you, your home, and your country." *The True Adventures of Junior G-Men* (1936–38) was part of a multiplatform attempt to reach younger listeners. Like *Gang Busters*, each episode began with loud sirens (though no gunfire) and a direct appeal: "Calling all Junior G-Men, calling all Junior G-Men!" The program urged its listeners to join the "Junior G-Men Corps," a club that distributed small badges and anticrime literature. It also inspired *Junior G-Men of The Air*, a 1942 Universal film serial.[74]

Younger audiences were also the primary target of comics such as *Special Agent J-8* and *Secret Agent X-9*. The latter was a newspaper strip begun in 1934 by King Features Syndicate. Though never wildly popular, it ran for sixty-two years and inspired two films during the late 1930s. The narrative centered on the adventures of a nameless secret agent who worked for an agency that was sometimes identified as the FBI. Written and drawn in the style of *Dick Tracy*, the strip depicted its protagonist as bold, brave, and decisive.[75] In 1936, Hoover's friend Rex Collier, a reporter for the *Washington Evening Star*, began writing *War on Crime*, a comic strip that purported to be "True Stories of G-Men Activities—Based on the Records of the Federal Bureau of Investigation—Modified in the Public Interest" and featured Hoover's official endorsement. The comic was a sanitized version of the Bureau's history; in recounting the Dillinger case, *War on Crime* emphasized the role of scientific policing procedures and intelligent evidence gathering as the immediate cause of locating public enemy number one, not the Bureau's accidental collaring of informant Anna Sage.[76] Other editorial decisions sought to present the G-Man as more family focused; despite Hoover's preference for hiring agents who were single, the G-Man of popular culture was often portrayed as a husband and father, emphasizing his investment in protecting the home.

The significance of early pop-cultural representations of the Bureau stems from more than the fact that they popularized the G-Man and made J. Edgar Hoover a household name. An equally important element of this story is the collection of values and ideals that accrued to the Bureau and Hoover. Because they were built around the new masculine identity that Hoover had produced, those cultural portrayals created a national image of the Bureau and its agents as professional, trustworthy, measured, analytical, athletic, and macho. Bureau agents became action heroes in suits rather than stuffy federal bureaucrats. The G-Man of popular culture played an important role in presenting agents as a force for good at a time when some Americans were becoming distrustful of the federal government as a result of the New Deal's legal and constitutional overreach. Furthermore, presenting G-Men as dependable family men helped underscore the paternalistic role Hoover envisioned for the Bureau as well as reaffirm male morality at a time when the stability of families seemed particularly tenuous—a 1940 survey estimated that as many as "1.5 million married women had been abandoned by their husbands" during the Great Depression.[77] Having masculinity so central to the G-Man's identity enabled Hoover and the Bureau to cement themselves as a central pillar of the national security apparatus.

In addition to making the G-Man a cultural icon, mass media representations of the Bureau also educated the public about various threats to national security, the Bureau's strategies for countering those threats, and how the general public could assist in that struggle. By advertising a curated version of the Bureau to a mass audience, those productions helped convince the public that the Bureau was both an essential part of the security apparatus and an ally of the average citizen. As such, they were central to the process by which the FBI came to be trusted by the public as the nation's foremost guarantor of national security, rather than feared as a secret police force.

Many of the activities of the Bureau's public-relations arm revolved around banging the drum for Hoover himself. Affixing his verbal or written signature to many of these dramatizations had the dual benefit of lending the products an air of authenticity and presenting Hoover as the ultimate example of the heroic G-Man. This policy extended to news stories; as *Collier's* noted in 1933, "In every newspaper and magazine article and radio broadcast recounting his field agents' activities there appears invariably the name of 'J. Edgar Hoover, Director of the United States Bureau of Investigation.'"[78] To Hoover, developing a cult of personality was essential to publicizing the Bureau, and he went to great lengths to ensure the public viewed him not only as the leader of the vaunted G-Men, but as their purest specimen. He wanted to be known as the living embodiment of the masculine legend he had created.

It is likely that part of the reason Hoover was so intent on displaying these credentials was because his manliness had been debated in the press. Around the time Franklin Roosevelt assumed office in 1933, a handful of pundits suggested that the new president was on the verge of replacing Hoover as director because he was not manly enough. As evidence of this effeminacy, reporters pointed to Hoover's appearance and personal habits. In the August 3, 1933, edition of the *Washington Herald*, columnist Peter Carter mentioned Hoover's expensive tastes and penchant for antiquing.[79]

In the August 19 issue of *Collier's*, Ray Tucker emphasized Hoover's supposedly feminine attributes:

> In appearance Mr. Hoover looks utterly unlike the story-book sleuth. He is short, fat, businesslike, and walks with a mincing step. His black hair, swarthy skin and collegiate haircut make him look younger than thirty-eight, but heavy, horn-rimmed spectacles give him an air of age and authority. He dresses fastidiously, with Eleanor blue as the favorite color for the matched shades of tie, handkerchief and socks. A little pompous, he rides in an expensive limousine even if only to a near-by self-service cafeteria.[80]

Had these criticisms appeared individually they might have been regarded as pernicious but ultimately innocuous; grouped together their impact was more insidious. Most historians have focused on Hoover's "mincing step" as the most caustic detail in Tucker's article, particularly since it was picked up by other news outlets. The knowing criticism seemed to hit its mark; Peter Carter's *Washington Herald* column from August 28 suggests that Hoover had been consciously lengthening his stride, attempting to make it appear more decisive and masculine.[81] Yet the characterization stuck; in a 1936 critique, Walter Trohan of the *Chicago Daily Tribune* wrote that "Hoover walks with a rather mincing step, almost feminine" and further questioned Hoover's claims to athleticism by noting that fishing was the only "active sport" in which he participated, "if it can be called that."[82]

However, Tucker's depiction held a bolder allusion to Hoover's femininity and sexuality, albeit a more hidden one. Tucker noted that Hoover's wardrobe was dominated by "Eleanor blue," a term coined by the press to describe the velvet day dress that Eleanor Roosevelt had worn to her husband's inauguration. The actual shade was more purple or violet. In fact, the Smithsonian Institution's description of the dress lists it as "lavender," a term which by 1933 had already entered the lexicon as a euphemism for male homosexuals.[83] It is safe to deduce that Tucker's mention was emasculating not only in linking the BOI director to the first lady, but as a coded reference to the director's rumored sexual preferences. Like much of the gossip surrounding the sexuality of Hoover—and, later, McCarthy and Cohn—it was an accusation hidden in plain sight. The average reader of *Collier's* might miss the insinuation, but those in the know would not. The overall air of suspicion was also underscored by Tucker's depiction of Hoover as "swarthy," a term that suggested deviation from racial norms as well as those of gender. In response to the *Collier's* article, a feature in *Liberty* magazine said Hoover's "compact body, with the shoulders of a light heavyweight boxer, carries no ounce of extra weight—just 170 pounds of live, virile masculinity."[84] Reportedly, the article had been planted by Hoover.

Hoover's attempts to emphasize his own vitality continued throughout his career. Interviewed in 1954, Hoover described his robust approach to life, claiming that "by nature, I express myself vigorously at all times. I'm not a soft, easy-going individual. I play tennis hard. I walk fast. And in my testimony [during a recent congressional hearing], I spoke as I usually do—with vigor."[85] This self-appraisal reveals the degree to which Hoover valued outward appearances, even by a point in his career when his power was firmly cemented. Particularly as he entered middle age and his body grew stouter, Hoover sought to portray himself as athletic, energetic, and decisive. The retrospective tone of the interview also reveals the degree to which Hoover attributed his success to that persona.

By the mid-1940s, Hoover had become so sensitive to rumors about his sexuality that he instructed all agents to immediately make him aware of such gossip. Those who failed to do so in a timely manner were reprimanded. Hoover's Official and Confidential file includes a number of memos on the topic, including a report on a "prominent New Yorker" who mentioned during an interview with the FBI that he had heard one "rumor to the effect that Mr. Hoover was a 'queer.'" Another entry in the file concerned a similar story being repeated in Cleveland, Ohio.[86] In both cases, local FBI agents were instructed to "censure" the individuals.[87]

Perhaps the most infamous example of the FBI working to stem gossip about Hoover's sexuality occurred in 1951. According to a memo from Assistant Director Louis Nichols to Clyde Tolson, a female FBI employee had made her superiors aware that while visiting a beauty shop she had heard the shop's owner claim that "the Director was a sissy, liked men, and was 'queer.'" One of her employees had concurred: "At the time that [the shop owner] referred to the Director as a 'queer,' the beautician . . . stated that she had also heard this about the Director." In the memo, Nichols suggested that two agents visit the salon to "take this scandal monger and liar on," a proposal that both Tolson and Hoover approved via handwritten comments in the margin.[88]

In addition to working to stem the spread of such talk, Hoover proactively forwarded an alternate narrative. Hoover knew how influential gossip could be—he even included a gossip column alongside the news and cartoons printed in *The Investigator*, the FBI's internal newspaper that he had created in 1933.[89] Using the same outlets he had relied on to create the legend of the G-Man, Hoover set out to create a legend around himself.

Through film projects, radio shows, comic strips, public addresses, newspaper articles, and friendly gossip columnists he fostered his cult of personality. One of the purest distillations of the persona Hoover was attempting to construct came in a syndicated report on the capture of Alvin Karpis:

> He is 41 years of age, black-haired and black-eyed, with no redundancy of person or conversation. His eyes are set away out on the corners of his face, suggesting a wide ambit of vision, which might take in, say, St. Paul and New Orleans in a single look. They are bright, luminous eyes, but they can become as flat and opaque as a poker chip when a momentary restraint is indicated. Through a long office day the mentally and physically athletic Mr. Hoover works like a trap-drummer—punching one of several octaves of buttons on his desk, summoning one of his avenging genii, grabbing a telephone like a shortstop fielding a hot grounder, barking a sharp staccato order and then relaxing, swinging around in his swivel chair and starting a heart-to-heart talk which makes you think he wears his heart on his sleeve, which he does, sometimes . . . He knows the minute details of personnel and operations of the Barker-Karpis gang the way Toscanini knows the score of "Lohengrin."[90]

Published at the zenith of Hoover's success in the War on Crime, that character sketch included nearly all the key characteristics that Hoover had striven to represent: attractiveness, intelligence, athleticism, preparedness, wisdom, and leadership. For Hoover, masculinity was an adaptable multitool that could forward his goals in nearly every situation. In constructing himself as a masculine hero, Hoover sought to embody a number of roles that would make him easily readable to the public. He could variably be a young bachelor about town, a crime-fighting wunderkind, a master of modern bureaucracy, a moral role model, a domestic guardian, or a blend of those identities.

One of the most explicit ways Hoover attempted to advertise his own manhood was in seeking to be regarded as a bachelor desired by women. Hoover's alliances with a number of gossip columnists allowed that image to be widely publicized. In exchange for details on the Bureau's operations, those columnists would present Hoover in a favorable light when reporting on his nights out at popular night clubs or floating rumors about his romantic life. Foremost among those contacts was Walter Winchell, the *New York Mirror* journalist who created the nation's first syndicated gossip column and whose Sunday evening radio broadcast was one of the nation's most popular during the 1930s and '40s. At the height of Winchell's popularity, his column and broadcast reached an estimated audience of fifty million Americans, two-thirds of the adult population.[91] Hoover biographer Curt Gentry has noted that Winchell "did more than any other man to perpetuate the myths of J. Edgar Hoover and his G-Men."[92] While that assessment perhaps underestimates Hoover's own role in that mythmaking, Winchell's assistance was profound. Winchell and Hoover began corresponding in April 1933 and met four months later, when Winchell went to Washington to "advise" President Roosevelt on the imminent threat of Nazism. As Hoover and Winchell's friendship grew they began spending leisure time together, including long nights out at the Stork Club, Winchell's favorite haunt.[93] The Stork's owner, the former bootlegger Sherman Billingsley, came to regard Hoover as one of his closest friends.[94]

Press coverage of Hoover's social life helped build his name recognition while also presenting him as accessible and relaxed. At the same time, Hoover's appearance in the society and gossip columns elevated his status by portraying him as belonging to a social elite populated by actors and actresses, musicians, sports stars, socialites, business magnates, and eminent politicians. Winchell had originally been hesitant to mention Hoover's nightclubbing, fearful of how his subject would react. But Hoover dismissed Winchell's worries, noting that "I do get some real relaxation and enjoyment in attending some of the night clubs, particularly when you have been with me, and I am looking forward to many evenings in the future when we can get together and have some real fun and settle the momentous questions of the nation."[95]

Winchell dedicated the entirety of his September 29, 1935, column to recounting Hoover and Tolson's trip to New York City to attend a boxing match between Joe Louis and Max Baer at Yankee Stadium. In it, Winchell described how he shepherded the top two G-Men on a tour of the city's hottest social clubs—including the Stork, Tony's, and the 21 Club—and introduced them to the owners. At the 21 Club, "Mr. Hoover and Mr. Tolson had their eyebrows lifted" by the bar's elaborate system for hiding alcohol during Prohibition. The G-Men's winking amazement at the criminal measures marked them as allies of the people—even the nation's top policemen recognized the absurdity of the Eighteenth Amendment. Winchell's column also stressed the presence of beautiful women at each stop, including girls who had recently featured in the Ziegfeld Follies and the actress Peggy Joyce, who "almost swooned as she fondled [Hoover's] paw in handshake and groaned: 'I suppose these handsome men are married and have their wives with them.'"[96]

Winchell often printed rumors that Hoover had been spotted out on the

FIGURE 4. Tolson and Hoover celebrate New Year's Eve 1936 at the Stork Club with a female friend (possibly actress and model Luisa Stuart). Credit: National Archives Still Photo Division.

town with an unidentified starlet.[97] Competing gossip columns strongly insinuated that Hoover was romantically involved with a number of women, including Lela Rogers (divorced mother of the actress Ginger Rogers), screenwriter Frances Marion, and Hollywood star Dorothy Lamour. A widely distributed photo from the Stork Club's 1936 New Years' Eve party depicts Hoover in a paper party hat, his hands up in mock surrender as a smiling blonde starlet points a toy gun at him.[98] More than once did columnists report that Hoover's engagement was imminent.

Hoover's nightlife had the desired effect on his public image, and soon his celebrity status was cemented. In October 1936, *Washington Post* gossip columnist Marylyn Reeve named Hoover as one of the city's most eligible bachelors, highlighting his local roots and athleticism. "He's a very busy person," Reeve wrote, "and when he has leisure, he plays as hard as he works . . . In his den he has a mounted sail fish he landed after a battle off the coast of Florida not long ago." The fact that Hoover lived in "a lovely old home" with his mother was presented as indicating his dedication to family.[99] Less than three years later, the *Los Angeles Times* referred to Hoover as one of the nation's most eligible bachelors in a front page article that included a gossipy description of his arrival in Los Angeles: "Hoover was met by a score of FBI agents and a mysterious woman in black. The woman, wearing a fashionable fluffy black dress and a wide-brimmed black hat, spent 10 minutes in close conference with Hoover at Grand Central Air Terminal. The woman would not disclose her name and Hoover just grinned. They both said 'no pictures,' and there were enough FBI agents there to make the order stick."[100] The suggestive detail about Hoover's smile is particularly telling in that it assumes that Hoover and the reader are in on the same joke; Hoover is positioned as concurrently supreme to the reader (in his ability to apparently date—or bed—the "mysterious," "fashionable" woman) and at the reader's level (in his understandable weakness for basic, manly pleasures).

Given his efforts to convince the public of his masculine credentials, it is not surprising that Hoover came to be regarded as a role model for young men. A 1940 *Washington Post* article cheekily reported on how "youngsters" in Hoover's new neighborhood were set on learning the director's habits and "cased" his house—with their official Junior G-Men badges at the ready—in the hope of catching a glimpse of the "Nation's No. 1 G-Man."[101] Though not a father, Hoover adopted a paternalistic persona for both himself and the Bureau. He freely dispensed advice to adolescents and their parents in speeches before the Boy Scouts, the Boys Clubs of America, and various commencements. In an illuminating 1938 article for *Woman's Day* magazine, Hoover ruminated on how he would treat a son if he had one:

> I'd like to see my son grow up to be a real man. He should take his part in good, rough, outdoor games. If he were a little noisier around the home than I liked I'd try to put up with it. Boys were noisy animals when I was one. If there were a litter of bats and rackets and fishing tackle in the hall closet I'd ask that it be set in order by the owner, but I wouldn't raise the roof about it. If he got into a fight I wouldn't punish him unless he had provoked it. Even then I'd find out if he had been warranted in provoking it. The last thing I'd do would be to punish him for standing up for his own rights. I might be a bit harsh with him if he didn't. Bruises in boyhood aren't tragedies; they are incidents in the process of growing up.[102]

Hoover used this venue to emphasize a number of positive characteristics about himself. In demonstrating his sympathy to the challenges of raising a boy, Hoover fostered a personal connection with the magazine's readership. But he also adopted a voice of expertise. Even though he did not in fact have a son, Hoover could assume such a position due to his perceived authority on issues of masculinity, particularly which qualities helped boys become "real men." Furthermore, Hoover's claim that character building begins at home reaffirmed the domestic space's honored position in America.

One telling detail of Hoover's list is its preoccupation with physicality and athleticism. Hoover implies that success could—and should—be physically embodied, echoing his own preoccupation with how his physicality was portrayed. Also noteworthy is his relatively libertine attitude towards a boy's appearance and behavior. In recalling that "boys were noisy animals when I was one," Hoover signals his grounding in a traditionalist, mainstream view of how boys became men, one that centered on the friction between innate urges and their management through moral discipline. But by advocating a relatively permissive approach, Hoover indicates his own boyishness, implying that he fulfilled such stereotypes when he was younger and that he still possesses the vitality and zeal they promoted. In Hoover's view, the goal was to positively channel that physicality rather than curb it.

Hoover's status as a moral role model fed another key element of his public persona: that of domestic guardian. That position can be seen as encompassing multiple meanings of the term "domestic," first as a sentinel against threats coming from within the United States and as a defender of the American home itself. Hoover rarely missed an opportunity to praise the sanctity of the family and their home, positioning the family unit as the foundation of society and the home as its most elemental building block. In a commencement address six months after the bombing of Pearl Harbor, Hoover was clear about the war's ultimate meaning: "No nation is stronger than its homes. The home is the cornerstone of democracy."[103] Undoubtedly, part of this focus on the nuclear family was an attempt to distinguish the United States from the community-based social structures of communism and the rampant nationalism of fascism. But for Hoover, privileging the home also helped make the Bureau's mission and tactics unimpeachable—how could any criticism be leveled at an agency whose primary purpose was to shield the hearth fires?

When addressing home security, Hoover referenced both protection from physical destruction and insulation from ideological sabotage. The home was a microcosm for the nation, Hoover told an audience in 1939: "The home still remains supreme as the basis of our social order. The very forces that attack the home attack the Nation, which is the aggregate of all our homes . . . In preserving the security of the home, we safeguard the security of the Nation. The time has come to erect defensive walls to protect our homes and our body politic from the insidious and malignant germs of foreign isms and the subversive forces of lawlessness."[104] In Hoover's vernacular, "foreign isms" was a catch-all term for a loosely defined collection of political, social, and religious beliefs that threatened national security. His metaphorical presentation of those isms as viruses referenced both their treacherous nature and their habit of spreading silently until reaching epidemic levels. It was the Bureau's role to identify symptoms, isolate their carriers, and destroy the disease.

Hoover never presented a comprehensive list of these threats—though it appears that those menaces included communism, socialism, atheism, and authoritarianism—and he never precisely defined exactly why those isms were so harmful as to classify them as "un-American." He told an audience in 1939, "A good citizen must be on guard against subversion in all its forms. Call it Communism, Fascism, or what you will—it is un-American." Employing both gendered and theological imagery, he continued, "Our patriotism can best be judged by our diligence in protecting American ideals from the rapists of justice and common decency . . . Here is a battle between priceless God-fearing principles on the one hand and pagan ideals and godlessness on the other."[105] A year earlier, Hoover had attacked those same ideological enemies in similarly religious language, noting that "both communism and fascism are the antithesis of American belief in liberty and democracy. There can be no room in this country for these destructive, anarchic, or despotic cults."[106] Identifying ideologies as the enemy—rather than specific nations or peoples—allowed Hoover to portray America's adversaries as constantly advancing, even if Nazi or Soviet soldiers were not making an amphibious assault up the Potomac. Those isms could be even more successful in undermining Americanism because they were silent assassins that could slip through defenses unnoticed. Furthermore, whereas protecting the nation from a military invasion was a purview of the Department of Defense, ideological warfare had become a specialty of the FBI.

In a 1940 speech to the Daughters of the American Revolution, Hoover explained his inexactitude: "You have noticed," he told his audience, "that I have not designated all of our ism enemies by name. There is a good reason; it is a part of present-day strategy among these different assailants of liberty to claim all good things for themselves and all bad things for the organization down the street, thus creating confusion while they attack our institutions. Therefore, the test of American citizenship lies in the ability to have nothing to do with any of them. The real test of citizenship is our devotion to the preservation of the American Democracy for which our forefathers fought and died, and which we are permitted to enjoy as a blessed heritage."[107] In refusing to coherently define these adversaries, Hoover gifted himself the ability to constantly change the target; the enemy became whomever or whatever he wanted it to be. This rhetorical slippage also seeped into Hoover's definition of Americanism. In defining what was American, Hoover rarely spoke in anything but generalities, alluding to a vague set of beliefs centered around (and policed by) the family, the church, and the law. The uncertain parameters allowed "Americanism" to become an elastic weapon, stretched and shaped to fit the current crisis.

Hoover genuinely believed that "foreign isms" were a threat to national security and the American way of life. He promoted this belief and worked to include it in cultural depictions of the Bureau. Those efforts helped the concept gain traction within the national discourse and influence the way Americans thought about domestic security. As he explained through his disease metaphor, the most dangerous aspect of foreign isms was that they spread surreptitiously and could quietly infect every corner of American life, including the home. The natural conclusion was that domestic spaces needed to be protected through policing. Thus, while Hoover was creating the legend of the G-Man and burnishing his own public image, he was helping to forward the legal framework that enabled domestic surveillance and promoted the growth of the national security and surveillance states.

The construction of the legal and social scaffolding of those apparatuses fundamentally altered Hoover's world (and the reality in which McCarthy and Cohn would come to operate). Most immediately, it expanded the powers of the FBI by granting it the legal right and technological capability to spy on domestic targets. At the same time, it familiarized the general public with the parameters and supposed necessity of domestic surveillance, including the concept that ideas were as open to prosecution as deeds, that the home was as much a battleground in the fight for freedom as any Western European or South Pacific front, and that the particulars of an individual's private life could be matters of national security. Finally, the way in which the framework was constructed further enshrined heteronormative, masculinized policies within the legal system and body politic.[108] These developments would prove to be central elements in fomenting the Second Red Scare and birthing McCarthyism.

*

In his efforts to turn the FBI into a bureaucratic juggernaut, Hoover was aided by larger forces promoting the development of the national security and surveillance states. The roots of those interrelated institutions are complex, varied, and deep. Recent examinations of them have focused on the passage of the National Security Act of 1947, but that emphasis shortchanges developments prior to World War II.[109] While some historians have drawn a distinction between the national security state and domestic surveillance, that artificial division overlooks their symbiotic relationship. Domestic surveillance was and is an essential aspect of the national security state. Furthermore, though the National Security Act and the National Security Agency were both products of the early Cold War, their foundations were laid during the first decades of the twentieth century.

One early landmark in the government's domestic surveillance program was the Mann Act. The Bureau's efforts to enforce the act, including the short-lived White Slave Division, set a precedent by which the agency expanded its purview to include the policing of moral standards. Those standards were most often violated behind closed doors, thereby necessitating (and justifying) government incursion into heretofore private spaces. Yet domestic surveillance was not put into widespread practice until later in the 1910s. The twentieth century's first significant antitreason law was the 1917 Espionage Act, which officials in the Department of Justice used to crush political dissent. Socialist Eugene V. Debs was among the critics of American involvement in World War I who ran afoul of the law, and was sentenced to a decade in prison for interfering with the work of army recruiters.[110]

In his position as head of the Justice Department's Radicals Division, Hoover used the Espionage Act to great effect during the Red Scare of 1919–20. The government was inspired to take a hard line against treason following a series of anarchist bombings in the spring of 1919, including an explosion that destroyed much of Attorney General A. Mitchell Palmer's house in Washington, DC. The resulting roundup—known to history as the Palmer Raids—led to the detention of approximately ten thousand resident aliens and the eventual deportation of 556 individuals. The bombings had been traced to an anarchist group led by Italian immigrant Luigi Galleani, and the government's belief that the anarchist movement was being inspired by foreigners was clear in the choice of Immigration Bureau agents to conduct the mission. As the operation unfolded, Hoover orchestrated raids via telephone in Washington. The roundup of suspected saboteurs was facilitated by Hoover's use of "telegraphic warrants," a new type of writ that did not require an official's signature.[111] Oftentimes a warrant was not even obtained; raids in New York City detained approximately 200 individuals even though only twenty-seven warrants had been issued.[112] When Palmer was criticized for the Department of Justice's role in the arrests, he attempted to evade questioning by explaining that Hoover "was in charge in this matter."[113]

One of the most infamous deportees was Emma Goldman, a Lithuanian-born Jew whose public statements reportedly inspired Leon Czolgosz to assassinate William McKinley. In a memo supporting her deportation, Hoover called Goldman and her associate Alexander Berkman "beyond doubt, two of the most dangerous anarchists in this country" and held that "if permitted to return to the community will result in undue harm."[114] True to Hoover's war against isms, Berkman and Goldman had never been charged with opposing the United States by their actions, only through their words; their prior prison sentences had resulted from vocal opposition to military conscription during World War I.

The raids themselves were only part of the Department of Justice's strategy against extremism during the First Red Scare. Concurrently, Hoover launched an unprecedented effort to gather and catalog information on persons considered a threat to the American state. The implications were astounding. A 1968 *Washington Post* article noted that "in a period of 100 days in 1919 [Hoover] and his associates put together 60,000 biographies on political 'radicals' and 'anarchists' who were the special targets of the Justice Department in that troubled postwar period. From those modest beginnings, the FBI collection of dossiers was expanded to nearly five million individual files by 1956."[115] Though nominally created to track political dissidents and domestic terrorists, the archive became an end in itself, with the FBI turning information—or even the possibility of information—into a weapon.

Developments during the 1920s and 1930s—including Prohibition, the New Deal expansion of government, and Hoover's own War on Crime—helped further law enforcement's incursions into the domestic sphere and expand the federal government's jurisdiction.[116] Since the late 1920s, Hoover had instructed Bureau agents to conduct limited domestic surveillance of antigovernment radicals, ignoring a 1924 ban on such activities by Attorney General Harlan Fiske Stone.[117] But the birth of the FBI's official domestic surveillance program can be traced to August 24, 1936, when Franklin Roosevelt and Hoover began discussing the gathering of "general intelligence information" about domestic threats to national security. According to Hoover's memo recounting the meeting, Roosevelt was concerned with "subversive activities in the United States, particularly Fascism and Communism," noting that though the Secret Service had planted informants in nearly every communist group, those agents were focused on monitoring threats against the president's life. In a meeting the following day, Hoover recalled, Roosevelt authorized Hoover to begin a survey of "Communist activities in this country, as well as Fascist activities." Roosevelt knew that such a directive would be controversial and declined to put the authorization in writing, noting that only he, Hoover, and Secretary of State Cordell Hull should be made aware of his request.[118] In Hoover's view, Roosevelt had authorized far-ranging investigations into subversive activity.[119]

Roosevelt's precise intentions are unclear, but he almost certainly did not mean to authorize the broad surveillance program the FBI coordinated against domestic political radicals and trade unionists. The directive's less-than-official nature granted Hoover leeway, but after Roosevelt's death Hoover had no evidence that the FBI had been granted such broad powers. As a result, historian Richard Gid Powers writes, Hoover became "violently defensive whenever the Bureau's authority for its secret operations was questioned. Hoover was forced to rely on vague presidential directives that he interpreted according to their spirit as elastic and comprehensive, but that were later dissected according to their letter as narrow and restrictive."[120] Though Powers makes it appear as though Hoover was stuck in a difficult position, in reality he was intent on pushing the limit of any restriction on his and the Bureau's power, as evidenced by his willful violation of Stone's 1924 ban.

While the secrecy of the program makes its size difficult to measure, the Bureau's public reports on domestic espionage cases illuminate the growth of domestic surveillance generally. In a 1940 report, Hoover detailed the increase in the FBI's involvement in espionage cases since the beginning of the war.

> In the five-year period preceding 1938, the FBI investigated . . . an average of 35 espionage matters each year. In the fiscal year 1938, 250 such matters were handled by the FBI, while in the fiscal year 1939, a total of 1,651 matters pertaining to the national defense were received for investigation. With the outbreak of war in Europe early in September and the Presidential Proclamation establishing a limited emergency, this type of work increased materially. On one day alone in May of 1940, a total of 2,871 complaints were received. During fiscal year 1940 a total of 16,885 national defense matters necessitating a follow-up investigation were received.[121]

Though the United States would not officially enter the war until late 1941, it is clear from Hoover's figures that the federal government was already on wartime footing. This preoccupation with domestic security is also evident in the 1938 creation of the House Un-American Activities Committee.

As Hoover was making that report, Congress was also demonstrating its concern about internal subversion through its passage of the Smith Act of

1940, which made advocating the overthrow of the US government illegal and requiring all noncitizen residents to register with the federal government. The urgency of conducting domestic surveillance during wartime—combined with the sheer size of the job—caused the Bureau to request public assistance with the task. Hoover called for citizen vigilance against threats to democracy, telling a public audience on the eve of World War II, "You can help by being ever alert in order that any suspected act of sabotage, espionage, or neutrality violation, designed to undermine internal defense, can be called to the attention of the Federal Bureau of Investigation."[122] Hoover also asked for the support of likeminded organizations such as the American Legion and the Daughters of the American Revolution in combating what he termed the "successful invasion of our country by any destructive influences of foreign origin."[123]

Though criticism of the Bureau's efforts at controlling subversion was largely drowned out by the relentless drumbeat of wartime patriotism, Hoover attempted to insulate the FBI from being condemned for its anti-espionage activities by noting that "the success of investigations of espionage and sabotage cannot be judged by prosecutions and convictions . . . Espionage and sabotage investigations must have for their objective the identification of the individuals involved, together with ascertaining their contacts, methods of operation, sources of information and related matters. The preventive aspect is of paramount importance."[124] That formulation gave Hoover the ability to claim the FBI's countersurveillance programs were working, even if they did not result in any visible judicial activity.

During World War II, the FBI came to be regarded as almost another branch of the military, dedicated to protecting the home front as the Army and Navy fought on foreign shores. As part of this battle, the Bureau secretly developed the custodial detention list in 1939, which Hoover described to a congressional committee as a database of "individuals, groups, and organizations engaged in subversive activities, in espionage activities, or any activities that are possibly detrimental to the internal security of the United States. The indexes have been arranged not only alphabetically but also geographically, so that at any rate, should we enter into the conflict abroad, we would be able to go into any of these communities and identify individuals or groups who might be a source of grave danger to the security of this country."[125] Though the list prompted a number of congressmen to voice concern about government overreach, it was never destroyed.

World War II also granted Hoover the opportunity to resume the Bureau's use of wiretaps, which it had abandoned following a 1939 court ruling. On May 21, 1940, President Roosevelt secretly affirmed the Bureau's right to run wiretaps, provided they were approved on a case-by-case basis by the attorney general. However, Attorney General Robert H. Jackson decided to avoid creating a paper record of his wiretap approvals, citing security concerns. As a result, Hoover was granted de facto carte blanche in running wiretaps.[126] Simultaneously, Hoover's call for community support was answered by a number of conservative organizations that relayed suspicions of subversive activities to the FBI. The most comprehensive partnership was with the American Legion, which provided reports on suspected radicals from 1940 to 1966.[127] By the end of World War II, Hoover administered a far-reaching domestic surveillance operation over which he had almost total control.

Hoover had assumed a place near the apex of American power by avoiding the accusations of immorality that had befallen his predecessors and turning a gender-based moral identity to his favor. In the process, Hoover served as an essential link between the burgeoning national security state and the new forms of masculinity then being defined, developments that can be seen in both his support for the gendered policies of the Bureau and his creation of the G-Man as a cultural icon. Those interrelated tasks were facilitated by Hoover's astute use of the mass media to publicize a sympathetic version of himself and his G-Men to the public. Furthermore, Hoover's creation of the G-Man as a moral figure also helped forward his concurrent efforts to expand the Bureau's surveillance powers. In order to make a mark in the postwar sociopolitical climate that Hoover had helped define, Joseph McCarthy and Roy Cohn would need to address the question of masculine identity and show how they, too, fit the parameters of surveillance state masculinity.

3

POPULIST MASCULINITY IN
THE AMERICAN HEARTLAND

Joseph McCarthy was not a boxer; he was a brawler. Any of the artistry that inspired Pierce Egan to dub boxing "the sweet science" was absent from McCarthy's pugilistic persona. As an amateur fighter while an undergraduate at Marquette University, McCarthy was "a wild slugger who would rush out of his corner at the first sound of the bell and start raining gloves on his opponent. He never left the offensive unless he was knocked to the ground."[1] Disregarding defense altogether, "inevitably he took a beating, but he would absorb punishment as if he enjoyed it, and keep lunging even when bloody and groggy."[2] His habit of grinning throughout these ordeals caused his peers to christen him "Smiling Joe." For a brief time he was the university's heavyweight champion, but he finished his amateur career with an even record of two wins and two losses.

It would be easy to draw parallels between McCarthy's boxing style and his political career: the proverbial rabid dog who refused to think strategically, blind to everything but his immediate goal.[3] And it is the conclusion at which many journalists and historians have arrived. Numerous critical examinations of McCarthy portray him as so power hungry that he unthinkingly launched full-frontal attacks on his enemies (both real and perceived) without any regard for collateral damage, even when the blowback could harm him.[4]

Such an interpretation misreads the man. Centrally, it overlooks the aspects of his character that allowed him to become, if only for a moment, one of the nation's most influential voices: his intelligence, his charisma, his work ethic. But in politics—as in the ring—he was a brawler. He did always seem to be on the offensive, and each punch he threw was intended to be a haymaker. Those tactics were the by-product of a complex blend of factors, including McCarthy's personality, his desire to project a certain public image, and his belief that directness had paid dividends in the past. His brash, bellicose style was a strategy that he thought was effective. And for many years it was.

His identity was the result of the collision between the values instilled during his upbringing and his ever-expanding ambitions. He was a man who desperately desired popularity and could be calculating in pursuing it. This is not to say he was inauthentic. There were numerous moments when he seemed genuinely sympathetic to the plight of others, particularly when those hardships were immediately visible to him. He had a talent for connecting with people who shared his working-class values and demonstrating his fidelity to both the values and their adherents through an unmatched work ethic. But he lacked the self-control and sense of propriety that guided J. Edgar Hoover, and the same values that served McCarthy so well in certain contexts ensured his doom in others. Central among these was his understanding of his role as a man, a philosophy that stressed physicality, labor, boldness, competitiveness, and the domination of women. This version of masculinity helped him achieve success early in his political career and eventually propelled him to Washington, DC. But it also prompted him to make the grave miscalculations that precipitated his spectacular downfall.

*

A complete and accurate reconstruction of McCarthy's early life is difficult because it is obscured by all the yarns he spun about himself. His tall tales seemed calculated to inflate his own legend, but a truthful account of his upbringing is fascinating enough. Joseph Raymond McCarthy was born on November 14, 1908, delivered by a midwife at his parents' farmhouse in Grand Chute, Wisconsin. He was the fifth child of Timothy and Bridget "Bid" McCarthy, out of seven children. Tim was a farmer, working 143 acres he had inherited from his Irish immigrant father. He was quiet, hardworking, and distrustful of excess. Bid was stocky, plain, devoutly Catholic, and had not received much formal schooling. Though neighbors recall Joe being her favorite child, they also note that she was never quick to coddle him.[5] And neither were his brothers, who often teased Joe for being awkward and gangly. Neighbors remember the McCarthy boys roughhousing often, and there is little doubt that Joe had to develop a certain fighting spirit to survive. The family attended church often, and throughout his life Joe was known for his unfailing attendance at Sunday mass.

Above all else, the McCarthy family valued the amorphous concept of "hard work," the combination of physical labor, industriousness, grit, and perseverance that is central to many working-class cultures. There was plenty of labor to be done on the farm: fields to be plowed, cows to be milked, horses to be fed. The family's white clapboard farmhouse lacked electricity and indoor plumbing. Tim McCarthy demanded much from his sons because the family's economic survival depended on their labor. Joe stood out because he worked harder than any of his brothers, refusing to rest until a job was complete. Years later, a neighbor remembered Joe as an exceptionally industrious young man who "worked like the devil" and once continued to help his father finish clearing hay even after losing his boot in the mud.[6]

This level of dedication served multiple purposes for young Joe. First, it appeased his father. Though later accounts of Tim's dictatorial nature have probably been exaggerated, he had high expectations of his sons' work ethic. Grinding through season after season on the farm led to Tim's approval. Furthermore, physical labor was a primary way by which a man's value was measured in Grand Chute, a small farming community. Though neighboring Appleton had grown into a small city thanks to its numerous paper mills, Grand Chute largely remained agricultural. In such environs, success in business and farming proved to be two of the only means of distinguishing oneself, and a lack of easily available capital meant that long hours of labor were the only way to find success. Like many rural dwellers, the people of Grand Chute also seemed to take pride in the simplicity of their lives, the things that might be regarded by more urban neighbors as backwards.

McCarthy's early education took place at the one-room Underhill Country School—a far cry from Hoover's experiences in the Washington school system. By most accounts McCarthy was quite smart and had a remarkable memory. He progressed at an accelerated rate but was also hyperactive: he couldn't sit still and he talked constantly. Impatient with his studies, McCarthy opted to leave school after finishing the eighth grade and work on the family farm. At the age of sixteen, he convinced his father to rent him an acre of land in order to establish his own business raising chickens.[7] McCarthy's work ethic paid off, and only a year later he was the proprietor of a thriving small business, with a large coop, hundreds of hens, and a used pickup truck to his name. He traveled the county and state, making deliveries and fostering business connections. But after a couple years, a difficult illness—possibly the flu—confined McCarthy to his bed for an extended period. The friends he hired to care for the chickens in his stead proved to be incompetent, and the enterprise collapsed in McCarthy's absence. Shortly thereafter, McCarthy took a job managing a recently opened grocery store in Manawa, thirty miles northwest of Grand Chute.

The same set of skills that helped McCarthy build his chicken concern made him a success in Manawa. Upon arriving he set out on a political campaign of sorts, knocking on doors to introduce himself and announce the store's opening. His popularity made the Cashway thrive, and the store became an after-work gathering place for residents of the small farming community. Even Manawa's rival shop owners would close their doors early in order to join the conversation at McCarthy's store. Cashway's outpost in Manawa soon became the chain's most profitable location, even though it was the smallest store the company owned. McCarthy's success was again a direct result of his work ethic and ability to connect with customers. His store kept longer hours than its competitors and offered to help anyone in need. When an illness infected most of the local chicken population, McCarthy pitched in at neighbors' farms. Though a transplant, McCarthy was a success because the people of Manawa liked him and adopted him; he was affable, gregarious, funny, and unpretentious.[8]

In Manawa, Joe boarded with Mrs. Frank Osterloth, a mother of grown children whose husband was a logger in the northern part of the state. It was largely through her prodding that Joe decided to return to school. Shortly before his twenty-first birthday he embarked on an accelerated course of study at Manawa's Little Wolf High School. By the spring of 1930 Joe had completed enough credits to graduate high school; he had earned his degree in a single school year.[9]

Building off his academic success, McCarthy began a degree in electrical engineering at Milwaukee's Marquette University in the fall of 1930. He chose the school because of its relatively inexpensive cost and its Catholicism. To pay for school, McCarthy took on a smorgasbord of part-time jobs: valet driver, dishwasher, short-order cook, gas station attendant, baker, truck driver, tire salesman, elevator operator, boxing coach. He also gambled—often and heavily—to earn money. Playing poker in the back rooms of Milwaukee's bars, McCarthy would raise the pot with reckless abandon, pushing large sums of money in with such confidence that his opponents would fold, fearing the strong hand that backed such boldness. More often than not, McCarthy had nothing. But he usually ended a night of poker with a profit. During one trip to Pittsburgh to watch a Marquette football game, he reportedly won enough money to pay a semester's worth of bills.[10]

McCarthy was popular at Marquette. An article in the school's newspaper about his feat of finishing high school in under a year increased his fame. He fashioned himself as something of a hustler, a persona that won him friends and admirers at the all-male university. He joined the school's intramural boxing team and fought in front of a crowd of nearly one thousand in his first bout. He engaged in arm-wrestling contests, betting money against all challengers. One of his favorite activities was patronizing burlesque clubs. McCarthy would buy a legitimate ticket with money cobbled together by his friends, then sneak through to open the establishment's back door to his waiting compatriots. By all accounts, McCarthy was an archetypical man's man at Marquette.[11]

Perhaps as a result of all these extracurricular activities, McCarthy's early grades in electrical engineering courses were far from stellar. But that course of study had ceased to appeal to him, and by the end of his second year he had settled on earning a law degree. Where engineering required precision and care, the law seemed more fluid, its practitioners successful when they were able to make connections with other people. And gregariousness was definitely one of McCarthy's talents. He became a member of Delta Theta Phi (a legal fraternity that provided its members with a library of past briefs and other study materials) and lived in its house on West Kilbourn Avenue, where he spent many nights drinking, smoking, carousing, and playing cards.[12] In the fall of 1932 McCarthy began at Marquette Law School, earning his degree in 1935.

During his senior year at Marquette, he ran for class president. McCarthy and his opponent, Charles Curran, made a public promise: regardless of what transpired during the campaign, each man would vote for the other on election day. When the votes were tallied, McCarthy ended up winning by two votes. "'Joe,' asked Curran suspiciously, 'did you vote for yourself?' 'Sure,' came the quick reply. 'You wanted me to vote for the best man, didn't you?'"[13] Curran eventually forgave the deception largely due to an act of kindness on McCarthy's part. When Curran's father passed away later that school year, McCarthy borrowed money and took time off from work to attend the funeral. "He did that for me," recalled Curran, "and he'll always be my friend."[14]

Upon graduation, McCarthy moved to Waupaca, a small city just southwest of Manawa. His plan was to set up a small law practice, make a name for himself, and then run for political office, an aspiration he had formulated at Marquette. After winning office furniture in a card game, he rented a workspace in the Loan and Abstract Building. But the warm welcome McCarthy received in Manawa was not echoed in Waupaca. His aggressiveness and ambition reportedly rubbed many residents the wrong way, and his tactics did not make him any friends in the town's small legal community. Waupaca attorney Ed Hart recalled, "I've always felt that Joe lived in a different moral universe. He asked himself only two questions: What do I want and how do I get it? Once he got rolling, you had to step aside. It was every man for himself, sort of what anarchy must be like."[15]

McCarthy jumped at the first opportunity to leave Waupaca. In 1936, he accepted a job with attorney Mike Eberlein in Shawano, a larger community northwest of Green Bay. McCarthy reasoned that the higher population would mean more political visibility. As right-hand man to the city's most prominent attorney, McCarthy was not an outsider for long; his association with Eberlein granted him immediate credibility. He accepted every invitation to address Shawano's businessmen's clubs and fraternal organizations, forging connections with everybody who was anybody and making a name for himself as a promising young attorney merely by presenting himself as one.

McCarthy quickly turned to politics. Even at the height of the New Deal, the Democratic party was an almost nonexistent in rural Wisconsin. Instead of regarding this deficit as a weakness, McCarthy seized on it as an opportunity. Less competition meant more notice from statewide party officers. He ran for district attorney in 1936 as a Democrat, losing in a landslide. McCarthy knew he had no chance of winning the race—he just wanted the publicity.[16]

For the next two years he steered clear of electoral politics and focused on his law practice, eventually becoming a named partner in the firm. In 1939 he declared his candidacy for a circuit judgeship, a position that did not require party affiliation.[17] McCarthy again faced an uphill climb against an entrenched and well-regarded opponent, Eric Warner. But McCarthy knew Warner was unpopular among many of the region's lawyers. McCarthy attacked his opponent on his salary and suggested that Warner was lying about his age. But McCarthy's real strength was that he campaigned relentlessly, making house calls on as many voters as time allowed, shaking hands and introducing himself as "Joe." A farmer described McCarthy's visit: "He didn't know me from Adam. But somehow he had learned my name, and my wife's name, and our kids' names, and our dog's name. By the time I got to the front door, he was handing my daughter a lollipop, and then Indian-wrestling with my boy . . . He wanted to know if I'd let him milk a cow; said he wanted to keep his hand in. He milked good."[18]

The anecdote captures many of the secrets to McCarthy's political success. He did his homework, came prepared, avoided talking politics directly, focused on topics both relevant and of interest to his audience, and asserted the authenticity of his working-class roots. It was pure Joe, and provided a stark contrast to Warner, an august jurist who disliked campaigning. Presenting himself as the epitome of working-class masculinity, McCarthy embodied the touchstones of that persona: toughness, strength, boldness, directness, vigor, industry. It was a shrewd political identity that was identifiable in his campaigning style, his approach to the judiciary, and his personality. McCarthy upset Warner by a comfortable margin.

Upon assuming his seat on the bench, McCarthy set to work clearing a crowded docket by adopting a pragmatic—critics would say slapdash—approach to outstanding cases. To his duties he brought an energy befitting the state's youngest circuit judge, sometimes keeping the court open past midnight in order to move through the inherited backlog. It was reported that he could conduct an entire divorce proceeding in under ten minutes. This energetic approach to work did not seem to make the quality suffer; McCarthy's decisions passed muster with the State Supreme Court at a higher-than-average rate. Soon he found himself ahead of schedule, and traveled the circuit to help lighten the load for other judges. It was a move less intended to provide support for his peers than to increase McCarthy's visibility, familiarize him with different parts of his district, drum up positive publicity, and curry political favor with influential Wisconsinites. Per usual, McCarthy did not mind taxing labor as long as he reaped the rewards.[19]

In his time as a circuit judge, McCarthy became more aware of his public image and concerned about the way he was portrayed in the press. He joined the Elks and Knights of Columbus, and continued to accept almost every speaking engagement that came his way. In June 1942, McCarthy's secretary Margaret Mary DeGroot sent a photograph of her boss to the Associated Press, explaining, "The local press asked Judge McCarthy to have an up-to-date picture taken. In view of the fact that a rather old picture of him has been run in connection with an Associated Press story recently, I thought you might like to have the enclosed picture for your files."[20] McCarthy had already sent the same, unsolicited photograph to the *Milwaukee Journal*.[21] Such proactive relations were less a product of vanity than of politicking; McCarthy knew fostering relationships with news outlets would pay dividends.

The young judge's concern for his public image can also be seen in the way he approached the question of military service at the outbreak of World War II. Already in his early thirties, McCarthy felt that his age and social standing merited special treatment. In January 1942, McCarthy sought a military job that would make use of his intelligence and talents.[22] This inquiry must have been unsuccessful, because a few months later McCarthy received a letter from the office of General Counsel John Lord O'Brian at the War Production Board, informing him that there were "no vacancies at the present time."[23]

Knowing that wartime military service would be essential to his political future, McCarthy set out to secure an officer's commission in whatever branch of service would have him. Here too he was unable to coax a satisfactory response from the military. Seemingly out of options, he joined the Marines. From the moment he signed his enlistment papers, he bragged that he had volunteered for the Marines as a buck private, even though he had requested—and received—an officer's commission.[24] The suggestion, of course, was that despite his political connections he wanted no special favors, and even took it upon himself to join the branch of the military that had a reputation as being the most demanding. McCarthy received dozens of notes applauding his decision, from both acquaintances and strangers. A friend, James Durfee, wrote that he "was particularly pleased to note that you had chosen the toughest branch of the service and that you had not asked for a reservation of a cushy desk job at Washington but that you had laid it on the line . . . The American people are getting fed up on pomposity and hypocrisy—they want courage in action and in thought. We of your own clan are particularly proud that you have led the way."[25]

This letter is also noteworthy for the sense of brotherhood that runs through it. The final line's reference to "we of your own clan" is multivalent. Like McCarthy, Durfee was a Wisconsin Catholic with Irish roots, and it appears that he was also an attorney. But this recognition of shared belonging extends beyond geographic, religious, ethnic, or professional ties. It appears to be an acknowledgment that—in deciding to join the Marines— McCarthy reaffirmed that his fidelity to a set of down-home, working-class values had remained central to his public identity even as he experienced professional and political success. Whether he actually held or adhered to that amorphous set of values is almost immaterial; the point is that Mc-Carthy was able to make others believe that he remained faithful to a way of life that kept him connected to the people he represented. Like the best politicians, McCarthy became a blank canvas onto which constituents projected what they wanted to see.

*

In his personal life as a young lawyer and judge, Joseph McCarthy continued to display many of the characteristics that had been an essential part of his identity as a student at Marquette. In his free time he drank, gambled, swam, hiked, skied, fished, hunted, and chased women. In short, he was one of the guys.

Much of McCarthy's personal correspondence during this time centers on planning trips and vacations with friends. These letters show a mixing of business and pleasure; notes from accountants and loan supervisors often end with a request for a drink or the suggestion of a fishing trip. Most notably, there is a certain male camaraderie in them, and gentle, frat-like ribbings can be found throughout. Often, this teasing centered around the topic of women. In a March 1941 letter, a friend jokingly asked McCarthy when he'd be getting married.[26] In dispensing advice to McCarthy on how his judicial correspondence should be handled while he was deployed with the Marines, court reporter Walter A. Evers counseled McCarthy to allow his secretary to "take care of your mail—except, of course, the perfumed portion."[27]

McCarthy did nothing to dissuade the perception that he was something of a tomcat. He claimed that he had little interest in marriage, asserting, "I can't work at politics if I have to call home every half hour."[28] Women were disposable; politics was forever. His friends seemed to accept him as a swinging bachelor; when McCarthy mentioned to Durfee that a girlfriend was having trouble getting her mother's permission to go away for the weekend with McCarthy and a group of his friends, Durfee wrote McCarthy that the mother's concerns were probably warranted, "knowing you as I do."[29] Acquaintances recall him having a revolving door of girlfriends; the relationships would start off strong but Joe would inevitably lose interest. Biographer Larry Tye claims that McCarthy had been engaged twice in his youth, but both relationships ended before he ran for Senate.[30]

McCarthy's romantic life in Wisconsin is relevant for a number of reasons. First, it demonstrates the degree to which he promoted his bachelorhood during his early days in the public eye. Rather than a young, debonair "bachelor about town," McCarthy showed himself as a man who was single because he was too involved with other pursuits to worry about a woman for longer than a night at a time. Second, his unconventional dating life establishes at least a modicum of plausibility for the accusations of homosexuality that would dog him later in life. Third, it plays into McCarthy's image as a brute who was ultimately too uncouth to attract a wife.[31] That reputation as a practitioner of brutish masculinity—or at least a rough-hewn, working-class version of it—seems to be deserved. The gambling never subsided, and it was rumored that his poker earnings accounted for most of his income when he was a lawyer.[32] Even after joining the circuit court bench he continued to gamble regularly. He also drank heavily, hard liquor rather than beer. And as his correspondence shows, his attitude toward women was less than enlightened.

McCarthy's correspondence also reveals his own efforts to define manliness. In a December 1942 letter endorsing his friend Mark Catlin Jr. for a commission in the Marine Corps, McCarthy wrote, "I have known Mr. Catlin rather well since I have been on the Bench. He is, in my opinion, good officer material. He has a very analytical mind and an unlimited amount of just plain guts. He has been active in athletics for some time and apparently is in excellent physical condition."[33] A country in crisis could only be defended by the toughest, most manly soldiers, and McCarthy saw evidence of manhood in his friend's analytic abilities, athleticism, physicality, and his possession of that ineffable quality, "guts." In a letter supporting a different friend's application to the Naval Officers Corps, McCarthy employed similar language: "Mr. Cohen is definitely far above the average young man in ambition, resourcefulness, and drive. He has a surplus of 'guts' and I do strongly feel that he is ideal Officer material."[34] McCarthy never elaborates on what exactly guts are, how they are earned, or why they are a desirable characteristic; he seems to trust that the Navy and the Marines both understand the value of this amorphous attribute.

In considering McCarthy's youth and young manhood as a whole, social class was among the most crucial influences on him and his sense of himself in the world. But it would also prove to be the major factor dividing him from one of his natural allies in Washington, J. Edgar Hoover. Hoover grew up in urban comfort, and as a result was led to believe that he had to actively craft his masculinity, warding off weakness through continual acts of vigor. For Hoover and members of his class, masculinity was something that had to be earned. For McCarthy, such vitality never had to be actively pursued—it was part and parcel of who he needed to become in order to be a success. Hard, sustained physical labor was not primarily thought of as a way to build vitality; it was the only way to earn a living and respect. The differences in the two men's upbringings are no small matter, particularly since they were perhaps the major element in Hoover's inability to fully embrace McCarthy as an equal. Though the two men were friendly, socialized together, and formed a political alliance, Hoover considered McCarthy too coarse to ever hold a position of true power.

*

Captain Joseph McCarthy resigned his commission in the Marine Corps in February 1945 so that he could return to Wisconsin and begin his campaign for the US Senate. He was officially discharged a full six months before the Japanese surrender. The 1946 election was actually McCarthy's second Senate race; in 1944 he had run for the Republican nomination even though military regulations prohibited him from speaking on behalf of his own candidacy while still on active duty. On primary day he was handily defeated by the incumbent, Alexander Wiley.[35]

McCarthy's opponent in the 1946 Republican primary was Robert M. La Follette Jr., the older son of legendary Senator Robert M. "Fighting Bob" La Follette Sr. Known colloquially as "Young Bob," La Follette had first been elected to his father's seat following a special election in September 1925. Originally a Republican, La Follette changed his allegiance and founded the Wisconsin Progressive Party with his younger brother Phillip in 1934.[36] Young Bob won reelection as a Progressive in 1934 and 1940, but the La Follettes' aspirations for a national Progressive Party never came to fruition, and the Wisconsin Progressive Party voted to liquidate in March 1946. Though courted by leading Democrats, La Follette decided to follow the majority of his fellow Progressives and rejoin the Republican Party.[37]

Though La Follette was a relatively popular senator and a member of the state's most famous political family, in 1946 he had a number of weaknesses McCarthy could exploit. He had alienated his traditional base by abandoning the Progressive Party, but had made few corresponding inroads among the conservative Republicans who distrusted the convenient timing of his ideological swing to the right. He was a subpar campaigner; taciturn and awkward, Young Bob had not inherited his father's easy way with voters. Perhaps most importantly, La Follette had been advised that the Republican nomination was his for the taking and consequentially chose to remain in Washington, D.C., during the summer of 1946. He did not return to Wisconsin until eleven days before the primary.[38]

Still, McCarthy remained a long shot. To defeat La Follette, he had to distinguish himself from an opponent who shared his outlook on nearly every major issue. McCarthy remarked on their few ideological differences, but was more focused on highlighting the personal characteristics that divided them. Despite having acquired the social capital of the upper middle class by this time, McCarthy actively cultivated a working-class identity rooted in purportedly manly qualities: his work ethic and hardscrabble roots, his easygoing personality, and his service as an "enlisted man." In so doing, he sought to portray himself as more in touch with the common Wisconsinite than his wealthy, fortunate son opponent.

McCarthy's dedication to hard work extended beyond cliché. His industriousness endeared him to working-class voters and projected a sense of authentic, toughened masculinity. McCarthy dramatized a cultural divide between blue-collar and white-collar workers, one in which manhood demonstrated a certain kind of authenticity. While J. Edgar Hoover worked to demonstrate that white-collar work could in fact promote masculine characteristics, McCarthy seemingly embraced the critique, suggesting that his blue-collar roots and working-class values would insulate him from the feminizing effects of white-collar employment. "While Mr. La Follette was in Washington working on a variety of projects," the New York Times wrote in the wake of the primary election, "Mr. McCarthy raced around [Wisconsin] talking to and shaking hands with anybody who looked old enough to vote for him."[39]

Depictions of McCarthy as a hard worker from a modest background dominated The Newspapers Say, a slick pamphlet he distributed during the campaign. Behind its bright red cover were decontextualized quotations from newspaper articles and interviews, depicting McCarthy as a hardworking, honest veteran who could provide Washington with a dose of much-needed common sense. It was long on biography and short on policy statements (the only legislative issue discussed was McCarthy's support for a bill authorizing increased benefits for veterans), choosing instead to massage McCarthy's public image. One section, quoting The Berlin Journal, stressed McCarthy's working-class roots, describing him as "largely a self-made man who had to come up the hard way, but it made him strong of mind and body and he will make a fine campaign, winning the voters away from the false Gods of bureaucracy, socialism, communism and back to the American way of life."[40] Quoting a political writer from Madison, the pamphlet noted that McCarthy was "born on a farm [and] lived there until past the age when most boys go to high school."[41] It also included The Shawano County Journal's contention that "McCarthy's personal initiative and capacity for hard work were responsible for his success as a farmer, grocery store manager, lawyer, judge, and as a soldier."[42]

On the campaign trail, McCarthy emphasized his years as a chicken farmer and grocery store manager more than his later success as a lawyer and judge. When he discussed his judicial record, his success was attributed to toil as much as an intellectual penchant for the law: "As a judge he administered justice promptly and with the combination of legal knowledge and good 'horse sense' for which the people admired him."[43] In choosing to highlight that quotation, the campaign also sought to emphasize McCarthy's agricultural background ("horse sense"), suggesting that even as a judge McCarthy used the values and common sense instilled by his rural upbringing. McCarthy further emphasized his modest background by deriding La Follette as "the gentleman from Virginia" because he had bought a farm outside Washington, D.C.[44]

To attract press and stress his approachability during the primary race, McCarthy crisscrossed the Badger State, always driving his own car and never deeming any town or hamlet too small to warrant a visit. He often wore casual attire—khaki pants and a work shirt. This strategy also underscored his willingness to toil for votes, as opposed to the barely campaigning La Follette. The message McCarthy tried to convey was clear: his working-class background gave him positive characteristics not available to the nepotistic La Follette. Five decades before President George W. Bush's reelection campaign popularized the phrase, McCarthy was the politician whom voters "most wanted to have a beer with." McCarthy's advocacy of self-sufficiency also influenced his political philosophy. Presenting himself as an anti–New Deal conservative, he charged that "Senator La Follette and the New Dealers believe that for every problem that confronts us there should be federal legislation or a federal bureau, while I believe that the less federal legislation, the less centralization of power, the more that is left to the individual state, the better we will be."[45] The campaign pamphlet echoed this sentiment, suggesting that McCarthy would bring a sense of efficiency and urgency with him to Washington, cutting through the restrictive red tape of the federal government.

In April 1946, Joe McCarthy's barnstorming campaign took him to the thriving small city of Sturgeon Bay.[46] His visit centered around a dinner hosted by the Door County Young Republicans at the Hotel Swoboda, an aging brick structure two blocks southeast of the city's main shipyards. The speech McCarthy gave that evening was similar to those he had delivered throughout the campaign. He focused on the makeup of the peacetime armed forces and the treatment of veterans, arguing that conscription be ended in favor of an all-volunteer force, that pay should be increased to attract enlistments, and that all soldiers be granted the opportunity to become commissioned officers. McCarthy also expressed his conviction that applicants to the army and navy academies should no longer require a political appointment. In addition, he pushed for an increase in aid to veterans, particularly to men who were "crippled or completely disabled."[47]

On the surface, McCarthy's proposals were moderate. But underneath his commentary ran a narrative thread that suggested a deeper theme of his candidacy. Each of McCarthy's propositions was based on a populist understanding of politics, one that attacked elitism, praised meritocracy, fed off voter distrust of the federal government, and purported to speak for the "common man." In this speech, McCarthy outlined a vision of the military that centered on what one newspaper termed an effort to "break down the caste system" governing the armed forces and grant opportunities for advancement to all men "when ability warranted." McCarthy's support for increased payouts to injured veterans was presented in the context of a welfare state run amok, with the candidate claiming that many veterans were allotted fewer funds than "relief clients."[48]

McCarthy's victory in the primary shocked observers not only in Wisconsin, but nationwide. The liberal political magazine *The Nation* opined that La Follette lost because Progressives had migrated to the Democratic Party, allowing the centrist McCarthy to seize the nomination. *The Nation* did not give much credence to McCarthy's campaign, claiming that his simplistic strategy was based on "taking any position that La Follette opposed."[49]

After securing the nomination, McCarthy continued this populist performance for the general election. During a debate between McCarthy and Democrat Howard J. McMurray, an audience member "asked McCarthy what background he had that could compare with the background of McMurray as a professor of political science. McCarthy got a hand when he said: 'I'm just a farm boy, not a professor.'"[50] One newspaper described McCarthy's general election performance as a continuation of "his pounding, dawn to dusk campaign," concluding that "true to the McCarthy pattern, his work paid off."[51]

McCarthy's populist credentials were also apparent in his personal characteristics. During the campaign he relied on the same personal touch that had made him a successful grocer in Manawa. The *Milwaukee Journal* reported in July that "the McCarthy method now is largely a personal contact one in which the firm handshake, the McCarthy smile and a personal, informal request for support are the fundamentals."[52] There was also a certain winking coarseness to McCarthy, an embrace of vulgarity that projected approachability even as it betrayed uncouthness. This approach had been apparent even in his nominal campaign in 1944, when the *Journal* reported this exchange between then-Captain McCarthy and a reporter: "Asked what the boys talk most about, the captain grinned and said: 'What do you think?' Next to that, what? 'The same thing,' retorted the captain."[53] This knowing exchange signaled to readers that McCarthy's elite status did not mean he had become disconnected from the people he sought to represent.

Suggestive language also found its way into the *Journal's* report on McCarthy's movements after he won the Republican nomination. After recounting McCarthy's late-night celebrations, the *Journal* described the scene that greeted a tired (and most likely hungover) Judge McCarthy at the courthouse the next morning: "Shirley [Foresman, McCarthy's secretary] brought the judge a cup of coffee from the jail downstairs. It was too hot to drink. 'Get me some ice, duchess,' the judge said. 'I don't have any ice, but I'll blow on it for you, senator,' she said. And so she did."[54] Here was McCarthy the bachelor, the lovable scoundrel winking and cajoling his way into the hearts of all he met: the soft misogyny of his pet name for his secretary, the compliant servitude of women in his life, the general desirability to women, the implied no-strings-attached sexual relationship with his employee. Again, the implication was that McCarthy was just one of the guys, if a more successful version than most.

Perhaps the most important showcase for McCarthy's populist masculinity was his military service. Captain McCarthy's actual service record was undoubtedly laudable, but candidate McCarthy needed a more rousing narrative to sell voters. There was a certain aggressive, militaristic tone to McCarthy's campaign; a *Milwaukee Journal* report described the approach McCarthy took while visiting a rural county in south-central Wisconsin as "hand to hand," a phrasing reminiscent of close combat.[55] Referencing McCarthy's service as the rear machine gunner on dive bombers in the Pacific, the 1946 campaign christened its candidate "Tail-Gunner Joe" and concluded a number of campaign materials with the exhortation that "Congress NEEDS A TAILGUNNER."[56] McCarthy's campaign posters featured a heroic photo of him in full flight gear, including a leather pilot's helmet and goggles resting atop his head. The image was taken from a low angle, with a half-smiling McCarthy gazing hopefully skyward.

The Newspapers Say pamphlet depicted McCarthy as a selfless war hero, quoting Admiral Chester W. Nimitz as claiming that McCarthy "although suffering from a severe leg injury . . . refused to be hospitalized and continued to carry out his duties in a highly efficient manner."[57] The same pamphlet reprinted Marine Corps Major General Field Harris's praise of

FIGURE 5. McCarthy at his campaign headquarters during the 1946 election. The photograph of McCarthy wearing flight gear was an important marketing tool for his campaign. Credit: Getty Images.

McCarthy: "I note with gratification McCarthy's unusual accomplishments during thirty months of active duty, particularly in the combat area."[58] The Nimitz "quotation" was actually from a citation the admiral had signed at the request of one of McCarthy's commanding officers, and which Mc-Carthy almost certainly had written himself. As a means of further burnishing his record, McCarthy attacked La Follette for not enlisting at the war's outbreak and charging that he made "bloated wartime profits" from his interest in a Milwaukee radio station.[59] He also chastised La Follette for his isolationist stance on foreign policy, suggesting that La Follette did not have the courage to commit American forces abroad.[60]

As a means of highlighting his own service as a "grunt," McCarthy repeatedly claimed that he had enlisted as a "buck private." A press release published in Wisconsin newspapers upon McCarthy's return from the Pacific claimed that "though automatically deferred from the draft, [McCarthy] left the bench and enlisted as a buck private in the Marine Corps. He was sent to an officer's training school, where he earned a second lieutenant's commission."[61] The wording—likely McCarthy's own—is particularly illuminating because it suggests that McCarthy had earned his promotion to the officer's ranks, rather than being appointed on the basis of his prewar profession. If McCarthy did not make himself out to be Wisconsin's version of Audie Murphy, he certainly exaggerated his military record enough to convince voters that his time in the Marines had provided experiences proving his masculine claims to toughness, resilience, fortitude, and strength.

The reality of McCarthy's time in the Marines was quite different. He began his service in August 1942 and was eventually assigned to Marine Scout Bombing Squadron 235 (VMSB-235). McCarthy spent two-and-a-half years as an intelligence officer, deploying with VMSB-235 to the South Pacific in late spring, 1943. His responsibilities were largely confined to briefing flight crews before their bombing runs over Japanese-held islands and debriefing them following their return. According to other Marines in the same area of operations, the most persistent enemy during their deployment was boredom. Though McCarthy would later lament the heart-wrenching letters he had to write to the parents and wives of deceased comrades, his unit emerged from the war without any fatalities.[62]

McCarthy actually earned the "Tail-Gunner Joe" nickname, though it was more sarcastic than laudatory. It arose from McCarthy's effort to break the military's record for the most ammunition expended in a single mission. Following an afternoon spent strafing coconut trees, McCarthy was "awarded" the record and the unit's public relations representative dashed off a press release to a few Wisconsin newspapers. When McCarthy received the resulting articles in the mail a few weeks later, he was said to have gleefully told his friends that the publicity was "worth 50,000 votes to me."[63] Though he was an intelligence officer, McCarthy did volunteer to serve as a tail gunner for as many as a dozen sorties, and his plane may have come under enemy fire a number of times, but he was certainly not the hero he described to voters.[64]

McCarthy consistently exaggerated his war record throughout his career. During the 1946 campaign, he reportedly told an audience that he walked with shoe orthotics because he had "ten pounds of shrapnel in [his] leg" from his military service.[65] McCarthy began his 1952 autobiography *McCarthyism: The Fight for America* by describing "the first trip which I had taken in the rear seat of an SBD to divebomb Japanese anti-aircraft on the then southern anchor of the chain of Japanese Pacific defenses at Kahili on the southern tip of Bougainville," noting that the plane dodged anti-aircraft fire as it made its bombing run.[66] In referring to the plane as "an SBD," McCarthy used military slang for the "Scout Bomber Douglas Dauntless," a dive bomber used by the Navy and Marines during the war. It was a vernacular choice that subtly indicated McCarthy's military bona fides.[67]

What McCarthy described as a war wound—the injury for which he was eventually awarded a Purple Heart—was actually the result of a hazing ritual onboard the *USS Chandeleur*, the seaplane tender that carried members of VMSB-235 from Hawaii to the New Hebrides. On June 22, 1943, many of the men aboard were participating in a ceremony marking their first time crossing the equator, sometimes called a "shellback" ritual. Each man who had yet to cross that latitude was forced to run through a line of oar-swinging sailors. The task was made more difficult because each initiate had to make their dash with a bucket attached to one of their feet. While running this gauntlet McCarthy slipped, fell down a flight of stairs, and broke some bones in his foot.[68] This hobbling was the only injury McCarthy received during the war.

McCarthy's self-portrayal as a tested veteran dovetailed perfectly with the other elements of his populist-influenced masculine performance. The centrality of that vision to McCarthy's masculinity was not simply the by-product of competitive bluster, nor was it the natural outcome of efforts to differentiate himself from La Follette and McMurray. It was a performance that enabled McCarthy to garner support from socially conservative voters concerned about labor disputes, the growth of federal bureaucracy under the New Deal, and the spread of communism. While McCarthy benefitted greatly from political circumstance—including mainline Republicans' distrust of La Follette and a split in the liberal-labor votes that would have typically gone to La Follette—his victories would have been impossible had McCarthy not worked to exploit the opportunities he was afforded.

A nationwide wave of strikes helped make labor relations a central issue in the 1946 midterm elections, with many voters fearing the economic ramifications of prolonged disputes between management and organized labor. Coal miners, meatpackers, steelworkers, machinists, teamsters, lumber workers, railroad engineers, and autoworkers all walked out in the eighteen months following the end of World War II. Approximately 4.6 million workers took part in work stoppages by 1946, more than any prior year.[69] Workers were facing cutbacks as a result of a return to peacetime productivity levels, and tensions were exacerbated by the return of servicemen to the labor force. According to labor historian George Lipsitz, "fears of another depression, accumulated resentments over wartime sacrifices, and anger over postwar reverses in wages and working conditions ignited strikes and demonstrations from coast to coast."[70]

One of the nation's most bitter labor disputes took place in the Milwaukee suburb of West Allis. The UAW-CIO Local 248 of the Allis-Chalmers Manufacturing Company, the state's largest union, walked out when they could not reach a new contract agreement with the heavy machinery manufacturer. The strike began on April 30, 1946, just as the primary campaign began. In retaliation, Allis-Chalmers accused Local 248's leadership of engaging in "a communist-inspired plot to disrupt American industry" and planted articles in the *Milwaukee Sentinel* alleging that the union was rife with communists.[71] The strike lasted for eleven months, and it was noted in the national press for its length and intensity. There is little doubt that the protracted battle influenced the electorate; the CIO's Political Action Committee actually urged its followers, many of whom had voted for La Follette on the Progressive ticket in 1940, to register as Democrats in 1946.[72] McCarthy highlighted his primary opponent's past support for unions, claiming that La Follette was "too subservient to organized labor."[73] In that context, McCarthy's efforts to claim the mantle of the "self-made-man" can also be read as anti-union because they suggested that he understood the value of self-sufficiency and was not looking for socialistic handouts.[74]

McCarthy's narrative of masculine self-sufficiency positioned him well to respond to conservative voters' frustration with the federal government, which by 1946 seemed to be doing little to deal with problems such as high prices, a shortage of sufficient housing, and an unsteady supply of consumer goods. The public was particularly frustrated by a meat shortage; livestock producers banded together to keep their goods off market, protesting the continuation of wartime price controls. President Truman acquiesced in mid-October, but not before significant damage was done to the Democratic Party's chances in the upcoming elections.[75] McCarthy took advantage of this sentiment by projecting an independent, can-do attitude. Newspaper coverage consistently portrayed him as a real-life Horatio Alger character who was able to pack "more activity and accomplishment in 13 years than most men have in a lifetime."[76] After his primary victory, McCarthy told one newspaper that "the people of Wisconsin, and especially the farmers, were fed up with the bureaucratic bungling and hamstringing they received from New Deal agencies which invaded every department of their lives."[77]

Another key factor in the 1946 campaign was voters' renewed fears of communism. The flame of American anticommunism had been fanned by former British Prime Minister Winston Churchill, who warned in his March 5, 1946, address in Fulton, Missouri, that a Soviet-hung "iron curtain" had fallen between Eastern Europe and the Western world and that communist spies were dedicated to promoting instability in the West. As a result, national security was at the electoral forefront; writing in the liberal-progressive newspaper *PM*, syndicated columnist Max Lerner echoed a popular opinion in claiming that Republicans had taken control of Congress "largely on the basis of a Red Scare."[78]

Wisconsin voters were certainly not immune to these fears. La Follette repeatedly sounded the warning alarm about communism and pledged to be the most voracious red hunter in the Senate. But his promises could not match McCarthy's pedigree as a (literal) fighter, with McCarthy's campaign working hard to present him as a strong, athletic veteran who had already proven himself capable of defending his nation.[79] In the general election, McCarthy employed red-baiting language to attack his Democratic opponent, Howard J. McMurray, noting that the communist *Daily Worker* newspaper had endorsed McMurray and dubbed him a fellow traveler ("meaning a communist," McCarthy helpfully explained).[80] In a show of loyalty to his new party, La Follette penned a number of editorials supporting McCarthy, promising that his former rival would be tougher on communism than the Democratic nominee.[81]

A final advantage of McCarthy's populist masculinity was that it made him approachable, relatable, and readable to a bloc of socially conservative voters who had become unsettled by momentous social and economic shifts. Though there is little evidence of voters' emotional responses to McCarthy, his improbable triumph in the primary and landslide victory in the general election make it reasonable to conclude that he established some kind of connection with the electorate. McCarthy had a talent for making personal connections—one newspaper described him as possessing "a seemingly inexhaustible supply of energy and an enthusiasm for meeting people."[82] In an era when mass media innovations like live radio broadcasts from far-flung locales and movie newsreels could make the world seem complex and unwieldy, McCarthy's personal touch and self-effacing attitude helped him court voters.

In positioning himself as representative of "traditional" values such as patriotism, industry, and self-sufficiency, McCarthy stood as a bulwark against the disconcerting, rapid changes apparent in society and culture.[83] Specifically, his masculine identity emphasized ideals many Americans feared were on the retreat. Whether McCarthy knew it or not, his embodiment of conservative values possibly helped assuage working-class Wisconsinites' fears that society was promoting laziness and entitlement.

McCarthy's masculine identity worked so well as a delivery vehicle for this balm precisely because the social changes implied by shifting gender norms were a concern of many conservative voters. Veterans returned to a nation in which women had experienced expanded commercial, civic, and social autonomy in their absence. In 1940, only 26 percent of women were part of the workforce; by 1945, that figure had increased to 36 percent.[84] Between 1940 and 1944, "the percentage of women in manufacturing jobs in the United States increased 140 percent," and though many women initially intended their employment to be temporary, by 1945 three-quarters of employed women reported that they wanted to continue to work outside the home.[85] Such desires increased stress on a tightening job market.

By early 1946, 3.25 million women workers had either quit or been fired, and workplace gender segregation was more pronounced that year than it had been in 1900.[86] Efforts to return women to the domestic sphere were regarded as necessary precisely because wartime upheaval had allowed women to encroach on "male" spaces.[87] Unsurprisingly, these attempts were inconsistent in their effectiveness—in the first year after the Japanese surrender, 2.75 million women *started* new jobs—and unable to stem the tide of gender-based social upheaval.[88]

Veterans were concerned about the labor market's social and moral impacts, too. As John D'Emilio and Estelle Freedman have noted, "The demands of wartime drew teenagers into the paid labor force while weakening the influence that family and community held over their behavior . . . Whereas [moral reformers] of the First World War focused on the dangers of prostitution, by the 1940s it was the behavior of 'amateur girls'— popularly known as khaki wackies, victory girls, and good-time Charlottes—that concerned moralists."[89] Moralists and mainstreamers alike were determined to reassert "traditional" gender divides.

In the unstable seas of postwar America, McCarthy's conservative values represented a safe harbor for many Wisconsin voters. His wartime experience helped him connect with fellow veterans and their families, and suggested he had the wherewithal to counter the expanding communist menace. His bachelor status and embrace of stereotypically male pursuits promised his fidelity to a paternalistic understanding of social order. His emphasis on self-sufficiency distinguished him from the seemingly entitled

La Follette and firmly affixed his personal story to the legends of Horatio Alger. Perhaps most importantly, McCarthy's efforts to emphasize his unassuming nature and connection with the people of Wisconsin spoke to voters who were growing increasingly frustrated with the impersonal nature of the federal government and the bureaucratic complexities of the New Deal.

When McCarthy began his Senate term in January 1947, he was the body's youngest member. The persona that McCarthy had cultivated during the election remained with him during his early days on Capitol Hill. Immediately following his victory, McCarthy told reporters, "I don't claim to be any smarter than the next fellow, but I do claim that I work twice as hard and that's what I intend to do in Washington the next six years." The *Milwaukee Journal* latched onto this self-characterization, noting that "there is no doubt that the hard driving, intensely ambitious McCarthy knows how to work. All the successes of this Outagamie County farm boy have been won the hard way."[90] Such praise was particularly noteworthy coming from the left-of-center *Journal*, which would eventually become a major opponent. For the time being, the *Journal* was happy to describe McCarthy in a way that would have been at home in the newly elected senator's campaign pamphlet, describing him as "dynamic, shrewd, engaging, and enterprising" and concluding that he fit into "the best Horatio Alger tradition."[91] A week later, the *Journal* continued its praise, describing a celebratory vacation McCarthy had taken with friends to the "tiny northern Wisconsin resort town" of Land O'Lakes. Again, the *Journal* stressed the senator-elect's athleticism, vigor, and ease with rugged pursuits, describing how McCarthy, "fit and trim at 198 pounds," easily outpaced two companions during a fourteen-mile hike.[92] Fawning depictions of McCarthy's athleticism and physical attributes were not limited to Wisconsin newspapers. A later article in the *US News and World Report* described him as "a dark, handsome, and athletic 6-foot bachelor . . . much in demand socially. He is gregarious and amiable, likes parties. The Senator likes riding. Last spring, at an outing of the National Press Club, he rode in a mule race and won."[93]

In opposition to the white-collar, refined masculinity of many of his peers in Congress, McCarthy was presented as the epitome of heartland manhood and self-sufficient bachelorhood. A brief item beside one of the *Milwaukee Journal's* longer profiles of McCarthy described a "Bachelor's Trick" that the senator had adopted: "Young Joe McCarthy, who . . . is now probably one of the nation's most eligible bachelors, has one bachelor's trick that you girls might be interested in. He presses his pants by putting them under his mattress at night. Also, instead of using a hone, like most staid married men, he sharpens his double edged bladed [sic] razor blade on the palm of his hand. He says it works fine."[94] Not only was McCarthy claiming to be a humble bachelor, but one that possessed the hands of a working man, rough enough to sharpen a razor blade. Again, McCarthy's supposed ruggedness was on display—as was his eligibility as a potential mate for some lucky girl. Friends from McCarthy's early days in Washington recall that he often went on dates, though most of the connections were brief and more physical than emotional. John W. Hanes, onetime special assistant to Secretary of State John Foster Dulles, recalled McCarthy's social behavior as boorish and often influenced by drink, noting that McCarthy was "rough" and "would fairly often get disorderly. He brought a succession of floozies, usually, out with him. If he didn't he was making passes at everybody in the house, including my sister."[95]

Photographs from 1946 appear to corroborate McCarthy's claims of working-class bachelorhood and the unpretentious visage he sought to project. On three different momentous occasions—the day he defeated La Follette, the day he met Wisconsin governor Walter S. Goodland, and the day he won the general election—McCarthy wore the same double-breasted, pinstriped suit and patterned tie, suggesting that he owned only one "formal" outfit. Though he tried to improve his wardrobe in Washington, he still sported suits that were "ill-fitting, poorly coordinated, and rarely pressed"—apparently the mattress trick wasn't that effective.[96]

As an eligible bachelor about town, McCarthy participated in a number of amusements that are stereotypically regarded as the purview of working-class men, including gambling and brothel visits.[97] These undertakings were certainly not part of his official public image—McCarthy even told inquiring reporters that he did not shoot craps—but rumors of them were rendered believable courtesy of his reputation as the embodiment of working-class manhood.[98] McCarthy spent many afternoons betting on horse races at one of the numerous tracks in the greater Washington area, often in the company of J. Edgar Hoover (and presumably Clyde Tolson).[99]

By most accounts these extracurricular distractions did not interfere with McCarthy's senatorial duties. Nor did they blunt his overall work ethic, at least initially. During a congressional recess in the fall of 1948, McCarthy and a friend harvested wheat at a farm in North Dakota. Signing on under an assumed name, McCarthy "ate German food, drank beer, cracked bad jokes, and earned everyone's respect."[100] It is unclear whether McCarthy needed money (his finances were often in disarray) or sought a working vacation from the pressures of public service. But his insistence on anonymity suggests that at least portions of his working-class public persona were authentic.

Though McCarthy's first three years in the Senate were unremarkable, a few key moments reveal much about his personality and how he was portrayed by the press. In each instance, McCarthy demonstrated his penchant for manipulating reporters, his violent temper, and his willingness to pugnaciously attack his opponents.

Senator McCarthy's first appearance in national headlines was the result of an ethics dustup soon after the beginning of his first term. After receiving a much-needed $20,000 loan from a Pepsi lobbyist, McCarthy advocated that wartime sugar rationing be eased. This quid pro quo was legal, though ethically questionable. McCarthy faced criticism from other senators, who derided him as the "Pepsi-Cola Kid." He fought back viciously, arguing (falsely) that there had never been a sugar shortage, fabricating figures, and claiming that the Department of Agriculture was planning to provide families with extra sugar for the purposes of canning (it was not). He even accused two senior colleagues from his own party—Vermont's Ralph Flanders and New Hampshire's Charles Tobey—of conspiring to lie about the amount of sugar available to consumers.[101] The sugar supply was ultimately decontrolled, but McCarthy's marginal victory surely did not warrant the resulting damage to his reputation in the Senate.

Around the same time—a five month period in 1947–48—McCarthy served as vice chairman of a joint committee studying housing, a position he earned by ensuring the vote was held on a day when his primary rival's supporters were out of town.[102] The committee was tasked with addressing one of the most vexing problems of the immediate postwar era, a crippling housing shortage nationwide. The dearth had its roots in the widespread construction slowdown during the Great Depression, but became a crisis due to postwar prosperity; because contractors could make large profits building golf courses, hotels, bars, and restaurants, there were fewer incentives to construct affordable housing. The results were shocking: by 1945, an estimated five million families were in search of a place to live. On average, they were unable to pay more than $6,000 to buy a house or $50 per month in rent.[103] Newspapers filled with classified advertisements from veterans seeking housing. A typical entry asked for "No sympathy or charity. Wanted: Just a Home. Whatever you have to offer. We aren't perfect, just normal people. Veteran, wife and child. Won't you please call us?" Another lamented, "Being a returned veteran I do want a home so my wife & I (no children or pets) can be together again. I'm sick of hotels & discouraged no end . . . rent to $60." A Mr. Berggren took a different approach, writing, "Attention, suckers. Drunken advertising exec. with gambling wife and moronic year-old brat want a modern 2-bedroom house or apt. immediately. Must be in first-class neighborhood."[104] Some observers viewed the housing shortage as a national security issue in addition to an economic one, arguing that the anemic housing market could undermine democracy by weakening the capitalistic system on which that freedom was built.[105]

At the heart of the congressional investigation stood the Taft-Ellender-Wagner (TEW) Housing Act, which was intended to promote the construction of fifteen million units of public housing over the next decade, including 500,000 that were to be built and operated by the federal government.[106] McCarthy was a vocal opponent of the bill, claiming that public housing interfered with the free market and promoted the growth of slums. When McCarthy schemed his way to the joint committee's vice chairmanship, the TEW Act had already passed the Senate but faced a difficult hurdle in the House, courtesy of an opposing coalition of contractors, bankers, and real-estate agents. Under the pretext of soliciting public opinion, McCarthy conducted formal public hearings in thirty-three cities across the country and eventually heard testimony from 1,286 witnesses.[107] The hearings, designed to attract as much media coverage as possible, became something of a national press tour for McCarthy, who staged press conferences and photo ops at every juncture.

They also allowed McCarthy's second foray into red baiting. Overall, the campaign against public housing centered on claims that the projects had a socialist bent. Conservatives allied with real estate interests noted the "socialist dangers" of public housing at both the federal and local levels, claiming that such plans were part of a communist conspiracy.[108] McCarthy's hearings played a central role in constructing that narrative, and he even used some of the subcommittee's budget to hire a public relations firm to broadcast that message. During the hearings themselves, McCarthy interrupted and intimidated witnesses who supported public housing, arguing that "the ultimate aim of . . . professional public housers is to socialize all housing under the guise of providing public housing for the underprivileged."[109] He also criticized the housing projects as possible havens for the communistic ideals that had spurred their construction. Touring the Rego Park Veterans Housing Project in Queens, McCarthy called it "a deliberately created slum area, at federal expense . . . a breeding ground for communists."[110] McCarthy presented himself as a populist advocate for veterans, piling scorn on superfluous middlemen who inflated the cost of housing and forestalled the mass production of homes by controlling the supply of building materials. It was a nimble piece of maneuvering; while advocating policies beneficial to the real estate lobby, McCarthy postured as a consumer advocate.

In the end, the public relations campaign worked, and both the House and Senate passed a more moderate version of the TEW Act. In the face of public pleas for housing, McCarthy had helped orchestrate a broad effort to torpedo any chance of a robust public housing system. Historians Roslyn Baxandall and Elizabeth Ewen conclude that "the Congressional hearings on housing, together with the public relations multimedia blitz of the private real estate lobby, succeeded in reframing the national discussion about affordable housing."[111] Fundamentally, those opposed to public housing made the TEW Act debate "a referendum on the fate of the New Deal's urban social provisions," thus granting McCarthy an opportunity to enact the anti–New Deal policies on which he had campaigned.[112] The housing developer William Levitt praised McCarthy in gendered terms that would have been at home in McCarthy's 1946 campaign literature: "Mr. McCarthy is first a veteran, second a US Senator, third a very aggressive young man typical of the type of leadership that you might expect in Washington from now on, and fourth, he exhibits a passionate interest in housing that almost amounts to a phobia. Parenthetically, I might add he is also a Republican."[113]

Not long thereafter, McCarthy became embroiled in a controversy surrounding the fate of German prisoners from the war. During the Battle of the Bulge, members of a German Panzer Division under the command of Colonel Joachim Peiper executed 353 American prisoners of war in what came to be known as the Malmedy massacre.[114] After the war, seventy-four German soldiers who had participated in the butchery were tried for war crimes. All were found guilty and more than half were sentenced to death by hanging, including Peiper. The defense attorney in the case, Army Colonel Willis M. Everett, was convinced that the Germans had not received a fair trial. During the appeal process, a number of them "testified that they were beaten severely and sadistically, not only by guards moving them around the prison, but by the staff of the war crimes investigating team, for the purpose of securing confessions."[115]

The publication of these accusations in American newspapers raised public ire, especially in German-heavy areas of the Midwest. In response, the Senate Armed Services Committee established a subcommittee to investigate the reports of misconduct. Though McCarthy was not on the Armed Services Committee, he asked to attend the hearings as an observer and was given the courtesy of being able to cross-examine witnesses.[116]

Even before the subcommittee investigation began, McCarthy argued that the death sentences of six German soldiers should be commuted because their confessions had been made under duress. Foreshadowing later behavior, McCarthy lost his temper during a May 1949 hearing when subcommittee members denied his request that Army investigators be given lie detector tests. He angrily exited the hearing room and later told the press that the inquiry was "a shameful farce." When the subcommittee report was published in October, McCarthy deemed it "a gross miscarriage of justice" and questioned the objectivity of subcommittee members due to their professional connections with the Army interrogation team.[117]

Ultimately none of the German soldiers was executed and all were spared significant jail time; in 1956, Peiper himself became the final prisoner paroled. The US government's desire to preserve positive relations with West Germany in the context of the Cold War greatly contributed to this leniency. Though some have regarded McCarthy's fiery advocacy as an effort to appeal to the large German-American constituency he represented, others have ventured that his interest can be largely traced to his hunger for publicity. Defending an unpopular group based on moral principles was sure to attract attention, and the primacy of the Cold War meant that supporting German soldiers (who were possible American allies against Soviet encroachment in Eastern Europe) was not as politically risky as it would have been a half-decade earlier.[118]

It was a miscalculation. McCarthy's public image was again sullied, largely because his actions were regarded as a direct attack on the integrity of the military. After making improved treatment for veterans one of the only substantive issues of his campaign, McCarthy had taken a stance that many derided as unpatriotic. The controversy must have illustrated to the young senator how potent accusations of being un-American could be. Another quirk of the Malmedy affair was that it may have been the root of the charge of anti-Semitism that later plagued McCarthy; more than once did he suggest that Jewish-American interrogators had mistreated their German prisoners due to "racial" animus.

Significantly, these early controversies demonstrated McCarthy's inability to moderate his temper when confronted with contrary opinions, even during relatively insignificant debates. McCarthy's short fuse and the angry accusations he made played an important role in how he came to be publicly perceived. One element that contributed to McCarthy's combative approach to the Senate was the friction between McCarthy's sense of himself as an outsider and his desire to belong. Though he prided himself on his working-class roots, McCarthy was intent on being accepted within an elite institution that has been described as "the world's most exclusive club." Because McCarthy could not rely on his class status as a basis for that acceptance, he appealed to masculine jocularity. The Senate of the late 1940s was the epitome of an old boys' network; there were no female Senators in the Eightieth Congress, and McCarthy himself served with only four female colleagues during his entire time on Capitol Hill.[119] McCarthy readily participated in the masculine amusements favored by his colleagues, including poker games, rounds of golf, hunting and fishing trips, and general carousing. To some degree, McCarthy must have felt his place at the proverbial senatorial table was deserved; even after publicly attacking a peer, McCarthy would show kindness to his opponent and expect to remain friends with him. Illinois senator Paul H. Douglas compared McCarthy to "a mongrel dog, fawning on you one moment and the next moment trying to bite your leg off."[120] But McCarthy himself seemed to regard the professional and personal sides of a relationship as distinct, a perspective that perhaps enabled the viciousness with which he fought political battles. In the case of the sugar rationing, housing subcommittee, and Malmedy controversies, McCarthy was not shy about launching personal attacks against his enemies, nor did he have any qualms about using tactics such as guilt by association, decontextualized quotations, and deliberate misinformation.

McCarthy's early days in the Senate affirmed his keen awareness of the power of the media and how he was portrayed in it. Though his talent for media manipulation would not reach its fullest expression until the early 1950s, McCarthy's deft handling of the national press was on display from the start. He even called a press conference on his first day in Washington, before his swearing-in.[121] McCarthy's greatest talent was his recognition that media coverage could drive the tenor of a story as much as actual happenings, and that statements to the press could influence an issue as much as—if not more than—statements made in the well of the Senate or in one of its hearing rooms. As a result, McCarthy rarely took any action without distributing a press release. Though his political identity largely relied on classic American tropes such as the self-made man and the war hero, his use of the media to advertise that image was distinctly modern. Unique, too, was his continued reliance on a practiced lack of sophistication, even after joining the Senate.

Most importantly, McCarthy recognized that the perception of an issue or event often had more influence over a dispute's outcome than the facts of the matter. Nowhere was his understanding of this distinction more visible than in his approach to the public housing hearings. A significant segment of the public wanted government-funded housing, but McCarthy was able to use the hearings to shift the public's perception.[122] In the view of housing historian Richard Davies, "In his role as Vice-Chairman of the Committee, [McCarthy] underwent an apprenticeship as [a] self-appointed inquisitor developing the sledge-hammer techniques he later used so effectively while seeking to exhume communist conspirators from the depths of the State Department."[123]

At the same time, the victories McCarthy won between 1947 and 1949 were minor, and often did not warrant the political capital he had expended to secure them. He had insulted colleagues, attracted the attention of the Ethics Committee, and earned a reputation as a hothead. In 1949, a poll of 128 members of Washington's press corps named him the worst senator.[124] Halfway through his term, with the 1952 election on the horizon, McCarthy was still in search of a way to make his mark.

4

THE POWER BROKER AS A YOUNG MAN

As a toddler, Roy Cohn was given a nose job. The purely aesthetic procedure was performed at the insistence of his mother, Dora. A small bump on
the ridge of Roy's nose had bothered her since the day of his birth in February 1927, and though nobody else in the family—including Roy's father—
saw a problem with it, Dora insisted on having the bump surgically removed. The Manhattan surgeon that Dora hired bungled the operation,
and as a consequence Roy had a scar on his nose for the rest of his life.[1]

He would carry other marks of his parents' influence to adulthood. Dora
and Al Cohn created a son in their own image, one obsessed with outward appearances, drawn to power, preoccupied with class standing, shot
through with ambition, and masterful at political deal making. These personal qualities enabled Cohn to deftly manage Washington power politics,
even before his twenty-fifth birthday. They also fostered a sense of entitlement that inspired the hatred of his rivals, who eventually came to regard
Cohn's background as noteworthy not for its record of youthful achievement but for its pattern of absurdity. It was a childhood that would be invoked by opponents in their attempt to explain his personality, including
his interpersonal relationships, gender identity, and sexual preferences. If
Hoover came of age as a middle-class Protestant moralist and McCarthy as

a blue-collar striver with a rough-and-tumble sensibility, Cohn was raised as an entitled opportunist who always believed he belonged among—but was never fully welcomed into—the nation's power elite.

As Joseph McCarthy made his way through his first term in the Senate, Roy Cohn was busy crafting a related political identity, one that also relied on masculine performance as a means of securing an increased foothold on power in the postwar security state. Like McCarthy, Cohn embraced anti-communism as a way to buttress his own masculine credentials, increase his public profile, and fuel his rise through the ranks of the federal government. Cohn also deftly used the media—specifically the gossip press—to craft and spread a public persona that would benefit his professional agenda. While McCarthy embraced his working-class background as a source of power (in that it allowed him to connect with citizens and advertise his populist bona fides), Cohn sought clout by advertising his upper-class credentials. At the same time, Cohn's experience demonstrates that a privileged background was not enough to ensure success. Cohn's first years in government employment show that a certain level of aggressiveness was required of all performers of surveillance state masculinity, regardless of class affiliation. In fact, an overreliance on well-trod upper-class routes to power such as wealth, familial connections, or an elite educational background could make displays of machismo all the more necessary. As he built press contacts and zealously hunted communists, Cohn was also intently constructing a professional and public persona that would allow him to join the power elite. Cohn's entry into that rarefied realm was contingent on a daily performance that hid his sexual and gender identities—both of which could be regarded as nonnormative—by emphasizing personal characteristics that projected a "traditional," heterosexual masculinity.

*

Cohn's blunt worldview was partially the product of his parents' mutually exploitative marriage. Albert Cohn, an assistant district attorney in the Bronx, needed to expand his personal fortune and monetary support for the Democratic Party in order to be named a judge. Dorothy Marcus, the daughter of a politically connected bank president, was quickly approaching the social irrelevance that accompanied being a middle-aged single woman. The pair's January 11, 1924, wedding was a calculated attempt by both parties to solve their problems: Al gained access to Dora's family money while Dora cemented her social status by marrying a well-known lawyer with a promising career ahead of him. The couple's five-week honeymoon in Europe was not a lovers' escape but a fulfillment of the expectations of the class to which they firmly felt they belonged.[2]

Unsurprisingly, the Cohns' arrangement of marriage-as-business-transaction did not bring happiness. One of Al's coworkers later recalled the pairing as "the most miserable marriage I've ever known," adding that Al and Dora "hated each other. Absolutely hated each other."[3] As loveless as the relationship was, Al Cohn's newly improved financial situation did allow him to soon become a county judge. His loyalty to his political allies served him well and his career progressed steadily. In 1929, he was appointed to Part III of the State Supreme Court by Governor Franklin D. Roosevelt. He joined the State Supreme Court's Appellate Division eight years later and held that position until his death in 1959.[4]

What fueled Al's rise was his role as a central cog in the Bronx's Democratic Party machine. When the party needed Al to rule a certain way for reasons political or personal, he followed through. When they needed his support for a specific candidate, he gave it. When the son of a friend and fellow Democratic operative killed a young woman in an automobile accident, Al made a late-night visit to the police station and "straightened it out."[5]

As Roy remembered it, Al was the "chief lieutenant" for Edward J. Flynn, Democratic Party operative, New York's secretary of state from 1929 until 1939, and chairman of the Democratic National Committee from 1940 until 1943. With the death of Kansas City's Tom Pendergast, Flynn became "the most powerful political boss in the country." He was "a devoted friend of Franklin Roosevelt [whose] influence on Roosevelt on political matters exceeded that of anyone inside or out of the administration."[6] Flynn was instrumental in convincing Roosevelt to select Harry S. Truman as a running mate in 1944 and in quarterbacking Truman's surprise victory in the 1948 presidential election.[7] And it was Flynn who in 1929 convinced then-Governor Roosevelt to appoint Al Cohn to a judgeship.

The only time Roy recalled his father abandoning his loyalty to Ed Flynn was in 1937, when Flynn proposed naming a Judge Callahan to a position on the State Appellate Court that Al coveted. Telling a ten-year-old Roy that he'd been passed over for the judgeship because he was not Irish, Al enlisted a pair of friends with influence over current governor Herbert Lehman to collect signatures supporting his appointment. The tactic worked and Al joined the appellate court on April 27, 1937. Personal loyalty was important, but not to the point that it should hinder professional gain.[8]

The favors Al performed for Ed Flynn and the Democratic Party were not confined to his judge's chambers. The Cohn family apartment at 975 Walton Avenue in the South Bronx became a meeting place for members of the borough's Democratic machine. Cohn remembered his address as "*the* building, where *everyone* lived. The district attorney, the most influential judges, the postmaster, the top businessmen."[9] As a result, Cohn was raised in an environment that intertwined the political and the domestic. Though Al did not appear in the newspapers or on the radio every day, his son still recognized his importance. While publicity was nice, a man did not have to be in the public eye to hold significant sway; major deals could be struck at a table in a linoleum-floored Bronx apartment kitchen.

Cohn quickly learned to trade on his father's power and name. Surrounded by the children of New York City's royalty at the Horace Mann School for Boys in the Bronx, Cohn made sure his peers knew that his family wielded its share of power.[10] As a teenager, "Roy would amaze his friends by putting in a spur-of-the-moment telephone call to the mayor's office and talking briefly to [New York City mayor] 'Bill' O'Dwyer."[11] He did not limit this demonstration of power and connections to his private circle of friends:

> A schoolmate of Roy's remembers Roy, age sixteen or seventeen, walking into a meeting where some of the younger boys were talking to an administrator. Roy said hello and went and picked up a telephone. The adult in charge asked, "Roy, what are you doing?" Roy replied, "I have to make this call. I'll only be a minute." The call went through and the other boys heard Roy say, "Is this the Twelfth Precinct? I want to talk to the officer in charge ... No, I want to talk to the officer in charge ... which lieutenant? ... Lieutenant O'Malley, my name is Roy Cohn. I'm the son of Judge Cohn. I'm sure you know who my father is. If you don't now, you certainly will. One of your officers [Roy gave the name and badge number] gave a traffic ticket to one of my teachers on the West Side Highway. My teacher was going forty-two miles an hour in a forty-mile-an-hour speed zone and that ticket has got to be quashed, torn up, and thrown away. Nothing less will do. He will not come down to your precinct. I don't want him to be disturbed. That's all there is to it." The schoolmate remembers, "Then he said call me when it was done or I will call you. Roy did not have a smile on his face, no expression of triumph, just all in a day's work at the age of sixteen or something."[12]

Beyond what this tale suggests about teenage Cohn's sense of entitlement, it is noteworthy that he did not choose to make the call from a more private location but did so in front of an audience that was sure to spread word of it. In addition to expressing his power to the officer at the other end of the line, Roy wanted his schoolmates to be aware of his sway. Additionally, there is little doubt that Roy learned this method of fixing problems through backchannels from his father and his father's friends.

For all of his father's influence, Cohn was truly his mother's son. From Roy's birth, Dora made it clear that she would mold Roy's childhood, reportedly telling him that the child was hers and Al would have no role in raising Roy.[13] And she stayed true to her word; family members remember little contact between Roy and his father. Dora did everything in her power to ensure her son was more in touch with his maternal roots than his paternal ones and would share her opinions on the family's entitled social status, the importance of outward appearances, and the value of well-placed social connections.

Dora Marcus Cohn had been born into wealth. Her father, Joseph S. Marcus, used $100,000 to charter the Bank of United States in 1913. The bank grew rapidly by catering to New York's sizable immigrant population, especially its Jewish community. Though the bank was a private institution, Joseph probably named his venture in an attempt to evoke the legitimacy of the federal government, a subtle misrepresentation aimed at attracting his fresh-off-the-boat target clientele. Immediately preceding the 1929 stock market crash, the bank had fifty-nine branches across New York City. Joseph's son Bernie (Dora's brother, and thus Roy's uncle) served as the bank's president and managed $25,250,000 of capital.[14] This success ended in December 1930, when rumors of the bank's troubles following a failed merger led to a run on a number of its branches. Though bank officials tried to calm its clients, New York State auditors formally shuttered the bank on December 11, 1930. To that date, it was the largest bank failure in American history; the debacle is now credited as the beginning of the national panic that would force the closure of hundreds of banks through March 1933. Six months after the bank's closing, Bernie and two partners were found guilty of misappropriating bank funds. Sentenced to three to six years in prison, Bernie was pardoned by Governor Lehman after twenty-seven months in Sing Sing, a reduction courtesy of lobbying by his brother-in-law Al.[15]

But the pardon could not salvage the family's reputation; the scandal made the Marcuses personae non grata in New York's Jewish community. The Bank of United States owed much of its growth to investment from Jewish residents of Brooklyn and the Bronx, and its failure caused significant hardship for the group with which the Cohns most closely aligned themselves. Dora remained an adamant defender of the family's position and good name. She told her son that Bernie was the scapegoat of an anti-

Semitic conspiracy, something Cohn professed to his dying day. But Uncle Bernie's experience taught Roy an important lesson, namely that even the loyalty of a community based on ethnic ties, shared memories of religious persecution, and cross-generational business relationships was not enough to insulate an individual from the cutthroat realities of power politics.[16]

Dora raised her son to act in a manner she thought appropriate to his station. She allowed him to treat his babysitters like servants and at expensive restaurants encouraged him to send back meals that were not completely to his liking, which he did. This absurd level of entitlement and false sense of maturity pervaded Cohn's life. As a boy, his daily attire was that of a middle-aged businessman, a full suit. His 1940 bar mitzvah was held at the Waldorf-Astoria on Park Avenue. To Dora, a family member recalls, Roy "wasn't her son. He was her crown prince and she was the queen."[17] In this royal family, there was little room for a king. Realizing who held the real power in the family, young Roy began to mirror his mother's contempt. Even as he relied on the Cohn family name to open doors throughout New York City, it is clear that Roy lost respect for his father due to Al's inability to control events at home as he did at work.

Nor were these two worlds—the domestic and the professional—practically separate. The one person who could halt Al's rise through the Democratic Party ranks was his wife. When Al was offered a major promotion to the State Court of Appeals in Albany, Dora informed her husband that she would not leave New York City, and Al declined the job. Later, Dora decided she was too good for the Bronx and lobbied Al to move to a Manhattan address. When he resisted, she moved anyway, leaving a note taped to the door: "Dear Al: I have moved to 1165 Park Avenue. Your furniture is there. Your supper is there. If you want to eat, go there tonight."[18] Al trekked to Manhattan.

Cohn's formal education in elite private schools reaffirmed his sense of entitlement. At both the Fieldston Lower School and then the Horace Mann School for Boys, he was an outstanding student whom teachers remembered for his exceptional intelligence, though he did not participate in any extracurricular activities.[19] Cohn's classmates noted his dutiful holding of his father's liberal Democratic line and recalled him boldly confronting a history teacher's anti-Semitism.[20]

Such boldness led Cohn to claim at the end of his junior year that he "had gotten all there was for me to get out of Horace Mann," and he convinced Horace Mann's headmaster to let him skip his senior year of high school.[21] He enrolled in Columbia University in January 1944, just before his seventeenth birthday. Through a combination of his own intelligence,

Columbia's lenient wartime requirements, and family connections, Cohn was able to skip a number of classes and graduate with both a bachelor's and a law degree in only three years. Because he was not yet twenty-one years old, Cohn had to wait nearly a year before being eligible for the state bar exam.[22]

Running alongside this youthful record of success remained the elemental friction between Cohn's desire for power and his privately expressed gender identity. While learning how to be accepted into the dual, often-overlapping worlds of social significance and political power, Cohn also displayed personal characteristics that were antithetical to his membership in both clubs, particularly his burgeoning homosexuality. The historical record has not preserved the content of the Cohn family's inner life, nor did Cohn ever dwell in his writing on precisely how the expectations of heterosexual masculinity shaped his youth. But it is possible to trace the influences and cultural attitudes a young man of Cohn's class and race would have encountered.

At some point Cohn discovered his sexual attraction to men. According to friend and coauthor Sidney Zion, Cohn's doctor claimed that Roy began having sex with other men at the age of sixteen, during his first year at Columbia.[23] His parents seem to have worried about their son's gender identity from a relatively early age. According to Cohn, his parents removed him from Fieldston because they agreed the curriculum was too nontraditional and effete after seeing their son partake in a sewing class during a parents' day visit. Cohn claims that he was thankful that "my father caught me doing knit-one, purl two," noting without a hint of irony that if the school "didn't have Parents' Day, who knows how I might have turned out?"[24]

And yet, FBI files show that Cohn attended Fieldston for a full five years, through sixth grade. His parents certainly were aware of the curriculum earlier than then; the school, founded by social reformer Felix Adler, was regarded as pedagogically liberal and adheres to a progressive educational platform to this day.[25] Perhaps Al and Dora started to worry about how the curriculum had affected their pubescent son when he began to display supposedly effete tendencies such as refusing to participate in athletics and continually worrying about his appearance.

The Cohn family's encounter with the Fieldston curriculum is noteworthy in that Cohn chose to both include the story in his autobiography and manipulate the demonstrable facts, illustrating the degree to which he was conscious of and concerned about the perception of his gender identity. Cohn attempted to highlight the unassailable nature of both his masculinity and his parents' desire that he adhere to society's expectations for young men. In brief, Cohn was rewriting history to make himself appear more masculine.

Al and Dora may have suspected that Roy was unlike other boys as he showed little interest in stereotypically male activities. His onetime baby-sitter Peter Bonan recalls that Roy was a "chubby little kid that everybody loved to kick around . . . he was not a boy's boy."[26] As Roy's cousin Eugene Marcus recalled:

> Roy was about thirteen . . . it was a lovely spring day. Al took his jacket off, rolled up shirt-sleeves. Roy, of course, was dressed always in a blazer, very correct . . . [Al] said, "Come on, Roy." I can remember it so clearly: "Put your jacket inside and come out on the driveway. I want to play catch with you."
> . . . But Roy was really annoyed. "All right," [Roy] said. You know how you throw to a little girl? That's how Al threw it to him. Roy muffed it by a mile, and then he just stood there and Al said, "Well, go after it. You didn't catch it. The least you can do is chase it." Well then, Dora, who was watching this exhibition, turned on Al and she said, "You have him running out into the road? There are cars [that] come by the road. You get the ball!" This was a quiet little street where cars come every half an hour. Al gave her one of those shrugs of his and he did. He got the ball. And Roy disappeared.[27]

This Cohn family enactment of a classic American scene speaks to Roy's lack of training in what American society considers even the most rudimentary modes of masculinity, with his cousin likening him to a little girl. This moment is made more significant by his age; he was thirteen, a point in his life when he was expected to make the transition from boy to man, publicly expressing and affirming his burgeoning manhood through his attire, interests, attraction to the opposite sex, and athletic ability.

Cohn's lack of masculine role models was due not only to his father's absence, but his mother's proactive efforts to mold her son. Numerous aspects of Cohn's personality can be directly attributed to his mother's influence, including his aloofness about monetary matters, obsession with aesthetics (both literally and how things *appeared* to others), general sense of entitlement, and poor treatment of those he regarded as beneath him.

This mother-son relationship would come to be regarded by many of Cohn's contemporaries through the lens of "momism," a term coined by the social critic Philip Wylie in 1942. Wylie held that modern mothers, freed from their traditional domestic duties by technological advancements and changing social mores, held an inordinate amount of influence over their sons. This overprotective attitude meant that the son was "shielded from his logical development through his barbaric period, or childhood . . . [and] cushioned against any major step in his progress toward maturity." Therefore, any sympathy the son would have for others was transmuted by the mother "into sentimentality for herself."[28] Momism became a pop-psychological phenomenon and deeply influenced the social conversation during the 1940s.

Whether or not Wylie's strident commentary applies, there is little doubt that Cohn's relationship with his mother fit a stereotype that had gained significant national traction during his adolescence. And it was perceived as such. Aspects of the relationship (particularly Cohn's decision to live with his mother through adulthood) were cited by his enemies and allies alike to explain his seemingly effete behavior. Realizing the prominence of this perception, Cohn strove particularly hard to counter it by publicly presenting himself as within the parameters of mainstream conceptions of manhood. Cohn's public presence as an anticommunist lawyer and Joe McCarthy's closest advisor proved to be the perfect stage upon which to perform that affirmation.[29]

As Wylie's theorizing demonstrates, idealized masculinity was defined in the negative as often as in the positive. No hindrance to a man's masculinity was greater than homosexuality, which was generally viewed as incompatible with the attributes that made men moral, Christian, and decent. It deeply troubled Americans during the interwar years that signs of homosexuality seemed to be everywhere. In their 1936 study *Sex and Personality*, Lewis Terman and Catherine Cox Miles outlined these harbingers of male queerness: "Too demonstrative affection from an excessively emotional mother, father who is unsympathetic, autocratic, brutal, much away from home, or deceased, treatment of the child as a girl, coupled with lack of encouragement or opportunity to associate with boys and take part in the rougher masculine activities; overemphasis of neatness, niceness, and spirituality."[30] As momism did, these concepts circulated in mass media, shaped the way parents raised their children, and helped define which characteristics were viewed as homosexual.

The clearest indication of latent homosexuality was a lack of interest in members of the opposite sex. Young men were supposed to be enamored with young women. The 1938 guidebook *Gentlemen Aren't Sissies* presented nearly all its life advice—from dining etiquette to athletic pursuits to career choice—in the context of a young man's relationship to women. Even the book's advice about automobile driving demonstrated a concern for the opinions of the fairer sex, admonishing young men to "resist all impulses to show Laura and her friends how good you are at stopping on a dime and receiving nine cents change. Most girls consider that rather adolescent."[31] The primary reason for undertaking any challenge was to impress a girl.

Though it is tempting to try to define Cohn's gender and sexual identities, it is both prudent and sufficient to conclude that he simply did not fulfill his society's expectations of masculine heterosexuality. And there is ample reason to believe that Cohn himself recognized this deficit. Though he never admitted to feelings of unworthiness, his conscious, consistent attempts to publicly portray himself as a paragon of masculinity—such as by emphasizing his prolific dating record and engaging in masculine banter with his peers and opponents—demonstrate his awareness that his "organic" gender identity was somehow lacking and would be an impediment to professional success. These expectations were made more explicit for Cohn because he grew up in a home where gender norms were in flux and came of age while attending an all-boys prep school during the hypermasculine World War II era. Because of their somewhat transposed gender roles, Al and Dora demonstrated a model of domesticity and romantic relationships directly opposed to the prevailing expectations of the era. It was only through popular culture and his experiences outside the home that Roy was able to learn how most American families were expected to operate. Additionally, it should not be forgotten that the Cohns' decision to transfer their son from Fieldston to Horace Mann was also one to move their son from a coeducational environment to an all-male institution.[32] While this change was possibly an attempt by the Cohns to toughen Roy, that plan may have backfired by isolating him from coed interactions; numerous friends would later comment on Cohn's awkwardness around women, which sometimes bordered on outright hatred.[33]

The societal emphasis on machismo on display during Cohn's time at Horace Mann intensified with the onset of World War II. Like all Americans of the period, the young men of Horace Mann were surrounded by depictions of a hypermasculine fighting force. Soldiers were portrayed as "more physical, sculpted, and aggressively masculine than in previous wars."[34] Such imagery became omnipresent in popular culture, including official representations in recruiting posters, newsreels, and general propaganda.[35] Coming of age at this moment placed even more burden on Cohn's gender identity. Most importantly, it prompted him to fully subscribe to the belief that men who sought power had to demonstrate their ability to fulfill traditional male roles. Cohn knew that he had to act a certain way to achieve the lofty goals of his upbringing. Even during his earliest days as a young lawyer, he set out to perform the tenets of masculinity that were demanded by the life to which he aspired.

If J. Edgar Hoover was working to construct a new form of white-collar masculinity and Joseph McCarthy embodied a populist-inflected, blue-collar masculinity, then Roy Cohn epitomized a masculine identity that sported a collar of gold. Cohn's manhood was white-collar in being partially founded on occupational status, upper-crust social connections, and ties to elite educational institutions. But Cohn himself had no fidelity to the Christian ethics that governed Hoover's managerial white-collar masculinity. While Hoover was dedicated (at least publicly) to preserving the rule of law, Cohn was wholly comfortable subverting it as necessary. Cohn's performance of masculinity—like his personality—was also more ostentatious than those of Hoover and McCarthy. Where Hoover was urbane, Cohn was uncouth. Where McCarthy was ingratiating, Cohn was judgmental. And though Cohn and McCarthy both exhibited a masculine brashness, they were divided by the class affiliations of the homes in which they were raised.

To Cohn, manhood was synonymous with power. Real men were influential: they socialized and conducted business with other powerful people; they knew the right phone numbers to call; they were connected to other people of significance. Their status allowed them to transcend the rules that limited others. Cohn seems to have relied on the constellation of personal characteristics composing his gold-collar masculine identity to overcome the obstacles presented by his ethno-religious, sexual, and gender identities. Performing his gold-collar masculinity allowed Cohn entry to powerful circles in the national security state while concurrently veiling aspects of his identity that would undermine his professional rise.

The most important element of Cohn's masculine performance was his anticommunism. During his relatively brief period working as a federal prosecutor, he consciously cultivated a reputation for being a virulent red hunter. That identity associated Cohn with a movement regarded as quintessentially masculine. Writing in 1955, sociologist Daniel Bell observed that "in these strange times, new polar terms have been introduced into political discourse, but surely none so strange as the division into 'hard' and 'soft' . . . Presumably one is 'soft' if one insists that the danger from domestic communists is small, [while] the 'hard' anticommunists insist that no distinction can be made between international and domestic communism."[36] Even left-of-center social commentators like the historian Arthur Schlesinger Jr. pointed to the softness of "doughfaced progressives" as a central obstacle in the fight against communism.[37] Like McCarthy, Roy Cohn wanted to be considered as "hard" as possible.

Fighting communism in the years following World War II was also a smart public relations move for individuals seeking power. "Red hunting in America," Edward T. Folliard of the *Washington Post* concluded in 1954, "has become an almost sure-fire way of rising from obscurity to head-line prominence."[38] Cohn thus forcefully rejected his familial pedigree and aligned himself with a more conservative anticommunist cabal to facilitate his professional advancement.[39]

Cohn constructed his masculine identity both socially and profession-ally. In both arenas he sought to project an image of a young man who was not only "going places" but had—in many ways—already arrived. Like Hoover and McCarthy, Cohn became adept at cultivating his public image by manipulating the press. Forming alliances with members of the media, he provided gossip columnists with information in exchange for positive press coverage about both his professional and personal endeavors. Using his father's connections and the personality traits instilled in him by his mother—brashness, egotism, and perseverance—Cohn spent his early professional career in New York and Washington expanding his Rolodex and developing personal skills that would ensure his position in the power elite.[40] Between the time he began working as a federal prosecutor in May 1948 and when he went to work for McCarthy in early 1953, Cohn dem-onstrated his penchant for managing the press, his talent for hunting com-munists, and, most importantly, his ability to integrate himself into the hypermasculine world of power politics.

Immediately after Cohn passed the bar exam, he used his father's connections to secure a position as an assistant attorney in the office of Irving H. Saypol, US attorney for the Southern District of New York.[41] Sometimes, Cohn was forced to anchor the office on a Saturday, a tedious duty that fell to the staff's youngest members. During his shift on Feb-ruary 19, 1949, Cohn received word that the Secret Service had arrested a man holding $10,000 in counterfeit money. At the arraignment, a re-porter asked Cohn whether the money was from a national counterfeiting ring; Cohn quickly responded that it was, though he had no evidence to back the claim. The resulting article on the front page of that evening's *New York World-Telegram* reported that "Assistant U.S. Attorney Roy M. Cohn said today that the arrest of three men last night by two city detectives . . . 'will lead us to some of the higher-ups in the national counterfeiting ring. Further investigation is being pursued vigorously and we expect further developments.'"[42] Cohn got lucky: the arrested man was indeed tied to a large counterfeiting operation that also printed phony stamps and dabbled in stolen drugs, furs, and whiskey. For the next eighteen months a steady stream of articles in major newspapers reported on the gradual collapse of the racket, almost always quoting information provided by Cohn.[43]

During that larger counterfeiting investigation Cohn approved a plea deal to suspend the prison sentence of Charlotte Whitehurst, a twenty-five-year-old divorcee from Virginia who was accused of making deliveries on behalf of the counterfeiters. As part of the deal, Whitehurst had to work in Virginia for a period of time and then return to Tennessee to live with her parents. The only justification for the deal that Cohn gave was that the woman had a "good family background."[44] The requirement that White-hurst live under her parents' roof suggested the state's faith in the institution of the family to rehabilitate a young woman who had been led astray. This minor event also fit well with Cohn's efforts to advertise his own masculinity, as it allowed him to present himself as benevolent and chivalrous, sensitive to the weak will of the female sex, and thus willing to forgive Whitehurst's crime.[45]

The publicity from the counterfeiting case raised Cohn's profile, and around New York City he began to be recognized as more than "Judge Cohn's son." Roy had become aware of the power of the press, and specifically gossip, from a young age. At thirteen, he had begun writing a gossip column for the *Bronx Home News* and as a teenager he acted as something of an apprentice to *New York Post* gossip columnist Leonard Lyons.[46] But the counterfeiting case was the first time Cohn had seen his name so prominently in print. He liked the exposure and the feeling of power that accompanied it; a fellow assistant attorney noted that for each indictment in Cohn's case files there was always a press release. That colleague also claimed that often the accused were indicted more than once so Cohn could distribute multiple press releases, noting that Cohn "was responsible for a hell of a lot of indictments that never went anywhere . . . Roy was the object of derision in the office as a publicity hound and someone who would indict anyone."[47]

Cohn's obsession with his media profile persisted throughout his career. In September 1952 he was elevated to being a special assistant to Attorney General James P. McGranery. Not surprisingly, news of the promotion was leaked to a number of major newspapers, most likely by Cohn himself.[48] On his first day, Cohn reviewed the official press release announcing his promotion as he waited to be sworn in (a procedure that was legally superfluous and occurred only because Cohn had demanded it) and noticed it did not include the "special assistant" portion of his new title. He walked out of the ceremony and demanded it be rewritten, as his parents waited with the attorney general.[49]

Cohn began to surround himself with influential reporters, beginning with Lyons, the nationally syndicated gossip columnist. Lyons familiarized Cohn with the chatty style of political reporting that centered around nightclubs as much as government buildings. More importantly, Lyons introduced Cohn to Walter Winchell, by then well established as the country's most popular gossip columnist. Winchell, along with conservative columnists Westbrook Pegler and George Sokolsky, would become one of Cohn's strongest cheerleaders and an essential figure in shaping the public's perception of Cohn.[50]

Lyons, Winchell, Pegler, and Sokolsky were all products of the national gossip industry that had exploded following the end of the Great War. The success of *Town Topics* and *Broadway Brevities* had spawned a host of imitators. Founded in 1919, the *New York Daily News* was one of the first tabloids to illustrate its articles on criminality, depravity, and corruption with graphic photographs. The newspaper's logo has always featured a camera, illustrating the importance of photography to its ethos. The *Daily News* was almost immediately successful, reaching a circulation of 400,000 in 1921, 800,000 in 1925, and 1.3 million 1930.[51] William Randolph Hearst tried to match the *Daily News*' success with his own tabloid, establishing the *New York Daily Mirror* in 1924.

But neither the *Daily News* nor the *Daily Mirror* could match the salaciousness of the *New York Evening Graphic*. Founded in 1924 by media mogul and fitness advocate Bernarr "Bodylove" Macfadden, the sensationalist, sex-obsessed *Graphic* strove to present the most salacious version of events it could and was replete with insinuation both in tone and content.[52] The *Graphic*'s photo editor Frank Mallen recalled that the only instruction he received from founding editor Emile Gauvreau was to feature "sex on every front page, big gobs of it. On the inside pages [Gauvreau] expected it to be spread out like butter over canapes."[53] The emphasis on sex was not surprising given that Macfadden was also the publisher of a number of trendy sex adventure magazines—including *True Story*, the most popular sex adventure magazine among residents of the Lynds' Middletown.

The *Graphic* is best remembered for two gifts it bestowed upon gossip journalism. First, it launched the careers of Walter Winchell, Louis Sobol, and Ed Sullivan. Winchell's work became a blueprint for the modern gossip column and allowed him to build the large following which would enable his friendships with Hoover, McCarthy, and Cohn. Second, the *Graphic* pioneered the use of "composographs": composite photographs depicting scenes that were either imagined (such as Rudolph Valentino's arrival in Heaven) or difficult to photograph (celebrity boudoir). The newspaper's first—and perhaps most infamous—use of the technique came during the 1924 divorce trial of Alice Jones Rhinelander and Kip Rhinelander, when it printed a front-page composograph in which a topless Mrs. Rhinelander displayed her body to the jury. The newspaper's hyperbolic depiction showed a model's bare back to the camera as a group of "jurors" leered at her naked torso.[54] The image was widely derided by media critics, but it caused a spike in sales. The *Graphic* reached the height of its popularity in the second half of the 1920s but was ultimately forced to close shop in 1932, undone by the Depression and cutthroat competition from other tabloids.

The *Graphic* was not the era's only newspaper to employ innovative, morally questionable tactics in its search for readership. The decade also saw the spread of what was termed "muscle journalism," which included "the gentle arts of kidnapping, wire tapping, burglary, bribery, plus cunning and unlimited nerve."[55] Its most fervent practitioners seemed to dominate the Chicago news scene of the late 1910s and 1920s, and specialized in covering gangland killings. The movement garnered enough cultural notoriety that it inspired *The Front Page*, a hit Broadway comedy and later the basis for two films. In applying the tactics of muscle journalism to the feminized realms of gossip journalism, columnists such as Winchell helped redraw gendered boundaries of the newspaper industry; because he had proven his masculine bona fides by undertaking tasks like assisting the FBI in its search for the missing Lindbergh baby and brokering negotiations between gangsters, Winchell could report on the social lives of Hollywood starlets without sacrificing his masculinity.

Winchell popularized Cohn as a relentless protector of American freedom, a "star Red prosecutor" intent on "Trapping Reds Coast-to-Coast."[56] In the summer of 1951 Winchell reported that he had watched "Federal Judge Sylvester Ryan and United States Attorneys Irving Saypol and Roy Cohn confound those 17 Reds in court," referring to a trial in which a number of "communist leaders" were tried for treason, including the mystery author Dashiell Hammett. Winchell's staccato report praised the prosecutors, tellingly presenting the judge as an ally of the prosecution rather than an impartial referee: "His Honor was Uncle Sam in person—great dignity. The Federal prosecutors and their walloping debunking clicked with the press box from 10:30 until prison-time. The United States marshals, all clean-cut people, look like Americans should . . . Betty Gannett, one of the accused Reds, is actually named Rifka Yareshefsky . . . One of the wifes [sic] (her husband got a break from the judge) mumbled, "You

S.O.B." at a United States attorney as she left."[57] Winchell underscored the "un-Americanness" of communism and anyone who subscribed to it; while the US marshals were "clean-cut," one of the accused communists had deviously Americanized her name.

Like his association with Winchell, Cohn's embrace of anticommunism was likely a calculated move to increase his public and professional standing. Cohn's career as an anticommunist prosecutor began in earnest with the case against Alger Hiss. While he had already broadened his notoriety through the counterfeiting case and a string of others, Cohn's prosecutions of communists placed him on the national stage. The Hiss case was also an important starting point for Cohn's extended residency in the public eye because it revolved around complex questions that were essential to the persona Cohn sought to craft, including issues of gender identity, sexuality, patriotism, and loyalty.

In testimony before the House Un-American Activities Committee (HUAC) in 1948, *Time* editor and former Soviet spy Whittaker Chambers charged a number of government officials with having communist ties.[58] Included in that list was Alger Hiss, a lawyer who had served the State Department during the Roosevelt and Truman administrations and had accompanied FDR to the Yalta Conference in 1945. When Hiss was charged with perjury, his case became a national cause célèbre.[59] Cohn claimed that he originally thought Hiss was the victim of a "HUAC witch-hunt," but soon changed his mind after seeing the evidence against him during a lunch with a number of FBI agents. In Cohn's own telling, he was a dedicated anticommunist from that moment forward.[60]

Yet the Hiss case also made apparent how anticommunism could help propel Cohn to a higher perch of power. Though his role in the prosecution was minor and largely consisted of writing memos, it gave him a front-row seat as the trial dominated the front pages of major newspapers and airtime on radio's most popular news programs.[61] If Cohn was searching for increased public exposure, chasing communists presented a unique opportunity.

In addition to clearly illustrating the degree to which the communist menace and those fighting it garnered attention, the Hiss case also delineated to Cohn the unmistakable correlation between communism and homosexuality in the public imagination. Chambers had preemptively admitted in a sealed letter to the FBI that he had engaged in homosexual activity while working as a Soviet spy, a confession that confirmed prejudices of that era. As historian David K. Johnson notes, "Though not publicly disclosed at the time, the rumor and innuendo surrounding the Hiss-

Chambers controversy not only associated the State Department with homosexuality but linked communism and homosexuality in the minds of many public officials, security officials, and opinion leaders."[62] Inevitably, the judgments of these leading voices eventually filtered down to the public. Throughout Hiss's two trials, rumors swirled that "the Hiss-Chambers relationship involved at least sexual jealousy if not behavior."[63] The rumors were pervasive enough to make it into a 1948 underground comic strip suggesting Hiss and Chambers were lovers.[64] If Roy Cohn harbored any doubts as to either the interrelationship between homosexuality and communism, or just how detrimental accusations of homosexuality could be to a government employee's career, being an immediate party to the Hiss case must have erased them.

Following Hiss's conviction, Cohn assisted Saypol with the prosecution of William Remington, a thirty-three-year-old government economist accused of passing sensitive information to Elizabeth Bentley, a Soviet spy. A wealthy, handsome, overachieving Ivy League graduate, Remington personified the East Coast establishment for which Cohn—like McCarthy—expressed disdain, even as he sought to join its ranks. Cohn's responsibilities in the case were drastically expanded compared to his role during the Hiss trial. He helped develop the list of witnesses, prepared them for trial, and led the in-court questioning. The Remington trial cemented Cohn's reputation as an anticommunist among the East Coast establishment while also demonstrating that the young prosecutor would use any means at his disposal to achieve his desired result.[65]

The first such tactic was coaching witnesses to provide misleading or false testimony. Roscoe C. Giles, an acquaintance of Remington's at Dartmouth, testified that they had attended Young Communist League (YCL) meetings together. The following day's newspapers headlined that Remington was "Linked to Red Recruiting."[66] However, Giles's earlier statements had not conclusively identified Remington as a member of the YCL. Furthermore, Giles himself had denied any involvement with the YCL, undermining his claims of access. It is likely that Giles's testimony had been coached by Cohn, meaning that "in its zeal to convict Remington the government allowed a witness to deliver mistaken, or deliberately false, testimony."[67] Though Giles's statements were later stricken from the record for having no probative value, his claims had already been widely distributed through the press. This tactic—soliciting easily disproven testimony for the purpose of generating favorable headlines—was one that Cohn and McCarthy used with gusto throughout their public careers.

Cohn also used familial and social connections to advance the case against Remington. When Cohn learned that defense witness Bill Goodman was married to a Cohn family friend and was the brother-in-law of a former classmate, Cohn allegedly called the classmate with a threat: "You better tell Bill Goodman not to testify, or we'll get him!"[68] Later, when a key witness for the prosecution was detained for fleeing the scene of an accident, Cohn telephoned the commissioner of the Connecticut State Police and "informed him they were holding an important witness in the Remington trial and demanded her immediate release. By 5:00 P.M., she was free without bond and back on the road."[69]

Not all of Cohn's achievements during the Remington trial resulted from dishonest methods. True to his reputation, Cohn performed with an adept tenacity inside the courtroom, using his vast knowledge of politics, culture, and law.[70] The jury returned a guilty verdict on Remington after only four-and-a-half hours of deliberation. Remington received the maximum sentence of five years imprisonment and a $2,000 fine, lost his appeal, and was eventually given additional time for perjury.[71] On November 22, 1954, three other inmates attacked Remington, bludgeoning his head with a brick. The acting warden told Remington's wife that "it was not a personal attack . . . but just the actions of a couple of hoodlums who got all worked up by . . . the publicity about communists."[72] Remington died of his injuries two days later, one of a handful of murders that can be at least partially blamed on McCarthyism.[73] If Cohn ever experienced remorse over Remington's death, there is no record of it. Notably, Cohn claimed that Remington's killing was not politically inspired, but "a turgid sexually motivated murder."[74] Given the paucity of evidence for this theory, perhaps Cohn was seeking to exonerate himself by pigeonholing Remington as the worst kind of traitor, both a communist and sexual deviant.

Cohn's reputation as one of the nation's foremost anticommunists was cemented by the trial of Julius and Ethel Rosenberg, a Jewish couple from New York who were accused of passing nuclear secrets to the Soviet Union. Once again, Cohn used all the tools at his disposal to earn a guilty verdict, including fabricating testimony and striking backroom deals. Writer and investigative journalist John Wexley noted his "firm conviction that it was Roy Cohn who was one of those most responsible for that mockery of justice called the trial of the People of the United States versus Julius Rosenberg, et al."[75] Whether the trial was a mockery or not, the publicity surrounding it allowed Cohn to position himself as a crusader for justice, the lone ranger who would stop at nothing to capture those who threatened the United States. In Cohn's words, "The Rosenberg case thrust me onto center stage for keeps."[76] It would also help put him on Joe McCarthy's radar.

During that trial, the twenty-three-year-old Cohn once again served as Saypol's primary assistant. He adopted extraordinarily brash positions, such as suggesting that Saypol pursue lines of questioning that risked exposing information the Atomic Energy Commission (AEC) considered sensitive.[77] Though opposed by AEC leaders—who considered Cohn reckless while admitting he was "a very bright fellow—one of the smartest to come down the pike in a long time"—those queries were asked of some witnesses.[78] Both syndicated columnist Drew Pearson and writers for the *New York Times* charged that Cohn fabricated testimony for government witness and former communist Harvey Matusow to use on the stand.[79] To the US Attorney's Office and Cohn in particular, nothing could stand in the way of bringing justice to suspected communists.

While plentiful evidence attested to Julius Rosenberg's guilt, the case against Ethel was far weaker. Much of it hinged on whether she had typed notes during meetings between her husband and her brother, David Greenglass. The question was so central because the resulting documents were eventually passed to Julius and David's Soviet contacts. In a 2003 interview, Greenglass claimed that Cohn had directed him to testify that his sister had served as the stenographer during those meetings. Greenglass complied, noting that at the time he did not realize the significance of his testimony. It is widely believed by historians and legal scholars that Greenglass's falsified claim was a key factor in the guilty verdict against Ethel.[80]

If his 1988 autobiography is to be believed, Cohn made his greatest mark on the Rosenberg case through his relationship with the trial's judge, Irving Kaufman. Cohn writes that his father was "instrumental in getting Irving Kaufman his federal judgeship [and] I was instrumental in getting Irving Kaufman assigned to the Rosenberg case."[81] As with many of Cohn's assertions, there is little evidence to support this claim, but it does illustrate Cohn's desire to be seen as the ultimate insider, even when his claims include a clear ethics violation.[82]

Even some historians convinced of the Rosenbergs' guilt have charged that Cohn improperly colluded with Kaufman *during* the trial and may have convinced the judge to impose a death sentence. Whispers of these improprieties grew so loud that the American Bar Association was forced to investigate the charges in 1977, though it cleared both men.[83] Cohn vigorously denied the charges, only admitting his guilt in his posthumously released autobiography, in which he claimed that "before, during, and after the trial, the prosecution team—particularly Irving Saypol and I—were in constant communication with Judge Kaufman. I mean private, or what the lawyers call *ex parte* communication, without the presence of the defense lawyers."[84] During these secret conferences, Cohn gauged Kaufman's opinion on various aspects of the case and worked to ensure the judge would impose the death penalty.[85] Cohn even went behind his boss's back and warned Kaufman that an overzealous Saypol planned to use a tactic that could result in a mistrial. Kaufman heeded Cohn's warnings and preemptively disallowed evidence Saypol had brought, possibly saving the government's case in the process.[86] By Cohn's own account, he was also successful in convincing Judge Kaufman to send both Julius and Ethel to the electric chair. During sentencing, Kaufman placed blame for the Korean War on the Rosenbergs and termed their crime "worse than murder."[87] After an extended appeal process, and despite a public outcry, they were executed just after 8:00 PM on June 19, 1953.

In the end, the Rosenberg trial stood as one of Cohn's proudest moments. For the remainder of his life, Cohn would seize any opportunity to highlight his role in it. His performance during the trial cemented his reputation as a tenacious anticommunist among the power elite. It also ensured that his first widespread exposure to the public came in a role that emphasized his moral strength, intellectual fortitude, and patriotic dedication. As the accusations of the government's use of improper tactics remained unknown—they were not widely reported until early 1955—Cohn found a place in the national consciousness as one of the men who helped bring down twentieth-century America's most infamous spies.

On the heels of the Rosenberg trial, Cohn was transferred to the Department of Justice in Washington. In his early days working for the attorney general he continued his anti-red crusade by heading a grand jury investigating the presence of communists among the nearly two thousand Americans employed by the United Nations.[88] Though incontrovertible evidence linking individuals to communist or so-called un-American activities was difficult to obtain, the mere insinuation of communist sympathies was enough to end careers and ruin lives. In May 1952, six UN employees were fired after being "investigated as security risks" by Cohn's grand jury, their contracts terminated even though they were not charged with a crime.[89] When the general counsel to the UN, an American named Abraham Feller, jumped from his twelfth-story apartment in the midst of the investigation, UN Secretary General Trygve Lie blamed his suicide on the stress involved in "defending United States members of the Secretariat 'against indiscriminate smears and exaggerated charges,'" a clear reference to the grand jury.[90] Undeterred by such allegations even as they caused schisms within the Justice Department, Cohn pressed on.

During this period, Cohn worked closely with the FBI. The resulting federal grand jury report—which the Truman administration reportedly tried to bury—praised Cohn and the cooperation of the FBI. Soon, the Republican-controlled House of Representatives began its own inquiry into the charges. According to the Chicago Daily Tribune, "The House investigation is expected to reveal the role played by Cohn in resisting pressure from high authorities. The grand jury report specifically singled out Cohn, commending him for 'unremitting zeal.' Hoover's Federal Bureau of Investigation was cited in the same report for its 'effective cooperation.'"[91] While Cohn and Hoover were not yet connected socially—at least not according to contemporary reports—they did seem to agree on the potency of the threat of communism.

As he built press contacts and zealously hunted communists, Cohn was also intently constructing a professional and public persona fit for the power elite. He accomplished this task through a daily performance that emphasized personal characteristics believed to be central to "traditional," heterosexual masculinity.[92] Cohn performed an aggressive, sometimes bawdy version of masculinity, obfuscating his more stereotypically feminine traits. He worked to prove to his fellow lawyers that he fit in with them. He dressed like his peers, slicking back his black hair and sporting traditional grey flannel suits that hid his gaudy personal style.[93] He partook in lavish multicourse dinners at Manhattan's finest restaurants, unwinding after work with a drink and ribald conversation.

On those nights out he would chase women just as much as his coworkers did. As one peer recalled, "Roy Cohn was a heterosexual then. I know that. I know that as a fact, he was a heterosexual."[94] Another assistant prosecutor claimed that Cohn was patronizing female prostitutes at the time, and "may have had trouble being with women who weren't" sex workers.[95] As his fame grew and he began to appear in gossip columns, Cohn embraced every opportunity to be photographed on dates with women (in groups or alone) at elite nightlife hotspots such as the Stork Club's Cub Room, where—like Hoover before him—he worked to befriend owner Sherman Billingsley.

The woman to whom Cohn was most consistently linked was Barbara Walters. In her memoir, Walters reported that Cohn asked her to marry him a number of times, even though their relationship had never been physical. Walters describes a date with Cohn during which he chose to abandon his car in the middle of West 52nd Street in Manhattan during rush hour rather than wait in traffic.[96] Cohn certainly realized that this desertion would inconvenience others, he simply did not care. In addition to illuminating aspects of his personality that were—by most accounts—dominant and essential, Cohn's frequent displays of arrogance suggest that he believed masculinist aggression to be a mark of influence and power.

The essentiality of female companionship in Cohn's masculine performance did not preclude him from developing a strong distaste for women, an element of his personality remembered by many friends and often (perhaps stereotypically) attributed to Cohn's complex relationship with his mother. Revealing his own prejudices about gender, Cohn once told a female acquaintance that he liked her because "you're tough and you're very smart. Most women are weak and they cry, blah, blah, blah . . ."[97] It is also conceivable that Cohn's habit of demeaning women intellectually while exploiting them physically endeared him to his hypermasculine coworkers in his early days as a prosecutor.

Though his ego may have incensed many of Cohn's coworkers, his ruthlessness impressed them. Cohn's no-holds-barred approach to communist hunting strengthened his masculine performance by demonstrating that he would go to any lengths—even illegal ones—in his anti-red quest. These methods allowed Cohn to position himself like a matinee cowboy with a vendetta against the Apaches. Such extremism was excused, even encouraged, because communists had replaced Nazis and fascists as the nation's most threatening enemy. Though it is possible that Cohn's radical tactics grew as much from his desire for power as they did from his need to be considered masculine, his aggressiveness conveniently helped him achieve both goals.

In the portion of his autobiography describing his early years as a prosecutor, Cohn emphasizes the mettle he displayed while navigating the challenges put to him by his older, gruffer bosses. Regardless of how many times a boss had him rewrite legal briefs, Cohn endured until he fully mastered the assignment.[98] Further initiation into the brotherhood was confirmed by superiors who would take his youthful arrogance with a wink and nod, such as the judge who advised, "Mr. Cohn, your [closing statement] was almost as good as you think it was."[99]

Dress rehearsals completed, Cohn seemed ready to move into an even brighter spotlight. On December 30, 1952, news reports emerged that Cohn was to join Joseph McCarthy's staff as the chief counsel of McCarthy's Senate Permanent Subcommittee on Investigations.[100] In the half-decade following the end of World War II, both McCarthy and Cohn had taken advantage of growing anxieties over social transformations and an uncertain global political situation to secure positions of influence in the emergent national security state. They had portrayed themselves as founts of masculinity, able to undertake the urgent task of defending the United States from enemies foreign and domestic. Now, the pressing question was whether those performances were primed for center stage.

5

SCANDAL AS POLITICAL ART

Joe McCarthy would have preferred to be someplace other than Wheeling, West Virginia. Republican Party officials had sent him there precisely because it was an undesirable assignment. For many conservatives, the man they had once viewed as a rising star had failed to live up to his promise in a disastrous fashion. In his first four years in the Senate, McCarthy had been the subject of numerous ethics investigations, had become roundly disliked by many of his peers and had been anointed the nation's worst senator. So when GOP leaders were creating the schedule for a weekend of events celebrating Lincoln's birthday, they saddled McCarthy with some of the least desirable slots. His first stop would be Wheeling, before continuing to Salt Lake City, Reno, Las Vegas, and Huron, South Dakota.

McCarthy flew to Wheeling on the morning of February 9, 1950. A cold front was sweeping in, with rain expected.[1] McCarthy made his way to the McClure Hotel, where he was to speak at an event sponsored by the Ohio County Republican Women's Club. Addressing approximately 275 party loyalists, McCarthy reportedly uttered a claim destined to change the course of history: "I have here in my hand a list of 205 that were known to the Secretary of State as being members of the Communist Party, and who nevertheless are still working and shaping the policy in the State Department."[2]

The bold assertion failed to make an immediate impact; most major newspapers did not mention it in their Friday editions, and the articles that did appear were subdued (the *Chicago Daily Tribune* placed a three-paragraph mention of the speech on page five, adjacent to an advertisement for cotton gloves aimed at Valentine's Day shoppers). The mainstream press did not take notice until McCarthy repeated the charges—with revisions—on Friday in Salt Lake City, claiming to know of fifty-seven communists currently employed by the State Department. By the time McCarthy reached Nevada on Saturday, the press had seized on the story. Ambushed at the Reno airport by a group of reporters seeking proof of his charges, McCarthy rummaged through his briefcase before claiming that he had left the list in his checked baggage.[3] He never did produce the document, but McCarthy encouraged the snowballing publicity by sending an open telegram to President Truman that reiterated his charges and argued that failure to investigate the State Department would "label the Democratic Party of being the bed-fellow of inter-national communism."[4] Despite the transparency of McCarthy's motives—it was an election year, after all—the news media continued to follow the story, intent on proving (or disproving) his assertions.

It was the beginning of a fifty-three-month period during which McCarthy stood as arguably the most influential—and most divisive—politician in the United States. As numerous historians have shown, while McCarthy did not invent the national hysteria that bears his name, he was able to achieve such prominence by exploiting, and seeming to understand as few did, a rising wave of mania over communist infiltration. McCarthy's allegations came at an opportune moment. The Wheeling speech happened a mere fifteen days after Alger Hiss had been sentenced to five years in prison for perjury, and only six days after atomic scientist Klaus Fuchs was arrested in London under suspicion of passing nuclear secrets to the Soviet Union.[5] Less than two weeks prior, President Truman had announced that American scientists were building a hydrogen bomb. Truman had also recently established a new highest tier of confidentiality for government information, "top secret."[6] In the atmosphere of early 1950, accusations of spying within the federal government were believable to both press and public.

But McCarthy's charges were built on more than fears of communism, as a major speech he made three months after Wheeling shows. In early

May, McCarthy appeared at the Midwest Council of Young Republicans convention in Chicago. His Saturday evening remarks were broadcast live to a national radio audience, evidence of how fully he had captured the nation's attention. In them he trained his aim on the Truman administration, deriding its investigation into communist subversives in the federal government as inadequate and dubbing it "Operation Whitewash." Throughout, McCarthy employed gendered language to label as effeminate both communists and those who were weak in fighting them. He claimed that Philip Jessup and Owen Lattimore, two government employees suspected of harboring communist sympathies, had ties to publications that "spewed forth the perfumed communist party line sewage."[7] He referenced the widely accepted association between homosexuality and communism, proposing the creation of a loyalty board under the direction of J. Edgar Hoover that would have "unlimited power to rid the government of the prancing mimics of the Moscow party line."[8] Turning to a class-influenced critique, McCarthy claimed that "the days of dilettante diplomacy are running out on Mr. [Secretary of State Dean] Acheson and his fancy comrades of the Kremlin."[9] Concurrently, McCarthy stressed that he possessed the machismo necessary to fight communism, answering "the accusation that his public investigation was embarrassing the United States before the world by saying that 'either I had to do a bare-knuckle job or suffer the same defeat that a vast number of well meaning men have suffered' in five years of trying 'to do this with kid gloves.'"[10]

Those linkages—communism with effeminacy and homosexuality, protectionism with machismo—were fundamental to McCarthy's public image and his arguments. Such associations were not accidental; they spoke to the anxieties of McCarthy's most ardent supporters, specifically their belief that the United States was becoming increasingly susceptible to communism due to a moral decline—a development apparent in the proliferation of homosexuals, "impure" women, emasculated men, blue-blooded bureaucrats, and even federal social programs. McCarthy's speeches reveal how fears of nonnormative gender and "deviant" sexuality overlapped with political radicalism in a moment of moral panic. To exploit that alarm, McCarthy employed tactics that were hallmarks of the flourishing gossip industry—insinuation, innuendo, guilt by association, sensationalism, coded language, and even photographic manipulation. Furthermore, he used that industry's columnists, magazines, and tabloids to eviscerate his enemies and promote his own masculine credentials. In both form and content, gossip was essential to the rise of McCarthy and McCarthyism.

*

No shortage of politicians and personalities had waved the flag of anticommunism since the end of World War II, including Representative Richard Nixon, Senator Pat McCarran, conservative pundit William F. Buckley, and J. Edgar Hoover himself. But none became as closely associated with the Second Red Scare as McCarthy. Why, then, did McCarthy emerge as the movement's most visible spokesperson, particularly considering his senatorial record prior to February 1950?[11] The answer to this question is multifaceted and complex, but largely centers on the way McCarthy mobilized his populist, masculine persona to address the concerns preoccupying American society in the early Cold War.

An oft-repeated legend maintains that McCarthy stumbled into anticommunism after searching for a hot-button political issue for his 1952 reelection campaign. That account holds that McCarthy was lamenting his reelection prospects during a January 1950 dinner with three influential Catholic friends—Father Edmund Walsh and Professor Charles Kraus of Georgetown University, along with lawyer William Roberts—who convinced him that the public fear of communist agents in the federal government would make a provocative issue around which to build his campaign. McCarthy, this story claims, seized on the idea. Thus converted, he made his Wheeling speech about a month later.[12]

Though the dinner almost certainly took place, the participants have different recollections of it, with one even remembering the conversation as light and apolitical. Yet the story of the dinner achieved a long afterlife in which it was marshalled to prove that McCarthy was an ideological mercenary who adopted anticommunism out of political expediency. Moreover, that version suggests that McCarthy's embrace of anticommunism was done on a whim, a reading that positions him as something of a happy idiot who stumbled onto a career-making issue rather than deliberately selecting it.

Neither perception—of McCarthy as mercenary nor of him as the beneficiary of dumb luck—can survive close scrutiny. As noted, McCarthy had red-baited his political opponents before this moment. More importantly, portraying McCarthy's rise as the by-product of blind fortune overlooks the calculated nature of both his selection of topic and his methods of attack. As a signature issue, anticommunism allowed McCarthy to play to his strengths while reaffirming key elements of his masculine persona, including his patriotism, militarism, toughness, and fidelity to the common man. It also allowed him to establish a continual presence in the national news; McCarthy's macho masculinity and anticommunism reinforced each other in his quest for the limelight.

Reflecting on McCarthy's success, the journalist Richard Rovere argued that McCarthy "simply persuaded a number of people that he was speaking the essential truth; he sent up such vast and billowing clouds of smoke that many men and women who were not abnormally gullible became convinced that there must be a fire beneath it all."[13] Extending Rovere's metaphor, how did McCarthy make *so much* smoke with so little fuel, and how was he able to make that smoke visible to the public? As such, the key to understanding McCarthy's influence lies in how he communicated his charges and the politics of the audience that heard them. Better than any other politician of his era, McCarthy understood the power of the press as a vessel for connecting with the public. McCarthy chased headlines for reasons beyond his ego; he sought them as a means of dictating the terms of political conversation and formulating a cult of personality around himself. In this effort, McCarthy became masterful at manipulating the media and the public by using tactics embraced by gossip journalists since the turn of the twentieth century.

Not only did gossip magazines, tabloids, and gossip columnists inspire many of McCarthy's tactics, they also ensured that the public was generally fluent in their vernacular. From those sources, Americans became more familiar with argumentative tactics such as insinuation, guilt by association, hyperbole, and alarmism, as well as tonal cynicism, underground slang, and photographic manipulation techniques. The Cold War dawned and the gossip magazine flourished at precisely the same moment, with each reinforcing the anticommunist ethos and masculinist gender politics of the other. As a result, the public was a prepared audience when it first encountered McCarthy and his tactics en masse, in February 1950.

The aesthetic mantle of the gossip magazine, once held by *Town Topics*, *Broadway Brevities*, and the *New York Evening Graphic*, was assumed by a series of "girlie," "true crime," and "true story" magazines in the 1940s and early 1950s. In particular, that era was a heyday for "true crime" magazines like *Headline Detective*, *Master Detective*, *Spotlight Detective*, *Crime Confessions*, and the long-running *National Police Gazette*.[14] Like the gossip magazines that would soon follow them, true crime magazines exploded in the late 1940s partially as a result of the end of wartime paper rationing. The colorful, cheaply printed periodicals fostered a market for sensationalized depictions of "real life" that emphasized violence, sex, danger, and intrigue. In so doing, they promoted the idea that state-sanctioned authority figures such as police detectives and FBI agents should embody the sort of macho masculinity that would be at home in the adventure stories of Edgar Rice Burroughs. By taking on prurient topics, they also provided readers with an expanded knowledge of slang terms, particularly those related to sex. Finally, their focus on revealing supposedly concealed narratives implicitly argued that mainstream publications were not providing the whole story to the reading public.

It was out of that immediate postwar cultural milieu that the golden age of American gossip magazines emerged. And at the moment when Joseph McCarthy was dominating political discourse in the early 1950s, no gossip magazine was more popular than *Confidential*, the best-selling brainchild of veteran girlie-mag publisher Robert Harrison. Harrison had impeccable tabloid credentials, having begun his career as a low-level errand boy at the *New York Evening Graphic* before ultimately serving as a reporter for the last eight months of its run. After rising through the ranks, Harrison began publishing his own girlie magazines—including *Beauty Parade, Eyeful, Titter, Wink, Whisper,* and *Flirt*—which combined photographs of pin-up girls with purportedly true tales of adventure and scandal.[15]

To that recipe *Confidential* added celebrity and political gossip, as well as consumer awareness stories. Harrison was inspired to begin publishing gossip about politicians after noticing the intensity with which his employees and family members watched news coverage of the 1950–51 Kefauver hearings on organized crime. Public interest was so great that during the month the hearings aired, more TV sets were sold than during the prior fifteen months combined.[16] It is likely that Harrison stole the name for his new magazine from the "Confidential" series of books by journalists Jack Lait and Lee Mortimer, bestsellers that revealed purportedly true stories of crime, vice, and corruption in major American cities.[17]

Adopting a populist tone, *Confidential* purported to speak for the common man by addressing issues it claimed were ignored by other publications. "Contrary to what you see in the movies," the magazine bragged in its first issue, "many newspapers don't print ALL the news without regard to whom it hurts. Too often, stories or photos a paper publishes are run with an eye to keeping advertisers happy. Advertising is a newspaper's life blood. If a situation arises necessitating a choice between offending a paying customer or reporting news as it happened, bet on the former."[18] *Confidential* promised its readers that it would not censor itself. Though it retained the true crime stories and cheesecake photographs that were mainstays of Harrison's other magazines, *Confidential* trained its spotlight on gossip about celebrities and political figures. The first issue hit newsstands in November

1952, with a bright red cover promising news that was "uncensored and off the record." The cover also signaled the magazine's direction, announcing that "athletes are lousy lovers" (under a photograph of Joe Louis), asking whether former New York City mayor William O'Dwyer was a "saint or sinner," and promising a story exposing "love in the U.N."

After that first issue sold poorly, Harrison courted Walter Winchell, trading positive coverage of the gossip columnist for Winchell's endorsement. Soon, *Confidential* was flying off of newsstands and on its way to becoming the most popular gossip magazine in America. In the summer of 1954, immediately following the close of the Army-McCarthy hearings, it had a circulation of one million issues.[19] By the time the magazine peaked in 1955, its newsstand sales surpassed those of *TV Guide, Life, Time, Look,* and the *Saturday Evening Post.* The magazine's July 1955 issue set the national record for newsstand sales.[20]

While stereotype holds that gossip magazines are largely consumed by women, circumstantial evidence suggests that *Confidential* and its slew of imitators enjoyed a broad readership across the gender spectrum. Advertisements in *Confidential* pitched products directly to men, including one that told readers, "You, too, may quickly and easily train for a new, success-winning *he-man* voice!"[21] The August 1955 issue of *On the Q.T.,* a *Confidential* clone, included competing advertisements encouraging men to look their best by purchasing the "'Manly' brand healthguard" (basically a girdle for men) or turning from a "sissy" to a "he-man" with help from the Jowlet Institute of Fitness Training.[22] One man who definitely read *Confidential* was McCarthy aide G. David Schine—he was seen hiding a copy of the gossip magazine within the pages of *US News and World Report* during the Army-McCarthy hearings.[23]

Like *Broadway Brevities* before it, *Confidential* advertised its willingness to identify the subjects of its gossip; a later tagline promised that the magazine "tells the facts and names the names." *Confidential* engaged in celebrity gossip at a level heretofore unseen in American publishing. Though movie fan magazines such as *Photoplay* and *Motion Picture* printed gossip and rumors, their primary effect was to buttress the film industry rather than critique it, and as a result their relationship with stars, agents, and studios was mutually beneficial. *Confidential* stood at the other end of the spectrum: critical, salacious, and harmful to its subjects' reputations. Harrison's strategy for avoiding lawsuits was to publish stories containing slightly less information than what the magazine knew (for example, reporting that a certain actor was engaged in an affair, but not revealing that the tryst was with an underage girl) in case it was needed to dissuade legal action.[24]

Emulating the methods of the governmental intelligence agencies that were sprouting in Washington (the CIA was founded in 1947, the NSA followed in 1952), *Confidential* cultivated an army of paid informants drawn from the ranks of city policemen, prostitutes, studio hands, agents, lawyers, bit actors, neighbors, hotel workers, and servants. Those contacts would relay information to the magazine's headquarters in New York City and, later, its satellite office in Hollywood. *Confidential's* reporters and informants employed surveillance tactics similar to those of Hoover's G-Men, including tape recorders disguised as wristwatches, hidden cameras inside handbags, and tapped telephone lines. As a result, *Confidential's* claims were well-researched and often constructed from multiple, corroborating sources. According to media historian Henry Scott, most of the magazine's stories "proved to be true."[25]

In content, perhaps *Confidential's* most noteworthy hallmark was its celebrity-style gossip about the so-called personal lives of politicians. During the nineteenth century, reporters had regarded the personal humiliations of politicians as fair game, and recounted in detail sex scandals involving Thomas Jefferson, Andrew Jackson, Daniel Sickles, and Daniel Webster. But a more refined, professional approach to political reporting developed at the outset of the twentieth century, and journalists began to adhere to an unwritten rule excluding embarrassing personal details about public figures. The reasons behind this détente can be partially traced to reporters' need for access; as the federal government grew and politicians and bureaucrats became protected by small armies of staff members, reporters were forced to cooperate with their political subjects, lest they be stonewalled. As late as the mid-1960s, President Lyndon Johnson's philandering was an open secret that Washington reporters never publicized; *Life* magazine correspondent Hal Wingo recalled that shortly after Johnson assumed the presidency in 1963 he cautioned a group of reporters that "you may see me coming in and out of a few women's bedrooms while I am in the White House, but just remember, that is none of your business."[26]

Confidential was able to break those unwritten rules partially because of its independent information-gathering operation, which enabled it to avoid kowtowing to politicians (and, in Hollywood, publicists and studio heads). The magazine's first issue included two stories exploring vice in the world of politics. Former New York City mayor and current US ambassador to Mexico Bill O'Dwyer was accused of having ties to organized crime, while "Love in the U.N.!" exposed a number of sex scandals, including some involving murder, suicide, adultery, and espionage.[27] In April 1953, *Confidential* reported on New York governor Thomas Dewey's 1946 pardon of mobster Lucky Luciano, claiming that it was a direct result of a deal Luciano had negotiated with Franklin Roosevelt.[28] Four months later *Confidential* suggested that former Boston mayor Andrew J. Peters had "corrupted" Starr Faithfull, a socialite who had been found dead in 1931.[29] Overall, *Confidential*'s reportage on the moral shortcomings of politicians helped undermine the deification of political leaders, contributing to a process that ultimately climaxed in the 1970s courtesy of the Watergate scandal and the Vietnam War.

An additional key element of the magazine was its explicit anticommunism, which it adopted even though Harrison claimed to be ignorant about politics generally and McCarthyism specifically, saying "that stuff is as foreign to me as Europe is."[30] *Confidential*'s politics were highlighted by editor Howard Rushmore, who joined the staff in 1952 on Winchell's prodding. Rushmore increased the amount of political coverage and used the magazine to publish a slew of anticommunist material, including numerous accusations that were stretches at best, libelous at worst.

The onetime film critic for the *Daily Worker*, Rushmore became a conservative darling after his firing from the communist newspaper. Rushmore remade himself into an expert on anticommunism and began writing for the *New York Journal-American*. During the 1947 House Un-American Activities Committee hearings, he provided testimony about the *Daily Worker*'s operations and identified communist sympathizers in Hollywood. Rushmore and his wife became friends with Winchell and Cohn, and sometimes dined with Cohn and Cohn's girlfriend at the Stork Club's exclusive Cub Room.[31] Immediately before joining *Confidential* on a full-time basis in 1954, Rushmore had worked as an investigator on McCarthy's staff.

A November 1953 article by Rushmore titled "Red Murder, Inc." warned, "In America this very minute 1,000 Benedict Arnolds, trained secretly in Moscow, await word to paralyze industry and liquidate top anti-Reds!" Rushmore claimed that the top four targets "marked for death by red murder squads" were J. Edgar Hoover, McCarthy, Winchell, and televangelist Bishop Fulton J. Sheen. Hoover was described as "the man who knows more about the Reds' top secrets than any other American . . . Visibly shaken by Hoover's practice of successfully planting his own agents in their midst, the Reds long ago decided that in any plan to take over America, the FBI head must die early." Similarly, Rushmore wrote that "the tireless efforts of Senator Joseph R. McCarthy to root communist agents out of Government has won him wide public support but at the same time made him one of the top targets on the Reds' 'purge' list . . . Startling proof that his name is high on the liquidation list was seen recently when his Senate subcommittee revealed that a military-trained communist had been assigned to knock off the Wisconsin Legislator."[32] That coverage not only stressed Hoover and McCarthy's anticommunist credentials, it also helped assert their masculinity, portraying them as bravely risking their own safety for that of the country.

Another defining characteristic of *Confidential* was its preoccupation with homosexuality; journalist Maurice Zolotow once said that Harrison and *Confidential* were both "queer for queers."[33] Under Harrison, the magazine became consumed with outing individuals (before that terminology existed) and printing stories related to homosexuality. Articles associated homosexuality with criminality and lawbreaking, and noted that gender inversion was homosexuality's most common symptom.[34] Some contemporary commentators attributed *Confidential*'s copious reporting on the topic not to Harrison's homophobia but his belief that such tales helped sell magazines. During the 1950s alone, *Confidential* reported homosexual rumors about Johnnie Ray, Tab Hunter, Van Johnson, Lizabeth Scott, Marlene Dietrich, Dan Dailey, the king of Sweden, the infamous bank robber Willie Sutton, Vanderbilt heir Peter Orton, and an entire dorm at Harvard University. In 1955, *Confidential* was prepared to run a report alleging that Rock Hudson had engaged in homosexual affairs until Universal Studios was able to convince it to bury that story and instead print one on the jail time actor Rory Calhoun had served for assault.[35] The frequency with which the magazine published stories on homosexuality—particularly exposés—helped popularize the notion that homosexuals, like communists, were both dangerous and lurking around every corner, even where one least expected to find them.

Confidential's articles on homosexuality also exposed its readership to a small dictionary of slang terms, including "lavender," "fire," "faggot," "scared," "lonesome," "wimpering" [sic], "double-gaited," "secret," "abnormal," "drag," "daughter," "gay," "woman," "Mary" (and other female names), "never married," "queer," and "lifelong bachelor." Gay women and lesbianism were written about using terms such as "tomboy," "going for dolls," "both sides of the street," "baritone babes," "lesbian," "strange girl," and "never married." They were often portrayed as wearing men's clothing and adopting aggressive stances. Centrally, *Confidential*'s use of that slang popularized its double meaning for a broad audience, allowing readers to recognize them when used in conversation or other publications.

The magazine's interests in political gossip and homosexuality often collided. In its third issue *Confidential* printed a story that all but accused former Illinois governor and Democratic presidential candidate Adlai

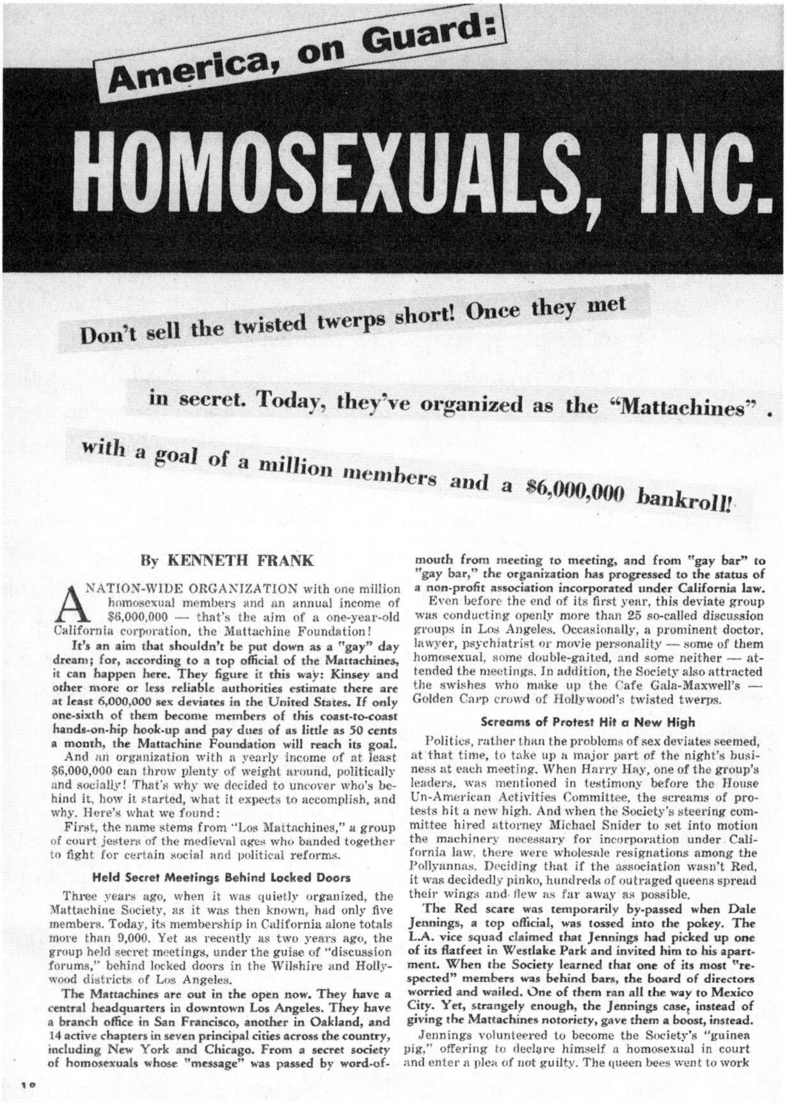

America, on Guard:

HOMOSEXUALS, INC.

Don't sell the twisted twerps short! Once they met in secret. Today, they've organized as the "Mattachines" . with a goal of a million members and a $6,000,000 bankroll!

By KENNETH FRANK

A NATION-WIDE ORGANIZATION with one million homosexual members and an annual income of $6,000,000 — that's the aim of a one-year-old California corporation, the Mattachine Foundation!

It's an aim that shouldn't be put down as a "gay" day dream; for, according to a top official of the Mattachines, it can happen here. They figure it this way: Kinsey and other more or less reliable authorities estimate there are at least 6,000,000 sex deviates in the United States. If only one-sixth of them become members of this coast-to-coast hands-on-hip hook-up and pay dues of as little as 50 cents a month, the Mattachine Foundation will reach its goal.

And an organization with a yearly income of at least $6,000,000 can throw plenty of weight around, politically and socially! That's why we decided to uncover who's behind it, how it started, what it expects to accomplish, and why. Here's what we found:

First, the name stems from "Los Mattachines," a group of court jesters of the medieval ages who banded together to fight for certain social and political reforms.

Held Secret Meetings Behind Locked Doors

Three years ago, when it was quietly organized, the Mattachine Society, as it was then known, had only five members. Today, its membership in California alone totals more than 9,000. Yet as recently as two years ago, the group held secret meetings, under the guise of "discussion forums," behind locked doors in the Wilshire and Hollywood districts of Los Angeles.

The Mattachines are out in the open now. They have a central headquarters in downtown Los Angeles. They have a branch office in San Francisco, another in Oakland, and 14 active chapters in seven principal cities across the country, including New York and Chicago. From a secret society of homosexuals whose "message" was passed by word-of-mouth from meeting to meeting, and from "gay bar" to "gay bar," the organization has progressed to the status of a non-profit association incorporated under California law.

Even before the end of its first year, this deviate group was conducting openly more than 25 so-called discussion groups in Los Angeles. Occasionally, a prominent doctor, lawyer, psychiatrist or movie personality — some of them homosexual, some double-gaited, and some neither — attended the meetings. In addition, the Society also attracted the swishes who make up the Cafe Gala-Maxwell's — Golden Carp crowd of Hollywood's twisted twerps.

Screams of Protest Hit a New High

Politics, rather than the problems of sex deviates seemed, at that time, to take up a major part of the night's business at each meeting. When Harry Hay, one of the group's leaders, was mentioned in testimony before the House Un-American Activities Committee, the screams of protests hit a new high. And when the Society's steering committee hired attorney Michael Snider to set into motion the machinery necessary for incorporation under California law, there were wholesale resignations among the Pollyannas. Deciding that if the association wasn't Red, it was decidedly pinko, hundreds of outraged queens spread their wings and flew as far away as possible.

The Red scare was temporarily by-passed when Dale Jennings, a top official, was tossed into the pokey. The L.A. vice squad claimed that Jennings had picked up one of its flatfeet in Westlake Park and invited him to his apartment. When the Society learned that one of its most "respected" members was behind bars, the board of directors worried and wailed. One of them ran all the way to Mexico City. Yet, strangely enough, the Jennings case, instead of giving the Mattachines notoriety, gave them a boost, instead.

Jennings volunteered to become the Society's "guinea pig," offering to declare himself a homosexual in court and enter a plea of not guilty. The queen bees went to work

1 0

FIGURE 6. *Confidential*'s May 1954 issue, published during the Army-McCarthy hearings, included a homophobic exposé of the Mattachine Society, one of the country's earliest gay rights organizations. Credit: Private collection.

Stevenson of homosexuality. Here, too, *Confidential*'s intelligence-gathering system had paid dividends: Harrison had first heard the rumor courtesy of contacts in the FBI.[36] Notably, the article never named the rumor (noting only that it "reflected on the manhood" of Stevenson) and instead adopted a tone of incredulity in discussing its spread: "It was the start of the nastiest, most widely circulated hearsay in the annals of rumor-mongering. By phone, on planes and trains, from the racket of factory assembly-lines to the quiet of hospital rooms, from the big-town sharpies to unsophisticated villages, it burned the ears of a nation."[37] McCarthy himself was aware of the rumors surrounding Stevenson as early as 1952. According to columnist Marquis Childs, McCarthy was prepared to make "a nationwide television attack on the Stevenson campaign. He was boasting he would say it was made up of pinks, punks and pansies." This quip also indicates that McCarthy was well-versed in homophobic slang such as "pink" and "punk."[38]

The tenor of *Confidential*'s report on Stevenson served the magazine's interests in two ways. First, it helped promote discussion of the magazine itself, positioning it as "in the know" and suggesting to its audience that they needed to read it in order to keep up with the latest gossip that was "burning the ears of a nation." Second, by not actually printing the rumor *Confidential* insulated itself from charges of libel. The magazine was more explicit in its accusations against former undersecretary of state Sumner Welles. In its May 1956 issue, *Confidential* detailed a January 1947 incident in which a drunken Welles propositioned a young man in a Cleveland hamburger joint.[39]

Confidential led a gossip magazine revolution and inspired over forty imitators, including *Uncensored, Top Secret, Inside Story, Celebrity, Suppressed, On the Q.T., Behind the Scene, Inside, Hush-Hush, Exposed, Private Lives, Rave, The Lowdown, Dynamite, Dare,* and *Tipoff*.[40] As their titles suggested, these magazines promised to cover not only traditional topics of gossip but to expose hidden truths. Many magazines took titles that appropriated the cloak-and-dagger language of the budding Cold War: *Suppressed, Tipoff, Hush-Hush, Inside*. A particularly telling title was *Top Secret*, a phrase that had entered the American lexicon only at the beginning of 1950 when President Truman authorized it as a security designation. Employing the security state's vernacular allowed the magazines to implicitly link themselves to the nation's most well-known and well-respected keepers of secrets and gatherers of information: the federal intelligence agencies tasked with protecting the United States from subversion.

Gossip has been a perennial presence in American society, but the Cold War zeitgeist of fear, anxiety, suspicion, and secrecy helped the 1950s gossip industry's wares seem more relevant. Key to their success was a renewed emphasis on the idea that *information itself* both held power and could be dangerous. During the early Cold War, the belief in the power of information was bolstered by an enduring fear of spies that began during World War II, a number of well-publicized espionage cases, and congressional

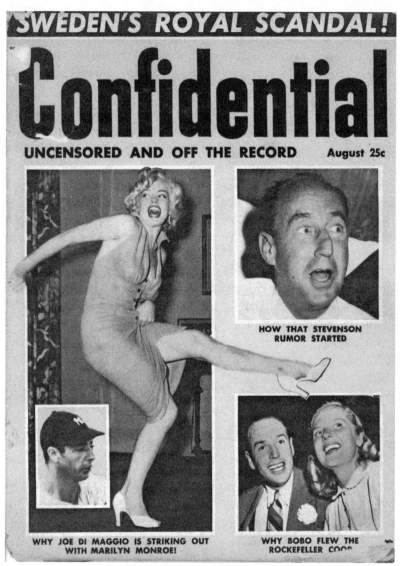

FIGURE 7. The August 1953 issue of *Confidential* included a story intimating that former Democratic presidential candidate Adlai Stevenson was homosexual. Credit: Private collection.

investigations into purveyors of ideas such as the Hollywood Ten. Even seemingly minor pieces of information—such as a coworker's flirtation with a left-wing union or a college roommate's academic interest in socialist economic policies—garnered newfound import since they could damage careers and ruin reputations.

The concept that thoughts and ideas could be threatening has a deep history. But in Cold War America communism came to be depicted in popular culture as an intellectual disease that could infect any host and brainwash individuals into socialist automatons. The cultural historian Matthew Dunne has noted that "the plots of nearly a dozen films, including *Invaders from Mars* (1953), *It Came from Outer Space* (1954), *Invasion of the Body Snatchers* (1956), *The Brain from Planet Arous* (1957), *I Married a Monster from Outer Space* (1958), and *The Brain Eaters* (1958) featured alien invaders who had the ability to mimic normal American citizens, control their minds, and turn them into cold, inhuman slaves." Information was so powerful that those who were infected with the communist plague needed to be quarantined and provided treatment.[41]

Gossip magazines promised their readers access to that powerful information. *Rave* advertised itself as "The Magazine of INTIMATE EXPOSÉ" and claimed to be "the magazine that's not for idiots," while *Tip-Off* declared itself the "magazine of inside exclusives."[42] The gossip industry also benefitted from the widespread belief that the full details of any major story—whether a celebrity romance or geopolitical intrigue—were never made available to the public. Gossip magazines fed off the sense that most public reports were incomplete, that behind-the-scenes motivations and actors were at play, and that only muckraking investigative reporters would reveal the unadulterated facts. *On the Q.T.* promised readers "stories the newspapers *won't* print" and claimed to be "the magazine that tells the WHOLE story," while *Whisper* advertised that it was telling "the stories behind the headlines."[43]

Confidential and its imitators relied on the tools of gossip—insinuation, guilt by association, euphemism, and hyperbole—to overcome two primary challenges. First, the magazines often needed to construct claims from shards of information, like building a house from an incomplete blueprint. Their sources were almost always tertiary to the central story: busboys who had caught a sliver of conversation, taxi drivers who had ferried home a drunken starlet, or jilted lovers passing on dirt about their former partner's new beau. Second, the claims had to be broad enough that the magazines could dodge libel charges. Presenting facts in a certain sequence, using specific watchwords, or pairing articles with telling illustrations allowed them to leave the task of drawing an explicit relationship to their readers. Another stylistic hallmark of *Confidential* was recycled gossip, constructing "composite-fact stories" by packing their exposés with tales already in circulation. These narratives served the publication's interests by offering "plausible chronologies for events that had a ring of truth about them because readers had probably encountered some aspect of them before in newspaper gossip columns, traditional fan magazines, other scandal magazines and tabloids, and even sometimes in feature stories of the mainstream press."[44]

The popularity of gossip magazines familiarized the general public with the linguistic and argumentative instruments they employed. *Town Topics*, *Broadway Brevities*, the *New York Evening Graphic*, *Confidential*, and similar publications popularized the tools of gossip as legitimate means of conveying information. Because of their experiences with gossip magazines, the public was able to recognize the implications of tactics such as insinuation and guilt by association. Even if the claims those tools enabled would not hold up in a court of law, they were often regarded as credible in the court of public opinion.

Furthermore, gossip magazines helped define and police the parameters of acceptable behavior. In spite of their reputation as vulgar and low-class, gossip magazines performed the socially conservative role that has long been ascribed to gossip generally. "At the group level," concludes social psychologist Eric K. Foster, "what begins as trusted exchanges in private becomes the knowledge, norm, and trust margins of communities, cultures, and other bounded social identities . . . Whispered gossip between members of one group perpetuates the inclusion of like members and the exclusion of members of another group, and the process is repeated innumerable times in innumerable private exchanges."[45] Gossip distributed through the national popular press had a similar impact, delineating which behaviors could lead to social exclusion. The establishment of such rules was particularly important in the context of postwar instability. *Confidential* consistently communicated that despite the rapid changes experienced in American society since the end of World War II, behaviors such as homosexuality, interracial marriage, nonmonogamous relationships, procreation out of wedlock, adultery, pederasty, and socialist sympathizing were unwelcome. Even though *Confidential* and its peers usually refrained from explicitly passing judgment on its subjects and their actions, the presence of a topic in the magazine marked it as "gossip-worthy" and thus deserving of public scrutiny.

As he sought to increase his political clout and public profile, Joe McCarthy came to marshal many of the same themes and tactics employed by *Confidential* and its competitors. At the same time, he continued to emphasize his populist masculinity. The hallmarks of that gendered identity were most apparent in the charges McCarthy leveled at the State Department. Even before Deputy Undersecretary of State John Peurifoy revealed in early 1950 that ninety-one homosexuals had been dismissed from the

State Department for being "security risks," the diplomatic corps had been regarded with particular suspicion. Conservative columnist Jack O'Donnell captured that wariness in his claim that "the foreign policy of the U.S., even before World War II, was dominated by an all-powerful, super-secret inner circle of highly educated, socially highly-placed sexual misfits in the State Department, all easy to blackmail, all susceptible to blandishments by homosexuals in foreign nations."[46] A June 1950 cartoon in the *New Yorker* played on public awareness of the recent dismissals, depicting a job candidate explaining his employment history: "It's true, sir, that the State Department let me go, but that was solely because of incompetence."[47] An anecdote related by columnists Joseph and Stewart Alsop from mid-1950 claimed that when a reporter asked a taxi driver to take him to the new State Department headquarters, the cabbie responded, "Fruits . . . The whole place is fulla fruits. Fruits and treachers."[48]

As a target, the State Department enabled McCarthy to emphasize his own masculine credentials while impugning those of his enemies. He often directed his most cutting invectives toward Secretary of State Dean Acheson, a Groton- and Yale-educated WASP emblematic of the type of bureaucrat McCarthy had come to loathe. Some of these attacks were direct; in critiquing Acheson for tolerating communist sympathizers within the State Department, McCarthy noted, "I hope the Secretary will have enough guts to stand up and say, 'This is my baby,' and take the blame for it. I suggest that Mr. Acheson stand up like a man."[49] McCarthy also condemned "egg-sucking phony liberals who litter Washington with their persons and clutter American thinking with their simple-minded arguments," impeding his investigation of subversives in the government.[50]

At other points, McCarthy used the language of class to critique the masculinity of his State Department opponents. In his keynote address to the 1950 Wisconsin State Republican Convention, McCarthy railed against Acheson as a man who sought to battle communism with "a lace handkerchief, a silk glove, and a Harvard accent, if you please."[51] McCarthy's analysis was noticed by the press; soon after McCarthy's Wheeling speech, syndicated columnist Holmes Alexander noted that the "rough young Senator from Wisconsin" was playing a key role in rehashing "the familiar American story of the snobby, supercilious dandy who gets his nose punched in by the boy from across the railroad tracks. It's the story of the comeuppance of the dude."[52]

Even J. Edgar Hoover's praise of McCarthy was based on the senator's masculine attributes. While he was vacationing with McCarthy during the summer of 1953, Hoover remarked:

McCarthy is a former Marine. He was an amateur boxer. He's Irish. Combine those, and you're going to have a vigorous individual, who is not going to be pushed around . . . The Investigating committees do a valuable job. They have subpoena rights without which some vital investigations could not be accomplished . . . I view him as a friend and believe he so views me. Certainly, he is a controversial man. He is earnest and he is honest. He has enemies. Whenever you attack subversives of any kind, communists, Fascists, even the Ku Klux Klan, you are going to be the victim of the most extremely vicious criticism that can be made.[53]

Hoover's description of McCarthy's pugilism was not merely based on collegiate stories. In Washington, McCarthy had engaged in a number of physical altercations. His most famous adversary was the syndicated newspaper columnist Drew Pearson, whose early support of McCarthy had waned after Pearson witnessed the brutishness with which McCarthy attacked his enemies. Over the course of 1950 Pearson published numerous columns attacking McCarthy and his allies, including one containing the charge that McCarthy knowingly employed a pervert on his staff. As a result, McCarthy trained his sights on the reporter.[54]

The rivalry erupted on December 13, 1950, at a dinner party at Washington's Sulgrave Club. Louise Ansberry, socialite and organizer of the party, had invited McCarthy without Pearson's knowledge. After trading barbs, Pearson tried to ignore McCarthy, but at the end of the night the two found themselves alone in the club's coat room. After more verbal jousting, a drunken McCarthy kneed Pearson twice in the groin, later claiming that he thought Pearson was reaching into his coat pocket for a weapon. The scuffle was finally broken up by Representative Richard Nixon, who later claimed to a friend that "if I hadn't pulled McCarthy away, he might have killed Pearson." Reporters quickly learned of the fight and wrote it up. Over twenty senators called McCarthy to praise him for giving Pearson what they regarded as a well-deserved beating. Senator Arthur V. Watkins, a future adversary, told McCarthy, "Joe, I've heard conflicting accounts of where you hit Pearson. I hope both are true."[55] Over the next few years Pearson and McCarthy relentlessly sued and countersued each other for libel. Pearson would take revenge years later, when he helped fuel rumors about the senator's sexuality.

McCarthy further emphasized his own gruff masculinity through attacks on homosexuals and homosexuality. In a speech to the Wisconsin Federation of Young Republicans in May 1950, McCarthy received a positive, snickering response when he winkingly referred to homosexuals in the

State Department as "individuals with particular mental aberrations as far as sex is concerned."[56] The comment did two forms of work; it underscored homosexuals as deviant while associating McCarthy with the "normal" from which they strayed. At the same time, McCarthy's own heterosexuality was being emphasized, with Walter Winchell reporting on McCarthy's romances with Bazy Miller and Jean Kerr (as Winchell had done with both Hoover and Cohn).[57]

Like many other politicians and public commentators, McCarthy linked homosexuality (or, in the parlance of the time, "sexual perversion") with communism. Early newspaper reports about McCarthy's claims about government subversives commonly identified him as making "charges of communism and sex perversion in the State Department." William Fulton of the *Washington Times-Herald* and *Chicago Daily Tribune* explicitly defined "McCarthyism" as "demands for cleaning communists and perverts out of the State Department."[58] In a speech before the American Society of Newspaper Editors, McCarthy forcefully stated, "I refuse to break ranks at the pitiful squealing of those who hold sacrosanct those communists and queers who have the American people in a hypnotic trance, headed blindly toward the same precipice."[59] Speaking in private to a pair of reporters, McCarthy was more direct: "If you want to be against McCarthy, boys," he said, "you've got to be a communist or a cocksucker."[60]

In the early months of 1950, Americans were particularly sensitive to the issue of sexual perversion due to the widespread perception that a recent spate of sex crimes had occurred against women and children, especially in urban areas. The second page of the November 20, 1949, edition of the *Pittsburgh Press* featured five separate stories reporting sex crimes. One week later, a widely distributed Associated Press article noted that the nationally recognized judge Samuel Leibowitz had joined Hoover and sexologist Alfred Kinsey to urge vigilance against "the current outbreak of child sex murders." In a December 1 press release, the American Legion urged Congress to "enact and have enforced rigid federal laws to exterminate the rape menace so prevalent in our country today." The legion's call was a reaction to the popular notion that there was not a "strong enough" law to prevent and punish sex crimes; newspapers reported numerous instances where a "convicted sex criminal" was released, only to continue attacking women and children.[61] Though it is difficult to determine whether a spike actually occurred, the perceived epidemic led twenty-one states to pass legislation targeting "deviants" between 1947 and 1955.[62]

Hoover had made a similar argument two years earlier, positing that "sex fiends [are] aided by weak laws." In a cover story for the *American Maga-*

zine, Hoover claimed that "the most rapidly increasing type of crimes is that perpetrated by degenerate sex offenders . . . at the rate of a criminal assault every forty-three minutes, day and night in the United States . . . Depraved human beings, more savage than beasts, are permitted to rove America almost at will."[63] Historian Philip Jenkins has observed that "some observers saw homosexuals as ipso facto dangerous, but even the most benevolent writers discussed homosexuality alongside other pernicious behaviors and conditions, so that a stigma was certain to be acquired."[64] In the American sexual imagination, "perversion" was an elastic concept that encompassed a variety of sexual dangers—from masturbation to rape to homosexuality—all of which were thought to stem from the inability of some men to control their sexual urges.[65]

Notably, many Americans traced the perceived proliferation of perversion to the New Deal, believing that the expansion of the federal government had replaced "traditional" values with the sinful ones of the nation's leaders.[66] That belief was particularly strong in the Midwest and West; "I can tell you exactly when the moral degeneration of America began," claimed a banker from Boise, Idaho. "It began with the election of Franklin Roosevelt."[67]

For similar reasons, both homosexuals and sex perverts were linked with communists in the public imagination. "The constant pairing of 'communists and queers,'" argues David K. Johnson, "led many [Americans] to see them as indistinguishable threats. Evidence that one group had infiltrated the government was seen as confirmation of charges that the other had as well."[68] The Hiss-Chambers case gave onlookers a specific example of that link; as Johnson notes, "both groups seemed to comprise hidden subcultures, with their own meeting places, literature, cultural codes, and bounds of loyalty. As people feared communist 'cells' within the federal government, they feared 'nests' of homosexuals."[69] Homosexuals were also feared on account of their supposed susceptibility to blackmail, even though the single recorded instance of homosexual blackmail affecting military policy occurred in 1907 in Germany.[70] When the liberal journalist Max Lerner asked government sources about homosexual blackmail in the United States, he was told that such cases could be neither confirmed nor denied, but that vigilance was appropriate because "J. Edgar Hoover says [homosexuals] are more vulnerable" to blackmail.[71]

Charges of sexual perversion, particularly at the State Department, became alarming to the Washington establishment. Columnists Joseph and Stewart Alsop took to the *Saturday Evening Post* to ask, "Why Has Washington Gone Crazy?" In the July 1950 piece, the elite Alsops defended the establishment and described highly qualified employees of the State Department who were preparing to resign instead of deal with attacks on their "intellectualism." The article specifically targeted McCarthy as an alarmist prone to "seeing a Red under every bed":

> A visit to the McCarthy lair on Capitol Hill is rather like being transported to the set of one of Hollywood's minor thrillers. The anteroom is generally full of furtive-looking characters who look as though they might be suborned State Department men. McCarthy himself, despite a creeping baldness and a continual tremor which makes his head shake in a disconcerting fashion, is reasonably well cast as the Hollywood version of a strong-jawed private eye. A visitor is likely to find him with his heavy shoulders hunched forward, a telephone in his huge hands, shouting cryptic instruction to some mysterious ally . . . The drama is heighted by a significant bit of stage business. For as Senator McCarthy talks he sometimes strikes the mouthpiece of his telephone with a pencil. As Washington folklore has it, this is supposed to jar the needle off any concealed listening device. In short, while the State Department fears that Senator McCarthy's friends are spying on it, Senator McCarthy apparently fears that the State Department's friends are spying on him.[72]

The Alsops also decried the "notion . . . loudly proclaimed in Chicago and points West . . . that the Government is now in the hands of perverts and traitors." They criticized Senator Kenneth Wherry's proposed investigation into the government's employment of homosexuals, calling the idea that "sexual perversion presents a clear and present danger to the security of the United States" a "vulgar folly."[73]

In pitting Eastern establishment intellectuals against the alarmist philistines of "Chicago and points West," the Alsops identified a key friction within the government at the outset of the Cold War: the Eastern establishment tended to see the regions of the nation distant from the traditional intellectual, cultural, and commercial capitals in the Northeast as provincial. And much of the conservative cabal spearheading investigations into subversives within the government hailed from Midwestern and Western states: McCarthy, Wisconsin; Wherry, Nebraska; Representative Noah Mason, Illinois; Senator Pat McCarran, Nevada; Nixon, California. As those men sought increased influence, they often relied on intertwined accusations of sexual perversion, elitism, and communism (or communist sympathies) to paint their opponents as anti-American and out of touch with the concerns of average, hardworking Americans. McCarthy's populist masculinity exemplified that approach, and it encouraged hatred from the long-established residents of the halls of power as much as it inspired loyalty from his blue-collar supporters.

In an August 8, 1950, speech on the Senate floor, McCarthy hit back at the blue-blooded Alsop brothers. He took particular umbrage at what he called their article's "sarcasm directed toward the people of the great Midwest and West, the heart of America." He claimed that "once the people of a Nation become complacent about moral degeneracy in its leadership, then that nation has not long to live. For example, the great Roman Empire came to an end when the ruling class became morally perverted and degenerate." Under the cover of immunity from charges of libel afforded senators speaking on the Senate floor, McCarthy insinuated that Joseph Alsop was a homosexual, noting that "I know some of your editorial staff and frankly can't believe that Senator Wherry's attempt to accomplish the long overdue task of removing perverts from our Government would be considered either 'vulgar' or 'nauseating' to them. I can understand, of course, why it would be considered 'vulgar' and 'nauseating' by Joe Alsop."[74] As a result, the *Saturday Evening Post* largely stopped publishing stories on McCarthy, becoming perhaps the only publication that McCarthy successfully intimidated.[75]

McCarthy's allies pointed to his successes in fighting so-called perversion nearly as often as they lauded his crusade against communism. Three months after McCarthy's charges in Wheeling, Representative Noah Mason, a former member of the House Un-American Activities Committee, claimed that McCarthy had already "forced the State Department to fire 91 sex perverts."[76] Partially as a result of McCarthy's charges, the Senate approved $10,000 for the investigation of "homosexuals and other perverts in government jobs," establishing a new task for an investigative subcommittee headed by North Carolina senator Clyde Hoey.[77] In so doing, McCarthy explicitly helped promote and expand the government-sponsored harassment of homosexuals that history has christened the Lavender Scare.

In establishing his masculine bona fides, McCarthy was aided by his relationship with J. Edgar Hoover and the FBI. Back in 1947, one of McCarthy's first actions upon arriving in Washington had been to contact Hoover. The two soon began spending time together socially, eating at Harvey's Restaurant near the Mayflower Hotel and visiting racetracks. McCarthy, accompanied by "a big blonde from his office," watched the 1949 Preakness Stakes with Hoover, who reportedly provided McCarthy with a tip on a horse.[78] (The horse lost.) They dined at each other's homes along with subordinates like Clyde Tolson, McCarthy's secretary Jean Kerr, and—later—

Roy Cohn (Hoover was reportedly the consummate guest, always presenting his host with a bottle of wine). In 1948, Hoover invited McCarthy to address that year's graduates of the FBI National Academy. When Jean Kerr vacationed in Hawaii two years later, Hoover assigned an off-duty FBI agent to escort her. After Kerr broke her hip in an accident and was forced to remain in Hawaii during her recovery, Hoover closely monitored her progress through telegrams from the Bureau's Honolulu office.[79]

The social relationship helped foster a professional one. Confidentially, Hoover directed his agents to provide McCarthy with notes on the Bureau's scores of files on suspected communists, even instructing them to comb through FBI records *after* McCarthy had publicly voiced an accusation in the hope of finding enough evidence to make the charge stick. In addition, Hoover provided McCarthy access to ex-communist witnesses such as Louis Budenz and recommended former FBI agents for staff positions with McCarthy. Lou Nichols, Hoover's public relations czar, helped McCarthy master the art of insinuation by suggesting that he use broader language in his accusations. Instead of using the difficult-to-prove charge that an individual was a "card-carrying communist," Nichols recommended employing language identifying his targets as "communist sympathizers" or "loyalty risks."[80]

Centrally, McCarthy's association with Hoover helped legitimize the previously obscure senator in the eyes of the American public. At the dawn of the Cold War, Hoover was arguably the most respected public servant in the nation. He was specifically lauded as the nation's foremost bulwark against communist subversion, so much so that in his May 1950 speech before the Midwest Council of Young Republicans, McCarthy lobbied for the creation of a loyalty board under Hoover's control.[81] That such a claim raised no major outcry is a testament to how much Hoover was trusted by the majority of Americans during that phase of his career. For a while, the relationship benefitted both men. McCarthy gained validation, legitimacy, and access to information that would help his anticommunist crusade. Hoover gained a key ally in the legislative branch and a way to surreptitiously leak material. But a partnership based on exchanging favors only works when both parties have power.

*

A significant part of McCarthy's appeal stemmed from his ability to forge an emotional connection with a large segment of the public, particularly members of the middle and lower middle classes who privileged conservative, populist values such as nationalism, kinship, regional pride, religious fidelity, self-reliance, and the amorphous yet powerful concept of "hard work." That loyalty resulted from the constituent elements of his populist masculinity: a straightforward communication style, easy way with people, veteran status, and his prominent self-placement on the nation's defensive ramparts. Supporters' emotional devotion to McCarthy is apparent in the hundreds of letters that were sent to Senator Arthur V. Watkins when he chaired a special committee investigating McCarthy in 1954. Because letters to McCarthy himself have either been lost, destroyed, or remain in sealed archives, the Watkins letters provide the best insight into how McCarthy's backers in the general public voiced their support. Pro-McCarthy voices praised him as "the greatest patriot of all" and "100% American."[82] Mrs. Joseph A. Drapeau of Salem, Massachusetts, echoed others with her opinion that "Senator McCarthy is a great American and a great patriot. His fight against communism is the greatest fight any man has ever waged in this country. He is fearless and has the get to go through with what he starts, no matter whose toes he steps on. I have every confidence in him and his methods because, no one can handle communists with kid gloves, that was proved over and over again."[83]

The emotions prompted by McCarthy and his crusade caused many letter writers to invoke a higher power. "How dare you crucify a man who has given his whole *being* to his country," Mrs. Naomi Barnard asked. "To take the path of *least* resistance is the *easy* way out. Joe McCarthy tackled the job that all of you know needed to be done but were afraid to face. Now that he has made the country aware of just what was going on, you want to get rid of him."[84] Similar notes were commonly replete with religious language. "Thank God" for Joe McCarthy and "God Bless Him" were common sentiments, with McCarthy often depicted as a martyr for the greater good. Among the biblical passages that were often cited by authors, Christ's admonition to "Let he who is without sin cast the first stone" was most frequent, suggesting that supporters recognized McCarthy's faults but still accepted his leadership.[85]

Part of the reason McCarthy engendered such loyalty was the way he communicated with people, specifically the assured tone of his allegations and the vernacular he employed when presenting evidence. McCarthy's hyperbolic accusations filled American newspapers. Secretary of Defense George Marshall was part of "a conspiracy so immense and an infamy so black as to dwarf any previous venture in the history of man."[86] Esther Brunauer, a State Department staffer whom McCarthy claimed was associated with a number of communist-front organizations, was "one of the most fantastic cases" McCarthy had ever encountered.[87] Haldore Hanson, a State Department official assigned to a program helping underdeveloped countries, was one of the "cleverest and smoothest" operators and "a man with a mission—a mission to communize the world."[88] Individuals McCarthy identified as communists were never "flirting" with communism or lower-level operatives; they were key players in a worldwide conspiracy.

McCarthy also demonstrated his willingness to commit to a position, even when the preponderance of the evidence stood against him. Though this strategy caused some observers to dismiss him as a stubborn demagogue, to his supporters it made him appear principled. A number of commentators likened McCarthy's tactics to that of the "big lie," a propaganda technique identified by Adolf Hitler in *Mein Kampf*—namely "the practice of telling a lie so profound that the general public will not believe that someone would fabricate such a falsehood and, as a result, will accept the lie as truth." In the public imagination, the big lie became associated with a phrasing often falsely attributed to Joseph Goebbels: "If you tell a lie big enough and keep repeating it, people will eventually come to believe it."[89] On the eve of the 1952 election, an editorial cartoon by Herblock depicted McCarthy whitewashing a fence while consulting a page titled "The Big Lie Technique" that had been ripped from a "Communist Handbook" held by a smiling Josef Stalin.[90] Even President Truman accused McCarthyist Republicans of using the big lie.

McCarthy's ability to connect with the public was also undoubtedly helped by the way his accusations employed the tools of gossip. McCarthy's numerous charges have been well-documented, but it is instructive to examine a few specific cases from the first year of his anticommunist campaign in this light.[91]

One of McCarthy's earliest targets was Owen Lattimore, a professor at Johns Hopkins University and adviser to the State Department who specialized in Central Asia and China. McCarthy deployed his typically hyperbolic language, claiming that Lattimore was the top Soviet spy in the United States and may "have done this nation incalculable and irreparable harm."[92] In a late March 1950 speech on the Senate floor attacking Lattimore, McCarthy positioned himself as a brave warrior willing to risk political and professional disaster in the search for justice. "In discussing this matter with some of my friends," he said, "they pointed out to me . . . that the road has been strewn with the political corpses of those who dared to attempt an exposure of the type of individuals I intend to discuss today . . . People have expressed a deep concern for fear I may quit in this fight. I want to assure them now that, in the words of John Paul Jones, 'I have just begun to fight.'"[93] McCarthy thus highlighted his toughness, his boldness, and his principled nature. He was a warrior like the Revolutionary War naval hero. He stressed his opponents' fortitude to inflate his own bravery in countering them. His suggestions about the danger of exposing Lattimore also appealed to a sense of conspiracy and nodded to the public paranoias of the Red Scare. Throughout his address, McCarthy used melodramatic language typical of gossip magazines, calling Lattimore's situation "fantastic," "unheard of," "sensational," "unbelievable," and "incredible." In addition to enlarging the significance of the service he was rendering, McCarthy's choice of terminology was also a clear attempt to inflame the passions of his target audience.

Lattimore returned to the United States from Afghanistan (where he was on a fact-gathering mission for the United Nations) to testify before a subcommittee of the Senate Foreign Relations Committee and vehemently deny McCarthy's charges. To counter Lattimore, McCarthy called former communist Louis Budenz as a witness. Budenz enjoyed widespread public trust because he had helped corroborate some of Whittaker Chambers's testimony against Alger Hiss. Under oath, Budenz claimed that Lattimore was "a member of a 'communist cell' and was assigned to help direct a Red conspiracy to betray China to the communists," basing his contention on Soviet communiques he claimed to have.[94] Budenz's testimony was largely hearsay and contained no hard evidence. He was cagey during cross-examination but was able to dodge all criticisms. The news media—including major publications such as *Time*—seemed to believe Budenz.[95] McCarthy then called Freda Utley, another ex-communist, to testify. Utley admitted that she did not know Lattimore and, like Budenz, could provide no hard evidence of his communist sympathies. But her testimony, too, found its way onto the front pages, including a headline in the *Washington Post* announcing that "Lattimore Acted Like a Red, Freda Utley Tells Senators."[96] McCarthy understood that headlines burned more brightly in the public consciousness than the more nuanced content beneath them.

Nowhere was McCarthy's faith in the narrative-determining power of headlines more apparent than during his 1950 investigation into the *Amerasia* affair. *Amerasia* was a small magazine focused on East Asian policy whose New York City offices were raided by federal agents in 1945, following suspicions that the magazine possessed classified government documents. Though the raid turned up thousands of pages of documents from the Department of State, the Navy, and the Office of Strategic Services, a thorough FBI investigation determined that none of them had been forwarded to a foreign power and the resulting punishment for *Amerasia*'s editors was relatively light. The incident was thought to be long settled when McCarthy dredged it up in 1950, charging that a government cover-up had hidden the extent of *Amerasia*'s crimes from the public. In so doing, McCarthy was building his own "composite-fact story," a tactic later popularized by *Confidential*, legitimizing charges by playing off (and repeating) previously known aspects of the case that had been reported by eminent voices.[97]

McCarthy called on Frank Brooks Bielaski, an ex-OSS agent who testified that the raid of the *Amerasia* offices had discovered a file of stolen information on the atomic bomb. Bielaski's claim was particularly alarming in the context of recent events; the Soviet Union's first successful test of an atom bomb had shocked Western analysts and caused widespread panic across the United States. Though Bielaski's testimony could possibly help explain how the Soviets caught up so quickly, his claim of a cover-up was thoroughly debunked under cross-examination later that day.

But McCarthy was largely unconcerned; he had taken steps to control the media narrative. Before Bielaski took the stand, McCarthy had released a preview of his testimony to the *Washington Star*, the capital's most popular newspaper. In so doing, McCarthy ensured that Bielaski's charges would be circulated before Bielaski was cross-examined.[98] McCarthy had learned this tactic from Lou Nichols, the FBI's master of public relations and one of Hoover's most trusted advisors.[99] For McCarthy and his FBI allies, the details of the situation were less important than the perception the media could create.

McCarthy's most explicit use of the tools of gossip came during the 1950 election cycle when he and his office used *From the Record*, a campaign mailer designed to look like a tabloid newspaper, to tar the reputation of Senator Millard Tydings.[100] McCarthy's extraordinary efforts to unseat Tydings had begun a few months prior, after the Maryland Democrat led an ethics investigation of the Wisconsin Republican. Tydings had famously vowed to embarrass McCarthy, saying, "Let me have [McCarthy] for three days in public hearings and he'll never show his face in the Senate again."[101] At the end of its inquiry, the so-called Tydings committee filed a three-hundred-page report concluding that McCarthy's investigations into communism represented "a fraud and a hoax perpetrated on the Senate of the United States and American people" and that they composed "perhaps the most nefarious campaign of half-truths and untruths in the history of the Republic."[102] William White of the *New York Times* noted that the report employed "terms of harshness rarely used in the Senate's history" and "cleared every person who had been accused by Senator McCarthy."[103] Then, in what *Washington Post* reporter Alfred Friendly termed "one of the most bare-fisted and personal denunciations ever delivered on the Senate floor," Tydings spent two-and-a-half hours attacking McCarthy, labeling his charges "a fraud, a hoax, and a deceit" and suggesting that his actions were deserving of censure.[104]

In retaliation, McCarthy and his staff spent much of the summer and early fall fighting to ensure Tydings would not be reelected. McCarthy's staff helped manage campaign contributions to Tydings's opponent, John Marshall Butler, often ferrying money from McCarthy's office to Butler's campaign headquarters in Baltimore. It is likely that McCarthy and his surrogates were responsible for outlining Butler's overall campaign strategy, including working with Jon M. Jonkel, a Chicago public relations director. McCarthy's staff also performed electioneering and publicity work on Butler's behalf.[105]

From the Record was the climax of those efforts. According to editor Ruth McCormick "Bazy" Miller, the idea for it had come from McCarthy himself. McCarthy enlisted employees at Miller's newspaper the *Washington Times-Herald* to produce the content under the direction of Garvin Tankersley, the assistant managing editor, with whom McCarthy often partied and caroused.[106] The mailer cloaked itself in legitimacy by imitating the formatting of widely read newspapers, citing purportedly reliable sources such as the *Congressional Record* and Federal Bureau of Investigation reports, and recycling content that had appeared in respected, mainstream publications like the *Cincinnati Enquirer, Chicago Daily Tribune,* and *Los Angeles Times.* It reprinted a letter from J. Edgar Hoover—describing him as a man whose "straightforward manner" had made his word "as good as gold throughout the nation"—as evidence that Tydings had lied about dealings with McCarthy.

At the same time, *From the Record* actively manipulated readers through cherrypicked quotations, exaggerated reports of malfeasance, a composograph, and a general tone of conspiracy. A front-page story announced that Tydings "Sponsored Lattimore Lectures on Soviet Russia," linking two of McCarthy's two favorite targets. The same article noted that Joseph E. Davies, Tydings's father-in-law, was the "former Ambassador to Russia and author of 'Mission to Moscow,'" without giving context for his service or the content of his book. The majority of the tabloid's articles were dedicated to illustrating the faults of the Tydings committee report, repeatedly using McCarthy's favorite epithet for it: "a whitewash."

Another headline declared, "Tydings Committee Blamed for High Korean Casualties," with the article reporting that critics "are holding Sen. Tydings . . . to blame for the horrible cost of the war in Korea . . . Tydings

COMMUNIST LEADER Earl Browder, shown at left in this composite picture, was a star witness at the Tydings committee hearings, and was cajoled into saying Owen Lattimore and others accused of disloyalty were not Communists. Tydings (right) answered: "Oh, thank you, sir." Browder testified in the best interests of those accused, naturally.

FIGURE 8. *From the Record's* composograph of Millard Tydings and Earl Browder. Credit: University of Maryland Archives.

is the head of this Senate committee which controls the Department of Defense, and which failed to provide this country with the necessary equipment to protect the soldiers, sailors, and marines who have been sacrificed in Korea." It was a clear iteration of McCarthy's tactic of aligning himself with enlisted soldiers in the face of supposed bureaucratic inaction. It also questioned Tydings's manhood and patriotism, referring to him as "the Administration's whimpering lapdog" and accusing him of failing to properly support the military. Like other tabloids, *From the Record* even positioned itself as a protector of consumer rights, complaining that the federal government was spending "more than $55 million annually" to publish books with titles such as "The Interaction of Sex, Shape, and Height Genes in Watermelons," even though Tydings had nothing to do with that program.

Taking a page out of the *New York Evening Graphic's* playbook, *From the Record* included a composograph at the bottom of page four (the mailer's back cover). The image combined a photograph of Tydings with one of former Communist Party USA leader Earl Browder, making it appear as if Tydings was listening thoughtfully while a chin-stroking Browder made a point. Maryland voters would have been able to immediately recognize both men, as Browder often appeared in the region's major newspapers. Though the caption identified the image as a "composite photograph" (perhaps to protect against a lawsuit), the image was clearly designed to suggest an alliance between the two men. In all, 303,206 copies of *From the Record* were distributed throughout Maryland the weekend before the election.

The strategy worked. Though Maryland leaned heavily Democratic—the *New York Times* reported there were approximately 600,000 registered Democrats to only 250,000 registered Republicans—Butler won with slightly more than 53 percent of the vote.[107] It was Tydings's first campaign defeat during his thirty years in elected office.

"Many factors figured in the defeat of Senator Millard E. Tydings," wrote James P. Connolly of the *New York Times* four days later, "but the campaign cry against the veteran Democrat that was most often emphasized was his clearance of the State Department of the McCarthy charges of Communist infiltration."[108] Tydings called for an investigation, claiming that the Butler campaign had been built around a "tissue of lies" epitomized by *From the Record* and its use of photographic manipulation. A bipartisan Senate subcommittee unanimously concluded that Butler's campaign had acted in a "despicable" manner and that McCarthy had been involved in those deceptions, but also acknowledged that it had no mechanism for removing either Butler or McCarthy from their positions. Tydings retreated to his farm, while Butler established himself as a conservative stalwart during two largely unremarkable terms in the Senate.

The triumph of McCarthy's approach is most clearly evident in the case of Philip Jessup, a Yale- and Columbia-educated diplomat and legal scholar whom President Truman nominated as a delegate to the United Nations General Assembly in October 1951, in part to initiate a showdown with McCarthy. In March 1950 testimony before the Tydings committee, McCarthy had claimed that Jessup, then an adviser to the State Department, had "an unusual affinity" for communist causes.[109] Jessup hit back, saying that "Senator McCarthy's charges and insinuations are not only false but utterly irresponsible and under the circumstances reveal a shocking disregard for the interests of our country."[110]

Jessup's nomination was sent to a Foreign Relations subcommittee composed of three Democrats and two Republicans. In testimony there, McCarthy charged that Jessup had been associated with numerous communist front organizations, including sponsoring a dinner held by the American-Russian Institute and serving on the advisory board for the American Law

Students' Association. In McCarthy's view, Jessup had followed "all the twists and turns of the communist line."[111] Most dramatically, McCarthy alleged that Jessup was culpable in China's embrace of communism. Subcommittee member J. William Fulbright (an Arkansas Democrat) repeatedly called for McCarthy to present hard evidence of Jessup's communist leanings, decrying McCarthy's reliance on "guilt by association" and attacks on Jessup's wife. Fulbright's tough questioning ultimately caused McCarthy to explode.[112] Jessup served as his own best defender, likening McCarthy's use of an apparently doctored photostat to the by-then-infamous Tydings composograph.[113]

It appeared that McCarthy's case had been thoroughly dismantled. But, shockingly, the subcommittee still voted against Jessup's nomination. Senator Guy Gillette, the Democratic subcommittee member who crossed party lines to hand Jessup a 3–2 defeat, praised Jessup as "a man of great mental ability, a man of honesty and integrity, a careful student of international affairs, a teacher of international law with a wide, though varied, experience in international affairs," and characterized McCarthy's charges against him as creating a "warped and distorted picture." At the same time, Gillette claimed that the public had a lack of confidence in Jessup, even if that perception was the result of a "concentrated campaign of unfair and unprincipled attacks made on him."[114] His justification illustrated a primary reason why the tactics of gossip were successful: public opinion was so powerful that it could transcend the limitations posed by basic facts. If McCarthy and his allies could control the public's perception of an individual, institution, or event, they could successfully forward their agenda. The tools of gossip made the facts of the matter mere inconvenience.

The 1952 midterm elections further demonstrated just how successful McCarthy's tactics had been. If McCarthy had embraced anticommunism as a means of securing reelection, the strategy had worked. Running against former US attorney Thomas E. Fairchild, McCarthy won 54.2 percent of the vote. Though a number of contemporary reports noted that McCarthy "trailed the rest of the Republican ticket"—meaning that Republican presidential candidate Dwight Eisenhower and gubernatorial candidate Walter Kohler both received more votes than McCarthy—he still won by a comfortable margin.[115] Furthermore, both Eisenhower and Kohler were moderates who could appeal to more liberal voters; McCarthy's brusque approach had little chance of convincing voters to switch parties. Nor was it intended to: McCarthy's strategy was predicated on mobilizing his conservative base, not appealing to a broader electorate.

The 1952 elections gave Republicans control of the presidency and both houses of Congress. In letters to the editor of the *Washington Post* prior to election day, numerous writers had opined that the vote was a referendum on McCarthy. Commentators from across the political spectrum held that support for any Republican candidate amounted to support for McCarthy.[116] In the opinion of Roy Cohn, "Except for Ike, no politician stood taller than McCarthy, and even more than Eisenhower it was McCarthy who [had] swung the Senate to the G.O.P."[117] The Republican majority in the Senate assured that McCarthy would be given a committee chairmanship, and with it a higher platform from which to shout his accusations.

McCarthy's reliance on the tools of gossip was not accidental, just as his embrace of anticommunism was not accidental. Employing such tactics fit McCarthy's brash personality, enabled him to exploit the multiple anxieties that had begun to asphyxiate America during the early Cold War, and allowed him to address a segment of the populace that was prepared to hear those fears voiced in such a language. His success in using those tools also helped usher in a new era in American politics, one in which the style in which a message was delivered would often prove as significant as the content it contained.

UNDER THE KLIEG LIGHTS

On September 29, 1953, Senator Joseph McCarthy was married at Saint Matthew's Cathedral in Washington, D.C. The 1,200 invited guests were joined by 3,500 well-wishers who crowded around the church to congratulate the forty-four-year-old groom and his bride, the former Jean Kerr (the senator's longtime secretary). McCarthy wore a black morning jacket with tails, an ascot, and striped pants, the bride a white dress with an empire bodice and a lengthy, cathedral-style train. Among those in attendance were Roy Cohn, Vice President Richard Nixon, Senators Barry Goldwater, T. F. Green, and John F. Kennedy, CIA Director Allen Dulles, former Minnesota governor Harold Stassen, Washington socialite Alice Roosevelt Longworth, movie star Constance Bennett, and professional boxer Jack Dempsey.[1] The star-studded, politically diverse guest list and wide media coverage demonstrated how McCarthy had successfully married politics and celebrity. Newspaper accounts explicitly mentioned that the groom kissed his bride not at the altar but in the limousine between the church and reception hall. The newlyweds spent their wedding night in Washington and left the next day for a three-week honeymoon in the British West Indies, a location kept secret for fear of harassment. That vacation ended after only one week, when Cohn (reportedly the only person with direct access to the couple) called McCarthy back to Washington on "urgent business": there had been a break in the McCarthy subcommittee's investigation of espionage at the Fort Monmouth US Army base in New Jersey.[2]

McCarthy returned to the United States at the height of his power. The Republican triumph in the 1952 elections had given him the opportunity to lead the Senate Permanent Subcommittee on Investigations, a body he used to torment so-called security risks in the federal government. He was supported by a number of influential newspaper columnists, including Walter Winchell, George Sokolsky, David Lawrence, and Westbrook Pegler. President Eisenhower's Executive Order 10450, authorizing the investigation of all federal employees for the purpose of ensuring their "complete and unswerving loyalty to the United States," had seemingly validated McCarthy's investigations. Later that October, a front page article in the *New York Times* reported that 1,456 government employees had been "Ousted by U.S. as Security Risks in 4-Month Period."[3]

The Fort Monmouth investigation promised to be McCarthy's most explosive inquiry yet. Approximately thirty miles south of Manhattan, the fort was home to the Army Signal Corps' research arm. It had been under investigation for nearly a decade for allegedly harboring a communist espionage ring, a claim made plausible by the fact that Julius Rosenberg had worked there during World War II. Now, aided by reports from the FBI, McCarthy's subcommittee seemed to be on the verge of cracking that ring open. Throughout the fall of 1953, McCarthy dominated the headlines, with reports claiming that the tough interrogative tactics he and Cohn employed were causing witnesses to wilt under pressure and confess their involvement in a wide-ranging conspiracy.[4]

At the same time, forces were in motion that would help ensure McCarthy and Cohn's downfall. Both men were attempting to secure preferential treatment from the Army for G. David Schine, a McCarthy staffer and friend of Cohn's who had recently been drafted. Cohn's repeated, threatening requests would put McCarthy and the Army on a collision course that ultimately exploded in a series of transformative congressional hearings in the spring of 1954. Elsewhere, in the pages of tabloid newspapers and magazines, the coded language of gossip columnists, and the low hum of cocktail party chatter, rumors were circulating that Cohn and McCarthy—and Hoover—had some of the same "perverted" sexual proclivities they denounced in their opponents. There were even whispers that McCarthy's recent wedding was an attempt to silence that talk. And although McCarthy's cult of personality had helped Republicans win major gains in 1952, members of the Eisenhower administration were entertaining the possibility that the rumors about him and his staffers were not so far-fetched after all.[5]

From the time Cohn joined McCarthy's staff in January 1953 to his resignation in the summer of 1954, the very circumstances that had enabled the ascendance of both men facilitated their downfall. Specifically, McCarthy and Cohn's opponents were able to portray the pair as "deficient" by appealing to the same understanding of surveillance state masculinity that had been essential to their rise. Those adversaries relied on many of the tactics and channels that McCarthy and Cohn had employed, including the use of hyperbolic accusations in the pages of gossip magazines and coded language in more august settings. The fact that those rumors gained traction speaks not only to their believability, but to the fact that the nation's dual fixations on national intelligence and aggressive masculinity were helping to establish and enforce the parameters of political discourse in an era of anxiety.

*

Seeing an opportunity to climb the rungs of power, Roy Cohn asked a mutual friend to introduce him to McCarthy in December 1952. Knowing that the senator had recently been appointed chairman of the Committee on Government Operations (CGO), Cohn hoped to convince McCarthy to hire him as general counsel for the CGO's most significant subcommittee, the Permanent Subcommittee on Investigations. A nervous Cohn thought he had blown the interview when the pair first met at New York City's Hotel Astor, but he got the job and joined the committee staff in January 1953.[6]

Both logistics and politics drove McCarthy's hiring of Cohn. McCarthy had built a reputation as a hunter of communists but lacked the field experience and legal skill necessary for the investigations themselves. Cohn had both; he was one of the most experienced anticommunist litigators in the United States and possessed an astute legal mind. Despite his relatively privileged background, Cohn was able to convince McCarthy that he shared the senator's well-publicized distaste for Washington's establishment elite.[7] While Cohn had attended one of New York's best prep schools and an Ivy League university, his uncouth demeanor was a far cry from that of the men who populated Washington's elite. Hiring the Jewish Cohn also helped McCarthy counter the charges of anti-Semitism he had been battling since 1950. Aware of that value, Cohn commonly referenced his religious background as a way of helping his boss.[8] For his own part, McCarthy was so sensitive to the oft-repeated accusation that he largely refrained from mentioning Julius and Ethel Rosenberg in public even though they were the most famous communist subversives of the period.[9] He also asked conservative columnist and friend George Sokolsky to investigate the roots of the anti-Semitism charge by polling leading members of the Anti-Defamation League (Sokolsky concluded that the ADL was not arrayed against McCarthy).[10] Despite those efforts, accusations of anti-Semitism continued to hound McCarthy; a headline in the January 1954 issue of *Confidential* asked, "Is Senator Joe McCarthy Anti-Semitic?"[11] Hiring Cohn also made sense because he enjoyed the support of two powerful McCarthy backers, Sokolsky and Hearst Corporation CEO Richard E. Berlin.[12]

Cohn's primary competition for the position was Robert F. Kennedy, a recent graduate of the University of Virginia Law School who had worked at the Department of Justice before leaving to manage his brother John's 1952 Senate campaign.[13] Robert's influential father Joseph had long been a McCarthy backer, but McCarthy was hesitant about hiring a fellow Irishman, and one from a famous Democratic family to boot. Furthermore, Joseph had already spent much of his political capital with McCarthy during John's campaign, during which McCarthy did the Kennedys a favor by not campaigning on behalf of Republican incumbent Henry Cabot Lodge in what proved to be an extremely close race. Knowing McCarthy had already helped one of his sons, Joseph Kennedy did not push the senator to hire Robert.[14] J. Edgar Hoover, Vice President–elect Nixon, and twenty senators attended a private party celebrating Cohn's hiring.[15]

Almost immediately, Cohn became McCarthy's most trusted confidant. "The union of McCarthy and Cohn was the partnership of kindred souls," journalist Fred J. Cook wrote, "each fueling the excesses in the other."[16] Cohn's immediate responsibilities included collecting informants, organizing depositions, preparing witness examinations, and managing the ever-present media. "He's a brilliant young fellow," McCarthy said of Cohn. "He works his butt off and he's loyal to me. I don't think I could make it without him."[17] Reporters quickly recognized Cohn's importance and wrote about him as the brains of McCarthy's operation, not only in regard to legal matters but in the entire structure of the pair's anticommunist campaign.[18] Nominally McCarthy's assistant, Cohn came to fill roles as the senator's secretary, legal counsel, stand-in, press liaison, business partner, organizer, adviser, travel agent, and confidante.

Cohn also populated McCarthy's staff with like-minded allies. One of Cohn's first acts was to suggest that the senator hire G. David Schine as an unpaid consultant. Schine was a young, handsome Harvard graduate and hotel heir whom Cohn had met in late 1952 through either George Sokolsky or Irving Saypol.[19] Born in the same year, Cohn and Schine had become fast friends and fixtures on the New York City nightlife circuit. The actress Piper Laurie, who was dating Schine at the time and would ultimately become engaged to him, recalls that when she went out with Schine and Cohn the latter "always had a pretty girl on his arm."[20] Schine was hired due to his purported expertise in fighting communism: he had written a six-page pamphlet on the topic that was placed next to the Gideon Bibles in each Schine-owned hotel. Cohn also claimed—erroneously—that Schine had developed a "psychological warfare program at present in use by the United States Navy."[21]

In actuality, the pamphlet and its author were widely regarded as farcical. At Harvard, Schine had hired a secretary to attend his classes for him and was chauffeured around campus in a limousine. In social circles he was best known for having what was perhaps the world's largest private collection of cigars.[22] As for the infamous pamphlet, journalist Richard Rovere noted that "it puts the Russian Revolution, the founding of the Communist Party, and the start of the First Five Year Plan in years when these things did not happen. It gives Lenin the wrong first name. It confuses Stalin with Trotsky. It confuses Marx with Lenin."[23] G. David Schine was many things, but an expert in anticommunism was not one of them.

So why did Cohn ask McCarthy to hire Schine? The question is made more intriguing by the fact that Schine's profile contained the establishment hallmarks that Cohn and McCarthy claimed to detest: his family was wealthy, he had attended elite, East Coast schools (Andover and Harvard), and he was nothing if not entitled.[24] Though numerous journalists and historians have opined that Cohn pushed for the hiring due to a sexual attraction toward Schine (or even because the pair were already involved), their partnership appears to have been primarily predicated on Cohn's desire to leverage the Schine family's social and media contacts to secure increased publicity.[25]

Cohn fully embraced his new boss's tactics, including his propensity for attacking the State Department as a haven for homosexuals. Less than a week after Eisenhower was inaugurated, Cohn led the questioning of State Department official John E. Matson before an executive session (a private meeting) of the Senate Permanent Subcommittee on Investigations.[26] Matson testified that numerous State Department officials had been involved in the removal of incriminating documents from the personnel files of Department employees accused of homosexual activity. In a couple of cases, Matson even identified the employees who continued to occupy spots on the payroll long after accusations had been leveled at them. Matson's claims led to the deposition of five other members of the State Department's Records Division who underwent aggressive questioning by McCarthy and Cohn. Two weeks after his appearance at the executive session, Matson testified at an open hearing of the committee, claiming that cover-ups and lax regulations were allowing the unchecked growth of "a flourishing clique of homosexuals" at the State Department.[27] McCarthy used Matson's testimony to justify his call for increased scrutiny of State Department officials, and accused Matson's boss of "incompetency" and perpetrating "the most inexcusable act I've ever seen on the part of an officer."[28]

In his first months working for McCarthy, Cohn also used accusations of homosexuality to attack Samuel Reber, a foreign service officer then serving as deputy high commissioner to Germany. A graduate of Groton and Harvard, Reber came under scrutiny when members of the Eisenhower administration began work at the State Department. On March 17 and 19, Reber underwent a "security investigation" during which he was subjected to a series of interviews and threatened with a polygraph test.[29]

It is unclear how McCarthy's staff learned about Reber's admission that he had engaged in homosexual activity while an undergraduate. But the information may have come from Hoover. Despite Hoover's claims to the contrary, the FBI did "collect and compile information about Reber, information placed in their Sex Deviates File, which existed for the express purpose of disseminating such information to purge gays from federal employment."[30] Though there is not currently enough evidence to prove that Hoover passed that information to Cohn and McCarthy, it seems likely. Cohn himself approached Reber, telling the diplomat that his past would be exposed if he refused to resign. Reber capitulated, and in late May retired.[31] Though contemporary news reports gave no reason why Reber had decided to step down, McCarthy later suggested that Reber had been "dropped" because he was exposed as a "security risk," a euphemism commonly applied to homosexuals.[32] In the wake of Reber's resignation Arthur Schlesinger Jr. summed up the establishment's fears in a letter to Adlai Stevenson, noting that at the State Department "people are being fired or forced to resign on the most extreme, tenuous and unsupported charges, whether political or sexual. The most eminent recent victim is, of all people, Sam Reber, who apparently is being forced out on a vague homosexual allegation, fifteen years old. And the thing is reaching the point where . . . the very fact of accusation makes a man, in the eyes of these thugs, a future risk."[33] Schlesinger's analysis is particularly noteworthy because he himself had been central to advocating a "hard" masculine approach to foreign policy in his 1949 book *The Vital Center*.

Perhaps Cohn's most powerful target during his early days working for McCarthy was Charles W. Thayer, a lifelong diplomat who had led the State Department's international broadcast division (commonly known as the Voice of America) from 1947 to 1949 before filling a variety of positions at the American consulate in Germany. The urbane, connected Thayer was a paragon of the establishment: he played polo, smoked a pipe, and had been educated at St. Paul's, a stuffy prep school in Concord, New Hampshire. Though Thayer graduated from West Point, he had resigned his Army commission after only a few months to join the foreign service.[34] McCarthy had begun investigating Thayer after receiving a series of anonymous letters accusing the diplomat of participating in homosexual activities and harboring communist sympathies. His investigation was not unprecedented; in the late 1940s, Hoover had Thayer investigated after the diplomat had incensed him by publicly complaining about the slow pace of Bureau security checks on prospective employees.

Thayer's governmental connections had enabled him to dodge Hoover's earlier attacks. He was the brother-in-law of another McCarthy target, Charles "Chip" Bohlen, and McCarthy claimed that Bohlen and other allies in the State Department had been instrumental in protecting Thayer from dismissal. That protective halo seems to have cracked after Hoover provided McCarthy and Cohn with a memo outlining what the Bureau had learned about Thayer's homosexuality.[35] When Thayer was ultimately forced to resign his post in late March, McCarthy claimed victory and suggested to the *Washington Post* that Thayer's downfall was a result of mistakes he had made while leading the Voice of America.[36] In actuality, Thayer's resignation had been part of a negotiated deal between conservative Republican members of Congress and the White House, with Thayer sacrificed in exchange for Bohlen's confirmation as ambassador to the Soviet Union. McCarthy was opposed to the agreement but was outmaneuvered by Republican leaders in the Senate.

Taking their scrutiny of Thayer a step further, McCarthy and Cohn began an investigation of the International Information Administration (IIA), an arm of the State Department that was charged with providing information about the United States to foreign audiences through libraries, print publications, and radio. Operating out of the Schine family's private suite at the Waldorf Towers in New York City, Cohn and Schine interviewed dozens of IIA employees in a search for communist agents or evidence that their publications had been infiltrated.[37] Although those interviews failed to produce any evidence of conspiracy, they allowed Cohn and McCarthy to create publicity for themselves while causing further headaches for the State Department.

The inquiry expanded in April 1953 when Cohn and Schine went to investigate the IIA's operations in Western Europe. The precise goal of the trip was unclear—seemingly even to Cohn and Schine. Early on, Cohn diplomatically claimed that the trip's purpose was "to collect evidence in the form of statements or of affidavits which would help the Senate committee to save the United States taxpayers money and to make the United States Information Service more effective."[38] However, Cohn would later hold that he and Schine were "looking into the information program and the people who work for it." Furthermore, in listing their qualifications for the job, Cohn pointed to his and Schine's anticommunist credentials rather than any kind of management or accounting experience.[39]

In practice, the trip was an anticommunist fishing expedition and publicity grab. Over eighteen days Cohn and Schine visited nine cities, rarely spending more than a dozen waking hours in each.[40] Though their inquiries were criticized for being notably brief—it took them a half-hour to determine that the 1,200 employees of Munich's Radio Free Europe were not communists—the pair "found time to call a press conference in almost every city."[41] At McCarthy's request, Hoover cabled his contacts in Europe ahead of Cohn and Schine's arrival. But Hoover seemed suspicious of the expedition and urged restraint, noting in his message to the legal attaché in Paris that "should [Cohn and Schine] contact you, extend usual courtesies but use caution and avoid any disclosure of confidential files."[42]

Foreign service workers privately groused about the damage Cohn and Schine's visit did to America's reputation and to morale in the State Department. The diary of a reporter who accompanied Adlai Stevenson on his 1953 world tour records that an embassy press officer in Vienna claimed that "the Cohn and Schine visit was disastrous to our prestige in Austria, especially as the Embassy had to give these two clowns the VIP treatment."[43] The mayor of Bonn said that "McCarthy has done more to hurt America abroad in 8 months than Soviet propaganda did in 8 years."[44] The diary shows that members of the diplomatic corps regarded McCarthyism with a mixture of fear and contempt. There was no question that McCarthy and his underlings were influential, with one diplomat telling Stevenson that "infiltration of the [State] Department by McCarthy spies is so widespread that Under-Secretary Bedell Smith must go over to CIA if he wants to file a confidential message to an Ambassador and not have it reported to McCarthy."[45] Though Cohn and Schine were feared, they were also regarded as easily fooled. Woody Walner, the American chargé d'affaires in Belgrade, "admitted he was somewhat appalled at the news that Cohn and Schine were coming to Belgrade and decided that the only way to handle them was to pick up the ball before they did. So they no sooner arrived at the airport than Walner announced 'Boys, you are now in the fightingest anti-Soviet country in Europe.' The boys were so impressed that they didn't cause much trouble during their visit."[46]

State Department officials were not the only ones nonplussed by Cohn and Schine's visit. In increasingly caustic reports, the European press dubbed the two Americans "scummy snoopers," "distempered jackals," and practitioners of "latter-day fascism."[47] After the pair's appearance in Rome, the *Manchester* (England) *Guardian* opined that "their limited vocabulary, their self-complacency, and their paucity of ideas, coupled with the immense power they wield, had the effect of drawing sympathy for all ranks of the United States diplomatic service who had to submit to this sort of thing."[48] When Cohn and Schine left England, the *London Evening News* published a snide farewell in the form of a poem based on an old vaudeville routine.[49]

While Cohn and Schine were regarded as an unfunny joke by the American diplomatic corps and European press, their actions reverberated in the United States. In the wake of their trip, the Eisenhower administration conducted a far-ranging review of the IIA. Hundreds of employees were fired or forced into retirement, the Voice of America saw a number of its foreign-language programs cut, and numerous IIA libraries overseas were either shuttered or purged of texts that could be regarded as communistic.[50] Bending to public pressure, Eisenhower also proposed a reorganization of the country's international information services that took the oversight of such programs away from the State Department, ultimately leading to the foundation of the United States Information Agency. Along with the Eisenhower Administration's efforts to purge the United Nations of homosexual employees and pressure allies into eliminating gay men and women from their own governments, Cohn and Schine's investigations of the IIA represented the internationalization of the Lavender Scare.[51]

Cohn and Schine's European trip was also noteworthy because of the way their relationship was portrayed by the media. European newspapers depicted them as hapless and confused, a pair of unsupervised boy scouts or bumbling honeymooners. There was much discussion of a spat between them in a German hotel lobby. The *Abendpost* of Frankfurt, Germany, re-

ported that following a disagreement stemming from Schine's lack of organization, "it was observed that Mr. Schine batted Mr. Cohn over the head
with a rolled-up magazine. Then both disappeared into Mr. Schine's room
for five minutes. Later the chambermaid found ash trays and their contents
strewn throughout the room. The furniture was completely overturned."[52]
The tone of those reports deliberately suggested a "lover's quarrel." One
British newspaper went so far as to title a story "Cohn and Schine, the
Two London Lovers."[53] Cohn and Schine were undoubtedly aware of the
possibility that their tour could be read in that light; when checking into
hotels, they asked for rooms that were adjoining but separate, repeatedly
emphasizing to all within earshot that they "don't work for the State Department."[54] Cohn repeated the same joke later in the trip when a hotel
assigned him and Schine to the same room.[55]

American newspapers reprinted many of the anecdotes. Some—
particularly those opposed to McCarthyism—began to suggest that Cohn
and Schine's connection extended beyond friendship. In so doing, those
writers and editors employed numerous forms of innuendo, some more
subtle than others. Piper Laurie, Schine's then-girlfriend, recalls reading
articles in a variety of Los Angeles newspapers which intimated that Cohn
had a sexual interest in Schine.[56] For the first time, Americans were exposed to the suggestion that Cohn was not as masculine as he wanted them
to believe. The overwhelming majority of prior media coverage on Cohn
had been positive, a narrative helped along by sympathetic columnists such
as Winchell and Sokolsky. Some commentators had even portrayed Cohn
as a saving grace, noting that his legal expertise and experience fighting
communists would help reign in some of McCarthy's more extreme tendencies.

Coverage of Cohn and Schine's Europe trip changed that narrative. It
made them seem inexperienced, ill-prepared, and unable to gauge the communist threat. It invited public scrutiny of their relationship. Centrally, it
raised questions about their manhood: even if Cohn and Schine were not
homosexuals, their behavior marked them as abnormal and transgressive.
Cohn had labored to construct a masculine persona as an intelligent, savvy,
and connected leader capable of handling complex situations. In Europe,
he was confused, inept, and incompetent. The trip's failure also invited further criticism of McCarthy, who had based his public image on blue-collar
strength but was now associated with two men whose entitled behavior had
raised eyebrows. It was a crack in a façade that would shatter during the
Army-McCarthy hearings.

In the summer of 1953, Schine was reclassified as draft eligible. His status had been reexamined courtesy of reporting by McCarthy's old foe Drew Pearson, who claimed that both Schine and Cohn had used flimsy excuses to avoid military service.[57] McCarthy and Cohn tried to secure Schine a posting that would allow him to retain his position as an adviser to the subcommittee, including Washington-based assignments with the Army and Navy or employment with the CIA or Department of Defense. Their efforts failed, and Schine entered the Army as a private in September.[58]

Cohn went to extraordinary lengths in trying to secure preferential treatment for his friend. He tried to have Schine commissioned as an officer, get him stationed near Washington or New York, and secure him concessions such as extra weekend passes and relief from the more menial tasks of an enlisted man. Over nine months, Cohn lobbied Army higher-ups through sixty-five telephone calls and nineteen meetings.[59] Increasingly frustrated by the Army's refusal to capitulate to his demands, Cohn resorted to vulgarly berating Army leaders, including Secretary of the Army Robert Stevens and Army General Counsel John G. Adams. Though Mc-Carthy did not have a strong opinion about Schine either way, the senator's loyalty to Cohn led him to support his chief counsel.[60]

While some have seen in Cohn's attitude a romantic obsession with Schine, a more likely explanation can be found in the aggressive masculinity that was elemental to Cohn's status as a power broker. Cohn had become so powerful and so adept at getting his way that he was likely shocked when the Army refused to immediately buckle under his usual tactics of backroom horse trading and outright bullying. Upon realizing the Army would not engage in a quid pro quo, Cohn reverted to brinkmanship in an effort to demonstrate that he, McCarthy, and their allies held more power than the Army.

Angered by Cohn's treatment, on March 11, 1954, Army representatives released to the press a list of Cohn's attempts to secure preferential treatment for Schine. Most significantly, the report delineated a number of Cohn's threats to Army leadership.[61] Originally seventy pages, the document was truncated to half that length when the Army decided to censor some of Cohn's more vulgar language, deeming it inappropriate for the public record.[62] The front page of the *New York Times* announced, "Army Charges McCarthy and Cohn Threatened It in Trying to Obtain Preferred Treatment for Schine."[63] The *Times* wrote that "the report quoted Mr. Cohn as threatening on one occasion to 'wreck the Army' and make certain that Robert T. Stevens was 'through' as the Secretary of the Army" and that "at another time . . . 'Mr. Cohn stated to Mr. Adams that he would teach Mr. Adams what it meant to go over his head'" before concluding that "the report is expected to spur growing demands for Mr. Cohn's ouster."[64]

The day after the report was released, McCarthy and Cohn called a press conference to deny the Army's claims. In addition, McCarthy "angrily charged the Army with attempted blackmail in an effort to stop his exposure of communists."[65] To support this charge, McCarthy and Cohn fabricated eleven internal memos, backdating them so that they appeared to be responses to Army attempts at "blackmail," and then released the phony documents to the press. The memos purported to include records of conversations in which numerous Army principals had made demands, including the charge that Army counsel John G. Adams had blackmailed Cohn and McCarthy into securing him a $25,000-a-year position in a New York City law firm.[66] During a March 14 appearance on *Meet the Press*, Cohn charged that the Army used Schine as a "bargaining point," suggesting it would grant the newly enlisted private special privileges if McCarthy and Cohn agreed to "get off the Army's back" about purported security failures at Fort Monmouth. Cohn also charged that the Army tried to tempt him and McCarthy with "a specific proposal . . . that we go after an Air Force base wherein Mr. Adams told us there were a number of sex deviates [and that such an investigation] would make excellent hearings for us."[67] Cohn's phrasing of the offer—that it would "make excellent hearings"—is telling in its implicit admission that the hearings were performative as well as probative, designed to attract attention as much as to solicit information.

Concerned with the escalating tensions, the other members of the Senate Permanent Subcommittee on Investigations called for a full inquiry into all charges and Cohn's conduct in particular. Four days later, during a heated closed-door meeting, an agreement was reached. The *New York Times* reported that the "subcommittee voted today for a complete public exposition of [McCarthy's] latest dispute with the Army. The Permanent Subcommittee on Investigations' decision requires a full inquiry, with sworn testimony, into charges of possible perjury and other misconduct in the controversy."[68] Emphasizing to the press that he had voluntarily relinquished his position of chair for the moment to Karl E. Mundt of South Dakota, McCarthy seemed confident that he could still quarterback the proceedings. The hearings were scheduled to begin on April 22, 1954.

FIGURE 9. McCarthy on the cover of the March 8, 1954, edition of *Time*. Credit: Ernest Hamlin Baker, Time, Inc.

*

In the lead up to the Army-McCarthy hearings there was a second drama playing out in the columns of little-read newspapers, oblique references by mainstream political reporters, cocktail party conversations, and the pages of gossip magazines. Stories claiming that McCarthy was a homosexual had circulated seemingly since the moment he entered the national spotlight in early 1950. And insinuations about Cohn and Schine clearly made a mark in the press following their spring 1953 trip to Europe. In the eighteen months preceding the start of the Army-McCarthy hearings these allegations had grown in both number and breadth of circulation. Though never explicitly reported in the mainstream press, they were distributed widely enough to influence the way audiences reacted to McCarthy and Cohn at the hearings. The rumors would shape the tenor of the hearings as much as the headline-grabbing squabbles over demands for special treatment and access to information. Rumors about McCarthy's homosexuality were made more believable by his association with Cohn, just as rumors about Cohn's homosexuality were made more believable by his association with McCarthy. It was a case of bidirectional guilt by association.

The rumors about McCarthy and Cohn are telling in their existence, their dissemination, their believability, and their impact. The fact of their existence speaks to the moment's anxieties and the way that McCarthy and Cohn's opponents thought their power could best be undermined. The way they were disseminated illustrates the growing power of a mass, polyphonic media to distribute rumor and insinuation to a broad audience. Their believability demonstrates the degree to which aspects of McCarthy's and Cohn's public personas could be read as insufficiently masculine, as well as the degree to which many Americans regarded homosexuals as a cabal that could infiltrate positions of power. And, centrally, the impact those rumors had on McCarthy and Cohn's ability to retain positions of influence in the burgeoning national security and surveillance states reveals the degree to which those entities were constructed around a paternalistic, homophobic understanding of gender and sexuality.

The origins of the rumors about McCarthy are nearly impossible to determine, but they seem to have begun in Wisconsin. There also does not appear to be any evidence of those rumors circulating before McCarthy's February 1950 charges made him a national political force. In one sense, the fact that the rumors seemed to blossom only after McCarthy attained national notoriety would suggest that they were born of an effort to discredit him. But it is possible that the rumors always existed but failed to enter the historical record until McCarthy was noteworthy enough to make them worth repeating in print.

The greatest purveyor of gossip concerning McCarthy's sexuality was his nemesis Drew Pearson. Pearson was a collector of all kinds of gossip about McCarthy, including stories about his drinking, gambling, financial improprieties, and sex life (including that McCarthy was sleeping with Jean Kerr long before their romance was public). But beginning in 1950, Pearson built an especially robust repository of information related to McCarthy and homosexuality, including affidavits from individuals who claimed to have had homosexual encounters with McCarthy or knew of people who said they had. Pearson first reported on the issue in a May 1950 radio broadcast in which he accused a McCarthy staffer of having been arrested for homosexual acts.[69] Pearson had previously attacked McCarthy for his actions during the Malmedy massacre trial, his acceptance of money from the Lustron Company and Pepsi-Cola, his inability (or refusal) to repay bank loans, his relationships with individuals thought to be tied to organized crime, his shady campaign financing, and his supposed granting of "quickie" divorces while a judge in Wisconsin. He had even sent two of his staff's best investigative reporters, Jack Anderson and Ronald May, to Wisconsin to dig up more evidence. Of all those accusations, McCarthy took the greatest umbrage at Pearson's claim of the homosexual staff member, complaining that "because [Pearson] failed to use the boy's name [he] had cast suspicion on every man who had worked in [McCarthy's] office."[70] Pearson knew of McCarthy's private reaction to the story because Fred Blumenthal, a researcher on Pearson's team, had been able to interview McCarthy without the senator knowing for whom he worked. Blumenthal's reconnaissance demonstrated to Pearson that stories about homosexuality were those that most angered his enemy. The story about the homosexual staff member would eventually be repeated in the course of a seventeen-part *New York Post* series criticizing McCarthy in September 1951.[71]

The earliest appearance in Pearson's files of a homosexual rumor about McCarthy himself is in a May 1950 letter from W. O. Berry of Waterloo, Iowa. Along with a note voicing support for Pearson, Berry enclosed a copy of an unsigned letter he had sent to "Mr. Jacob [sic] R. McCarthy" accusing the senator of perversion: "And as for sex perverts—That is a fine subject to discuss and have made public—People are saying that you are no angel in that respect yourself. Your low-level thinking boomeranged. Supposed [sic] you do some thinking with the front part of your brain and give the base of your brain a rest. We are all sick of your vulgarity."[72] Though Berry does not directly accuse McCarthy of homosexuality, it is reasonable to assume his reference to "perverts" was such an allusion, considering how the term was being used by government officials and members of the media. Berry's letter to McCarthy was perhaps prompted by Pearson's radio broadcast about a homosexual on McCarthy's staff, as it was sent a little less than a fortnight after that show had aired. Despite its vagueness, Berry's accusation demonstrates that rumors about McCarthy's "perversion" had been circulating as early as the spring of 1950.

That same month, Pearson exchanged correspondence with Bill Evjue, editor of the Madison, Wisconsin, *Capital Times* and a longtime McCarthy critic. It appears that Pearson was contacting as many McCarthy opponents as he could in search of ammunition. Evjue pushed Pearson to pursue the homosexuality angle, claiming that a contact had heard that "McCarthy is receiving a lot of letters asking why he remains a bachelor and why he has shown no affinity for women."[73] In addition, Evjue provided Pearson with an anonymous letter signed "A University Student," positing that McCarthy's obsession with homosexuality and ribald jokes meant that "the Senator is a victim of repressed homosexuality himself."[74]

The most valuable evidence came from individuals who claimed to have witnessed sexual contact between McCarthy and other men. In a handwritten, signed statement witnessed by May and Anderson, a man named R. Garth Lewis stated that his friend William McMahon, an official with the Milwaukee County Young Republicans, "described to me an experience which [McMahon] had with Senator Joseph McCarthy. McMahon told me that he had spent a night—or part of it—with Senator McCarthy in a hotel room in Wausau, Wisconsin, during or about the time the Young Republicans State Convention was being held in that city. McMahon further stated to me that he, McMahon, and Senator McCarthy had engaged in sexual acts with each other in their hotel room. McMahon also showed me what he said were the hotel receipts, which he had saved. I also know it to be common talk among some homosexuals in Milwaukee whom I ran across in the White Horse Inn in Milwaukee on several occasions that Senator McCarthy has engaged in homosexual activity at other times."[75] Though the statement was undated it appears to have been made during the fall of 1951. Both Anderson and May attempted to contact McMahon and confirm the story but were apparently unsuccessful.[76]

On October 20, 1951, Anderson summarized for Pearson the dirt he had collected in Wisconsin, including a report that upon learning of his election to the Senate, McCarthy "burst into a hotel room, ecstatic with joy, and kissed the young Republican president, Lloyd Tegge, on the mouth." Anderson also provided the address of an eyewitness to that incident.[77] Anderson's inquiries into McCarthy's sex life were not solely focused on homosexuality; he also relayed to Pearson a rumor that McCarthy had been sleeping with Mickey Johnson, another one of his secretaries.[78]

Pearson's interest in gossip on McCarthy became so well known that allies in Washington began to share information with him. In December 1951 Senator William Benton of Connecticut forwarded to Pearson a letter he had received from a lieutenant in the US military. The officer claimed that McCarthy had picked him up at "the Wardman Bar [in Washington, DC] and took me to his home. While I was half drunk he performed sodomy on me . . . A number of other officers I know have had similar experiences with him." The writer—whose name is censored in the archival copy of his letter—concludes by saying, "If you want me to testify for you, I will be glad to do so."[79] It appears that similar stories were circulating around Wisconsin at the time; journalists for the *Milwaukee Journal* later reported they had been offered affidavits from other men who claimed to have had sexual relations with McCarthy, but the newspaper declined to print them.[80]

The rumors reached J. Edgar Hoover courtesy of Attorney General J. Howard McGrath, who contacted the Bureau director after being handed the lieutenant's letter by Senator Carl Hayden of Arizona. Hoover then contacted McCarthy, who asked the FBI to investigate the letter's source. McCarthy seemed to think the letter may have been written in the offices of either Pearson or Benton, and suggested the FBI analyze the typewriters in both offices.[81] Likely with an eye to his ongoing legal battle with Pearson, McCarthy wanted to ensure the FBI's investigation would be (in Hoover's words) "very circumspect" so that McCarthy could pin any public leak on Pearson.[82] In a memo to his deputies at the FBI, Hoover reported that McCarthy was "very anxious to have [the investigation] done most thoroughly and that he expected a lot more [rumors] like this before the election."[83] The subsequent enquiry uncovered another letter, written in November 1951 and signed by a civilian, that repeated similar accusations about McCarthy, notably that he "hung around bars for the purpose of taking men to his one bedroom apartment."[84] Hoover ultimately concluded that both letters were forgeries, likely produced because "the homosexuals are very bitter against Senator McCarthy for his attack upon those who are supposed to be in the government and are retaliating in this manner."[85] McCarthy also fought back against Pearson directly. He called for his supporters to boycott one of Pearson's radio sponsors, the Adam Hat Company, and initiated a number of civil suits against Pearson.[86] Fred Blumenthal alerted Pearson that McCarthy had assigned two of his own investigators to research Pearson's background. Notably, the news made Pearson worried that McCarthy would bring to light an old accusation that Pearson had sexually propositioned an African American boy.[87] In February 1951 Pearson sent his lawyers an affidavit with "the real facts" about that encounter in preparation for a slander suit that never came.[88]

Despite this treasury of evidence, Pearson never accused McCarthy of homosexuality in his column, on the radio, or during television appearances. Given that Anderson and May were having difficulty attaining sworn affidavits from the men who claimed to have had sexual relations with McCarthy, Pearson may have been concerned about his ability to defend himself against a libel suit. He instead chose to pass on the information he had collected to someone who would print it, *Las Vegas Sun* owner and editor Hank Greenspun.

Greenspun was a fervent anticommunist but also styled himself as a defender of individual liberties. As a result of those commitments, he had used his daily editorial column to criticize McCarthy, whom he dubbed "the Wisconsin cry baby."[89] When McCarthy came to Las Vegas to stump for George "Molly" Malone in 1952, he retaliated, calling Greenspun "a former communist" and chastising his newspaper as a local iteration of the *Daily Worker*.[90] Greenspun, who was in the audience, approached the stage and attempted to shout down McCarthy. A smiling, surprisingly calm McCarthy tipped his cap to the crowd and walked offstage, leaving an unoccupied microphone that Greenspun then put to use as he verbally eviscerated McCarthy for the better part of an hour.[91]

Following that incident, Greenspun contacted Pearson and Bill Evjue for information he could use against his new archenemy. Pearson shared his file on McCarthy's alleged homosexual encounters, and Greenspun immediately put the rumors to work in a column on October 25, 1952. He first discussed allegations against two members of McCarthy's staff, Charles Davis and Ed Babcock, claiming that Davis had been dishonorably discharged from the Navy for "admitted homosexuality" and Babcock had been arrested on charges of homosexual solicitation by a vice squad in Washington. In providing the names of the two men, Greenspun took a step that Pearson had declined to. Greenspun then turned to McCarthy himself. "Joe McCarthy is a bachelor of 43 years," Greenspun wrote, "he seldom dates girls and if he does, he laughingly describes it as window dressing." Drawing directly from Pearson's files, Greenspun leveled the charge that McCarthy had "engaged in illicit acts" with William McMahon during a Young Republicans convention, and reported that "it is common talk among homosexuals in Milwaukee who rendezvous at the White Horse Inn that Sen. Joe McCarthy has often engaged in homosexual activities." In conclusion, Greenspun pointed to a piece of supposed evidence his readership had heard themselves: "the persons in Nevada who listened to McCarthy's radio talk thought he had the queerest laugh. He has. He is."[92]

It is difficult to know how quickly and how broadly Greenspun's claims spread. Greenspun forwarded a copy of his October 25 column to Pearson, indicating in an attached note that it had become his most famous article.[93]

McCarthy biographer David Oshinsky claims that "by 1953 those rumors were freely discussed on Capitol Hill" and that "newsmen and even senators joked about 'the boys' in McCarthy's office."[94] Though it appears that McCarthy was deeply troubled by the rumors, he was advised by a lawyer for the Anti-Defamation League that a libel lawsuit against Greenspun would inevitably lead to McCarthy being forced to answer to the accusers' claims under oath. Apparently not willing to risk further publicity or memorialization in a court record, McCarthy declined to sue at that juncture—though he would later charge Greenspun with "inciting violence" when he predicted that McCarthy would meet a violent end (the suit was dismissed). When McCarthy married Jean Kerr in September 1953, rumors flew that he had done so to help quell gossip about his sexuality. Regardless of the accuracy of *that* rumor, the talk did seem to make McCarthy more aware of his sexual persona; during a 1954 trip to Milwaukee, McCarthy reportedly rushed out of the Mint Bar upon learning that it was a "hangout for queers."[95]

Pearson did use his nationally syndicated column to hint at a romantic relationship between Cohn and Schine.[96] Here, too, Pearson was drawing on information he had been provided by friends and researchers; Justus Lawrence, a New York City public relations official and friend of Pearson's, wrote in April 1953 to corroborate the reports of Cohn and Schine bickering like spouses in Europe, claiming that "the same incident happened at the Boca Raton Hotel, owned by Myer Schine, father of David, recently this winter when both boys were visiting there. There was a tremendous fight in which Schine, 6′ 4″, hit little Cohn, who is an elongated midget."[97] In July 1953 Pearson presented the pair as "a 'vaudeville' team . . . two slapdash young men . . . who zoomed across Europe last winter [sic] exuding drama and headlines at every stop," making a point of noting that each man was single. He described Schine as "a handsome, haughty 25-year-old kid with a dreamy look in his eye, who sometimes slaps Cohn around as if they were dormitory roommates" and derisively referred to the pair as "McCarthy's two junior G-Men."[98] That same month, Pearson reported that observers thought Cohn and Schine's "operations [in Europe] were a bit unusual" and opined that McCarthy's fellow senators "are wise-cracking in Capitol cloakrooms that Senator McCarthy's staff would be a good place for a budding young psychiatrist."[99]

The following March, on the eve of the Army-McCarthy hearings, Pearson recounted the Cohn-Schine spat in Frankfurt and asked, "Why the persistent attachment of Cohn for Schine? Why was he almost savage in his demands that Schine be transferred back to New York? Answer: The two have been inseparable friends for some time."[100] By using the term "for" to characterize Cohn's feelings for Schine rather than the more grammatically appropriate "to," Pearson implied a more dependent relationship. Pearson's passing suggestions had more weight because of his reputation; readers had come to expect Pearson's columns to include personal gossip.

In the wake of publishing those intimations Pearson received a handful of letters from individuals either echoing or buttressing his charges. On June 2, 1954, a reader from Lancaster, Pennsylvania, wrote to report that "everywhere I hear that McCarthy, Cohn, and Schine are homosexuals. It has been intimated in your column and in the Alsops'. Isn't there any way in which you can break this story and completely wreck this terrible man?"[101] A month later, Pearson exchanged letters with Philip H. Bagby, a former foreign service officer who purported to have evidence of Cohn and Schine participating in homosexual activities.[102] Around the same time, a man whose old college roommate knew the Schine family wrote to Pearson with evidence of Schine's effeminacy, including his "fear of physical pain," his (earlier) efforts to dodge military service, and "the time that David was beaten at tennis by a young girl."[103]

Pearson and his readers were not the only ones interested in the rumored Cohn-Schine coupling. Two decades after McCarthy's death, *Washington Post* reporter Murrey Marder recalled that "among the reporters there was certainly [a] lot of arched eyebrows and suspicions and so forth. And there were some vague innuendos that would come up from time to time . . . There was also a cover for that even then, though, and that was the fact that Schine was so rich. So even then, even among the sniggerers, the question was whether it was because Schine was so rich and picking up the bills with the hotel chain money, or was it a homosexual relationship or a combination of the two of them."[104] In their column on March 15, 1954— four days after the Army released its account of Cohn and McCarthy's attempts to secure preferential treatment for Schine—Joseph and Stewart Alsop reported that "the country and the Congress have been shocked as seldom before by the sordid tale of Sen. McCarthy, committee counsel Roy Cohn, and their pet, Pvt. David Schine. The shock would be immeasurably greater, however, if the Army Department had told the whole story." The Alsops claimed that one of the key pieces the Army had excised from its report "contained certain suggestions as to the nature of the McCarthy-Cohn-Schine relationship," that "the implication is clear that Cohn possessed a peculiar power over McCarthy," and wrote of "Cohn's feverish desire to be of service to Schine."[105]

At the White House, members of the Eisenhower administration who had become increasingly frustrated with McCarthy and his endless hunt for subversives in government searched for a way to weaken him and his allies. The files of Assistant Secretary of Defense Fred Seaton contain a hand-written note illustrating the lengths to which White House staffers had gone to locate damaging material on McCarthy and his staff. The slip of paper appears to be an early 1954 note that Seaton may have written during a phone conversation: "Chauffeur of Shine [sic] knows of Cohn-Shine [sic] / thinks ready to testify / drove Ft. Dix-Cohn to Philly points + N.Y. / engaged in homo-sexual acts in back of car." The note closes by listing the phone number and address of the driver, Percy B. West.[106] Seaton's papers do not appear to include any further reference to Shine's chauffeur and no testimony was ever taken. But the note demonstrates that the Eisenhower administration and the Department of Defense were both interested in using charges of homosexuality to confront McCarthy. The strategy was not the sole purview of political columnists and gossip journalists.

Though the topic was never openly discussed in major news outlets, rumors about McCarthy's homosexuality did enjoy some level of distribution. The two most important vehicles were both reprints of Greenspun's writings. In April 1954 the Las Vegas Sun published Greenspun's columns on McCarthy as a booklet. It included a series of pieces that Greenspun published in February 1954 that featured further attacks on McCarthy's politics, methods, and character. Greenspun questioned McCarthy's masculinity, placing the word "man" in quotations when it referred to McCarthy and writing that the senator's "normal gait . . . is a little bit to the left of manly." He also repeated his accusations of homosexuality, including the claim that Jean Kerr had blackmailed McCarthy into marriage after learning of his "frailties." Playing on Schlitz beer's famous marketing slogan, Greenspun referred to McCarthy as "the queer that made Milwaukee famous."[107]

Shortly thereafter, Greenspun's columns were reworked into an article for the gossip magazine Rave. Rave typically mixed the celebrity gossip of Confidential with a healthy smattering of pin-up photographs. Its June 1954 cover story promised a look "Inside Jane Russell," the Hollywood sex symbol who had recently starred alongside Marilyn Monroe in Gentlemen Prefer Blondes. That issue, which hit newsstands in May, also featured "Secret Lives of Joe McCarthy," a fifteen-page tour-de-muckraking that printed what Greenspun had collected from Pearson in a slightly reorganized narrative. Subtitled "The Incredible Story Washington Tells in Whispers," the article gave readers access to information about McCar-

SECRET LIVES OF

JOE McCARTHY

The incredible story Washington tells in whispers

As readers of this magazine should know, it's only once in a blue moon that RAVE touches politics or politicians. This is one of those times when the moon is a big, bright blue. The article you're about to read was written by Hank Greenspun, editor and publisher of The Las Vegas Sun, and ran in that newspaper in February of this year. Although it is unquestionably the most startling and explosive story to come out of Washington in 25 years, no magazine or newspaper in America has dared to reprint it.

THE NEWSPAPERS of the country are not playing fair with the American people. There is a great deal of information which many papers possess, and which is not being printed, so that the people might better be in a position to realize what is taking place in the country today.

What is the strange hold which McCarthy has on government officials? Why does the newspaper industry, almost to a man, fear him? Who is McCarthy?

McCarthy has been operating through a defense mechanism caused by a guilt complex. When McCarthy started on his first large

SENATOR JOE McCARTHY
"Where does his allegiance lye?"

59

FIGURE 10. *Rave's* June 1954 issue reprinted Hank Greenspun's allegations that McCarthy was homosexual. Credit: Private collection.

thy's sexual proclivities that was purportedly well-known among capital insiders.[108] Like much political gossip during the early Cold War, it characterized the federal government as a citadel full of secrets.

A second gossip magazine, *Celebrity*, featured a cover story in its August 1954 issue provocatively titled, "The Men in McCarthy's Life." Released in mid-June, at the tail end of the Army-McCarthy hearings, the *Celebrity* article made no explicit reference to McCarthy's sexuality. But it was certainly suggestive. The article's opening line, "The men who have figured importantly in Sen. Joseph McCarthy's life are, in a way, strange bed-fellows," placed the group in a metaphorical boudoir.[109]

Again, it is difficult to discern how large of an audience was exposed to the McCarthy rumors. *Celebrity* lasted for just eighteen months, and circulation figures are not available for *Rave*, which published only twenty-three issues between April 1953 and January 1958.[110] That said, a five-year run would suggest that the magazine had a large enough readership to remain financially viable for much of that period. The magazine's circulation must also have been significant enough to worry the subjects of its salacious stories, as it attracted libel suits from Hollywood stars Humphrey Bogart, James Mason, and Terry Moore.[111]

The papers of Utah senator Arthur V. Watkins contain some of the only documentary evidence that the rumors about McCarthy's sexuality reached a general audience. In his role as the head of the senatorial subcommittee investigating charges of misconduct against McCarthy following the conclusion of the Army-McCarthy hearings, Watkins received hundreds of letters from writers across America expressing their opinion on McCarthy. Many of those letters reference the masculinity of McCarthy, his associates, and his opponents, and a handful explicitly refer to McCarthy's sexuality. On August 7, 1954, a writer from Muncie, Indiana, asked Watkins if it would be possible for his subcommittee to use the Greenspun articles in the *Las Vegas Sun* and *Rave* as evidence against McCarthy.[112] Demonstrating his awareness of the rumors, Watkins replied that "articles from magazines cannot be accepted [by the subcommittee] unless presented by the author, who can verify his charges."[113] A letter from a writer in Coulter, Pennsylvania, enclosed the *Las Vegas Sun*'s booklet and threatened, "If the statements in the covers of this book are true and you men do not fire that Jesuit Joe McCarthy, clear out of Washington, as far as pertaining to having any thing to do with the legislation, then all who has [sic] had any thing to do with this foreign-controlled representative, are as dumb as an ox, or just as crooked as he Joe McCarthy is. Don't think the people are not getting next to what is going on behind those closed doors, and if continued much longer there will be some fireworks in this country. If the Senate wishes to retain the good graces and respect of the people in this country, then you men will fire Joe McCarthy out on his —, bag and baggage."[114] Beyond the aggressive posturing and anti-Catholic prejudice, what is noteworthy about this letter is the writer's firm belief that the government was harboring a classified agenda hidden from citizens, a sentiment likely fostered by the larger spirit of secrecy and suspicion.

By the time the Army-McCarthy hearings began, public discourse had been influenced by a firmly established and rarely questioned set of beliefs about the relationship between national security and gender identity. Central among these was the conviction that a specific form of masculine identity (and an intertwined heterosexual identity) was a prerequisite not only for protecting America's welfare generally, but for countering communists specifically. Though the concept had deep roots in American political history, it was popularized during the First Red Scare, matured as a result of J. Edgar Hoover's leadership of the FBI, and enjoyed its most recent resurgence courtesy of McCarthy and Cohn's employment of homophobia as a tool in their anticommunist inquiries. Concurrently, many—if not most—Americans had been introduced to the idea that something was amiss with the gender and sexual identities of McCarthy, Cohn, and Schine. There is no evidence that a majority of Americans thought of the three men as gay or even that a majority were aware of the rumors of their homosexuality. But there appears to have been enough evidence, conjecture, and insinuation published in the media to suggest that the gender and sexual identities of all three men were atypical, even if that abnormality was amorphous and ill-defined. Finally, a large number of Americans seem to have been open to the idea that the full story of the McCarthy-Cohn-Schine relationship had not been exposed. Part of this suspicion was likely born of the Cold War's general obsession with secrecy and intelligence, but it also had roots in a more specific understanding of information as a key weapon in the fight against international communism, the increasing popularity of gossip magazines, and the emergence of political intrigue as a source of gossip. Furthermore, those suspicions seemed to be confirmed by the Army's detailed dossier on the behind-the-scenes actions of McCarthy and Cohn on behalf of Schine. That document fed off the same political-cultural zeitgeist that had fueled the growth of gossip magazines: the pervasive narrative that every piece of mainstream news had "more" to it, a secret sequence of events known only by the informed few. In many ways, the Army-McCarthy hearings promised to bring light to the shadows.

*

The hearings proved to be a political disaster for both McCarthy and Cohn. The majority of analysis about them—both from contemporary commentators and historians—has focused on the famous "have you no decency" charge that the Army's lawyer Joseph Welch directed at McCarthy, viewing the moment as the climax of a national feeling of disgust with McCarthy and Cohn's tactics. In those tellings, McCarthy's fall was the product of his deviation from acceptable political decorum; McCarthy's lack of politesse led to his downfall rather than his political beliefs themselves. But that rendering proves myopic. McCarthy and Cohn fell as much because they failed to live up to the standards of surveillance state masculinity that they had helped define. They had claimed the title of national defenders on the basis of their manhood; the hearings made their failings on that front visible to an unprecedented audience.

The hearings were an elaborate performance staged for millions of spectators. In the words of media historian Thomas Doherty, "the Army-

McCarthy hearings proved a media milestone not only because of the inherent significance of the event but because television coverage itself determined the meaning of the event . . . what was new and surprising to senators and spectators alike was that the duel was as much televisual as political."[115] Live television coverage was provided by two of the four major networks, ABC and DuMont, while CBS and NBC broadcast highlights every evening.[116] Just as the Kefauver hearings had inspired Robert Harrison to make political gossip a focus of *Confidential*, they motivated ABC news director Fritz Littlejohn to provide gavel-to-gavel coverage of the McCarthy hearings. It has been estimated that 45 million viewers watched at least a portion of the hearings live, while 120 million people watched the nightly roundups or read print coverage. In Boston, the ABC affiliate reported its highest ratings to date, and in early May the live coverage on ABC and DuMont accounted for 60 percent of all television viewership.[117] The *New York Herald Tribune* described the rapt attention of viewers in Manhattan: "Most noticeable in bars and restaurants in the midtown area was the silent attention which the hearings received. The normal buzz of conversation was hushed . . . Many saw part of the proceedings on television sets in the windows of radio and electrical-appliance stores. One group of three men, out for lunch, stopped for 'just a minute' to see the show. After twenty minutes one of them said, 'Come on, let's go. I'm hungry.' One of his companions silenced him with, 'Look, you, this is important. I'm going to stay till they break for lunch even if I have to go without.' The three stayed."[118] Ultimately, 188 hours of live coverage were aired, and the hearings became the most-watched live event to that point in television's infant history.

For many viewers, television promised more than wide distribution. Even prior to the hearings, interested observers had opined that television would expose a "truth" about McCarthy that had been obfuscated by print reporters. In a 1952 letter to the editor of the *Washington Post*, one writer objected to how an Associated Press story had covered McCarthy, arguing, "It should be obvious to you and the Associated Press that television is going to impose a standard on you such as you have never been obliged to meet before. A great many of your readers know perfectly well that Senator McCarthy didn't give a 'free-swinging speech to a cheering, overflow crowd.' Granted we took our prejudices with us—but we were there."[119] The letter expressed a common assumption in the early years of television, that the medium's immediacy promised two revelations. First, it would provide audiences with a view of events that was unfiltered by the biases of newspaper reporters and radio commentators. To many, television promised to prevent journalists' manipulations. Second, there was a belief that television would reveal the truth about those who appeared on it. Television—especially live broadcasts—projected a certain aura that provided viewers with a novel way to interact with national events. Furthermore, many viewers expressed a faith in the medium regardless of their views on McCarthy himself; some believed that live television would reveal him to be a bullying demagogue, while others were convinced it would expose the degree to which the national press had treated him unfairly.

Those sentiments resurfaced when it was announced that the late 1954 hearings on whether the Senate should censure McCarthy would not be televised. The office of censure committee chairman Arthur Watkins was flooded with citizen correspondence protesting the decision, with many writers arguing that televisual coverage was necessary because print journalism was inherently biased and would not provide a "truthful" or "accurate" report.[120] Mrs. E. S. Hersh of Bayville, New Jersey, wrote to express her frustration:

> How else are we to know except by television? We can not tell by reading the newspapers. Proof of that was at the other hearing [the Army-McCarthy hearings]. We all listened and watched every day at the other hearings and then at nite would read the accounts of it in the papers. Two from Phila and one from NY, daily[,] and the paper accounts were never as it actually happened. They were all against Joe McCarthy and the reporters of these papers either wrote what they hoped had happened or else it was their interpretation of what did happen. None of it being true. I will never believe any thing I read in a newspaper again . . . Please have the hearings televised.[121]

Other writers opposed the ban for reasons including worries over censorship (which was often called a "communist" or "Nazi" tactic), a belief in the public's right to know, and a desire to "expose the truth." Again, those who voiced faith in television's power to "expose the truth" occupied both sides of the McCarthy issue, with some believing that the "truth" would expose a communist conspiracy against McCarthy, while others trusted that "the more people who see McCarthy in action," the more they will realize his "evil" nature.[122] Referring to the upcoming censure hearings, an editorial in the conservative-leaning *New York Daily News* opined that it was "waiting with no little interest to see whether a lot of anti-McCarthy newspapers will slant and discolor their reports of this investigation. They were doing a pretty vicious job of slanting on the McCarthy-Cohn-Schine-Stevens hearings, until they woke up to the fact that the television audience was checking up on their dishonesty . . . *The News*, of course, did not slant its reports."[123]

The Army-McCarthy hearings dominated the news cycle across television, print, and radio. Each morning's *New York Times* carried a front-page article and included a transcript of highlights within the front section. Radio listeners in major metropolitan areas could hear much of the proceedings broadcast live, especially the afternoon sessions.[124] The hearings were so packed with photojournalists that Chairman Mundt was forced to declare "the flash-bulb period" to be over before witnesses could speak.[125]

The nonstop media attention made it clear to the participants that they were performing for an audience beyond the crammed caucus room. They would have been particularly aware of television due to the large camera setups and hot Klieg lights that had been installed. Undoubtedly, each participant did his best to adopt a posture that would endear him to that audience and demonstrate his predisposition to leadership. And the metrics by which those performances were gauged were particularly focused on questions of masculinity. If McCarthy and Cohn had become accustomed to performing surveillance state masculinity, then during the hearings that performance became more literal. They, like the other men in the room, sought to display what Cold War America believed to be the markers of masculinity: confidence, boldness, aggressiveness, heterosexuality, strength, preparedness, intelligence, stoicism, and wit.

A tone of masculine jousting pervaded the hearings. Every primary participant was male, as was every witness. In a space largely given over to verbal communication, many of the participants tried to dominate by raising their voices and shouting each other down with "points of order" and other bits of parliamentary procedure. These efforts fit with social psychologists' findings about how men try to use the volume and timbre of their voice to control conversations and retain hegemony.[126] The participants' habit of trading barbs can even be seen as a contemporary version of "flyting," which was "a North European tradition of a ritual exchange of insults or boasting between two parties which is both crude and often scatological, but at the same time skilled and creative."[127] Though Mundt was nominally chair, his control over the proceedings was tenuous and the major players rushed to fill the resulting vacuum.

Both McCarthy and Cohn tried to continue their masculine performances. Cohn attempted to demonstrate his intelligence, wit, and resolve, laughing at the appropriate moments while trying mightily to dictate the tenor of his testimony. As was his wont, Cohn often sought to make his power felt through backchannels. He privately told Robert Kennedy that he planned to "get [Democratic committee member and McCarthy opponent Henry M.] Jackson."[128] He also threatened Kennedy physically; some contemporary reports noted that the two men had a physical altercation outside the caucus room after one day of testimony in early May.[129]

McCarthy's own performance during the hearings was somewhat paradoxical. In most instances he was combative, an old pugilist trying to enact his will through brute force. He commonly shouted over his opponents and was snidely dismissive, as in this exchange with Joseph Welch, the Boston lawyer hired to represent the Army at the hearings:

> MR. WELCH: Have you some private reservation when you take the oath that you will tell the whole truth that lets you be judge of what you will testify to?
>
> SENATOR MCCARTHY: The answer is that there is no reservation about telling the truth.
>
> MR. WELCH: Thank you, sir. Then tell us who delivered the document to you!
>
> SENATOR MCCARTHY: The answer is no. You will not get the information.
>
> MR. WELCH: You wish then to put our own interpretation on your oath and tell us less than the whole truth?
>
> SENATOR MCCARTHY: . . . You can go right ahead and try until doomsday. You will not get the names of any informants who rely upon me to protect them.[130]

This sort of verbal jousting was not uncommon, both in content and tone. McCarthy attempted to position himself as the ultimate guardian of the "truth," echoing his earlier appeal for citizens with information on subversives to circumvent an unsympathetic government and send their evidence directly to him. He also employed blunt, absolutist language (e.g., "until doomsday") as a means of illustrating his assuredness and dedication to his cause. When not fortifying his own masculinity, McCarthy was busy questioning the virility of his adversaries. In one exchange, McCarthy repeatedly suggested to Stevens that he could ask for a recess if he became tired; not wanting to appear weak, Stevens refused.[131]

McCarthy also continued to gay-bait his opponents. The hearings' first full day featured the testimony of Major General Miles Reber, who charged that Cohn had pressured him to commission Schine as an officer in the Army. General Reber was the brother of Samuel Reber, the State Department official whom Cohn and McCarthy had forced into retirement after learning of his admission that he had participated in homosexual activity decades prior. As a means of countering General Reber's accusations, McCarthy asked him, "Are you aware of the fact that your brother was allowed to resign when charges that he was a bad security risk were made against him as a result of the investigations of this committee?"[132] The meaning of the phrase "security risk" was clearly known by all present, as subcommittee counsel Ray Jenkins had employed the term earlier that day in referencing the investigation into homosexuals at Fort Monmouth.[133] General Reber corrected McCarthy, stating that his brother had "retired" rather than "resigned" and claimed that he had not previously heard that his brother had been under investigation by McCarthy's subcommittee. McCarthy then moved onto another point, apparently satisfied that his characterization of Sam Reber as a "security risk" had made it into the record.

Concurrently, there were moments when McCarthy sought to forge a connection with his Army opponents as men. At times, McCarthy appeared to smile knowingly at his adversaries, as if all were participating in some grand joke. These flashes often emerged when the hearings approached the back-slapping atmosphere of the proverbial locker room. On the hearings' second day, Secretary of the Army Robert T. Stevens testified that McCarthy had once requested "a few weekends off for David Schine . . . perhaps for the purpose of taking care of Dave's girl friends."[134] The winking phrasing caused those present to burst into laughter, including McCarthy and, a beat later, Cohn. On another occasion, when Army counsel John G. Adams testified that there were rumors of a "homosexual ring of generals" on a base in an unnamed southern state, Senator John McClellan and counsel Ray Jenkins interrupted Adams's testimony to make the secretary confirm that the southern state in question was neither of their home states—Arkansas and Tennessee, respectively. After this interlude received a chuckle from the audience, Senator Mundt asked Adams to confirm that the base was also not in South Dakota, joking that some might mistakenly locate it in "the south." Riotous laughter followed, including from McCarthy and Cohn.[135]

Masculinity was not only of concern to the men in the hearings, it was also of central import to those who watched them on television. Again, the correspondence sent to Arthur Watkins in late 1954 is illustrative. Writers often referenced McCarthy's masculinity, whether they were defending or attacking him. One writer from New Mexico noted that Americans were "entitled to hear and to see McCarthy defend such conduct as becoming a Senator and especially as a *man*."[136] Another letter in support of McCarthy capitalized the key term: "as it stands now, McCarthy is the Man in this country. If we only had more like him. Any Man that upset the Commies as he has, they are afraid of him so we must keep him in the Senate where he can do the most good."[137] Others described McCarthy as "the big[g]est man in the Senate today" and "the greatest patriot of all" who "shines out as a man, the greatest man in Washington today."[138]

An attorney from Houston defended McCarthy's brash demeanor, writing that "I was reared among the rattle snakes of southwest Texas and I do not know how their deadly attack can be successfully dealt with by sweet-tempered, indulgent, peaceful, quiet, bashful, congenial and compassionate attitude toward them, and it is my opinion that anyone who condemns Senator McCarthy for dealing with communist sympathizers as he has done is guilty of 'negligent homicide' as it applies to the Government of the United States of America."[139] Another Texan echoed, "It takes a rough and tough fighter to fight subversion. You cannot fight such with a powder puff."[140] Writers with similar viewpoints opined that though McCarthy might be gruff, uncultured, and use rough language, at least he was on the side of right. Furthermore, he needed to be tough to successfully counter his dishonorable communist opponents.

The commentary of a writer in Wichita, Kansas, showed that McCarthy's blue-collar masculine persona had influenced his political reputation: "McCarthy is tough, a fighter. He came up the hard way, the admirable way. He knows the America for which he is fighting, the place where you can go as far as you want, if you have the ambition and ability and work hard enough. You couldn't be weak and stand up to the concentrated attack McCarthy has taken from the communist conspiracy and those dupes who have been sold a bill of goods by the communists."[141] A writer from South Orange, New Jersey, likened McCarthy to three of the era's paragons of masculinity: the Marine Corps, the nation's general-cum-president, and the country's finest boxer, writing, "I believe that the fiery McCarthy with a talent for hunting Communists should be encouraged. So he does miss a few swings so what, so did the Marines so did our Great President so did Jack Dempsey. But McCarthy never quit pitching did he? I also think that the Secretary of the Army was the weakest man we ever had at the head of the bravest Army in the world."[142] A writer from upstate New York expressed his opinion that manhood was essential to successfully governing the United States and asked Watkins, "When, Senator, are we going to stand up and act like MEN?"[143]

It was also common for citizens who wrote to Watkins *criticizing* Mc-

Carthy to use gendered language. A writer from Greensboro, North Carolina, condemned McCarthy by writing that "he should be censored [*sic*]. What has happened to the manhood of the Senate? Do we have a bunch of namby-pambies in the Senate? Are they afraid of McCarthy? Haven't they the courage or the character to stand up to him?"[144] One writer described McCarthy and his staff as "a group of 'so-called men' too contemptible to describe."[145] Another letter referenced a recent car accident that McCarthy was in: "Speaking of bravery—the *cowardly* Senator McCarthy allows himself to be hospitalized because of an elbow scratch!!!"[146] Similarly, the anti-McCarthy writers used gendered language to positively describe his opponents as "real men," "red-blooded courageous Americans," and congratulated them on their "manly defense of America."[147] One writer praised Watkins directly: "I'm glad that we have at least one Senator who is not a coward and has [the] manly principles to oppose McCarthyism."[148]

The most damning indictment of McCarthy and Cohn's masculinity came via the television coverage of the hearings, both the live broadcast and the nightly recaps. The pair's greatest problem was that their televisual avatars did not match the personas depicted in favorable newspaper reports. Though both men had previously appeared on television news shows such as *Meet the Press*, the hearings were the first opportunity for a widespread audience to see them for an extended period of time and in a less-scripted format. Similarly problematic was the fact that as the "accused," McCarthy and Cohn spent the hearings constantly on the defensive, legitimizing the charges against them by suggesting to the audience that a defense was necessary.

Cohn was largely silent until he took the stand, but his body language betrayed his discomfort. When the camera turned to him, he was usually looking down and rarely smiled. The broadcast image of Cohn was of a pudgy young man with a puffy visage, swollen lips, and large ears. The shadows across his face caused by his deep-set eyes and heavy brow were made darker by his slumped posture. His eyes constantly searched the room, as if seeking a route of escape. It was a drastic departure from the newspaper photographs of Cohn out on the town, double-dating with Schine. A number of times, especially when McCarthy made particularly glaring errors of judgment, television cameras captured Cohn in silent torture, seemingly searching for a convenient hole in which to hide.

When Cohn did open his mouth, he came across as arrogant and entitled. In a series of self-aggrandizing moments, Cohn referred to himself in the third person, declaring that "Roy Cohn is here speaking for Roy

Cohn, to give the facts."[149] Further complicating Cohn's statements was his heavy New York accent, which undermined his public image by making him sound more like a stevedore than a major player in the halls of power.

Cohn's constant denials and use of confusing legalese could not match the knowing telegenic repartee of Army counsel Joseph Welch, a grandfatherly figure who seemed to wink at the camera as he delivered each quip, no matter how biting. Newspapers ran columns dedicated to recounting Welch's wit, emphasizing how his deft use of folksy vernacular enabled him to build a connection with the public.[150] Cohn was woefully unable to engage in such banter, establishing a disparity between himself and Welch that clearly injured Cohn's sense of pride and hurt his standing as a legal expert and skillful litigator.

Though the persona McCarthy had cultivated was less glamorous than Cohn's, the Wisconsinite still had a certain reputation to uphold with respect to both his investigative prowess and capacity for leadership. On television, he failed to project either. Audiences had come to expect a certain suaveness from their detective heroes, even if hard-boiled crime fiction and Hollywood film noir had depicted investigators who were less clean-cut than Hoover's G-Men. Furthermore, there was a certain level of refinement they expected from those entrusted with leading the country.

On the contrary, McCarthy appeared frumpy and disheveled. His combover failed to hide his receding hairline and bald spot, and his ill-fitting suits always appeared wrinkled. In Cohn's words, "with his easily erupting temper, his menacing monotone, his unsmiling mien, and his perpetual 5-o'clock shadow, [McCarthy] did seem the perfect stock villain. Central casting could not have come up with a better one."[151] McCarthy seemed uncertain, peppering his questions and statements with numerous "ums" and "ahs." Worse, McCarthy mistakenly seemed to think his asides were as witty and charming as Welch's. New York Times columnist James Reston took McCarthy to task on May 30:

> The Senator from Wisconsin is a bad-mannered man. No session ever goes by without somebody being cut down by his sharp tongue. Testimony can go along smoothly for an hour, but as soon as the Wisconsin Senator enters it, there is usually a quarrel. Nobody escapes his aim—not the President of the United States, or the Secretary of the Army, or even the members of the subcommittee or its counsel. He tells Senator Symington before 10,000,000 people or more; "Oh, be quiet!" He refers contemptuously to the 63-year-old Mr. Welch as "this young man." He invites Government employees to defy the order of the President and the Attorney General. He slurs the honorable

family name of Joseph Alsop, and refers to any newspaper that opposes him as *The Daily Worker* . . . At one time or another he has accused almost everybody who has opposed him of telling lies, usually for bad motives. He presents himself as legislator, investigator, policeman, jurist and judge, and discusses anticommunism as if he invented it.[152]

To his growing number of detractors, television coverage had revealed McCarthy not as the scrappy defender of freedom he purported to be, but a bully with, as Welch famously said, "no sense of decency."

Most importantly, McCarthy and Cohn's opponents attacked their masculinity with subtle though deliberate suggestions that they were homosexuals. That queering began on the hearings' first day, when Stevens identified McCarthy and Cohn's efforts on behalf of Schine as a "perversion of power."[153] Given the implications of the term "perverted," it is highly likely that Stevens (or his speechwriters) selected it for its insinuative value. The phrase led the headlines the next day, with appearances on the front pages of the *New York Times*, *Baltimore Sun*, *Los Angeles Times*, and *Washington Post and Times-Herald*. The *Post and Times-Herald*'s headline actually read "McCarthy and Aides Perverted Power to Force Promotion of David Schine, Stevens Testifies in Army Inquiry," and was placed above a photograph depicting Cohn and McCarthy facing each other and leaning in, almost as if for a kiss. The layout meant that a quick look could have led a reader to initially see only "McCarthy and Aides Perverted."[154]

McCarthy and Cohn also had their sexuality called into question via their association with David Schine, whose sexuality became a recurring topic. Less than a week into the proceedings, Ray Jenkins was questioning Secretary Stevens about whether he was aware of the preferential treatment Schine had received while in the Army, including being exempt from working in the base kitchen, not wearing his uniform on base, and riding in the cab of a truck while his fellow soldiers remained in the truck bed. At one juncture, Jenkins asked Stevens, "Did it come to your attention that this private, David Schine, was hiring his fellow soldiers and paying them money to clean his rifle?"[155] At the suggestion that Schine had his (male) peers "clean his rifle," the audience and participants in the normally stern proceedings erupted in laughter. Many of the senators, including McCarthy, enjoyed a loud laugh, though Cohn sat stone-faced. Whether the double-entendre was intended or not, the vast majority of those present were clearly aware of the rumors surrounding Schine and Cohn.

Two days later, Joseph Welch questioned McCarthy associate Jim Juliana. Cohn and McCarthy had previously introduced into evidence a

FIGURE 11. Joseph McCarthy, flanked by Roy Cohn and G. David Schine, during the 1954 Army-McCarthy hearings. Credit: Eve Arnold, Magnum Photos.

photograph depicting Schine and Stevens smiling at each other, an apparent attempt to suggest that such goodwill would have been impossible had Stevens been pressured in the way the Army had described. After some investigation the Army legal team discovered that the photograph was a cropped version of a larger image that actually showed Stevens smiling at a third person, Colonel Kenneth Bradley. Juliana, the McCarthy staff member who had enlarged the image for use during the hearing, was called to the stand to identify who had instructed him to crop the photograph. Like everybody else in the room, Welch knew Cohn was behind the alterations. He was just having trouble getting Juliana to admit it under oath.[156]

This moment led to the famous "pixie-fairy" exchange. After Juliana repeatedly plead ignorance as to the photograph's precise origin, Welch asked whether he thought the photograph "came from a pixie."[157] Whether Welch's comment was planned or born of a moment of frustration is uncertain, though it did fit with other sarcastic quips he had made throughout the hearings. What is clear is that at least some of the laughter that followed was directed at Cohn. For Cohn, this moment was only worsened when Joe McCarthy oafishly suggested the Army's counsel was an expert in such matters. Seeing an opening, Welch sharpened his barb by replying that a "pixie is a close relative of a fairy" and asked if his definition had "enlightened" McCarthy.[158]

By the mid-1950s the terms "fairy" and "pixie" had long occupied a place in American English as code for "homosexual man." The former had dated to the end of the nineteenth century and had recently been printed in Norman Mailer's best-selling novel *The Naked and the Dead* as slang used by soldiers.[159] It also had appeared in gossip tabloids from *Broadway Brevities* to *Confidential*, and had been explicitly banned "when used in a vulgar sense" by the "Profanity" section of the Hollywood Production Code.[160] The journalist Frank Mallen used "fairy" to reference male homosexuals throughout *Sauce for the Gander*, his 1954 memoir of working for the *New York Evening Graphic*. "Pixie" was of more recent vintage, with crime novelist James M. Cain's 1937 novel *Serenade* being one of the first uses in print.[161] Welch was thus referencing a shared cultural vernacular that was likely understood by many of those watching the hearings, perhaps even a majority. He was also suggesting that in addition to partaking in homosexual affairs, Cohn possessed a particularly feminine character. And even if some members of the television audience did not immediately catch the reference, the resulting cocktail party conversations—"Why did everyone laugh at that exchange?"—would have fostered talk about Cohn's homosexuality and, possibly, the rumors surrounding McCarthy.

Though there were other coded references to Cohn and Schine's alleged homosexuality during the hearings, the pixie-fairy exchange was uniquely important. It was the hearings' most explicit reference to rumors that Cohn, McCarthy, or Schine was gay. Furthermore, such an exchange was only possible because of years of gossip that had circulated either in coded language or through underground channels. Finally, it aired the rumors to a live nationwide audience. Due to the limitations on their distribution, Greenspun's columns, the reprinted booklet, the *Rave* article, and even the more mainstream, subtle references to McCarthy and Cohn's rumored queerness never fostered enough of a critical mass to profoundly influence the national conversation. The television feed of the hearings, on the other hand, was immediately seen by millions and thus had a greater chance of affecting public discourse about McCarthy and Cohn than any previous iteration of the rumors.

The insinuations continued. Exactly one month after the pixie-fairy exchange Cohn was again the target of innuendo, this time while on the witness stand:

> MR. JENKINS: In all fairness, Mr. Cohn, isn't it a fact that [Schine] is one of your best friends? We all have our best friends. There is no criticism of you on that account.
>
> MR. COHN: No, of course not, sir.
>
> MR. JENKINS: We have friends whom we love. I do. And the relationship between you and Dave Schine has been very close for the past two years, hasn't it?
>
> MR. COHN: Yes, sir. He is one of a number of good friends I am proud to have.
>
> MR. JENKINS: Have you known him socially?
>
> MR. COHN: I have.
>
> MR. JENKINS: Visited in his home?
>
> MR. COHN: Yes, sir.
>
> MR. JENKINS: Has he visited in your home?
>
> MR. COHN: Yes, sir.
>
> MR. JENKINS: And perhaps you have double-dated together. There is no reflection on anything about that. You are both single men as we understand it.
>
> MR. COHN: We have been on double dates, sir . . .[162]

The signals were subtle, but to anyone aware of the rumors about Cohn and Schine, the reasons were clear why Jenkins included the word "love," took care to place each man in the other's home, and referenced both men's marital status. At another point, when questioning Army counsel John G. Adams, Jenkins asked if Adams tried to "break the news gently" to Cohn that Schine would probably be shipped overseas, once again causing the audience to laugh at the hint that the Cohn-Schine relationship was so close as to necessitate a certain degree of tenderness when Adams delivered the bad news.[163] Jenkins's suggestive remarks are particularly illustrative because they ran counter to his normally diffident approach to questioning witnesses; by that point in the hearings even the timid Jenkins had embraced a more aggressive tone.

But such innuendo was not the sole purview of the lawyers. Senator Mc-

Clellan hinted at a possible sexual relationship between Cohn and Schine at the outset of his interrogation of the former:

> SEN. MCCLELLAN: First I will ask you if you have any special interest in Mr. Schine?
>
> MR. COHN: I don't know what you mean by 'special interest.' He is a friend of mine.
>
> SEN. MCCLELLAN: I mean in friendship or anything else that would bind you to him closer than to the ordinary friend.
>
> MR. COHN: Nothing. He is one of a number of very good friends whom I have. I am fortunate to have a large number.[164]

By beginning his questioning in that manner the Arkansas Democrat not only reminded the audience about Cohn's questionable sexuality, he alluded to the idea that homosexuality was a condition that could cause the "sufferer" to act illogically, to be so "bound" to their desires that they would transcend the limits of common decency (as Cohn had in dealings with the Army), not to mention other responsibilities. In addition, McClellan's use of "bind" is noteworthy given its hint of sadomasochism, which was explicitly associated at the time with the sexual practices of homosexual men.[165] In the McCarthy-Cohn-Schine relationship, who was controlling whom?

The timing of McClellan's questioning of Cohn is particularly noteworthy. Earlier that day, during an executive session of the committee, a wide-ranging discussion had ensued about how much longer the hearings would—and should—continue. Much of that debate centered around whether McCarthy's or the Army's legal teams planned to call more witnesses, and at one point this seemingly innocuous exchange occurred:

> SENATOR SYMINGTON: Who is the witness that you are not going to insist on calling up in public? We are not having secrets, are we?
>
> MR. WELCH: No. Are you talking about a witness we asked for yesterday?
>
> SENATOR MUNDT: Yes.
>
> MR. WELCH: It is a former chauffeur for Private Schine.

Welch is clearly referencing Percy B. West, the chauffeur who claimed to have seen Cohn and Schine "engaged in homosexual acts" in his limousine. It is unclear whether Symington, a passionate opponent of McCarthy, knew that Welch's proposed witness could so testify. But Symington's teasing nod to "having secrets" and his prompting Welch to revisit the possibility of calling West suggests that Symington knew the chauffeur's testimony would be damaging to Cohn and McCarthy. Even though Welch did not ultimately call West, the fact that he raised the possibility of doing so was a clear shot across the bow of Joe McCarthy.[166]

Unsurprisingly, similar insinuations found their way into articles by key newspaper columnists. In spite of Winchell and Sokolsky's steadfast support, the majority of editorial news coverage of McCarthy and Cohn during the hearings was critical. A *Washington Post and Times-Herald* editorial the day after Welch's "no sense of decency" outburst noted the prevailing opinion that "Senator McCarthy has been shown to have used the investigating power conferred on him by the Senate in improper and overbearing ways; and Mr. Cohn has been shown to have been absurdly importunate in behalf of his friend, Private Schine."[167] Winchell was so concerned about how his two friends were being portrayed that he threatened *Washington Post* reporter Murrey Marder one afternoon, warning, "We're going to get you."[168]

Those threats did not have their intended effect, and the press's attitude toward McCarthy and Cohn became increasingly negative as the hearings progressed. Before going to work for McCarthy, Cohn's public image had been that of a smart, determined warrior against communism, a young bachelor about town whose great failing was perhaps that he was a little too ambitious. Questions about his tactics and manhood had begun to emerge during his trip to Europe with Schine and had reached a fever pitch after the Army released its record of his actions in March. Media representations of Cohn gradually began to describe an irresponsible, vulgar twerp more interested in himself than anything else. This narrative hit a high point during the hearings. Edward R. Murrow's *See It Now* broadcasts—especially the infamous "Report on Senator Joseph McCarthy" from March 9, 1954— emphasized Cohn's "crude behavior and arrogance" and how the negative aspects of his personality had come to overshadow his intelligence and dedication. Murrow critiqued McCarthy similarly, as an unethical bully.[169]

Around the same time, Drew Pearson became emboldened in raising questions about the masculinity and sexuality of McCarthy, Cohn, and Schine. In a number of columns, Pearson highlighted Cohn's efforts to dodge military service, a biographical detail the young lawyer had long attempted to hide.[170] On May 4, Pearson harped on the fact that Schine "hired a fellow private to clean his rifle" while he was in the Army, and also referenced "the man who cleaned Schine's rifle at Fort Dix," an innuendo that made a pun of the military base's name.[171] On June 5, Pearson took his brashest shots yet, writing that during Cohn and Schine's tour of Europe "the two McCarthy gumshoes seemed unusually preoccupied with investigating alleged homosexuals" and reprinted the anecdote that "the pair also made a show of registering for separate hotel rooms, remarking loudly that they didn't work for the State Department." Pearson further noted that Cohn and Schine had borrowed $600 to buy perfume in Paris, an anecdote which feminized the pair both as shoppers and as poor managers of money.[172]

In addition to shaping public opinion, that negative press coverage may have influenced J. Edgar Hoover to cool his relationship with McCarthy and Cohn. While Hoover had originally lent both men his support, his patience had begun to thin after they had convinced FBI agent Frank Carr to join McCarthy's investigative team. Hoover was particularly worried about McCarthy and Cohn gaining too much access to proprietary Bureau information—including the names of confidential informants—should they continue to siphon agents away from the FBI.[173] Hoover had cast a long shadow over the hearings. He was spoken of reverently throughout, with individuals on all sides praising him as the nation's preeminent anticommunist. In later letters remarking on the hearings, some citizens noted that they relied on Hoover's opinion to shape their own: "J. Edgar Hoover thinks McCarthy's work has been of value," wrote one citizen, "that's good enough for me."[174] But others had come to view McCarthy and Hoover as inevitable rivals, especially if McCarthy's investigations began to encroach on the Bureau's territory. Communism clearly was a threat, wrote one, "but let's not resort to the hysterical and poorly organized methods of a McCarthy. Instead, we could use the expert services of J. Edgar Hoover and our fine FBI."[175]

At some point in the spring of 1954 Hoover decided to step back from his association with McCarthy and Cohn. A deft student of public opinion, Hoover was evidently quick to realize how disastrous the hearings were becoming for his allies. Hoover's rejection of McCarthy was subtle but clear. Two weeks into the hearings McCarthy produced a carbon copy of what he claimed was a letter written by Hoover to the Army warning them about potential security issues at Fort Monmouth. Secretary Stevens refused to read the letter without express permission from Hoover, noting that it was marked "personal and confidential."[176] It was a key piece of evidence that could prove McCarthy's charge that the Army had ignored warnings about security risks at Monmouth; Hoover simply had to certify its authenticity. But Hoover sent word to the committee that he had never sent such a letter, and a chastened McCarthy was forced to admit that what he possessed was a "summary of a memorandum."[177] Though McCarthy believed he was able to wriggle out of the controversy without too much damage to his reputa-

FIGURE 12. *Washington Post* cartoonist Herblock skewered McCarthy for both the cropped photograph and the supposed letter from J. Edgar Hoover. Credit: The Herb Block Foundation.

tion, the fact remained that Hoover had refused to help his friend in a time of need.[178] Hoover's actions signaled more than the cessation of a political alliance; they marked a key moment in the anticommunist center-right's rejection of McCarthy. In relying on their masculine personas to secure positions of influence in the national security state, McCarthy and Cohn had followed a script legitimated by Hoover. But the public queering and feminization of both men that culminated during the hearings meant that their membership in what one historian has called the "imperial brotherhood" of national security leaders was becoming tenuous.

Perhaps the final nail in McCarthy and Cohn's political coffin was struck outside the caucus room. In June, Vermont senator Ralph Flanders addressed the issue of McCarthyism on the floor of the Senate, referring to McCarthy as "Dennis the Menace" after the destructive comic strip character and clearly referencing the rumors of homosexuality surrounding McCarthy and his staff:

> But the committee has not yet dug into the real heart of the mystery. That mystery concerns the personal relationships of the Army private, the staff assistant, and the Senator . . . Then, there is the relationship of the staff assistant to the Army private. It is natural that [Cohn] should wish to retain the services of an able collaborator, but [Cohn] seems to have an almost passionate anxiety to retain him. Why?
>
> And, then, there is the Senator himself. At times he seems anxious to rid himself of the whole mess, and then again, at least in the presence of his assistant, he strongly supports the latter's efforts to keep the Army private's services available. Does the assistant have some hold on the Senator? Can it be that our Dennis, so effective in making trouble for his elders, has at last gotten into trouble himself? Does the committee plan to investigate the real issues at stake?[179]

Flanders had enunciated certain words and phrases to amplify their impact, drawing out "passionate anxiety" and "hold" to alert his audience to the intent behind his seemingly innocuous questions. His remarks received extensive press coverage, and were widely discussed on Capitol Hill. Shortly after Flanders's speech, former New York congressman Vito Marcantonio denied having political ties with Cohn by saying, "I am not the type that would want anything from any character who, according to Senator Flanders, has permitted his 'almost passionate anxiety to retain Private Schine' to embarrass our national government in the eyes of the world. Cohn knows what I mean."[180] McCarthy and Cohn were unable to sue Flanders because the Vermonter was covered by senatorial immunity from charges of libel stemming from utterances made on the Senate floor—a protection that McCarthy himself had relied on during his anticommunist diatribes.

Flanders's speech was a climactic moment in the career of the gossip about McCarthy and Cohn. Though Flanders had not explicitly charged that either Cohn or McCarthy was homosexual, he had clearly referenced the ongoing rumors in a prominent and formal setting. As a result, those rumors had entered not only the consciousness of the general public, but the official record of its political debates. They had journeyed from the lowest of brows to the highest, and had captured an element of the national zeitgeist en route. Flanders continued his attack on McCarthy and was the driving force behind the censure committee hearings convened in the fall of 1954. Ultimately McCarthy was not officially censured, but his peers passed a resolution stating that "the conduct of the Senator from Wisconsin, Mr. McCarthy, is unbecoming a Member of the United States Senate, is contrary to Senatorial traditions, and tends to bring the Senate into disrepute."[181]

On the afternoon of Flanders's speech, an irate McCarthy used the hearings to respond. Returning to a favored tactic, he charged that Flanders was a religious and racial bigot.[182] This time, however, McCarthy's claims were largely ignored by the press and his fellow senators; they had become inured to his bombast. At least on Capitol Hill, the tide had turned against McCarthy and Cohn. Soon, nearly every member of the Permanent Subcommittee on Investigations was calling for Cohn's resignation.

Even before he joined McCarthy's staff, Cohn had employed homophobia, a masculine aggressiveness, and the tools of gossip to forward his anticommunist and professional agendas. As McCarthy's most trusted aide, Cohn continued using those tactics and urged his boss to do the same, whether in the investigation of the International Information Administration, the inquiry into espionage at Fort Monmouth, or the pair's dealings with the Army. And for a period, that strategy seemed to work; using the media to manipulate discernable facts and promote their own masculine credentials while disparaging those of their rivals paid great dividends for McCarthy and Cohn.

The great irony, then, is that rumors about McCarthy and Cohn's sexuality circulated along similar pathways: gossip columns, tabloids, gossip magazines, and subtle references in more conservative outlets. Those rumors influenced the tone and verbiage of the Army-McCarthy hearings, which to many Americans promised to reveal the truth behind the secret operations of the growing federal apparatus. At the same time, letters from citizens who followed the hearings, commentary from reporters attending them, and the words and actions of the participants themselves show that masculinity was used as a measure of the principals' fitness to defend the United States. In the end, McCarthy and Cohn's failure was as attributable to the way their sexual and gender identities were perceived as it was to their refusal to remain within the limits of decency.

EPILOGUE

THE LONG LIFE OF SURVEILLANCE STATE MASCULINITY

Facing mounting criticism from the members of the Senate Permanent Subcommittee on Investigations, Roy Cohn resigned as the chief counsel on July 20, 1954. Joseph McCarthy claimed that "the resignation of Roy Cohn must bring great satisfaction to the communists and fellow travelers. The smears and pressures to which he has been subjected make it clear that an effective anticommunist cannot long survive on the Washington scene."[1]

Eight days later, a farewell party was held for Cohn in the ballroom at New York City's Hotel Astor, the hotel at which he and McCarthy had first met. Over two thousand guests each paid seven dollars to attend the five-hour dinner, which had been organized by Rabbi Benjamin Schultz and sponsored by the Joint Committee Against Communism, which counted as members the New York branches of the American Legion, Veterans of Foreign Wars, Catholic War Veterans, and AMVETS. Schultz opened the proceedings by recognizing Cohn for "his battle for his God and country, which has inspired America," and noting that he had to turn away six thousand additional requests for tickets to the dinner. A dozen commemorative plaques were presented to Cohn by various conservative-leaning organizations. Speakers included columnist George Sokolsky, conservative radio personality Fulton Lewis, chairman of the American Jewish League Against

Communism Alfred Kohlberg, conservative writer William F. Buckley, and Fordham Law School professor Godfrey Schmidt.[2] On the dais sat numerous members of the conservative movement, including Judge Robert J. Morris, former Notre Dame Law School dean Clarence Manion, financier E. F. Hutton, and Robert Vogeler, an American businessman who had been imprisoned by Hungarian communists for seventeen months. McCarthy was the night's keynote speaker.

Both Cohn and McCarthy were treated to numerous standing ovations during the event, and attendees had to be asked to refrain from rushing the stage.[3] Cohn was cast as "the American Dreyfus," a reference to the infamous turn-of-the-century French case fueled by anti-Semitism. The mainstream press, particularly the *New York Times*, was continually attacked by speakers. Another favored target was Senator Ralph Flanders.[4] In praising Cohn, Rabbi Schultz struck a populist tone, noting that "Roy Cohn could be elected to almost any office in America today . . . Cohn is the symbol of the people's revolt against politicians soft on treason, professors soft in the head, and writers talking softly about Hiss and Oppenheimer . . . The people know that the loss of Cohn is like the loss of a dozen battleships." As the *Christian Science Monitor* knowingly predicted, though McCarthy "may be slipping politically, McCarthyism will not be easily swept away."[5]

And neither would surveillance state masculinity. In the six decades since the conclusion of the Army-McCarthy hearings, the idea that the United States' leaders should possess a hard, masculine toughness has continued to influence political culture and speak to the potency of the approach embraced by Hoover, McCarthy, and Cohn. Furthermore, that period has demonstrated the staying power of gossip as a source and carrier of political information, leading to a political culture in which the line between rumor and reality is continually blurred.

Though he officially dodged censure by his peers in the Senate (the resolution passed by that body employed the less-damning term "condemn"), McCarthy's power had clearly eroded. He continued to push an anticommunist agenda, but was regarded as a pariah in Washington and throughout the rest of the country. By August 1954, McCarthy's net favorability rating had fallen to −15 after enjoying a high of +21 eight months prior.[6] A survey of college newspaper editors in the spring of 1955 found that the vast majority considered McCarthyism a "dead issue."[7] McCarthy's biographer David Oshinsky writes that "his life became a nightmare . . . He lost interest in his senatorial duties, avoided his constituents, and skipped the Republican National Convention in 1956."[8] His health failed as his fondness for liquor morphed into alcoholism, and in late 1956 he was treated for hepatitis, alcohol withdrawal, and cirrhosis of the liver. On May 2, 1957, at the age of forty-seven, McCarthy died at Bethesda Naval Hospital in Maryland. A high mass in his honor was held at St. Matthew's Cathedral—where he had been married less than four years prior—and attended by Hoover, Cohn, Richard Nixon, and seventy-seven senators.[9] The following day McCarthy was buried in St. Mary's Parish Cemetery, along the banks of the Fox River in Appleton, Wisconsin.

Many accounts of McCarthyism end with the man's death, but the political moment named for Joseph McCarthy long outlived him. As the turnout at Cohn's "retirement party" demonstrated, the nation did not lack for virulent anticommunists. The movement that had coalesced around McCarthy reorganized after his downfall and once again embraced J. Edgar Hoover as its spiritual leader. In the spring and summer of 1956, Hoover was moving to expand the government's investigation into subversives through the FBI. In a meeting at the White House on March 8, 1956, Hoover obtained the implicit approval of President Eisenhower and the National Security Council to use extralegal means to hunt communist subversives, including wiretapping, mail surveillance, bugging, and "surreptitious entry" into offices and homes.[10] Two months later, the Bureau began developing the counterintelligence program that would come to be known as COINTELPRO, a broad-ranging initiative aimed at disrupting and bringing down all kinds of subversives. COINTELPRO would ultimately encompass 2,340 covert operations against organizations of all political stripes, including various communist-affiliated groups, the Ku Klux Klan, the Nation of Islam, unions, the Black Panthers, the Young Lords, the Student Nonviolent Coordinating Committee, and the Southern Christian Leadership Conference.

Though Hoover had been interested in extralegal means of countersubversion throughout his time at the Bureau and had received presidential approval for them from President Roosevelt, the need to garner Eisenhower's support meant that such activities could have ceased (or at least significantly subsided) in the mid-1950s. But McCarthyism's amplification of the communist threat to both the American citizenry and the federal government meant that Eisenhower was in a position to support extraordinary (and extrajudicial) efforts to counter it and any other form of subversion. COINTELPRO was not a direct outgrowth of McCarthyism, but McCarthy's anticommunist instigating helped create the ideal conditions for Hoover to forward his vision of domestic surveillance.

Hoover himself had also done plenty to foster that zeitgeist. The impact of his direct engagement of the general public as allies against subversion—and what Hoover defined as the various "foreign isms" threatening the United States—cannot be overestimated. In short, the experience of antiespionage activities during World War II prepared Americans for the anxieties of the Cold War, accustoming them to regarding their fellow citizens with suspicion. Along with moments such as the First Red Scare, wartime domestic surveillance and countersubversion also acquainted the American public with the concept of prosecuting a suspect—either in a legal court or that of public opinion—on the basis of their beliefs rather than their actions.

In constructing and publicizing the G-Man, Hoover helped establish many of the parameters under which the national security state operated, specifically its marrying of bureaucratic efficiency and aggressive masculinity. At every turn, a paternalistic, assertive version of masculinity was written into the social and legal framework that would become the national surveillance and security states. In both his bureaucratic leadership of the FBI and the cult of personality he constructed around himself, Hoover was essential in promoting that understanding of masculinity. Hoover's actions helped define the parameters of masculinity under which McCarthy and Cohn labored, particularly regarding how men engaged in "protecting America" were supposed to act and be. As a bureaucrat and public figure, Hoover's outlook legitimized, codified, and cemented the alliance between national security and the myopic understanding of masculinity that had come to hegemonic dominance since the turn of the twentieth century.

As the establishment of COINTELPRO demonstrates, Hoover shrewdly exploited the anxieties over subversion that had been fueled by McCarthyism. In that way, Hoover and McCarthy supported each other's quests for power. At the same time, it can also be argued that McCarthy and McCarthyism ultimately played a role in the desanctification of Hoover. As a result of McCarthy's overreach, Americans become more suspicious of government figures using personal information against individuals (such as Hoover's use of wiretaps to undermine the Civil Rights Movement). In hindsight, McCarthy's downfall can be seen as an opportunity, a point at which the federal government could have stemmed the growth of the national surveillance and security states. But McCarthyism became a closet of horrors in which Americans stored their fears of government overreach and expanding federal oversight—once the man had died, many believed that his tactics would die with him. The actions of Hoover and the FBI clearly proved that assumption to be false. Referring to the era as "McCarthyist" captures one element of it, but such nomenclature ultimately promotes a false periodization; McCarthy's tactics did not accompany him to the grave but became folded into the fabric of American political culture and continue to influence the structure of political discourse to this day.

The strongest evidence of Hoover's reliance on surveillance state masculinity as a source of political power can be seen in the way he is remembered today. During his lifetime, Hoover's opponents sought to use rumors about his purported queerness to undermine his political and social status. In death, those rumors have grown only more bold and become more widespread. The most infamous—and lasting—claim is that Hoover enjoyed wearing women's clothing. That specific rumor can be traced to Susan Rosenstiel, the ex-wife of Lewis Rosenstiel, a liquor magnate and friend of both Cohn and Hoover. In speaking with journalist Anthony Summers, Mrs. Rosenstiel claimed to have witnessed Hoover dressed as a woman while in attendance at two "homosexual orgies" hosted by Roy Cohn at the Plaza Hotel in New York City. Mrs. Rosenstiel claims she had been invited to the small sex parties by her bisexual husband (whom she also claims to have once found "in bed" with Cohn). The details Mrs. Rosenstiel provided about the two parties she witnessed are telling. The first meeting supposedly took place in 1958:

> According to Mrs. Rosenstiel, Edgar was dressed up as a woman, in full drag. "He was wearing a fluffy black dress, very fluffy, with flounces, and lace stockings and high heels, and a black curly wig. He had makeup on, and false eyelashes. It was a very short skirt, and he was sitting there in the living room of the [hotel] suite with his legs crossed. Roy [Cohn] introduced him to me as 'Mary' and he replied, 'Good evening,' brusque, like the first time I'd met him. It was obvious he wasn't a woman, you could see where he shaved. It was Hoover . . . The next thing, a couple of boys come in, young blond boys. I'd say about eighteen or nineteen. And then Roy makes the signal, we should go to the bedroom . . . And they go into the bedroom, and Hoover takes off his lace dress and pants, and under the dress he was wearing a little, short garter belt. He lies on the double bed, and the two boys work on him with their hands. One of them wore rubber gloves."[11]

A year later, Mrs. Rosenstiel returned to the Plaza for another one of Cohn's parties.

> Cohn ushered [Mr. and Mrs. Rosenstiel] into a suite to find Edgar, again attired in female finery. His clothing this time was even more outlandish. "He had a red dress on," Susan recalled, "and a black feather boa around his neck.

He was dressed like an old flapper, like you see on old tintypes. After about half an hour some boys came, like before. This time they're dressed in leather. And Hoover had a Bible. He wanted one of the boys to read from the Bible. And [the boy] read, I forget which passage, and the other boy played with [Hoover], wearing the rubber gloves. And then Hoover grabbed the Bible, threw it down and told the second boy to join in the sex."[12]

Susan Rosenstiel's story caused a sensation when Summers's book *Official and Confidential: The Secret Life of J. Edgar Hoover* was published in 1993. Tabloids and gossip magazines picked up on the story, and political cartoonists had a field day squeezing the plump Hoover into negligees and stilettos. Part of what made Rosenstiel's story so compelling and memorable was that it featured nearly every stereotype about gay men: the chasing after young boys, the over-the-top sense of style, the gaudy makeup, the antireligious fervor, the adoption of a female name (and the one of the Virgin Mother, at that). FBI historian Athan Theoharis identified a number of problems with Mrs. Rosenstiel's story, including the absurdity of a woman being invited to a "gay orgy," the fact that she never raised the issue of her husband's supposed homosexuality in their divorce proceedings, and the convenient fact that all the principals were deceased by the 1990s.[13]

As the story is almost certainly falsified, the relevant historical question becomes why it has persisted in American culture. For one, the story is decadent; it is tempting to believe that a man whose power was largely based on collecting secrets about other people would harbor such an astounding secret himself. The story also seems to confirm widely held prejudices about both Hoover and homosexuals, namely that Hoover himself was gay and that homosexuals engage in sex practices mainstream American culture considers extreme or abnormal. Another explanation of the rumor's staying power goes back to surveillance state masculinity. In a post-Vietnam, post-Watergate world shot through with irony and distrust of the federal government, in some way it makes sense that a man who cultivated a public persona of heroic masculinity, piety, moral sanctity, and professionalism would prove to be the stereotypical opposite of his claims. In that sense, the wide acceptance and dissemination of the gossip about Hoover dressing as a woman confirms the centrality of masculinity to both his public image and his professional success. Regardless of the story's factuality, it is poignant that the legacy of a man whose rise to power was facilitated by his adept handling of gossip is now irrevocably linked to a rumor he cannot control.

Cohn and Hoover remained close even after Cohn returned to New York. One of Cohn's law partners recalls that Cohn and Hoover often had long conversations over the telephone, and that Cohn was an annual recipient of Hoover's famous Christmas gift of a box of Cuban cigars—a bit of contraband to which Hoover retained access despite the embargo with the communist outpost in the Caribbean. When the federal government began investigating Cohn for insurance fraud in the 1960s, Hoover supposedly forwarded Cohn information on the government's case. Said a lawyer in Cohn's office, "I think he was getting information from Hoover during the government prosecution . . . I think it is pretty clear that one of the things that Hoover did during Roy's trial was to feed information to Roy on the government case."[14] For his part, Cohn served as a middleman between the FBI and gossip journalists, planting information from Hoover with columnists like Liz Smith.[15]

Cohn eventually enjoyed a second act as a high-powered lawyer, representing luminaries such as Yankees owner George Steinbrenner, Studio 54 proprietors Steve Rubell and Ian Schrager, and organized crime bosses Carmine Galante, John Gotti, and Tony Salerno. During the 1960s, 1970s, and first half of the 1980s Cohn served as a bridge between the celebrity and political worlds in New York City. He continued to hold court at the 21 Club and was a regular visitor to the Reagan White House. His creative accounting practices—he took a relatively small salary from his law firm but covered nearly all of his purchases with an expense account—caused his tax return to be audited by the Internal Revenue Service twenty years in a row. When he contracted HIV/AIDS in the 1980s he refused to acknowledge his diagnosis due to its association with homosexuality, maintaining both in private and in public that he was suffering from liver cancer. Only weeks before his death in 1986 Cohn was disbarred by the state of New York, stemming from allegations that he had cheated clients out of money, including Susan Rosenstiel's ex-husband Lewis.[16]

Cohn's most famous client will prove to be the one with the most lasting influence. In 1973, Cohn met the real estate developer Donald J. Trump at Le Club, a trendy members-only bar, restaurant, and disco on Manhattan's East Side. Soon thereafter, Trump hired Cohn to defend the real estate company Trump and his father owned against charges of racial discrimination brought by the Department of Justice. Though the Trumps' settlement with the federal government forced them to diversify the apartment buildings they owned, Cohn and Trump declared victory. In the aftermath, Cohn taught Trump that the media narrative of an event was more important than the event itself. *Village Voice* reporter Wayne Barrett recalls that by the mid-1970s, Cohn "became Donald's mentor, his constant advisor on every significant aspect of his business and personal life."[17] Reportedly, a photo of Trump hung on the wall of Cohn's office; Trump had signed it, "To Roy, my greatest friend. Donald."[18]

It has been reported that Trump cut Cohn from his inner circle after learning that his mentor had been diagnosed with AIDS.[19] Yet Cohn's influence on Trump has continued throughout the real estate mogul's business career and into his entry into politics. Early in Trump's successful 2016 run for president, he tapped Roger Stone as an adviser to his campaign. Stone, a notorious conservative political fixer who sports a tattoo of Richard Nixon between his shoulder blades, was a close friend of Cohn's and regarded Cohn as a mentor ever since the pair worked together on Ronald Reagan's 1980 presidential campaign. Stone also uses his masculinity as a political tool: for a 2008 *New Yorker* profile, Stone was photographed with his shirt off, flexing a pectoral muscle in a pose reminiscent of Bernarr Macfadden.[20]

In many ways, Donald Trump is the ultimate practitioner of surveillance state masculinity in his masculinist persona, his weaponization of propriety information, and his employment of the tools of gossip.[21] From one perspective Trump embodies the masculinity of Roy Cohn: the appeal to wealth and connections, the single-minded pursuit of power, the equation of manhood with authority. But Trump's political base is more reminiscent of the populist constituency that helped launch Joe McCarthy to the Senate in 1946: uneducated, conservative white men who are distrustful of the government and fearful of losing their social and economic status to "outsiders." In appealing to that audience, Trump has fully embraced masculinist rhetoric, peppering his speeches with pugilistic, bellicose bombast directed at enemies real and perceived. To wit, Trump is the only American presidential candidate to have publicly referenced the size of his penis. Responding to a barb from Republican primary rival Marco Rubio, Trump commented, "[Rubio] referred to my hands—'if they're small, something else must be small'—I guarantee you there's no problem. I guarantee."[22] Among his supporters, Trump's misogynistic and racist comments are taken as a measure of his boldness and willingness to speak his mind, qualities that resonated with voters who view "political correctness" as tiresome, effete, and overly sensitive.

Much of Trump's political career is built on his expert use of the tools of gossip. For the majority of his first presidential campaign Trump's team was able to avoid spending significant funds on television advertising because he was already dominating the twenty-four-hour news networks. Trump often employed classic gossip magazine tactics such as hyperbole, insinuation, and guilt by association. His use of Twitter to speak directly to his followers mirrors McCarthy's use of gossip magazines and tabloids; as an unofficial channel Twitter allows Trump to employ a vernacular that speaks to his supposed "authenticity" as a populist firebrand.

Trump commonly stretched the truth or told outright lies at his campaign stops, taking to heart Cohn's doctrine that presentation was more memorable than content. This approach extended into his presidency: *Washington Post* fact-checker Glenn Kessler has argued that Trump made over 10,000 "false or misleading claims" by his twenty-eighth month in the White House.[23] As president, Trump has even relied on the manipulation of images. During a 2019 Oval Office briefing, Trump displayed a map of the possible path of Hurricane Dorian that had been altered in an effort to corroborate his unfounded claim about the storm's likelihood of striking Alabama.[24] The resulting mini-scandal—dubbed "Sharpiegate" by the media—was quickly forgotten as the news cycle moved on to cover other Trumpian absurdities.

Trump's most common target is what he delights in calling the "Fake News Media," a phrase that seems to encompass any news outlet with which Trump happens to disagree at that moment. But like Hoover, McCarthy, and Cohn before him, Trump has fostered symbiotic relationships with a number of sympathetic media figures, most notably gossip journalists from right-wing websites such as Breitbart.com and InfoWars.com. His requited romance with the Fox News show *Fox and Friends* is legend, with the daytime program's three hosts fawning over the president in exchange for privileged access to him and his administration. Sean Hannity, one of Fox News's most popular hosts, has joined Trump onstage at campaign-style rallies during his presidency. At the outset of Trump's third year in office, historian Nicole Hemmer opined that Fox News "is the closest we've come to having state TV."[25]

Trump's association with the supermarket tabloid the *National Enquirer* has been nothing short of an alliance. He reportedly planted stories about his presidential rivals in the *Enquirer*, including one suggesting that Ted Cruz was engaged in an extramarital affair and another claiming that Dr. Ben Carson had paralyzed some of his patients for life during botched surgeries.[26] Articles have appeared in the *Enquirer* under Trump's byline, usually providing an "inside look" into what makes Trump so successful. Trump has also used the *Enquirer* as a source of legitimate journalism, once citing a story the tabloid had published linking the father of Ted Cruz to John F. Kennedy's assassin Lee Harvey Oswald. In the summer of 2016, when former *Playboy* model Karen McDougal shopped a story about her affair with Trump, the *Enquirer* paid $150,000 for her story and then buried it, hoping to ensure it would not be told before election day.[27] In the end, the *Enquirer* was the only American newspaper with a circulation of over 200,000 to endorse Trump in the 2016 general election. In the wake of Trump's victory, the *New York Post* reported that David J. Pecker, the chairman and CEO of the *Enquirer*'s parent company American Media, was being considered for an ambassadorship.

The history of the *Enquirer* serves as a fitting end to this examination. The *Enquirer* was established in the mid-1920s as a broadsheet newspaper titled the *New York Evening Enquirer*, its founder having secured a loan from William Randolph Hearst. Three decades later, the failing newspaper (by then known as the *New York Enquirer*) was purchased by a young investor named Generoso Pope Jr. Pope had experience in the publishing industry courtesy of his father, who had risen from employment as a day laborer to own the Italian-language newspaper *Il Progresso Italo-Americano*. For the first five years of the younger Pope's leadership the renamed *National Enquirer* floundered along, its circulation hovering around 17,000 copies. But in 1957 Pope decided to follow the lead of gossip magazines like *Confidential*, *Top-Secret*, and *Rave* and turn the *National Enquirer* into a sensationalist tabloid. From 1957 to the mid-1960s the *Enquirer* focused on gore- and sex-filled stories not unlike those that populated the *New York Evening Graphic* in the 1920s. It was not until 1967 that the *Enquirer* moderated its approach in an effort to expand its distribution to supermarkets.

One enduring mystery about the *Enquirer*'s success was where Pope came up with the funding to buy the magazine, particularly since he had been cut off from his family's fortune following his father's death in 1950. A recent investigation by *DuJour* magazine confirmed a longstanding rumor that approximately half of the money came from Pope's godfather, Mafia boss Frank Costello. The remainder of the funds had been put up by a friend of Pope's from his days at the Horace Mann School: Roy Cohn.[28]

ACKNOWLEDGMENTS

Much of the research for this project was made possible by generous support from the Lyndon B. Johnson Presidential Library Foundation, the Harry S. Truman Presidential Library Foundation, the Charles Redd Foundation for Western Studies, the Brown University Department of American Studies, and the Brown University Graduate School. Brian Greenspun and William Straw provided access to important research materials, as did the incomparable Ernie Lazar. Steven Remy kindly shared an advance chapter from his book *The Malmedy Massacre*. Steve Lenius was helpful in introducing me to the work of Robert Bienvenu. Steven Payne of the Bronx County Historical Society helped by searching the records of the *Bronx Home News*. Claire Potter provided insightful comments on an early version of this book's fifth chapter. The largesse of Henry Scott profoundly improved the sections of this work on the magazine *Confidential*. I benefited from the expertise of archivists and librarians at a variety of institutions, including the Milwaukee Public Library, the Marquette University Archives, the Wisconsin Historical Society, the Lyndon B. Johnson Presidential Library, the Dwight D. Eisenhower Presidential Library, the Harry S. Truman Presidential Library, the New York Public Library, the University of Maryland Archives, the Hoover Institution at Stanford University, and the Brigham Young University Archives.

I am indebted to the friends and mentors I met at the Ohio State University, especially the patient, compassionate Judy Wu. Perhaps the greatest gift Ohio State bestowed on me is the friendship of William Sturkey, whose skill as a historian is only equaled by his generosity as a person.

At Brown University, I was fortunate to be mentored by Elliott Gorn, Robert Self, and Samuel Zipp. Elliott helped me formulate this project in its earliest stages and inspired me to think creatively about masculinity's place in American culture. Robert pushed me to be more precise with my historical claims and deepened this project's engagement with the historiography of twentieth-century America. Sandy improved the project's claims about American identity formation and helped nurture its narrative core.

At St. Olaf, my work on this book has been supported by a number of colleagues, including Tim Howe, Steve Hahn, and DeAne Lagerquist. The generous Eric Fure-Slocum provided insightful comments on the book's introduction and first chapter. St. Olaf librarians Ezra Plemons, Maggie Epstein, and Kim Follett were key to helping me locate resources in the final stages of working on the manuscript. The Dean's Office and the Faculty Life Committee both provided backing as the book made its way to print.

I am deeply grateful for the talented, hardworking staff at the University of Chicago Press. I was originally attracted to the press by Doug Mitchell, who encouraged this project at an early stage. He was an intellectual dynamo and is sorely missed. Tim Mennel showed me what a great editor can do for a book, and I am indebted to him for his insight, his patience, and his sharp editorial eye. Susannah Engstrom was a perfect guide through the finer points of the publishing process. Michael Koplow significantly improved the manuscript in its final stages. The detailed comments by the two anonymous readers engaged by the press were of great help in positioning my argument and considering its impact on readers.

Two mentors have been so essential to my intellectual and professional growth that I don't quite know how to thank them. Jack Chatfield deepened my appreciation for the past and embodied what I seek to become as a teacher, scholar, and human being—I miss him dearly. Kevin Boyle's warmth and empathy are boundless, and his advice on how to approach this profession has buoyed me throughout my career.

I would be lost without the support of my friends and family, including Barbara Fournier, Hank Corinha, Lauren Elias, Doug and Lorelei Starck, Suvadip Bose, Ben Koren, Christopher Meatto, and Michael Peart.

As far back as I can remember, my father fostered my love for history. He read *Sam the Minuteman* to me before I could read myself, brought me on weekly visits to the Andover Public Library to explore the Cornerstones of Freedom series, and put *The Best and the Brightest* in my hands when I expressed an interest in the Vietnam War. I would not be a historian without his encouragement. My mother has been a constant source of support, and her passion for the arts has not only influenced my work as a cultural historian but has fundamentally changed the way I see the world.

Finally, to Lindsay, my favorite gossip partner: This book would not exist without you. Being with you is the best decision I've ever made.

ABBREVIATIONS

ARMY-MCCARTHY HEARINGS: Special Senate Investigation on Charges and Countercharges Involving: Secretary of the Army Robert T. Stevens, John G. Adams, H. Struve Hensel and Senator Joe McCarthy, Roy M. Cohn, and Francis P. Carr, DOC-TYPE: Hearings—Digital Collection, HEARING-ID: HRG-1954-OPS-0013, LexisNexis Congressional Hearings Digital Collection

DDE LIBRARY: Dwight D. Eisenhower Presidential Library, Abilene, KS

HST LIBRARY: Harry S. Truman Presidential Library, Independence, MO

JEHMC: J. Edgar Hoover Memorabilia Collection, National Law Enforcement Museum, Washington, DC

MCCARTHY FBI FILE: *FBI Records: The Vault*, "Sen. Joseph (Joe) McCarthy," https://vault.fbi.gov/Sen.%20Joseph%20%28Joe%29%20McCarthy

MCCARTHY PAPERS: Papers of Joseph R. McCarthy, Marquette University Archives, Milwaukee

MPL MCCARTHY: Milwaukee Public Library, McCarthy Clippings File

PEARSON PAPERS: Papers of Drew Pearson, Lyndon B. Johnson Presidential Library, Austin

WATKINS PAPERS: Arthur V. Watkins Papers, L. Tom Perry Special Collections, Brigham Young University Archives, Provo, UT

NOTES

INTRODUCTION

1. Michael Straight, *Trial by Television and Other Encounters* (New York: Devon Press, 1979), 126.

2. The term "McCarthyism" now refers to a moment in the early Cold War during which government authorities employed extraordinary, extrajudicial methods to combat purported communist subversives, often starting with the congressional investigation into the entertainment industry that began in 1947. The term is thus often employed to refer to events predating Joseph McCarthy's February 1950 rise to national prominence. In more recent political discourse, "McCarthyism" and "McCarthyist" reference politicians and movements that rely on unsubstantiated accusations to appeal to populist sentiments.

3. Margaret Chase Smith, "Declaration of Conscience," June 1, 1950, *Congressional Record*, 81st Congress, 2nd Session, 7894–7895.

4. Army-McCarthy Hearings, 1954, part 13, p. 15, April 30.

5. It was in 1885 that *Town Topics*—arguably the United States' first gossip magazine—was founded. The Army-McCarthy hearings occurred in 1954.

6. I use the terms "queer" and "sissy" as they were employed in contemporary government documents and media reports, as well as the personal reflections of participants: "queer" was often a derogatory term for individuals exhibiting or suspected of harboring same-sex attraction, and a "sissy" was a man whose gender identity was considered to be less than fully masculine. The term "queer" has a particularly labyrinthine history, but for the majority of the 1885–1954 time period, it carried a dual, derogatory meaning of "strange, peculiar, odd" or sexually attracted to (and perhaps in active sexual relationships with) individuals of their own sex, or—usually—both. The slippage is why the word gained traction; its inexactness provided deniability. Though the term "queer" was applied to men and women alike during the 1885–1954 era, it was most commonly used to refer to men. See Stephen Heath, "Queer," in *The Keywords Project*, a University of Pittsburgh and Jesus College—Cambridge Collaborative Research Initiative, http://keywords.pitt.edu/key words_defined/queer.html. For a scholarly examination of J. Edgar Hoover's "queerness," see Claire Potter, "Queer Hoover: Sex, Lies, and Political History," *Journal of the History of Sexuality* 15, no. 3 (September 2006): 355–381.

7. On consumerist masculinity's predecessor, "producerist manhood," see Stephen Kantrowitz, *Ben Tillman and the Reconstruction of White Supremacy* (Chapel Hill: University of North Carolina Press, 2000), 106, and Martin Summers, *Manliness and Its Discontents: The Black Middle Class and the Transformation of Masculinity, 1900–1930* (Chapel Hill: University of North Carolina Press, 2004).

8. Surveillance state masculinity was dominant from approximately 1898 to 1989: it began with the War of 1898, found its fullest expression during the early Cold War, and was possibly replaced by an alternative form of masculine leadership in conjunction with the rise of "soft power" foreign relations following the fall of the Soviet Union—though Donald Trump and his administration have given new life to many of its key elements.

9. Surveillance state masculinity is closely linked to "Cold War masculinity," but its roots run deeper than the post-1945 geopolitical struggle. I contend that the hallmarks of Cold War masculinity—a fear of being perceived as "soft," the need to publicly perform machismo, a predilection toward brinksmanship—predated the Cold War itself. While surveillance state masculinity achieved its climactic moment of expression at the 1954 Army-McCarthy hearings, it had been crescendoing since at least the end of World War I. Such a periodization, including both the interwar period and the early Cold War, allows an investigation of how the emergence of the American security state related to concurrent shifts in gender politics more completely than one that includes only the post-1945 conflict between the Soviet Union and the United States. Although it argues for a shift in timeline and terminology, this project is not a corrective to the work of historians of Cold War masculinity—centrally K. A. Cuordileone and Robert D. Dean—but an extension of it, a reframing that provides a deeper context for those investigations. By taking a longer view, I seek to capture how the gradual eclipse of "producerist manhood" unfolded in the halls of power. See K. A. Cuordileone, *Manhood and American Political Culture in the Cold War* (New York: Routledge, 2005); Robert D. Dean, *Imperial Brotherhood: Gender and the Making of Cold War Foreign Policy* (Amherst: University of Massachusetts Press, 2001); Kristin L. Hoganson, *Fighting for American Manhood: How Gender Politics Provoked the Spanish-American and Philippine-American Wars* (New Haven: Yale University Press, 2000).

10. Related books that take a different approach include Margot Canaday, *The Straight State: Sexuality and Citizenship in Twentieth-Century America* (Princeton: Princeton University Press, 2009); Douglas M. Charles, *Hoover's War on Gays: Exposing the FBI's "Sex Deviates Program"* (Lawrence: University Press of Kansas, 2015); David K. Johnson, *The Lavender Scare: The Cold War Persecution of Gays and Lesbians in the Federal Government* (Chicago: University of Chicago Press, 2006); Jessica Pliley, *Policing Sexuality: The Mann Act and the Making of the FBI* (Cambridge, MA: Harvard University Press, 2014).

11. Three key elements distinguish this book from similar works. First, it focuses on high-powered individuals as a means of understanding longitudinal developments in politics, media, gender, and sexuality. Second, it positions gossip as an essential binding component in the marriage of security state politics and gendered identity. Third, it argues that the roots of the "hard masculine toughness" that was essential to Cold War liberalism run much deeper than the Cold War itself (see note 9 above).

12. Charles L. Ponce de Leon, *Self-Exposure: Human-Interest Journalism and the Emergence of Celebrity in America, 1890–1940* (Chapel Hill: University of North Carolina Press, 2002).

13. On the transition from "character" to "personality" in regard to the construction of masculinity, see Summers, *Manliness and Its Discontents*, 8, and Michael S. Kimmel, *Manhood in America* (New York: Oxford University Press, 2008), 145. On that revolution more generally, see Warren Susman, "'Personality' and the Making of Twentieth-Century Culture," in *Culture as History: The Transformation of American Society in the Twentieth Century* (New York: Pantheon, 1984).

14. Michael J. Hogan, *A Cross of Iron: Harry S. Truman and the Origins of the National Security State, 1945–1954* (New York: Cambridge University Press, 1998), 2. See also Aaron L. Friedberg, *In the Shadow of the Garrison State: America's Anti-statism and Its Cold War Grand Strategy* (Princeton: Princeton University Press, 2000), and Douglas T. Stuart, *Creating the National Security State: A History of the Law That Transformed America* (Princeton: Princeton University Press, 2008).

15. Hogan, 255.

16. Alfred W. McCoy, *Policing America's Empire: The United States, the Philippines, and the Rise of the Surveillance State* (Madison: University of Wisconsin Press, 2010), 16–17.

17. McCoy., 21–24, 34–35.

18. Kimmel, 88–89; emphasis in original.

19. Jackson Lears, *Rebirth of a Nation: The Making of Modern America, 1877–1920* (New York: Harper, 2009), 8.

20. Alan Trachtenberg, *The Incorporation of America: Culture and Society in the Gilded Age* (New York: Hill and Wang, 1982). For the argument that Americans spent the half-century following the Civil War on the hunt for new ways of organizing society, see Robert Wiebe, *The Search for Order: 1877–1920* (New York: Macmillan, 1967).

21. On consumerism and personal identity at the turn of the twentieth century, see Daniel Horowitz, *The Morality of Spending: Attitudes Toward the Consumer Society in America, 1875–1940* (New York: Ivan R. Dee, 1992); Jackson Lears, *Fables of Abundance: A Cultural History of Advertising in America* (Boston: Basic Books, 1995); Susan Strasser, *Satisfaction Guaranteed: The Making of the American Mass Market* (New York: Pantheon Books, 1989).

22. For a fuller description of this transformation in gender, see Peter Filene, *Him/Her/Self: Gender Identities in Modern America*, 3rd ed. (Baltimore: Johns Hopkins University Press, 1998), 3–122.

23. Sherwood Anderson, *Perhaps Women* (New York: H. Liveright, 1931), 7, 42.

24. Summers, *Manliness and Its Discontents*, 9. See also Anthony Rotundo, *American Manhood: Transformations in Masculinity from the Revolution to the Modern Era* (New York:

Basic Books, 1993), 282–286; Gail Bederman, *Manliness and Civilization: A Cultural History of Gender and Race in the United States, 1880–1917* (Chicago: University of Chicago Press, 1996), 10–20; Tom Pendergast, *Creating the Modern Man: American Magazines and Consumer Culture, 1900–1950* (Columbia: University of Missouri Press, 2000), 1–18; Lewis A. Erenberg, *Steppin' Out: New York Nightlife and the Transformation of American Culture* (Chicago: University of Chicago Press, 1984), 237–238.

25. Kimmel, 89.

26. Bederman, 7. For another historian's understanding of social constructivism, see Joan W. Scott, "Gender: A Useful Category of Historical Analysis," *American Historical Review* 92, no. 5 (December 1986). My understanding of masculinity can also be likened to that defined by John Pettegrew in *Brutes in Suits: Male Sensibility in America, 1890–1920* (Baltimore: Johns Hopkins University Press, 2007), "I advance a feminist view of masculinity as a mind-set developed through language, habit, and knowledge and therefore remediable through those same cultural forms." Pettegrew, 2.

27. This concept—including its contingencies—was first introduced by the philosopher Judith Butler, who termed it "gender performativity." Judith Butler, *Gender Trouble: Feminism and the Subversion of Identity* (New York: Routledge, 1990).

28. Kimmel, 4.

29. "Hegemonic masculinity" stems from a theory introduced by the Australian sociologist R. W. Connell. Though the term has sometimes denoted a form of masculine domination that renders women subservient within a patriarchal society, I use it to reference the way society defined the constellation of characteristics of an ideal man. I do not consider hegemonic masculinity to be a fixed concept, but specific aspects of it remained relatively stable during the era covered by this book. R. W. Connell, *Gender and Power* (Stanford, CA: Stanford University Press, 1987). See also R. W. Connell and James W. Messerschmidt, "Hegemonic Masculinity: Rethinking the Concept," *Gender and Society* 19, no. 6 (December 2005): 829–859.

30. On the "crisis theory" of American manhood, see Bryce Traister, "Academic Viagra: The Rise of American Masculinity Studies," *American Quarterly* 52, no. 2 (June 2000), esp. 287–291. Traister does not distinguish between historians who have seen the crisis as cyclical (and thus bubbling up during periods of upheaval, such as the 1890s, 1950s, and 1990s) and those, like Michael Kimmel, who argue that American men are constantly in crisis. A strong overview of the field is James Gilbert, *Men in the Middle: Searching for Masculinity in the 1950s* (Chicago: University of Chicago Press, 2005), chap. 2. An analysis focused on heterosexual white men is Daniel Wickberg, "Heterosexual White Male: Some Recent Interventions in Cultural History," *Journal of American History* 92, no. 1 (June 2005): 136–157.

31. Gilbert, *Men in the Middle*.

32. For an overview of this process, see John D'Emilio and Estelle B. Freedman, *Intimate Matters: A History of Sexuality in America*, 2nd ed. (Chicago: University of Chicago Press, 1997). On how sexuality shifted in New York City during the half-century before World War II, especially from a gay male perspective, see George Chauncey, *Gay New York: Gender, Urban Culture, and the Making of the Gay Male World, 1890–1940* (New York: Basic Books, 1994). On the intersection of sexuality, class, and race in the era of modernization, see Mary Ting Yi Lui, *The Chinatown Trunk Mystery: Murder, Miscegenation, and Other*

Dangerous Encounters in Turn-of-the-Century New York (Princeton: Princeton University Press, 2004). On the intersection of criminality, gender, and sexuality, see Angus McLaren, *The Trials of Masculinity: Policing Sexual Boundaries 1870–1930* (Chicago: University of Chicago Press, 1997).

33. On sexuality during the Great Depression, see Michelle Mitchell, "A 'Corrupting Influence': Idleness and Sexuality during the Great Depression," in *Interconnections: Gender and Race in American History*, ed. Carol Faulkner and Alison M. Parker (Rochester, NY: University of Rochester Press, 2012). On World War II's impact on sexuality, see Alan Bérubé, *Coming Out under Fire: The History of Gay Men and Women in World War II* (New York: Free Press, 1990) and Canaday, *The Straight State*.

34. Melanie Tebbutt, *Women's Talk: A Social History of "Gossip" in Working-Class Neighbourhoods, 1880–1960.* (Aldershot, England: Scolar Press, 1995), 20.

35. Kathleen A. Feeley, "Gossip as News: On Modern U.S. Celebrity Culture and Journalism," *History Compass* 10, no. 6 (2012): 467.

36. Patricia Meyer Spacks, *Gossip* (New York: Alfred A. Knopf, 1985), 34.

37. Spacks, 4.

38. Joke Hermes, *Reading Women's Magazines: An Analysis of Everyday Media Use* (London: Polity Press, 1995); Graeme Turner, *Understanding Celebrity*, 2nd ed. (London: SAGE, 2014), 121–143.

39. Neal Gabler, *Winchell: Gossip, Power, and the Culture of Celebrity* (New York: Knopf, 1994), 80–81.

40. Kathleen A. Feeley and Jennifer Frost, "Introduction," *When Private Talk Goes Public: Gossip in American History* (New York: Palgrave Macmillan, 2014), 7.

41. Feeley, "Gossip as News," 468. Feeley is referring to Mary Beth Norton, *In the Devil's Snare: The Salem Witchcraft Crisis of 1692* (New York: Vintage, 2003); John Demos, *Entertaining Satan: Witchcraft and the Culture of Early New England* (New York: Oxford University Press, 1982); and Terri L. Snyder, *Brabbling Women: Disorderly Speech and the Law in Early Virginia* (Ithaca, NY: Cornell University Press, 2013). The Salem witch trials also serve as the setting for Arthur Miller's 1953 play *The Crucible*, which has been widely read as a critique of how the social panic enabled by gossip and rumormongering facilitated the growth of McCarthyism.

42. Feeley, "Gossip as News," 468.

43. Molly M. Wood, "Diplomacy and Gossip: Information Gathering in the US Foreign Service, 1900–1940," in *When Private Talk Goes Public: Gossip in American History*, ed. Kathleen A. Feeley and Jennifer Frost (New York: Palgrave Macmillan, 2014), 140.

44. Wood, 151–152.

45. Ponce de Leon, 4.

46. Feeley and Frost, *When Private Talk Goes Public*, includes a variety of essays on the history of gossip in the United States. See also Ponce de Leon, *Self-Exposure*. Details on the rise and fall of *Confidential* magazine can be found in Mary Desjardins, "Systemizing Scandal: *Confidential* Magazine, Stardom, and the State of California," in *Headline Hollywood: A Century of Film Scandal*, ed. Adrienne McClean and David A. Cook (New

Brunswick, NJ: Rutgers University Press, 2001), and Henry E. Scott, *Shocking True Story: The Rise and Fall of* Confidential, *America's Most Scandalous Scandal Magazine* (New York: Pantheon Books, 2010).

47. The cultural critic Sue Brower reported in 1990 that the American gossip magazine the *Star* estimates that each copy is read by an average of 3.3 readers. The publishers of *People* magazine estimated a similar "pass-thru" rate in the late 1980s. Sue Brower, "Inside Stories: Gossip and Television Audiences," in "Culture and Communication: Language, Performance, Technology, and Media," ed. Sari Thomas and William A. Evans, special issue, *Studies in Communication* 4 (1990): 225–235.

CHAPTER 1

1. Robert S. Lynd and Helen Merrell Lynd, *Middletown: A Study in Modern American Culture* (New York: Harcourt, Brace, Jovanovich, 1929), 239. The Lynds estimated that one in five Middletown households subscribed to *The American Magazine*, a general-interest monthly; a slightly smaller number received *The Saturday Evening Post*, *McCall's*, and *Ladies' Home Journal*.

2. Lynd and Lynd, 242.

3. Lynd and Lynd, 242.

4. Lynd and Lynd, 499.

5. Lynd and Lynd, 500.

6. Lynd and Lynd, 501.

7. The lot is now occupied by the Capitol Hill United Methodist Church's parking lot. Though a number of biographers describe the house as stucco, the only photograph of the building that I have seen (from the Library of Congress and reprinted in Kenneth Ackerman's *Young J. Edgar*) shows clapboard siding. Kenneth D. Ackerman, *Young J. Edgar: Hoover and the Red Scare, 1919–20* (Falls Church, VA: Viral History Press, 2011).

8. Most biographers have understood Hoover as a brilliant, successful bureaucrat who was ruthless in his pursuit of power. Where they differ is in assessing the roots, character, and significance of Hoover's approach. Richard Gid Powers argues that such ambition made Hoover the most powerful political figure in the twentieth century. Richard Gid Powers, *Secrecy and Power: The Life of J. Edgar Hoover* (New York: Free Press, 1987). Curt Gentry positions Hoover as a righteous Victorian driven to defend the country from corrupting ideas and persons that did not fit with his traditionalist mindset. Curt Gentry, *J. Edgar Hoover: The Man and the Secrets* (New York: W. W. Norton, 2001). Athan Theoharis and John Stuart Cox emphasize how Hoover's authoritarianism helped erode constitutional guarantees. Athan G. Theoharis and John Stuart Cox, *The Boss: J. Edgar Hoover and the Great American Inquisition* (Philadelphia: Temple University Press, 1988). Douglas Charles and Jessica Pliley have recently illuminated how Hoover marshaled the FBI's bureaucratic prowess to combat obscenity, surveil and harass homosexuals, and "police morality." Charles, *Hoover's War on Gays*; Pliley, *Policing Sexuality*. My own perspective is closest to the work of Claire Bond Potter, who demonstrates how the War on Crime was as much of a cultural crusade as it was a judicial one. Claire Bond Potter, *War on Crime: Bandits,*

G-Men, and the Politics of Mass Culture (New Brunswick, NJ: Rutgers University Press, 1998). Where this book is singular is in mapping how Hoover's approach to surveillance and publicity helped inspire other political leaders—namely McCarthy and Cohn—to wield similar weapons.

9. Powers, *Secrecy and Power*, 6–8.

10. Gentry, 63.

11. Dickerson N. Hoover, Sr., letter to John Edgar Hoover, April 19, 1904, J. Edgar Hoover Collection, National Law Enforcement Museum, Washington, DC, as quoted in Powers, *Secrecy and Power*, 12.

12. Powers, *Secrecy and Power*, 8.

13. Powers, *Secrecy and Power*, 12.

14. George E. Allen, as quoted in Gentry, 63.

15. Though he apparently did not mind the nickname, the adult Hoover would not allow anybody but his closest friends to call him Speed. Two of those select few were Frank Baughman and Clyde Tolson.

16. Some records list him as 5'7", while others record a height of 5'10". In a *New Yorker* profile, Hoover is described as "almost six feet tall." Jack Alexander, "Profiles: The Director—II," *New Yorker*, October 2, 1937, 21.

17. Gentry, 65.

18. See US Census Bureau, "Table 13, Population of the 100 Largest Urban Places: 1900," https://www.census.gov/population/www/documentation/twps0027/tab13.txt.

19. Powers, *Secrecy and Power*, 9.

20. Powers, *Secrecy and Power*, 22.

21. Jack Alexander, "Profiles: The Director—II," *New Yorker*, October 2, 1937, 21.

22. "Central High School Report of J. E. Hoover, 1911–1912," JEHMC.

23. Hester O'Neill, "J. Edgar Hoover's Schooldays (Part 4)," *American Boy and Open Road*, September 1954, 22; J. Edgar Hoover, "Debate Memorandum Notebook," JEHMC.

24. Jack Alexander, "Profiles: The Director—II," *New Yorker*, October 2, 1937, 21.

25. Powers, *Secrecy and Power*, 30–31; Gentry, 61–62.

26. Central High School classmate of Hoover's, as quoted in Gentry, 66.

27. "Population, Housing Units, Area Measurements, and Density: 1790 to 1990," United States Census Bureau, https://www.census.gov/prod/www/decennial.html.

28. Daylanne K. English, *Unnatural Selections: Eugenics in American Modernism and the Harlem Renaissance* (Chapel Hill: University of North Carolina Press, 2004), 37.

29. Peter Quartermain, *Disjunctive Poetics: From Gertrude Stein and Louis Zukofsky to Susan Howe* (Cambridge: Cambridge University Press, 1992), 10.

30. Howard P. Chudacoff, *The Age of the Bachelor: Creating an American Subculture* (Princeton: Princeton University Press, 1999).

31. In this formulation, "white-collar jobs" include "clerical workers, salespeople, government employees, technicians, and salaried professionals," with an increase from "756 thousand to 5.6 million." See figures in S. P. Hays, *The Response to Industrialism* (1957), as quoted in Jeffrey P. Hantover, "The Boy Scouts and the Validation of Masculinity," in *The American Man*, ed. Elizabeth Hafkin Pleck and Joseph H. Pleck (Englewood Cliffs, NJ: Prentice Hall, 1980), 291.

32. Kate Upson Clark, *Bringing Up Boys: A Study* (New York: Thomas H. Crowell, 1899), 102.

33. Clark, 114, 117–120. Clark did not even mention boxing—Joe McCarthy's chosen sport—presumably because of its violent nature and proletarian associations.

34. Clark, 78–80.

35. Frank Orman Beck, *Marching Manward: A Study of the Boy* (New York: Eaton & Mains, 1913), 41, 54–55.

36. Hantover, 289.

37. James E. West, "The Real Boy Scout," *Leslie's Weekly*, no. 114 (1912), 448.

38. Beck, 96.

39. Originally the New England Society for the Suppression of Vice, the New England Watch and Ward Society became so successful stemming the distribution of morally questionable literature, films, dramatic productions, and music that they gave birth to a new phrase: "banned in Boston." Ironically, the label often spurred overall sales and was sought by authors, publishers, and filmmakers. See Neil Miller, *Banned in Boston: The Watch and Ward Society's Crusade against Books, Burlesque and the Social Evil* (Boston: Beacon Press, 2010).

40. Chauncey, *Gay New York*, 147.

41. "Anthony Comstock Dies in His Crusade," *New York Times*, September 22, 1915, 1. See also Anna Bates, *Weeder in the Garden of the Lord: Anthony Comstock's Life and Career* (Lanham, MD: University Press of America, 1995); Nicola Beisel, *Imperiled Innocents: Anthony Comstock and Family Reproduction in Victorian America.* (Princeton: Princeton University Press, 1997). Numerous online sources claim that while a law student, J. Edgar Hoover became "obsessed" with Comstock and his tactics. But no trustworthy sources corroborate that claim. Furthermore, it does not appear that the Bureau maintained any meaningful relationship with the NYSSV following Hoover's elevation to director, despite their common interests. On John S. Sumner, see Jay A. Gertzman, "John Saxton Sumner of the New York Society for the Suppression of Vice: A Chief Smut-Eradicator of the Interwar Period," *Journal of American Culture* 17, no. 2 (June 1994): 41–47.

42. Allan Hoben, *The Minister and the Boy: A Handbook for Churchmen Engaged in Boys' Work* (Chicago: University of Chicago Press, 1912), 4.

43. A recent examination of the way muscular Christianity operated at the nexus of gender, race making, and religious iconography is Rachel McBride Lindsey, "'The Mirror of All Perfection': Jesus and the Strongman in America, 1893–1920," *American Quarterly* 68, no. 1 (March 2016): 23–47.

44. Hoben, 106.

45. William Byron Forbush, *The Boy Problem in the Home* (Boston: Pilgrim Press, 1915), 257.

46. Pierce arrived at this conclusion after polling eight college professors about "the twelve greatest men in all the world since Christ." Of the ninety-six names he received in response, there was no overlap and "the only one who was not really a Christian was Napoleon." Jason Noble Pierce, *The Masculine Power of Christ, or, Christ Measured as a Man* (Boston: Pilgrim Press, 1912), 5–6, 8.

47. Hoben, 11.

48. Eugene C. Foster, *The Boy and the Church* (Philadelphia: Sunday School Times Company, 1909), 53.

49. Foster, *The Boy and the Church*, 119.

50. Foster, *The Boy and the Church*, 138.

51. Pierce, 11.

52. Pierce, 14.

53. Robert Warren Conant, *The Virility of Christ: A New View* (Chicago:the author, 1915), 14, emphasis in original.

54. Conant, 63–64.

55. Pierce, 2.

56. Conant, 330.

57. Clifford Putney, *Muscular Christianity: Manhood and Sports in Protestant America, 1880–1920* (Cambridge, MA: Harvard University Press, 2003), 11.

58. Putney, 198.

59. Hoben, 81.

60. Hoben, 74–76.

61. Hoben, 79–80.

62. David Macleod, *Building Character in the American Boy: The Boy Scouts, YMCA, and Their Forerunners, 1870–1920* (Madison: University of Wisconsin Press, 1983), 29.

63. Hoben, 69–70. Of course, the great irony here is that in the mid to late twentieth century the YMCA would become known in certain circles as a location where men sought to meet other men for sex.

64. Don Whitehead, "Hoover's 30 Years With FBI—From Hack Bureau To Top Agency," *St. Petersburg Times*, May 9, 1954, 11-A.

65. Richard Harwood, "J. Edgar Hoover: A Librarian with a Lifetime Lease," *Washington Post*, February 25, 1968, D1.

66. Powers, *Secrecy and Power*, 15.

67. Session Records of First Presbyterian Church of Washington, D.C., courtesy of Reverend Jerry Wheat, Archives Representative, National Presbyterian Church, Washington, D.C.

68. Don Whitehead, "Hoover's 30 Years With FBI—From Hack Bureau To Top Agency," *St. Petersburg Times*, May 9, 1954, 11-A.

69. Upton Sinclair's introduction to his novelization of *Damaged Goods*, as quoted in Alan Axelrod, *Selling the Great War: The Making of American Propaganda* (New York: Macmillan, 2009), 118.

70. Powers, *Secrecy and Power*, 33. Despite the organization's name, men were welcomed as honorary members of the Women's Christian Temperance Union.

71. Gentry, 68. Among the sanitarium's specialties was treating neurasthenia, a condition characterized by weakness, nervousness, and fatigue whose prevalence was thought to be at partially a by-product of the stresses of "modern living." White-collar men were believed to be at particular risk because their work was not physical. By the time Dickerson Sr. arrived, the sanitarium was run by Jesse Coggins and Cornelius DeWeese, doctors with extensive experience treating mental disorders. See Kevin Leonard, "Once a Laurel Landmark, Sanitarium Now Forgotten," *Baltimore Sun*, July 10, 2014, http://www.baltimoresun.com/news/maryland/howard/laurel/ph-ll-history-sanitarium-0619-2014
0710-story.html#page=1.

72. Gentry, 67.

73. Andy Logan, "That Was New York—Talk of the Town," *New Yorker*, August 14, 1965, 37–91.

74. Andy Logan, *The Man Who Robbed the Robber Barons* (New York: W. W. Norton, 1965), 130.

75. Logan, *The Man Who Robbed*, 131–132.

76. Mann would later claim that the election had been stolen from him by Radical Republican interests. Logan, *The Man Who Robbed*, 101–102; Robert R. Rowe, "Mann of Town Topics," *American Mercury*, July 1926, 272.

77. In 1926, *The American Mercury* reported that Mann's favorite dinner consisted of "three English mutton chops festooned with baked yams and a lettuce-tomato-cucumber salad, washed down with not less than two bottles of vintage champagne." Robert R. Rowe, "Mann of Town Topics," *American Mercury*, July 1926, 272.

78. Logan, *The Man Who Robbed*, 20, quoting a December 1895 issue of *Town Topics*.

79. "Mann Would Reform the Four Hundred," *New York Times*, August 1, 1905, 7.

80. Logan, *The Man Who Robbed*, 139.

81. Logan, *The Man Who Robbed*, 139. See also Stephanie Foote, "Little Brothers of the Rich: Queer Families in the Gilded Age," *American Literature* 79, no. 4 (December 2007): 701–724.

82. "Saunterings," *Town Topics*, February 16, 1893, 7.

83. *Town Topics*, January 5, 1893, 1. It appears that the final issue carrying such a banner was that of April 20, 1893, which advertised a circulation of "over 80,000."

84. Edwin Post, *Truly Emily Post* (New York: Funk & Wagnalls Company, 1961): 143. Tuxedo Park, a gated community northwest of Manhattan, was a haven for a number of Gilded Age elites including J. P. Morgan.

85. "Other People's Money," *Town Topics*, February 16, 1893, 23.

86. *Town Topics*, August 22, 1895, 27–28.

87. All advertisements appear in *Town Topics*, January 5, 1893, 26.

88. *Town Topics*, April 27, 189327.

89. *Town Topics*, February 16, 1893, 23.

90. Logan, *The Man Who Robbed*, 24–28.

91. Robert Love, "Shakedown!: The Unfortunate History of Reporters Who Trade Power for Cash," *Columbia Journalism Review* 45, no. 2 (May/June 2006): 47–51; Mark Caldwell, "New York's School for Scandal Sheets," *New York Times*, April 21, 2006, A25; Laura Claridge, *Emily Post: Daughter of the Gilded Age, Mistress of American Manners* (New York: Random House, 2008): 167.

92. Will Straw, "Remembering the Creator of Modern Gossip Journalism," *Huffington Post*, February 8, 2016, huffingtonpost.ca/will-straw-phd/gossip-king-stephen-g-clow_b_916 9414.html.

93. Will Straw, "Traffic in Scandal: The Story of *Broadway Brevities*," *University of Toronto Quarterly* 73, no. 4 (Fall 2004): 950.

94. "'Brevities' Owners Indicted for Fraud," *New York Times*, May 6, 1924, 8.

95. "Night No. 5 in Fairyland," *Broadway Brevities and Society Gossip*, May 1924.

96. "Night No. 11 in Fairyland," *Broadway Brevities and Society Gossip*, November 1924, 32; ellipsis in original text.

97. "Night No. 11 in Fairyland," *Broadway Brevities and Society Gossip*, November 1924, 35–36. Despite its successes at the newsstand, *Broadway Brevities* was eventually shut down when Clow's extortion scheme was revealed. The investigation had partially resulted from the efforts of the New York Attorney General's Office to control the production and distribution of vulgar publications. After a two-year stint in the Atlanta Federal Penitentiary, Clow tried to relaunch *Town Topics* but had little success. Impoverished, his marriage failed and he eventually died in Bellevue Hospital in June 1941. "Stephen Clow Dies at 67," *New York Times*, June 7, 1941, 19.

CHAPTER 2

1. Brian Burrough, *Public Enemies: America's Greatest Crime Wave and the Birth of the FBI, 1933–34* (New York: Penguin Press, 2004), 538–542. Note that the "cuffs" had been forgotten by the FBI agents in their rush to arrest Karpis, and the outlaw and his associates had to be bound with ties borrowed from the agents' necks.

2. "Karpis Captured in New Orleans by Hoover Himself," *New York Times*, May 2, 1936, 1; "Hoover Leads 20 Agents in Arresting Nation's No. 1 Outlaw," *Washington Post*, May 2, 1936, 1.

3. Burrough, 538–542.

4. Alvin Karpis and Bill Treat, *The Alvin Karpis Story* (New York: Ishi Press, 2011), 230.

5. "J. Edgar Hoover Is Quizzed about Work as Sleuth," *Chicago Daily Tribune*, April 17, 1936, 3.

6. "Hoover Leads 20 Agents in Arresting Nation's No. 1 Outlaw," *Washington Post*, May 2, 1936, 1.

7. Lemuel F. Parton, "Beer Bottle Fingerprint Led to Karpis Gang Doom: Writer Learns How J. E. Hoover's Men Work in Battle against Organized Criminals," *Los Angeles Times*, May 14, 1936, 21.

8. "Seize Karpis; Fly Him Away," *Chicago Daily Tribune*, May 2, 1936, 1. The same term was utilized by the *Los Angeles Times* and the *Atlanta Journal-Constitution*.

9. J. Edgar Hoover, as quoted in "Karpis Begs to Be Killed," *Los Angeles Times*, May 4, 1936, 14.

10. J. Edgar Hoover, as quoted in "Karpis Frightened So He Couldn't Talk," *Washington Post*, May 3, 1936, M4.

11. "Seize Karpis; Fly Him Away." *Chicago Daily Tribune*, May 2, 1936, 1.

12. Powers, *Secrecy and Power*, 41–42. The connection was Hoover's cousin, William Hitz, who had worked for Attorney General Thomas Gregory before becoming an associate justice in the District of Columbia's Supreme Court.

13. Jack Alexander, "Profile: The Director—II," *New Yorker*, October 2, 1937, 21. While there is little reason to doubt Alexander's description, his conclusion that Hoover's superiors considered his work "so important" that they "persuaded him to spend the period of the World War at his desk" does signal that the journalist had been fed lines from the FBI's public-relations representatives.

14. Ovid Demaris, *The Director: An Oral Biography of J. Edgar Hoover* (New York: Harpers' Magazine Press, 1975), 51. Hoover would also remain known for his sense of style throughout his life, with the *Washington Post* naming him one of DC's ten best-dressed men in 1950. Gregory Carmichael, "Washington's List of Ten Best-Dressed Men," *Washington Post*, January 1, 1950, S5.

15. On public calls for morality policing, see Pliley, 85.

16. Section 2 of the White-Slave Traffic Act held that anyone caught disobeying it "shall be deemed guilty of a felony, and upon conviction thereof shall be punished by a fine not exceeding five thousand dollars, or by imprisonment of not more than five years, or by both such fine and imprisonment, in the discretion of the court." Passed on June 25, 1910, the act has never been repealed; each count now carries a maximum penalty of ten years in prison. See US Legal Code Title 18, part I, chapter 117, subsection 2421. Original text of the act can be found in Senate Document 702 of the 61st Congress, 3rd Session (December 13, 1910).

17. Pliley, 132–135. Pliley notes that during that same period there were only 6,335 convictions under the Mann Act. But too much focus on the ratio of prosecutions to convictions overlooks the impact the Bureau had in merely signaling that the state condemned such conduct. Convictions were not the only way to influence behavior.

18. J. Edgar Hoover, "Accomplishments of the Federal Bureau of Investigation, United

States Department of Justice, during the Fiscal Year Ending June 30, 1940," July 31, 1940, 3, Marquette University Archives.

19. James H. Hallas, *Doughboy War: The American Expeditionary Force in World War I* (Boulder, CO: Lynne Rienner Publishers, 2000), 1.

20. On the history of the Obscene File, see Douglas M. Charles, *The FBI's Obscene File: J. Edgar Hoover and the Bureau's Crusade against Smut* (Lawrence: University Press of Kansas, 2012). On the 1923–25 Clean Books Crusade, see Paul S. Boyer, *Purity in Print: Book Censorship in American from the Gilded Age to the Computer Age*, 2nd ed. (Madison: University of Wisconsin Press, 2002), 99–127. Boyer notes that the Clean Books Crusade partially backfired on the New York Society for the Suppression of Vice and its leader John S. Sumner, who were both ridiculed for attempting to police reading materials, and identifies the crusade as the beginning of the downfall of the influential NYSSV.

21. FBI memo of August 25, 1944 (FBI document 80-662-[40?]), as quoted in Charles, *The FBI's Obscene File*, 22.

22. J. Edgar Hoover, "Pioneering in Honesty," commencement address delivered at Oklahoma Baptist University, Shawnee, May 23, 1938, 7, Marquette University Archives.

23. J. Edgar Hoover, "No More Cops!," *Los Angeles Times*, March 6, 1938, I2.

24. Potter, *War on Crime*, 189–194.

25. See Alfred McCoy, *Policing America's Empire* (Madison: University of Wisconsin Press, 2009).

26. Federal involvement was justified due to the Mann Act's explicitly interstate nature and the fact that obscenity was regulated by policing the federally controlled postal system.

27. Hoover in a May 1925 memo to Special Agents in Charge, as quoted in Powers, *Secrecy and Power*, 144.

28. "A Byte Out of History: 'Machine-Gun Kelly' and the Legend of the G-Men," the Federal Bureau of Investigation: Stories: September 29, 2003, https://www.fbi.gov/news/stories/2003/september/kelly092603. The timeline forwarded in this FBI legend matches other media monikers for Bureau agents, including an August 1933 *Collier's* piece which exclusively refers to them as "D of J men" (Ray Tucker, "Hist, Who's That?," *Collier's* 92 (August 19, 1933): 15, 49). Hoover himself repeated elements of the Kelly story in a syndicated newspaper column. J. Edgar Hoover, "G-Heat Stays Hot," *Los Angeles Times*, June 5, 1938, I10.

29. Angel Kwolek-Folland, *Engendering Business: Men and Women in the Corporate Office, 1870–1930* (Baltimore: Johns Hopkins University Press, 1994), 47.

30. Pettegrew, 16.

31. Pettegrew, 40.

32. Cindy Sondik Aron, *Ladies and Gentlemen of the Civil Service: Middle-Class Workers in Victorian America* (New York: Oxford University Press, 1987), 188.

33. Kwolek-Folland, 48–49. She continues, "Religion could create success not only because it was morally proper but because it made a man stronger, both physically and mentally. In turn, evidence of moral propriety was proof of related business skills and hence manliness."

34. According to biographer Richard Gid Powers, "By the end of his first year Hoover had let sixty-one employees go and closed five out of fifty-three field offices; he was also able to return $300,000 of his $2.4-million appropriation. At the end of the decade, his staff was down to 581, 339 of them agents, far below the Bureau's peak figure of 1,127 (579 agents) in 1920, and he had reduced the number of field offices to thirty. At the end of 1932, the number of field offices would reach a low of twenty-two." Powers, *Secrecy and Power*, 151.

35. Kwolek-Folland, 73. In this telling, scientific management also played into a gendered understanding of business management: "To the extent that the work process could be measured, and to the extent that it was governed by technological developments and increasing job specialization, it was less possible to imagine a place for the self-made man of character, for social mobility through work, for the opportunity to prove one's manhood by grappling with the vicissitudes of business life, or for physical skill and stamina . . . Rational management closed a crucial door for self-evaluation by locking out a central tenet of middle-class notions of manhood. However, systematic management's mechanic view of society suggested alternative avenues for the expression of masculinity: acquiring specialized knowledge, developing such ascribed masculine qualities as rationality, and gaining power over others if not over oneself. Masculinity could be expressed through rational application of mechanical business laws of profit and loss, maximized use of time, and separation from more menial, clerical, female labor." Kwolek-Folland, 73–74.

36. For Hoover's own description of the idea special agent applicant, see J. Edgar Hoover, "The Work of the Bureau of Investigation," *American Journal of Political Science* 2, no. 2 (March–April 1931): 103.

37. C. D. White, "Report on Applicant for Position as Special Agent: Clyde Tolson," February 7, 1928 (document 76-9524-15, FBI Files, National Archives). The "no particular interest in women" comment came from John Martyn, executive secretary for the secretary of war.

38. Potter, *War on Crime*, 49. Hoover's favoritism for such organizations was so well-known that some newspapermen began referring to special agents as "Hoover's Boy Scouts." Walter Trohan, "J. Edgar Hoover: The One-Man Scotland Yard," *Chicago Daily Tribune*, June 21, 1936, D1.

39. J. Edgar Hoover, "Your Task as a Citizen: Address before the National Convention of the United States Junior Chamber of Commerce," Tulsa, OK, June 21, 1939, 1, Marquette University Archives.

40. In 1935, these principles influenced the curriculum of the newly formed FBI Police Training School, which instructed law enforcement officers from across the nation on proper investigative methods. See "A Milestone in Police Training: Seventy-Five Years Ago," Federal Bureau of Investigation—Stories, July 29, 2010, http://www.fbi.gov/news/sto ries/2010/july/national-academy.

41. Powers, *Secrecy and Power*, 223–224.

42. The Bureau's intramural basketball team was successful and even won the 1932 Government League title. See George D. Riley, "The Federal Diary," *Washington Post*, January 2, 1933, 4.

43. Don Whitehead, *The FBI Story: A Report to the People* (New York: Random House, 1956), 70–71.

44. This notion is examined more fully in Pettegrew, *Brutes in Suits*.

45. Powers, *Secrecy and Power*, 265.

46. J. Edgar Hoover, "Your Future Task: Address at Commencement Exercises of the University of the South," Sewanee, TN, June 9, 1941, 2, Marquette University Archives.

47. Hoover's interest in the media had deep roots; at the age of eleven, he had published his own newspaper (price, one cent) in which he reported the goings-on in his household and the Seward Square neighborhood. See Powers, *Secrecy and Power*, 20–22.

48. Hoover to Melvin Purvis, August 18, 1931 (attached to memo from V. W. Hughes to Hoover, August 15, 1931, FBI file 67-7489-168), as quoted in Potter, *War on Crime*, 54.

49. Walter Winchell, "Winchell on Broadway," *New York Daily Mirror*, September 24, 1935, 10.

50. J. Edgar Hoover, "Editorial Comment: The Task of the Teacher," *Phi Beta Kappan* 22, no. 7 (March 1940), 329–330; J. Edgar Hoover, "Is There a Spy Menace?," *Atlanta Journal-Constitution*, July 14, 1940, B2; J. Edgar Hoover, "Juvenile—or Public—Delinquency?," *Los Angeles Times*, December 19, 1937, J10; J. Edgar Hoover, "The Woman in Crime," *Los Angeles Times*, October 17, 1937, J2; J. Edgar Hoover, "Is the Army Breeding Criminals?," *Los Angeles Times*, March 11, 1945, F4.

51. J. Edgar Hoover, "Fifty Years of Crime: Corruption Begets Corruption: Address before the National Fifty Years in Business Club, Nashville, Tennessee, May 20, 1939," *Vital Speeches of the Day*, June 1, 1939, 507.

52. J. Edgar Hoover, "Firearms Training in the FBI," *Leatherneck*, September 1939, 5–8.

53. J. Edgar Hoover, "M-Day for the FBI," *Los Angeles Times*, August 11, 1940, 14.

54. J. Edgar Hoover, "The Cost of Crime," *Chicago Sun*, January 16, 1938, SM2.

55. J. Edgar Hoover, "We Prove Them Innocent," *Chicago Sun*, October 29, 1944, MS2.

56. Mary Elizabeth Strunk, *Wanted Women: An American Obsession in the Reign of J. Edgar Hoover* (Lawrence: University Press of Kansas, 2010), 25.

57. Emma Bugbee, "J. Edgar Hoover Asks Women to Aid in Crime Fight," *New York Herald Tribune*, May 18, 1938, 15.

58. "J. Edgar Hoover Pleads for Family Religious Life," *New York Herald Tribune*, January 2, 1948, 10.

59. J. Edgar Hoover, "Pioneering in Honesty: Commencement address delivered at Oklahoma Baptist University," Shawnee, May 23, 1938, 7, Marquette University Archives.

60. Erica J. Ryan, *Red War on the Family: Sex, Gender, and Americanism in the First Red Scare* (Philadelphia: Temple University Press, 2015).

61. J. Edgar Hoover, "Address at the Opening Session of the 22nd Annual National Convention of the American Legion," Boston, September 23, 1940, 3–4, Marquette University Archives.

62. J. Edgar Hoover, "Men of Tomorrow: Address before the Boy Scout Day Celebration at the New York World's Fair," New York, June 29, 1939, 3, Marquette University Archives; emphasis in original.

63. Hoover, "Men of Tomorrow," 3; emphasis in original.

64. J. Edgar Hoover, "Your Task as a Citizen: Address before the National Convention of the United States Junior Chamber of Commerce," Tulsa, June 21, 1939, 1, Marquette University Archives.

65. J. Edgar Hoover, "Your Future Task: Address at Commencement Exercises of the University of the South," Sewanee, TN, June 9, 1941, 1, Marquette University Archives.

66. Hoover, "Your Future Task," 1.

67. Hoover, "Your Future Task," 4–5.

68. Stock response signed by Hoover and distributed in reply to fan mail about *G-Men*, as quoted in Richard Gid Powers, *G-Men: Hoover's FBI in American Popular Culture* (Carbondale, IL: Southern Illinois University Press, 1983), 53.

69. Early agents of the Bureau had been issued firearms, but the practice had been dropped in 1924.

70. According to script notes, Gregory was a "strong-faced man of about thirty-nine, very young for his important post." Powers, *G-Men*, 61. Thirty-nine was Hoover's exact age the year the film was released.

71. Powers, *G-Men*, 61.

72. *Queen of the Mob* featured an appearance by Hedda Hopper, a mid-level actress who would later make her name as one of the nation's most popular gossip columnists.

73. Now largely a relic of Hollywood history, the film serial (or simply "serial") was a live-action production released in multiple parts that usually featured a hero such as Dick Tracy, Zorro, Flash Gordon, or Captain Marvel. Most serials were composed of fifteen chapters of fifteen to twenty minutes each that would be shown at a movie theater during multifeature shows designed to attract adolescent audiences. For more, see Buck Rainey, *Serials and Series: A World Filmography, 1912–1956* (Jefferson, NC: McFarland Books, 2010).

74. Full episodes of *Gang Busters*, *This Is Your FBI*, and *The True Adventures of Junior G-Men* are available at the Internet Archive, www.archive.org.

75. The strip's original writer was Dashiell Hammett, author of *The Maltese Falcon* and future McCarthy target. After the 1930s, the FBI name was dropped in favor of an anonymous secret agency. See Bruce Canwell, "Craft and Tradecraft," in *Secret Agent X-9* (San Diego: IDW Publishing, 2015), 5.

76. Powers, *G-Men*, 134. Note too that Rex Collier was one of the original writers for the *G-Men* radio program.

77. Susan L. Cook and Karen Krupar, "Defining the Twentieth Century and Impacting the Twenty-First: Semantic Habits Created through Radio and Song: A Review of General Semantics," *Et Cetera* 67, no. 4 (October 2010): 416.

78. Ray Tucker, "Hist, Who's That?," *Collier's*, August 19, 1933, 49.

79. Peter Carter, "Peter Carter Says . . ." *Washington Herald*, August 3, 1933.

80. Ray Tucker, "Hist, Who's That?," *Collier's*, August 19, 1933, 49.

81. Peter Carter, "Peter Carter Says . . . ," *Washington Herald*, August 28, 1933. The phrase "mincing step" was used by critics throughout the rest of Hoover's life to suggest his homosexuality. In 1967, Mr. William Reinbold used almost that exact phrase in a letter to the liberal newspaper columnist Drew Pearson: "For a long time I have heard the persistent rumor that J. Edgar Hoover is a homosexual. That may be unbelievable to many but it is by no means impossible[.] His misogyny, his mincing walk, his vindictiveness, the fact that he is usually seen in public with one handsome male are at least superficial signs." William Reinbold to Pearson, folder "Federal Bureau of Investigation," box G-273 (1 of 3), Pearson Papers.

82. Walter Trohan, "J. Edgar Hoover: The One-Man Scotland Yard," *Chicago Daily Tribune*, June 21, 1936, D1.

83. The Smithsonian actually describes it as "lavender (??)." "Eleanor Roosevelt's 1933 Inaugural Ceremonies Dress, 1933," https://americanhistory.si.edu/collections/search/object/nmah_491671. On use of the term "Eleanor blue," see Blanche Wiesen Cook, *Eleanor Roosevelt*, vol. 2: *The Defining Years, 1933–1938* (New York: Viking Press, 1999), 14. On the history of the word "lavender" as a marker of homosexuality, see Gershon Legman, "The Language of Homosexuality," in *Gay/Lesbian Almanac: A New Documentary*, ed. Johnathan Ned Katz (New York: Harper & Row, 1983), 571–584; and Judy Grahn, *Another Mother Tongue: Gay Words, Gay Worlds* (Boston: Beacon Press, 1984), 3–17.

84. *Liberty* magazine, as quoted in Richard Harwood, "J. Edgar Hoover: A Librarian with a Lifetime Lease," *Washington Post*, February 25, 1968, D1.

85. Don Whitehead, "Hoover's 30 Years with FBI—From Hack Bureau to Top Agency," *St. Petersburg Times*, May 9, 1954, 11-A.

86. "Memo: FBI Agent to Conroy, 27 June 1944," Official and Confidential File, folder 75, as quoted in Theoharis and Cox, *The Boss: J. Edgar Hoover and the Great American Inquisition* (Philadelphia: Temple University Press, 1988), 208; "Memo: FBI Agent to Hoover, 30 June 1943," Official and Confidential File, folder 75 (reel 12, frame 750 of University Publications microfilm).

87. Theoharis and Cox, *The Boss*, 208–212.

88. "Memo: FBI Assistant Director Louis Nichols to FBI Associate Director Clyde Tolson, 20 June 1951," as quoted in Athan Theoharis, *From the Secret Files of J. Edgar Hoover* (Chicago: Ivan R. Dee, 1993), 353–354.

89. *Washington Post*, January 2, 1933, as cited in Potter, *War on Crime*, 48.

90. Lemuel F. Parton, "Beer Bottle Fingerprint Led to Karpis Gang Doom: Writer Learns How J. E. Hoover's Men Work in Battle Against Organized Criminals," *Los Angeles Times*, May 14, 1936, 21.

91. Samuel Bernstein, *Mr. Confidential: The Man, His Magazine, & the Movieland Massacre that Changed Hollywood Forever* (West Hollywood, CA: Walford Press, 2006), 50.

92. Gentry, 512.

93. Gabler, *Winchell*, 197–202. Winchell even helped Hoover capture Murder, Inc., hitman Louis "Lepke" Buchalter, serving as a go-between during the negotiation of Lepke's surrender. See Gabler, 274–280.

94. Gentry, 329.

95. Hoover to Winchell in August 8, 1935, letter, as quoted in Gabler, 202.

96. Walter Winchell, "Walter Winchell on Broadway: G-Men about Town," *New York Daily Mirror*, September 29, 1935, 10.

97. Potter, *War on Crime*, 128–130.

98. Some have suggested that the woman in the photo is Luisa Stuart, a model and soap opera actress. Stuart gained renewed fame in the early 1990s when she claimed to Hoover biographer Anthony Summers that she witnessed Hoover and Clyde Tolson holding hands in a limousine on New Years' Eve 1936.

99. Marylyn Reeve, "Lawyer, G-Man, Sailor, Diplomat Offered as This Week's 'Eligibles,'" *Washington Post*, October 4, 1936, S4.

100. "Murphy Goes East 'Til July," *Los Angeles Times*, May 28, 1939, A1. Hoover was also named one of the world's ten most eligible bachelors by the Bachelors Clubs of America in 1952. A good measure of Hoover's enduring celebrity status is that Marlon Brando made the same list. "Here They Are, Girls!: World's Most Eligible Bachelors Chalked Up," *Los Angeles Times*, February 19, 1952, 10.

101. Jessie Ash Arndt, "Boys in Neighborhood Turn Heat on J. Edgar Hoover," *Washington Post*, July 30, 1940, 13.

102. J. Edgar Hoover, "If I Had a Son . . . ," *Woman's Day*, June 1938, Marquette University Archives.

103. J. Edgar Hoover, "Our Future: Address at Commencement Exercises of the University of Notre Dame," South Bend, IN, May 10, 1942, 4, Marquette University Archives.

104. J. Edgar Hoover, "Law Enforcement in a Crisis: Address before the Annual *New York Herald-Tribune* Forum," New York, October 24, 1939, 1, Marquette University Archives.

105. J. Edgar Hoover, "Law Enforcement in a Crisis: Address before the Annual *New York Herald-Tribune* Forum," New York: October 24, 1939, 2, Marquette University Archives.

106. J. Edgar Hoover, in a September 19, 1938, speech to the American Legion in Los Angeles, as quoted in "'Twin Ism Evils' Hit by J. Edgar Hoover," *New York Times*, September 20, 1938, 25.

107. J. Edgar Hoover, "The Test of Citizenship: Address to the 49th Continental Congress of the Daughters of the American Revolution," Washington, DC, April 18, 1940, 7, Marquette University Archives.

108. This point is thoroughly made in Canaday, *The Straight State*.

109. See Stuart, *Creating the National Security State*; Hogan, *A Cross of Iron*.

110. Debs eventually served half that time. See Nick Salvatore, *Eugene V. Debs: Citizen and Socialist* (Urbana: University of Illinois Press, 1982).

111. Powers, *Secrecy and Power*, 104.

112. Theoharis and Cox, *The Boss*, 59. For more on anarchism in America, see Kenyon Zimmer, *Immigrants against the State: Yiddish and Italian Anarchism in America* (Urbana: University of Illinois Press, 2015).

113. Betty Medsger, *The Burglary: The Discovery of J. Edgar Hoover's Secret FBI* (New York: Vintage, 2014), 523.

114. J. Edgar Hoover, "Memorandum for Mr. Creighton," August 23, 1919, Emma Goldman Papers, University of California–Berkeley, cited in Kathy E. Ferguson, "Discourses of Danger: Locating Emma Goldman," *Political Theory* 6, no. 5 (October 2008): 735–761.

115. Richard Harwood, "J. Edgar Hoover: A Librarian with a Lifetime Lease," *Washington Post*, February 25, 1968, D1.

116. Of particular significance in this expansion of federal jurisdiction was the 1932 Federal Anti-Kidnapping Law, or Lindbergh Law, which made kidnapping a federal crime in the wake of the abduction and murder of Charles Lindbergh Jr.

117. Theoharis and Cox, *The Boss*, 151.

118. As quoted in Theoharis and Cox, *The Boss*, 150–151. The recounting of these two meetings comes from two confidential memoranda filed by Hoover to his Official and Confidential File on August 24 and 25, 1936.

119. Theoharis and Cox, *The Boss*, 151.

120. Powers, *Secrecy and Power*, 274.

121. J. Edgar Hoover, "Accomplishments of the Federal Bureau of Investigation, United States Department of Justice, during the Fiscal Year Ending June 30, 1940," July 31, 1940, 2–3, Marquette University Archives.

122. J. Edgar Hoover, "Law Enforcement in a Crisis: Address before the Annual *New York Herald-Tribune* Forum," New York, October 24, 1939, 3, Marquette University Archives.

123. J. Edgar Hoover, "Address at the Opening Session of the 22nd Annual National Convention of the American Legion," Boston, September 23, 1940, 3, Marquette University Archives.

124. J. Edgar Hoover, "Accomplishments of the Federal Bureau of Investigation, United States Department of Justice, during the Fiscal Year Ending June 30, 1940," July 31, 1940, 3, Marquette University Archives.

125. Hoover testimony before House Appropriations Subcommittee, November 30, 1939. Curt Gentry notes that the custodial detention list was "periodically revised to include new enemies [and] later renamed the Security Index (SI) and the Administrative Index (ADEX), and it eventually spawned such other specialist lists as the Reserve (or Communist) Index, the Agitator Index, and the Rabble Rouser Index." Gentry, 213.

126. Theoharis and Cox, *The Boss*, 171.

127. Theoharis and Cox, *The Boss*, 193–198.

CHAPTER 3

1. Jack Anderson and Ronald W. May, *McCarthy: The Man, the Senator, the "Ism"* (Boston: Beacon Press, 1952), 23.

2. Lately Thomas, *When Even Angels Wept: The Senator Joseph McCarthy Affair—a Story without a Hero* (New York: Morrow, 1973), 10.

3. Even the path of McCarthy's boxing career is a tempting metaphor for his post-Wheeling political trajectory—he started off hot but eventually fell back to earth.

4. Examples of this approach to McCarthy can be seen in Anderson and May, *McCarthy*; Richard H. Rovere, *Senator Joe McCarthy* (New York: Harcourt, Brace, 1959); Thomas C. Reeves, *The Life and Times of Joe McCarthy* (New York: Stein and Day, 1982); and William Bragg Ewald, *Who Killed Joe McCarthy?* (New York: Simon and Schuster, 1984). Anderson's original pitch for his book on McCarthy was entitled, "The Wild Man from Wisconsin." See folder "Anderson—McCarthy Outline," box G221, 2 of 3, Pearson Papers.

5. David Oshinsky, *A Conspiracy So Immense: The World of Joe McCarthy* (New York: Oxford University Press, 2005), 3–6. My understanding of McCarthy is very similar to that developed in Oshinsky's magisterial, evenhanded biography. But where Oshinsky is interested in a full character study, here I have focused on the ways in which McCarthy helped foment and embody a key shift in political identity.

6. Anderson and May, 8.

7. Oshinsky, 6–7.

8. Oshinsky, 9.

9. Oshinsky, 9–10; Michael O'Brien, *McCarthy and McCarthyism in Wisconsin* (Columbia: University of Missouri Press, 1981), 10.

10. Oshinsky, 13.

11. Oshinsky, 13; Jeffrey S. Kinsler, "Joseph McCarthy, the Law Student," *Marquette Law Review* 85, no. 2 (Winter 2001): 469–470.

12. See Kinsler, 470.

13. Anderson and May, 26–27.

14. Oshinsky, 14.

15. Ed Hart, as quoted in Oshinsky, 16.

16. Oshinsky, 19.

17. "Deposition of Senator Joseph McCarthy in the case of *Pearson v. McCarthy et al.*," September 26, 1951, F132, box 1 of 4, Pearson Papers. Mike Eberlein, McCarthy's law partner, also coveted the circuit court seat and may have privately secured McCarthy's support, only to be leapfrogged by McCarthy at election time. See Oshinsky, 19–20.

18. Anderson and May, 38–39.

19. Oshinsky, 25–27.

20. M. DeGroot to Associated Press, June 23, 1942, General Correspondence Folder "A," box 1, series 1, McCarthy Papers.

21. McCarthy to *Milwaukee Journal*, June 22, 1942, General Correspondence Folder "Mi–Mz," box 3, series 1, McCarthy Papers.

22. McCarthy to Klapp, January 1, 1942, General Correspondence Folder "K," box 3, series 1, McCarthy Papers.

23. Letter from War Production Board to McCarthy, March 9, 1942, General Correspondence Folder "Ba–Bo," box 1, series 1, McCarthy Papers.

24. Blair Fraser, "The Spectre of Senator McCarthy," *Maclean's*, May 15, 1953, 87.

25. Durfee to McCarthy, June 6, 1942, General Correspondence Folder "D," box 1, series 1, McCarthy Papers.

26. Kaminsky to McCarthy, March 15, 1941, General Correspondence Folder "A," box 1, series 1, McCarthy Papers.

27. Evers to McCarthy, June 8, 1942, General Correspondence Folder "E," box 1, series 1, McCarthy Papers.

28. Oshinsky interview with Urban Van Sustern, as quoted in Oshinsky, 29.

29. Durfee to McCarthy, December 31, 1940, General Correspondence Folder "D," box 1, series 1, McCarthy Papers.

30. Larry Tye, *Demagogue: The Life and Long Shadow of Senator Joe McCarthy* (Boston: Houghton Mifflin Harcourt, 2020), 41–42. As Tye writes, "His first fiancée was Mary Louis Juneau, a dark, statuesque coed at Milwaukee's Mount Mary College . . . The other engagement was to Maybelle Counihan, a short, attractive Irish American nurse from Milwaukee who moved to Appleton because of Joe and remained his friend longer than the others."

31. At least one woman did seem to be taken with McCarthy. In a March 1942 letter from McCarthy to Mrs. Bohatschek, his former housecleaner, McCarthy rebuffed what he viewed as her advances: "Dear Mrs. Bohatschek. I have just received your letter of March 27th, in which you ask that I pick you up, etc. Frankly, Mrs. Bohatschek, when I hired you to take care of the house, I wasn't looking for a girl friend. Your letters and phone calls are a nuisance and I must insist that you stop." Yet she kept writing, apparently sending letters on June 6 and June 13, 1942. See McCarthy to Bohatschek, March 28, 1942, General Correspondence Folder "Ba–Bo," box 1, series 1, McCarthy Papers.

32. Memo: Anderson to Pearson, January 3, 1953, folder "McCarthy—(Finances)," box G212 (3 of 3), Pearson Papers.

33. McCarthy to United States Marine Corps, December 22, 1942, General Correspondence Folder "Caa–Caz," box 1, series 1, McCarthy Papers.

34. McCarthy to Chief of Navy Personnel, July 7, 1942, General Correspondence Folder "Cb–Cz," box 1, series 1, McCarthy Papers.

35. "Candidate But 'Won't Talk,'" *Milwaukee Journal*, July 21, 1944, p. 1143, MPL McCarthy.

36. Phillip won the governorship as a Progressive in 1934 and was reelected in 1936, but lost to Republican Julius P. Heil in 1938.

37. One of the primary factors influencing Wisconsin Progressives to end the party was the fact that La Follette would probably not win reelection to the Senate as a third-party can-

didate. See W. H. Lawrence, "Progressives of Wisconsin Slated to Rejoin the Republican Party," *New York Times*, March 17, 1946, 1.

38. Patrick J. Maney, *"Young Bob" La Follette: A Biography of Robert M. La Follette, Jr., 1895–1953* (Columbia: University of Missouri Press, 1978), 287.

39. "M'Carthy's Record Like Alger Story," *New York Times*, August 15, 1946, 16.

40. *The Newspapers Say: A Brief News and Editorial History of Judge Joe McCarthy, Regular Republican Candidate for the U.S. Senate* (Appleton, WI: McCarthy for Senator Club, 1946), 9, courtesy of the Wisconsin Historical Society, Madison.

41. *The Newspapers Say*, 1.

42. *The Newspapers Say*, 3.

43. *The Newspapers Say*, 3.

44. Maney, 290–292.

45. "Hand to Hand for McCarthy in Rock County," *Milwaukee Journal*, July 26, 1946, p. 1144, MPL McCarthy.

46. Powered by the shipbuilding industry, the city's population had increased by nearly 30 percent between the 1940 and 1950 censuses. According to the Door County Historical Society, during World War II a new vessel was launched by Sturgeon Bay shipyards an average of every five days. United States Census Bureau, "Number of Inhabitants: Wisconsin," in *Census of Population and Housing, 1950*, https://www.census.gov/prod/www/decennial.html.

47. "McCarthy Wants No Man-Heavy Forces," *Door County Advocate*, April 19, 1946, 4.

48. "McCarthy Wants No Man-Heavy Forces," *Door County Advocate*, April 19, 1946, 4.

49. "La Follette's Folly," *The Nation*, August 24, 1946, 200–201.

50. "McCarthy, McMurray Stage a Verbal 'Slugfest.'" *Milwaukee Journal*, October 23, 1946, p. 1146, MPL McCarthy. It seems that McCarthy's own academic training was regarded as unsuspicious because he claimed to have paid his own way through school by performing so many blue-collar jobs and because he retained his working-class personality.

51. "New Senator 'Vote Getter': McCarthy Knows Self," *Milwaukee Journal*, November 6, 1946, p. 1146, MPL McCarthy.

52. "Hand to Hand for McCarthy in Rock County," *Milwaukee Journal*, July 26, 1946, p. 1144, MPL McCarthy.

53. "Candidate But 'Won't Talk,'" *Milwaukee Journal*, July 21, 1944, p. 1143, MPL McCarthy.

54. "Getting to Bed Is Out for Fellow Who Licks La Follette; Well Wishers Won't Allow It," *Milwaukee Journal*, August 14, 1946, p. 1144, MPL McCarthy. Though the term "blow job" has more recent origins—*Green's Dictionary of Slang* coincidentally claims that one of its earliest uses was in a 1948 underground comic strip depicting oral sex between Whittaker Chambers and Alger Hiss—the use of the term "blow" to suggest a sexual act has much deeper roots. According to *Green's Dictionary*, the sexualized usage can be traced as far back as the seventeenth century, though it was not until the 1930s that the term "blow" was used to refer to *oral* sex. See entries for "Blow" and "Blow Job," in Jonathon Green, *Green's Dictionary of Slang* (London: Chambers Harrap Publishers, 2010).

55. "Hand to Hand for McCarthy in Rock County," *Milwaukee Journal*, July 26, 1946, p. 1144, MPL McCarthy.

56. Anderson and May, *McCarthy*, 83–85.

57. *The Newspapers Say*, 10.

58. *The Newspapers Say*, 11.

59. Both accusations were absurd. As David Oshinsky notes, no reasonable person would have expected La Follette to enlist; he was a forty-six-year-old senator when Pearl Harbor was attacked. Furthermore, there was no evidence of war profiteering via WEMP. Oshinsky, 44. See "Hand to Hand for McCarthy in Rock County," *Milwaukee Journal*, July 26, 1946, p. 1144, MPL McCarthy.

60. "La Follette's Folly," *The Nation*, August 24, 1946, 200–201.

61. Rovere, 93. As Rovere notes, McCarthy's claim that he enlisted in the Marines was repeated in the *Congressional Directory*'s biographical sketch of him until repeated questions about its accuracy led to its deletion in 1948.

62. Oshinsky, 62.

63. McCarthy, as quoted in Oshinsky, 32.

64. Larry Tye argues that McCarthy did not falsify his war record to the degree many journalists and political opponents charged, citing McCarthy's wartime diary and letters from McCarthy's comrades following the war. McCarthy undoubtedly deserves credit for volunteering for missions when he could have safely remained on-base. But given that McCarthy was already intent on building a Senate-worthy résumé while in the Marines, all his claims to valor must be read with a degree of skepticism—to wit, William Evjue of the *Madison Capital Times* collected letters from veterans who served in the Pacific with McCarthy who regarded his claims of war heroism as farcical. See Tye, 54–56; "Capt. Jack Cannon to William Evjue," December 1949, box G222 (1 of 3), folder "19. McCarthy—Marine Corps Record," Pearson Papers.

65. Robert H. Fleming, "McCarthy War Injury? Just Felled by a Bucket," *Milwaukee Journal*, June 8, 1949, p. 1187, MPL McCarthy.

66. Joseph McCarthy, *McCarthyism: The Fight for America* (New York: Devin-Adair, 1952), 1.

67. For a more recent exploration of this phenomenon, see Phil Klay's short story "OIF" in *Redeployment* (New York: Penguin, 2014), 73–76.

68. "Medical Record of Senator McCarthy," May 27, 1952, box 5, David Lloyd Files, Staff Member Files, HST Library.

69. Irving Richter, *Labor's Struggles, 1945–1950: A Participant's View* (Cambridge, UK: Cambridge University Press, 2003), 48. Richter notes that "measured by total time lost, there were 116 million man-days of idleness resulting from stoppages, or 1.45 percent of total working time. By comparison, the total strike idleness at the height of the CIO's sitdown strikes in 1936–7 was only 0.5 percent of total working time, one third that of 1946."

70. George Lipsitz, *Rainbow at Midnight: Labor and Culture in the 1940s* (Urbana: University of Illinois Press, 1994), 99–100.

71. The *Sentinel* ran articles examining the question of communists in the CIO for fifty-nine straight days, all under the byline of "John Sentinel," which the newspaper claimed was a reporter's pseudonym. In reality, the series was penned by the public relations arm of Chalmers-Allis. The *Sentinel*'s charges eventually led UAW president Walter Reuther to pledge to expel all communists from the union's rolls. Allis-Chalmers's campaign was successful, and on March 24, 1947, the strikers returned to work without a contract. Within a month, Allis-Chalmers had fired the union's most active members and soon thereafter Reuther placed the union under administrative control. See Julian L. Stockley, "'Red Purge': The 1946–47 Strike at Allis-Chalmers," *Wisconsin Academy of Sciences, Arts, and Letters* 76 (1988): 17–31.

72. James Reston, "La Follette Loses His Seat in Senate," *New York Times*, August 15, 1946, 1.

73. Dewey L. Fleming, "Issues Ignored in Wisconsin," *Baltimore Sun*, July 13, 1946, 7. In the wake of the election, the *New York Times* opined that "the explanation of Mr. La Follette's loss seems to lie primarily in the loss of labor support, not so much to Mr. McCarthy in the Republican primary, but to Mr. McMurray, the unopposed candidate in the Democratic primary. Mr. McMurray received over 56,000 votes, most of them in the industrial areas, and it was generally conceded that most of these votes would have gone to Mr. La Follette, who is opposed by some labor factions but whose support in the past has usually come from the very groups that chose to go into the Democratic primary to vote for Mr. McMurray. The vote by counties indicated the importance of the switch from Mr. La Follette in the populous industrial counties. In the 1940 election Mr. La Follette had a majority in the three southeastern counties—Milwaukee, Racine and Kenosha—of 61,831. In yesterday's voting, while he was expected to carry these counties again, he lost them by 10,651, more than twice the majority by which he lost to Mr. McCarthy." See James Reston, "La Follette Loses His Seat in Senate," *New York Times*, August 15, 1946, 1.

74. The 1945–46 strike wave prompted members of the 80th Congress that convened in January 1947 to introduce scores of laws intended to limit the power of unions, including the Taft-Hartley Act. Passed over the veto of President Truman, Taft-Hartley largely neutered the resurgent union movement.

75. Alonzo Hamby, *Beyond the New Deal: Harry S. Truman and American Liberalism* (New York: Columbia University Press, 1973), 136–137.

76. "McCarthy to Address G.O.P. Meet Here," *Door County Advocate*, April 5, 1946, 1.

77. "Farmers Fed Up with New Deal Says M'Carthy," *Chicago Daily Tribune*, August 15, 1946, 1. La Follette biographer Patrick J. Maney has argued that antifederalist sentiment was crucial in Young Bob's primary loss.

78. Max Lerner, as quoted in Hamby, 157.

79. A persistent misinterpretation has held that the chief reason McCarthy defeated La Follette was the support of communists who feared La Follette's anti-red stance. This falsehood has been thoroughly debunked by historians and political scientists; see Oshinsky, 46–48, and Maney, chap. 16.

80. "McCarthy, McMurray Stage a Verbal 'Slugfest,'" *Milwaukee Journal*, October 23, 1946, p. 1146, MPL McCarthy.

81. Maney, 299–300.

82. "Wisconsin Senate Nominee Was High School Wonder," *Boston Daily Globe*, August 18, 1946, C36.

83. This is not to suggest that either La Follette or McMurray were progressive advocates for change, only that they lacked the easy persona that made McCarthy familiar to voters, even though he was a relatively new face.

84. James T. Patterson, *Grand Expectations: The United States, 1945–1974* (New York: Oxford University Press, 1996), 32.

85. Lipsitz, 49.

86. Patterson, 33.

87. Lizabeth Cohen, *A Consumer's Republic: The Politics of Mass Consumption in Postwar America* (New York: Alfred A. Knopf, 2003). On women being forced back into limiting, domestic roles, see 133–150, passim.

88. Lipsitz, 51. Lipsitz argues that women's workplace experiences forced them to organize as a defense against unfair treatment by their employers and male coworkers, including unequal pay, longer working hours and harsher working conditions, and outright sexual harassment. These experiences would set a more explicit foundation for later efforts at political organization. See also Dorothy Sue Cobble, *The Other Women's Rights Movement: Workplace Justice and Social Rights in Modern America* (Princeton: Princeton University Press, 2004).

89. D'Emilio and Freedman, *Intimate Matters*, 260–261. See also Marilyn E. Hegarty, *Victory Girls, Khaki-Wackies, and Patriotutes: The Regulation of Female Sexuality during World War II* (New York: NYU Press, 2007).

90. "'Work' Is McCarthy's Formula for Success," *Milwaukee Journal*, November 10, 1946, p. 1146, MPL McCarthy.

91. "New Senator 'Vote Getter': McCarthy Knows Self," *Milwaukee Journal*, November 6, 1946, p. 1146, MPL McCarthy.

92. "'Work' Is McCarthy's Formula for Success," *Milwaukee Journal*, November 10, 1946, p. 1146, MPL McCarthy.

93. *US News and World Report*, April 14, 1950, 40, "Internal Security—Senator Joseph R. McCarthy charges (Section no. 1)," box 69, George Elsey Papers, Truman Presidential Library.

94. "Bachelor's Trick," *Milwaukee Journal*, November 10, 1946, p. 1146, MPL McCarthy.

95. John W. Hanes oral history from the John Foster Dulles Collection at Princeton University, as quoted in Oshinsky, 56.

96. Oshinsky, 55.

97. Oshinsky, 69.

98. "Ohioan Revises Dice-Game Story about McCarthy," *Toledo Blade*, August. 3, 1951, 3.

99. Oshinsky, 56.

100. Oshinsky, 57.

101. Oshinsky, 65–66. Flanders would prove to be one of McCarthy's harshest critics throughout his career, routinely launching personal attacks against him during speeches on the Senate floor.

102. Tye, 86–87.

103. Oshinsky, 67.

104. Classified advertisements, as quoted in Jack Smith, "Give Me Shelter: LA's Post-WWII Housing Shortage Foreshadowed the Crisis of the 1980s," *Los Angeles Times*, September 17, 1989, 6. There is no record as to whether Berggren's unique method paid off.

105. Samuel Zipp outlines this connection more explicitly, arguing that housing "seemed to be the beam on which prosperity and abundance precariously balanced; with the Cold War, these appeared as not merely economic concerns but matters of national security. Material abundance became an all-encompassing symbol in these years, an ideal around which the new global contest between capitalism and communism turned. The very idea of ever-increasing prosperity became a bulwark of national identity, a shared pursuit expected to gather diverse peoples into a secular faith, a communal belief in which, ironically, the raw materials of belonging were individualism, self-reliance, and the freedom of consumer choice. With the Cold War, material abundance became a medium in which the war by other means was joined." Samuel Zipp, *Manhattan Projects: The Rise and Fall of Urban Renewal in Cold War New York* (New York: Oxford University Press, 2010), 271.

106. Mary Spargo, "Truman Prods House to Act on Housing Bill," *Washington Post*, May 7, 1948, 1, 3.

107. Roslyn Baxandall and Elizabeth Ewen, *Picture Windows: How the Suburbs Happened* (New York: Basic Books, 2000), 90.

108. Baxandall and Ewen, 93.

109. *Congressional Record*, 80th Congress, 2nd Session, 1948, part 2, 1230, 2823.

110. Anderson and May, 145.

111. Baxandall and Ewen, 104.

112. Zipp, 272.

113. William Levitt, "The Builder and Banker, a Partnership in Democracy," *United States Investor* 46 (1947): 1948.

114. "Malmedy Massacre Investigation," Report of Subcommittee of the Committee on Armed Services, United States Senate, 81st Congress, 1st Session (Washington: United States Government Printing Office, 1949), 2. For a full historical account of the Malmedy massacre trial, see James Weingartner, *A Peculiar Crusade: Willis M. Everett & The Malmedy Massacre Trial* (New York: NYU Press, 2000), and Steven P. Remy, *The Malmedy Massacre: The War Crimes Trial Controversy* (Cambridge, MA: Harvard University Press, 2017).

115. Weingartner, 10. Although most contemporary reports state that the number of German soldiers tried was seventy-three, the "Malmedy Massacre Investigation" Report of the Subcommittee of the Committee on Armed Services refers to seventy-four defendants, https://www.loc.gov/rr/frd/Military_Law/pdf/Malmedy_report.pdf, 4.

116. Oshinsky, 74.

117. McCarthy, as quoted in John Fisher, "Senate Unit Clears Army in War Trial," *Chicago Daily Tribune*, October 15, 1949, 1, 4. Ironically, the subcommittee report insinuated that Soviet agents may have been behind efforts to question the investigative team's strategy and thus discredit American claims of democracy. Though McCarthy was not named, it was not the last time that he was accused of being a communist agent. See Weingartner, 196.

118. Remy, *The Malmedy Massacre*.

119. Those four female Senators were South Dakota's Vera C. Bushfield, Maine's Margaret Chase Smith, Nebraska's Eva Kelly Bowring, and Nebraska's Hazel Hampel Abel, most of whom served partial terms. In a June 1950 speech titled "Declaration of Conscience," Smith famously attacked McCarthy's tactics, making her one of the earliest critics of McCarthyism.

120. Paul H. Douglas, *In the Fullness of Time: The Memoirs of Paul H. Douglas* (New York: Harcourt Brace Jovanovich, 1972), 251.

121. Oshinsky, 59.

122. For context on the push to paint government social welfare programs as "communistic" or "socialistic" in the immediate postwar era, see Stuart Ewen, *PR!: A Social History of Spin* (New York: Basic Books, 1996), esp. chap. 15. Ewen's brief analysis of McCarthy's use of the housing hearings as a public relations gambit is on 368–369.

123. Richard O. Davies, *Housing Reform during the Truman Administration* (Columbia: University of Missouri Press, 1966), 69.

124. He also earned that dubious honor in 1951, earning the "support" of 75 percent of the members of the press gallery who were queried. See "Newsmen Pick Worst Senator," *Milwaukee Journal*, August 10, 1951, 2.

CHAPTER 4

1. Nicholas von Hoffman, *Citizen Cohn* (New York: Doubleday, 1988), 52. Cohn's obsession with his appearance and how others perceived him would remain a constant in his life. During the 1960s and '70s he had numerous facelifts and other cosmetic procedures, commonly arriving at social engagements and court dates with the stitches in his face still visible. See Barbara Walters, *Audition: A Memoir* (New York: Alfred A. Knopf, 2008), 114–115. Von Hoffman's well-researched biography of Cohn is a compelling study of the man and his quest for power. But where von Hoffman is focused on Cohn's status as a kingmaker at the intersection of politics, crime, and celebrity in New York, I understand his import more in terms of how he shaped the vernacular in which American political identity is expressed.

2. "Albert Cohn Marries," *New York Times*, January 12, 1924.

3. Von Hoffman, 50.

4. "Justice Albert Cohn Takes Office," *New York Times*, April 3, 1929; "Justice Albert Cohn Promoted," *New York Times*, April 28, 1937.

5. Roy Cohn, as quoted in Sidney Zion, *The Autobiography of Roy Cohn* (Secaucus, NJ: Lyle Stuart, 1988), 23–24.

6. David McCullough, *Truman* (New York: Simon & Schuster, 1992), 371.

7. McCullough, 403, 779.

8. Zion, 19–22.

9. Roy Cohn, as quoted in Zion, 18.

10. Cohn's classmates at Horace Mann included Generoso Pope, son of an industrial magnate and the eventual founder of the *National Enquirer*; Anthony Lewis, future *New York Times* columnist; and Si Newhouse, heir to the Condé Nast fortune and later the company's CEO.

11. "The Self-Inflated Target," *Time*, March 22, 1954, 26.

12. Von Hoffman, 57–58.

13. Von Hoffman, 51.

14. "Bank Opened in 1913 Grew by Mergers," *New York Times*, December 12, 1930, 2.

15. Christopher Gray, "Streetscapes: The Bank of United States in the Bronx; The First Domino in the Depression," *New York Times*, August 18, 1991; "3 In Bank of US Guilty; Face Maximum of 7 Years; Disagreement on Pollock," *New York Times*, June 20, 1931, 1; von Hoffman, 48–49.

16. Roy Cohn, as quoted in Zion, 24–25.

17. Von Hoffman, 59.

18. Von Hoffman, 55.

19. "Character Investigation on Cohn, Roy M," Roy Cohn FBI File, box 23, pp. 11–22.

20. Horace Mann classmate of Roy Cohn's, as quoted in von Hoffman, 62–63.

21. Roy Cohn, as quoted in Zion, 35–36.

22. Von Hoffman, 75.

23. Zion, 243.

24. Roy Cohn, as quoted in Zion, 30.

25. "Who We Are," Ethical Culture Fieldston School, https://www.ecfs.org/en/who-we -are/.

26. Peter Bonan, as quoted in von Hoffman, 68.

27. Eugene Marcus, as quoted in von Hoffman, 53–54. As von Hoffman had it, the quote appears to show Cohn requesting that his father throw the ball to him underhanded, as it places quotation marks around the sentence, "You know how you throw to a little girl?" I believe these quotation marks to be misprinted, and thus something Marcus said to von Hoffman rather than something Roy said to his father.

28. Philip Wylie, *Generation of Vipers*, with new annotations by author (New York: Reinhart, 1955 [1942]), 208.

29. In the 1955 reprint, Wylie notably connected "momism" to the moment's biggest news story: "Today, as news photos abundantly make plain, mom composes the majority of

Senator McCarthy's shock troops—paying blind tribute to a blind authoritarianism like her own . . . The tragic Senator stalks smiling to the podium and leads the litany of panic, the rituals of logic perverted, the induced madness of those the gods have marked for destruction. 'McCarthyism,' the rule of unreason, is one with momism: a noble end aborted by sick-minded means, a righteous intent—in terrorism fouled and tyranny foundered." Wylie, 196n.

30. Lewis M. Terman and Catherine Cox Miles, *Sex and Personality: Studies in Masculinity and Femininity*, 320, as quoted in Julia Grant, "A 'Real Boy' and Not a Sissy: Gender, Childhood, and Masculinity, 1890–1940," *Journal of Social History* (Summer, 2004), 838.

31. Norton Hughes Jonathan, *Gentlemen Aren't Sissies* (Chicago: John C. Winston Company, 1938), 168. Norton's guide made some effort to push back against the belligerent, macho masculinity that had taken hold among lower- and lower-middle-class youths, noting that "good manners don't class you as a 'sissy.' Being courteous and presentable doesn't make you effeminate any more than acting rudely and dressing like a hobo makes you a 'he-man.' A gentleman is an honorable man. You can't be anything finer than that" (4). However, this call for balance would not have been applicable to young Roy Cohn; he needed no instruction to avoid dressing "like a hobo."

32. Roy's move from Fieldston to Horace Mann can also be seen in the context of a long-standing pattern of "institutionalizing" boys in schools dedicated to military and industrial training as a way of correcting overly effeminate behavior. Roy's switch partially fits the pattern of rehabilitative institutionalization prescribed by contemporary child psychologists and health care providers. See Grant, 840–841.

33. Von Hoffman, 364, 438.

34. Robert A. Nye, "Western Masculinities in War and Peace," *American Historical Review* 112, no. 2 (April 2007): 423.

35. Christina S. Jarvis, *The Male Body at War: American Masculinity during World War II* (DeKalb: Northern Illinois University Press, 2004), 56–85.

36. Daniel Bell, "Interpretations of American Politics—1955," *The Radical Right*, ed. Daniel Bell (Garden City, NY: Doubleday & Company, 1963), 54–55. Also see the introduction to Cuordileone, *Manhood and American Political Culture in the Cold War*.

37. Arthur Schlesinger Jr., *The Vital Center: The Politics of Freedom* (New York: Da Capo Press, 1949), 38–46.

38. Edward T. Folliard, "The Partnership of Cohn & Schine," *Washington Post and Times-Herald*, March 21, 1954, B3. Note that in 1954 the *Washington Post* purchased the *Washington Times-Herald*, and from that point until 1973 the newspaper was officially known as the *Washington Post and Times-Herald*.

39. There is, of course, an outside possibility that Cohn actually experienced a significant change in his political outlook. He noted the Alger Hiss trial as a major factor in his swing from left to right. Though he died a registered Democrat, Cohn often bragged that he never voted for a Democratic candidate for president and actually claimed to have placed moles in the Democratic party during the 1972 presidential campaign (see von Hoffman, 175, 407). He also served as an inspiration and role model for numerous Republican operatives and leaders. See Jeffrey Toobin, "The Dirty Trickster," *New Yorker*, June 2, 2008. That said,

Cohn never seemed driven by ideology, a fact that becomes particularly apparent when juxtaposing his public comments and his private life.

40. I am consciously using the term "power elite" as defined by sociologist C. Wright Mills: a group of individuals who occupy positions of dominance in the nation's economic, military, and political realms and make decisions based on their self-interest that have far-ranging consequences for the country and, by extension, the world. See C. Wright Mills, *The Power Elite* (New York: Oxford University Press, 1956).

41. Zion, 40–41. Saypol was a family friend. He is credited by Nicholas von Hoffman and others with helping Roy Cohn dodge the draft and lighten his military service. Specifically, the Scripps-Howard news service reported that Cohn had skipped 44 percent of his physical drills while in the National Guard and that Saypol had signed "many of the excuses [Cohn] had submitted." See von Hoffman, 73–74. For his part, Cohn claims he was instrumental in getting Saypol his position as U.S. attorney by vouching for him to *National Enquirer* founder Generoso Pope, who in turn recommended Saypol to local powerbrokers including Ed Flynn and mobsters Frank Costello and Gaetano Lucchese. See Zion, 60–65.

42. "4th Man Held After Cops Nab 3 With $10,000," *New York World-Telegram*, February 19, 1949, 1.

43. See, for example, "Eastern 'Aid' Held; Biggest Blow against Counterfeiting Ring," *Chicago Daily Tribune*, July 9, 1949, 11.

44. "Judge Suspends Sentence on Va. Woman in N.Y.," *Washington Post*, August 15, 1950, 6.

45. It is also plausible that Whitehurst received easier treatment due to her heterosexuality, whiteness, and age, all of which marked her as a likely candidate for rehabilitation. The fact that she was the only woman arrested with a group of eight men and that her arrest was made in New York City also played into contemporary fears that young women would be corrupted by city living; returning to the rural confines of eastern Tennessee could set her back on the right path.

46. Von Hoffman, 76. The majority of the pieces in the *Bronx Home News* were published without a byline, but if Cohn did indeed write for the newspaper it is likely he contributed to "Bokays and Brikbatz" (a Yiddishization of "Bouquets and Brickbats"), a recurring column covering largely harmless gossip from the borough. The characterization of Cohn as Lyons's apprentice comes from the entertainment columnist Jack O'Brien. Von Hoffman, 76.

47. Anonymous coworker of Roy Cohn's, as quoted in von Hoffman, 77–78.

48. "The Self-Inflated Target," *Time*, March 22, 1954, 25.

49. Von Hoffman, 133; Zion, 85–86. See also "The Self-Inflated Target," *Time*, March 22, 1954, 25.

50. Walter Winchell, "Trapping Reds Coast-to-Coast," *New York Daily Mirror*, August 25, 1952. This Winchell column was also printed in the *Washington Post* as "Walter Winchell . . . Of New York: Man about Town," August 25, 1952, 19. On Pegler and his support of McCarthy, see Finis Farr, *Fair Enough: The Life of Westbrook Pegler* (New Rochelle, NY: Arlington House Publishers, 1975), 213.

51. Alan Betrock, *Unseen America: The Greatest Cult Exploitation Magazines, 1950–1966* (Brooklyn: Shake Books, 1990), 8.

52. On Macfadden, see William R. Hunt, *Body Love: The Amazing Career of Bernarr Macfadden* (Bowling Green, OH: Bowling Green State University Popular Press), 1989.

53. Frank Mallen, *Sauce for the Gander* (White Plains, NY: Baldwin Books, 1954), 55.

54. The Rhinelander divorce trial centered on the question of whether Alice Jones had deceived her husband by not admitting her "Negro" ancestry before their marriage. Mrs. Rhinelander's attorney had her display parts of her body—including her cleavage and legs—to the all-white, all-male jury to argue that Mr. Rhinelander had to be aware of his wife's race. See Elizabeth M. Smith-Pryor, *Property Rites: The Rhinelander Trial, Passing, and the Protection of Whiteness* (Chapel Hill: University of North Carolina Press, 2009), 202.

55. "The Press: Muscle Journalist," *Time*, March 31, 1941, 40.

56. Walter Winchell, "Trapping Reds Coast-to-Coast," *New York Daily Mirror*, August 25, 1952. Winchell's penchant for blending political and social gossip was on display in same column, which asked, "Does the FBI know that a top Red (in the Soviet Embassy) has a New York apartment for his Dollpuss, an Hungarian import?"

57. Walter Winchell, "Walter Winchell . . . Of New York: Broadway Heartbeat," *Washington Post*, July 13, 1951, C7; ellipses in original, which in this context amplify the chattiness and immediacy of Winchell's tone. They also can intimate that something is being left unsaid, more than Winchell could safely print.

58. This powerful committee featured Richard M. Nixon, then a young congressman from California.

59. Hiss was charged with perjury because the statute of limitations on espionage had already expired. See Johnson, 32.

60. Zion, 49–50.

61. See, e.g., C. P. Trussel, "Alger Hiss Admits Knowing Chambers; Meet Face to Face," *New York Times*, August 18, 1948, 1. Chambers repeated his charges on the radio program *Meet the Press*, which caused Hiss to sue Chambers for slander and made national news of the news program itself. See Allen Weinstein, *Perjury: The Alger Hiss Case* (New York: Random House, 1997), 141–142.

62. Johnson, 33.

63. Johnson, 32.

64. Bob Adelman, *Tijuana Bibles: Art and Wit in America's Forbidden Funnies, 1930s-1950s* (New York: Simon and Schuster, 1997), 125.

65. The most complete telling of the Remington saga is Gary May, *Un-American Activities: The Trials of William Remington* (New York: Oxford University Press, 1994).

66. See *New York Post* and *New York World*, January 5, 1951, as well as *Washington Evening Star* and *New York Times*, January 6, 1951. The front page of *The Washington Post* from January 6 announced that "Ex-Classmate Says Remington Got Him into Red Youth Group."

67. May, 226.

68. May, 196. Seemingly unafraid, Goodman testified anyway.

69. May, 282.

70. May, 284.

71. May, 264–265.

72. May, 308.

73. May, 310. See also Ellen Schrecker, *Many Are the Crimes: McCarthyism in America* (Boston: Little, Brown, 1998), 361. In addition to "a few murders," including Remington's, Schrecker connects approximately a dozen suicides to the Red Scare and McCarthyism, including those of Abraham Feller (discussed below), Stanford University biologist William Sherwood, and blacklisted actor Philip Loeb.

74. Zion, 57.

75. John Wexley, *The Judgment of Julius and Ethel Rosenberg*, revd. and updated ed. (New York: Ballantine Books, 1977), 487.

76. Zion, 59.

77. Ronald Radosh and Joyce Milton, *The Rosenberg File*, 2nd ed. (New Haven: Yale University Press, 1997), 148–149.

78. Diary of Atomic Energy Commission president Gordon Dean, as quoted in Radosh and Milton, 149.

79. Drew Pearson. "The Washington Merry-Go-Round: More on Mysterious Matusow." *Washington Post and Times-Herald*, February 5, 1955, 37; Wexley, 419. *New York Times* articles on February 1 and 6, 1955, also reported these charges. See Edward Ranzal. "Anti-Red Witness Confesses He Lied; His Charge That Roy M. Cohn Prefabricated Parts of Testimony Is Denied." *New York Times*, February 1, 1955, 12. See also Anthony Leviero, "Role of Informers Now under Inquiry; Matusow Case Raises New Questions about Ex-Communists as Witnesses," *New York Times*, February 6, 1955, E7.

80. "The Traitor," *60 Minutes II*, CBS (New York: CBS, December 5, 2001). See also Walter Schneir, *Final Verdict: What Really Happened in the Rosenberg Case* (Brooklyn: Melville House, 2010), 140. Greenglass suggests that he was presented with an almost-impossible choice: if he did not testify against his sister, his wife would have been arrested and tried for treason herself.

81. Zion, 65.

82. Other historians have posited that Kaufman, a Jew, was chosen to insulate the U.S. government from charges of anti-Semitism in the prosecution of the Jewish Rosenbergs. This explanation mirrors one of the reasons Joseph McCarthy subsequently chose to hire Cohn.

83. Von Hoffman, 101.

84. Zion, 68. Cohn justifies this behavior by explaining that in nearly every case the prosecution communicated directly with the assigned judge. This practice only ceased, he claims, following the Watergate scandal, when "everybody and his brother became sensitive to the Canon of Ethics."

85. Von Hoffman, 101–104; Radosh and Milton, 278–279, 428.

86. Radosh and Milton, 536–537n.

87. Radosh and Milton, 3–4.

88. These inquiries ran concurrent to a similar investigation by the Senate Subcommittee on Internal Security. For a more extensive discussion of this period, see James Barros, *Trygve Lie and the Cold War: The UN Secretary-General Pursues Peace, 1946–53* (DeKalb: Northern Illinois University Press, 1989); von Hoffman, 114–122. The "nearly two thousand" figure comes from "Bunche Denounces 'Pressures' on U.N.," *New York Times*, November 14, 1952, 4.

89. Edward Ranzal, "U.N. Ousts 6 American Aides after Security Risk Inquiry," *New York Times*, May 25, 1952, 1.

90. Thomas J. Hamilton, "Secretary General Says Aide Sought Justice for Those Accused of Subversion," *New York Times*, November 14, 1952, 1. See also "Leap Kills UN Legal Chief," *Chicago Daily Tribune*, November 14, 1952, 1.

91. Willard Edwards, "How Officials Fought to Bar U.N. Red Expose," *Chicago Daily Tribune*, December 5, 1952, 2.

92. Paradoxically, critics have read this masculine need to conform as rhyming with traits that were seen as essentially feminine by 1950s psychologists: "In his need for 'belongingness,' in his deference to the group, in his acceptance of the therapeutic ideals of cooperation and conflict resolution, the organization man looked remarkably feminine in psychological disposition." Cuordileone, *Manhood and American Political Culture in the Cold War*, 119. See also Barbara Ehrenreich, *The Hearts of Men: American Dreams and the Flight from Commitment* (New York: Doubleday, 1983), 32–35.

93. Cohn began to dress more ostentatiously in public during the late 1960s, when such style was closer to the norm, following the death of his mother. Among other flamboyant choices, Cohn appeared on *60 Minutes* in an orange plaid dinner jacket. See von Hoffman, 22.

94. Von Hoffman, 78.

95. Von Hoffman, 79. Cohn's experiences with female prostitutes apparently continued into the early 1960s. He would sometimes brag to his friends about his bedroom talents after such an encounter. See von Hoffman, 143, 310. Similar stories were also relayed to Sidney Zion, Cohn's coauthor on *The Autobiography of Roy Cohn*. "I was in the same room with him, both of us fucking these broads," Zion quotes a Cohn associate as recalling. "He called for girls every town we were in, from Buffalo to Paris." See Zion, 242.

96. Walters, 97–98.

97. Roy Cohn, as quoted in von Hoffman, 364.

98. Zion, 41.

99. Zion, 44.

100. Jack Steele, "Plans to Probe Red Influences on Campus," *Boston Daily Globe*, December 30, 1952, 1, 15.

CHAPTER 5

1. "Weather Forecast Map for the United States," *Chicago Daily Tribune*, February 9, 1950, 2.

2. "205 Reds on Job in State Dept. McCarthy Says," *Chicago Daily Tribune*, February 10, 1950, 5. In his authoritative biography of McCarthy, David Oshinsky quotes "several witnesses" as reporting McCarthy's words as, "While I cannot take the time to name all of the men in the State Department who have been named as members of the Communist Party and members of a spy ring, I have here in my hand a list of 205 . . . a list of names that were known to the Secretary of State and who nevertheless are still working and shaping the policy of the State Department." Oshinsky also notes that McCarthy denied speaking those words; McCarthy claimed that his actual phrasing was "I have in my hand 57 cases of individuals who would appear to be either card-carrying members or certainly loyal to the Communist Party." See Oshinsky, 109.

3. Oshinsky, 111.

4. "Telegram from Senator Joseph McCarthy to President Harry S. Truman," February 11, 1950, General File on McCarthy, Joseph, box 111, President's Secretary's Files, HST Library.

5. "Dr. Fuchs Held in London Jail; Trial on Friday," *Washington Post*, February 4, 1950, 1. The next day, the *New York Times* reported that Fuchs's arrest "caused much less excitement [in London] than it did in the United States," a development underscoring the anticommunist mania that had overtaken Americans. "Britain Unexcited over Fuchs Arrest," *New York Times*, February 5, 1950, 2.

6. Executive Order 10104 added the new "top secret" designation as the highest level of security, exceeding "secret," "confidential," and "restricted."

7. "McCarthy Says Truman Offered 'Phony Files,'" *Boston Daily Globe*, May 7, 1950, 1.

8. "McCarthy Says Truman Offered 'Phony Files,'" *Boston Daily Globe*, May 7, 1950, 1.

9. "McCarthy Accuses Truman of 'Deceit,'" *Los Angeles Times*, May 7, 1950, 24.

10. George Eckel, "McCarthy Scorns 'Phony Files Offer,'" *New York Times*, May 7, 1950, 35.

11. Similarly, why is the Second Red Scare commonly known as "McCarthyism" rather than "McCarranism" or "HUACism"? Historian Ellen Schrecker argues that "had observers known in the 1950s what they have learned since the 1970s, when the Freedom of Information Act opened the Bureau's files, 'McCarthyism' would probably be called 'Hooverism.'" See Schrecker, *Many Are the Crimes*, 203.

12. For a more detailed recounting of this story and its factual shortcomings, see Oshinsky, 107–108.

13. Rovere, 21–22.

14. Will Straw, "Introduction," *Cyanide and Sin: Visualizing Crime in 50s America* (New York: Andrew Roth, 2009).

15. Bernstein, *Mr. Confidential*. Harrison would eventually redesign *Whisper* as a *Confidential* clone, using it to publish stories that were too crude for his flagship gossip magazine. See Samantha Barbas, *Confidential Confidential: The Inside Story of Hollywood's Notorious Scandal Magazine* (Chicago: Chicago Review Press, 2018), 102.

16. Bernstein, 47–48.

17. The four books were *New York Confidential* (1948), *Chicago Confidential* (1950), *Washington Confidential* (1951), and *USA Confidential* (1952). *Washington Confidential*, which topped the nonfiction bestseller lists the summer it was published, portrayed a city overrun by homosexuals and claimed there were "at least 6,000 . . . on the government's payroll." John Kelly, "Commies, Clip Joints, Easy Women: The World of 'Washington Confidential,'" *Washington Post*, January 9, 2016, https://www.washingtonpost.com/local/commies-clip-joints-easy-women-the-world-of-washington-confidential/2016/01/09/d1fc2db4-b332-11e5-9388-466021d971de_story.html; Jack Lait and Lee Mortimer, *Washington Confidential* (New York: Crown, 1951), 116.

18. "Too Hot to Print!," *Confidential*, December 1952, 20; emphasis in original.

19. Scott, *Shocking True Story*, 34.

20. Theodore Peterson, *Magazines in the Twentieth Century* (Urbana: University of Illinois Press, 1956), 82.

21. *Confidential*, August 1953, 53; emphasis in original.

22. *On the Q.T.*, August 1955, 2–3. Along with a free "muscle meter," the Jowlet Institute also offered potential customers a free "photo book of STRONG MEN," a provocative detail considering its advertisement of a booklet filled with what some might consider soft-core pornography.

23. Drew Pearson, "Washington Merry Go Round: 'Malinkov' at Golf Club," *Bakersfield Californian*, May 17, 1954, 36.

24. Scott, *Shocking True Story*, 40.

25. Scott, *Shocking True Story*, 40. There is some debate about the veracity of the tape recorder hidden in a wristwatch; Scott presents it without comment while Bernstein holds that the story is untrue. Regardless, the fact that *Confidential*'s admirers and targets believed the magazine had access to such technology (and that such a rumor was widely spread) speaks volumes about the publication's impact on gossip journalism.

26. Hal C. Wingo, "Presidential Privilege," *New Yorker*, April 23, 2012. "[Johnson] had just made it clear," Wingo wrote, "that he wanted the same cover the press had given [President John F.] Kennedy, and the rules were stacked in favor of the President. We knew he was right about the rules, at least for then." See also Robert Dallek, *Flawed Giant: Lyndon Johnson and His Times, 1961–1973* (New York: Oxford University Press, 1999), 186–187. It is possible that Johnson's adultery—as well as Kennedy's—would have been reported by *Confidential* had the magazine still been in its heyday in the 1960s. Another infamous, possibly apocryphal story detailing the alliance between celebrities and reporters tells of a group of reporters playing cards on a train when a naked Babe Ruth ran through, closely followed by an angry woman wielding a knife. "It's a good thing we didn't see that," one reporter said, "otherwise we'd have to report it." See Brad Schultz, *Sports Media: Planning, Production, and Reporting*, vol. 1 (New York: Taylor & Francis, 2005), 18.

27. Michael Stephenson, "The O'Dwyer Story!," *Confidential*, December 1952, 21–23, 45–47; Jim Johnson, "Love in the U.N.!," *Confidential*, December 1952, 32–33, 58–59.

28. Brad Shortell, "Governor Dewey's Biggest Blunder!," *Confidential*, April 1953, 10–11, 54.

29. Johnson Caldwell, "How Boston's Ex-Mayor Peters Corrupted Starr Faithfull!," *Confidential*, August 1953, 10–11, 51–52. Though rumors about Peters's connection with Faithfull had long circulated—the two were actually distant relatives—*Confidential* made the story fresh by publishing a letter from Faithfull's father that the magazine claimed proved Peters's involvement in her death.

30. Scott, *Shocking True Story*, 23.

31. Harvey Matusow, *False Witness* (New York: Cameron & Kahn, 1955), 128. Matusow does not identify Cohn's girlfriend.

32. Howard Rushmore, "Red Murder, Inc." *Confidential*, November 1953, 38–39, 62–63.

33. Zolotow, as quoted in Bernstein, 3.

34. Scott, *Shocking True Story*, 82.

35. In short, Universal gave up a lesser star in its effort to protect a more valuable one; mainstream publications did not report on Hudson's sexuality until his 1985 death from AIDS. See Bernstein, 118–122. The story exposing Calhoun's prison record appeared in "Movie Star Rory Calhoun: But for the Grace of God, Still a Convict!," *Confidential*, May 1955.

36. Scott, *Shocking True Story*, 81.

37. Joseph M. Porter, "How that Stevenson Rumor Started!," *Confidential*, August 1953, 41–43, 59–60.

38. Marquis Childs, *Witness to Power* (New York: McGraw-Hill, 1975), 67.

39. Truxton Decatur, "We Accuse . . . Sumner Welles: A Confidential Report," *Confidential*, May 1956, 12–15. Stories about Welles's sexuality had circulated in Washington since the early 1940s, but when Welles was forced to resign his position in 1942 following rampant rumors about his drunken proposition of a Pullman porter, most news reports attributed the change to anti-Soviet sentiment in the Roosevelt administration. The only reporter to allude to the real reason for Welles's downfall was Drew Pearson, who referenced "stories of divorce, domestic infelicity, and sex rumors." Even a decade later, the authors of the bestselling gossip guide *Washington Confidential* only referred to it as a blind item. See Gail Collins, *Scorpion Tongues: Gossip, Celebrity, and American Politics* (New York: Morrow, 1998), 151–152.

40. Betrock, *Unseen America*, 28.

41. Matthew W. Dunne, *A Cold War State of Mind: Brainwashing and Postwar American Society* (Amherst: University of Massachusetts Press, 2013), 70. See also Paul S. Boyer, *By the Bomb's Early Light: American Thought and Culture at the Dawn of the Atomic Age* (Chapel Hill: University of North Carolina Press, 1985); Tony Shaw and Denise J. Youngblood, *Cinematic Cold War: The American and Soviet Struggle for Hearts and Minds* (Lawrence: University Press of Kansas, 2010).

42. *Rave*, August 1955; *Tip-Off*, June 1957.

43. *On the Q.T.*, August 1955, emphasis in original; *On the Q.T.*, November 1960, emphasis in original; *Whisper*, March 1955.

44. Desjardins, "Systemizing Scandal," 212.

45. Eric K. Foster, "Gossip," in *Encyclopedia of Human Relationships*, ed. Harry T. Reis and Susan Sprecher (Los Angeles: SAGE Publications, 2009), 769.

46. Jack O'Donnell, as quoted in Max Lerner, "Scandal in the State Department: XI—Sex and Politics," *New York Post*, July 21, 1950, 2.

47. Alan Dunn, "It's true, sir . . . ," *New Yorker*, June 17, 1950, 21.

48. In the era's slang, a "treacher" was a "traitor." Joseph and Stewart Alsop, "Why Has Washington Gone Crazy?," *Saturday Evening Post*, July 29, 1950, 60.

49. McCarthy, as quoted in "Aides of Acheson Under New Attack," *Los Angeles Times*, March 14, 1950, 14.

50. McCarthy in a speech before the American Society of Newspaper Editors, April 20, 1950, as quoted in "Senator Declares His Attack Made Him 'A Revolving S.O.B. Automatically,'" *Washington Post*, April 21, 1950, 1.

51. McCarthy, as quoted in "Wisconsin GOP Hails McCarthy as He Urges Acheson Be Fired," *Boston Daily Globe*, June 10, 1950, 2.

52. Holmes Alexander, "No Tears Are Falling for State Department," *Los Angeles Times*, March 24, 1950, A5. "Dude" was a term long applied to easterners who could not handle the supposedly rough-and-tumble life in the west.

53. Officially, McCarthy and Hoover held it was just a coincidence they were staying at the same La Jolla, California, hotel at the same time. Hoover's quote can be found in I. F. Stone, *The Haunted Fifties* (New York: Vintage, 1969), 23–24.

54. "Memo to Pearson from F.B." in folder "McCarthy et al.—Law Suit I," box G221 (2 of 3), Pearson Papers. Pearson had made no shortage of enemies during his time as a journalist—a letter simply addressed "S.O.B., Washington DC" was correctly delivered to Pearson's office—but his diary entries show that he seemed to regard McCarthy as particularly dangerous. See "Memoirs (unpublished)," box G211 (1 of 3), Pearson Papers; and Drew Pearson and Tyler Abell, *Drew Pearson Diaries 1949–1959* (New York: Holt, Rinehart and Winston, 1974).

55. Oshinsky, 179–182.

56. *Milwaukee Journal*, May 8, 1950, as quoted in Edwin R. Bayley, *Joe McCarthy and the Press* (Madison: University of Wisconsin Press, 1981), 79.

57. Walter Winchell, "Walter Winchell on Broadway," *Zanesville Signal*, March 7, 1951, 4.

58. From a *Chicago Daily Tribune* and *Washington Times-Herald* article series beginning February 5, 1951, as quoted in Bayley, 154. See also "McCarthy Says Truman Offered 'Phony Files,'" *Boston Daily Globe*, May 7, 1950, 1.

59. McCarthy in a speech before the American Society of Newspaper Editors, April 20, 1950, as quoted in "Senator Declares His Attack Made Him 'A Revolving S.O.B. Automatically,'" *Washington Post*, April 21, 1950, 1.

60. McCarthy, as quoted in Bayley, 73.

61. Articles and press release from folder "Sex Crimes (1 of 2)," box F170 (3 of 3), Pearson Papers.

62. Angus McLaren, *Sexual Blackmail: A Modern History* (Cambridge, MA: Harvard University Press, 2002), 248.

63. J. Edgar Hoover, "How Safe Is Your Daughter?," *American Magazine*, July 1947, 32.

64. Philip Jenkins, *Moral Panic: Changing Concepts of the Child Molester in Modern America* (New Haven: Yale University Press, 1998), 61.

65. As John D'Emilio and Estelle B. Freedman demonstrate, narratives of "perversion" stemmed from the attempts of late nineteenth-century medical professionals to classify homosexuality, but it eventually entered the mainstream lexicon as a means of describing a variety of sexual desires and practices considered deviant. D'Emilio and Freedman, 129–130.

66. Historian David K. Johnson has noted that "what leaders of both the Red and Lavender scares feared most was not communism as defined in the Soviet Union as much as the communism of the New Deal and all it implied—that Americans were becoming a nation of immoral, materialistic bureaucrats." Johnson, 97.

67. Johnson, 97–98.

68. Johnson, 31.

69. Johnson, 33.

70. On the so-called Harden-Eulenburg affair, see James D. Steakley, "Iconography of a Scandal: Political Cartoons and the Eulenburg Affair," in *History of Homosexuality in Europe & America*, ed. Wayne R. Dynes and Stephen Donaldson (New York: Garland, 1992), 328–337.

71. Max Lerner, "'Scandal' in the State Dept. V—The Problem of Blackmail," *New York Post*, July 14, 1950, 2. Assistant Director of the FBI Lou Nichols denied that Hoover had gone out of his way to support the homosexual blackmail theory but noted that any homosexuals caught in the FBI's employ would be dismissed.

72. Joseph and Stewart Alsop, "Why Has Washington Gone Crazy?," 21.

73. Joseph and Stewart Alsop, "Why Has Washington Gone Crazy?," 21, 61.

74. "Senate: Tuesday August 8, 1950," *Congressional Record*—Senate. 81st Congress, 11979.

75. Bayley, 161–163.

76. See "Expose of Reds Is Described as Just Beginning," *Chicago Daily Tribune*, May 3, 1950, 5.

77. The other impetus for the investigation was "testimony by a Metropolitan Police officer that there are an estimated 5000 homosexuals in Washington, 75 percent of [which] are in Government service." See "$10,000 Voted to Investigate Perversion in U.S. Agencies," *Washington Post*, June 8, 1950, 1. Hoey was unhappy to learn of the subcommittee's new task: "'God damn. I don't want to investigate that stuff,' he told Francis Flanagan. 'It's baloney and I don't want to get involved in it.'" Johnson, 101–102.

78. "Memo from FB to Pearson," June 21, 1950, folder 34. McCarthy, Jos. (continued) General (folder 1 of 2), box G222 (3 of 3), Pearson Papers.

79. Kerr's two-month absence led to speculation that she had gone to Hawaii to deal with a pregnancy, possibly from a liaison with McCarthy. Rumors about the two had already been circulating, with Jack Anderson noting in December 1950 the likelihood that McCarthy and Kerr were sleeping together. "Memo: Anderson to Pearson," December 16, 1950, folder IV "McCarthy—(Background Info)," box G221 (2 of 3), Pearson Papers. The "abortion" rumor about Kerr is briefly discussed in Ralph de Toledano, "The Real McCarthy," *American Conservative*, April 25, 2005, http://www.theamericanconservative.com /articles/the-real-mccarthy/. De Toledano claims that though there was no truth to the abortion rumor, Kerr's fall did damage her pelvis so badly that she was left unable to have children. Following their marriage, McCarthy and Kerr adopted a baby girl.

80. Gentry, 379.

81. "McCarthy Says Truman Offered 'Phony Files,'" *Boston Daily Globe*, May 7, 1950, 1.

82. "Gerald M. Galvin to Arthur V. Watkins," September 29, 1954, box 56, folder 9, Watkins Papers. For examples of "100% American" epithet, see box 54, folder 15, Watkins Papers.

83. "Mrs. Joseph A. Drapeau to Arthur V. Watkins," August 18, 1954 box 54, folder 15, Watkins Papers.

84. "Naomi Barnard to Arthur V. Watkins," October 1, 1954, box 55, folder 7, Watkins Papers, emphasis in original.

85. For numerous examples of this use of sectarian language, see box 55, folder 12, Watkins Papers.

86. "McCarthy to Unmask Gen. Marshall," *Washington Post*, June 13, 1951, 5.

87. "Brunauers, McCarthy Targets, Suspended from U.S. Posts," *Washington Post*, April 11, 1951, 3.

88. "Aides of Acheson Under New Attack," *Los Angeles Times*, March 14, 1950, 14.

89. Hitler used the concept to refer to Jews who (in his view) blamed Germany's defeat in World War I on German general Erich Ludendorff. Of course, the concept was later applied to Hitler himself and his attempts to blame Jews for economic depression in Germany. See Joel T. Nadler and Tiffany Edwards, "The 'Big Lie' Technique," in *The Encyclopedia of Deception*, ed. Timothy R. Levine (New York: SAGE Publications, 2014), 77–79.

90. *Washington Post*, November 2, 1952, B4.

91. Fuller treatments of McCarthy's accusations and their role in the larger postwar Red Scare can be found in Victor S. Navasky, *Naming Names* (New York: Viking Press, 1980); William L. O'Neill, *A Better World: The Great Schism: Stalinism and the American Intellectuals* (New York: Simon and Schuster, 1982), especially chap. 9; Oshinsky; and Schrecker, *Many Are the Crimes*.

92. Alfred Friendly, "Lattimore Acted Like a Red, Freda Utley Tells Senators," *Washington Post*, May 2, 1950, 1; "McCarthy Labels 4 Pro-Red," *Boston Daily Globe*, March 14 1950, 1, 10.

93. McCarthy, as quoted in Oshinsky, 144–145.

94. "Budenz Identifies Lattimore as Red," *Los Angeles Times*, April 21, 1950, 1.

95. Oshinsky, 152–153.

96. Alfred Friendly, "Lattimore Acted Like a Red, Freda Utley Tells Senators," *Washington Post*, May 2, 1950, 1.

97. See Desjardins, 211–212.

98. *Washington Star*, May 4, 1950.

99. Gentry, 379.

100. "From the Record," folder 2: "Clippings, 1946–1950," box 2, series 3.2, Millard Tydings Papers, Special Collections, University of Maryland at College Park.

101. Tydings, as quoted in Oshinsky, 119.

102. "Majority Report of the Subcommittee of the Committee on Foreign Relations Pursuant to Senate Resolution 231," as quoted in "Excerpts from Text of Majority Report on Charges by Senator McCarthy," *New York Times*, July 18, 1950, 16.

103. William S. White, "Red Charges by M'Carthy Ruled False," *New York Times*, July 18, 1950, 1.

104. Though Tydings suggested that McCarthy be censured, he did not introduce a resolution to do so. Alfred Friendly, "Tydings Fires 2½-Hr. Blast at McCarthy from Floor," *Washington Post*, July 21, 1950, 1.

105. "Maryland Senatorial Election of 1950," Report of the Committee on Rules and Administration, United States Senate, 82nd Congress, 1st Session (Washington, DC: United States Government Printing Office, August 20, 1951), 5.

106. "Maryland Senatorial Election of 1950," Report of the Committee on Rules and Administration, United States Senate, 82nd Congress, 1st Session (Washington, DC: United States Government Printing Office, August 20, 1951), 5. Bazy Miller and Tankersley were later married, and the former Mrs. Miller, now known as "Bazy Tankersley," served as a bridesmaid for Jean Kerr at her 1953 wedding to McCarthy.

107. William Graf, "Statistics of the Congressional Election of November 7, 1950" (Washington, DC: United States Government Printing Office, 1951), 13. Political scientists Adam Berinsky and Gabriel Lenz argue that McCarthy did not have as much influence on the outcome of senatorial elections as many observers have concluded. In the Butler-Tydings race, they note that Maryland had recently voted Republican in national elections—though their model does suggest that McCarthy's greatest impact was likely here. See Adam J. Berinsky and Gabriel S. Lenz, "Red Scare?: Revisiting Joe McCarthy's Influence on 1950s Elections," *Public Opinion Quarterly* 78, no. 2 (January 2014): 369–391.

108. James P. Connolly, "Maryland: M'Carthyism," *New York Times*, November 12, 1950.

109. Alfred Friendly, "Insults Fly at Hearing on Loyalty," *Washington Post*, March 10, 1950, 1.

110. Jessup statement to Tydings committee of March 20, 1950, as quoted in "The Texts of Ambassador Jessup's Statement and of the Senator McCarthy Letters," *New York Times*, March 21, 1950, 24.

111. McCarthy, as quoted in "Congressmen Ask Jessup Rejection," *Los Angeles Times*, October 8, 1951, 8. See also Oshinsky, 211–213.

112. Richard L. Strout, "McCarthy Clashes with Fulbright at Hearing on Jessup," *Christian Science Monitor*, October 2, 1951, 1.

113. Richard L. Strout, "Jessup Brands McCarthy Charge False," *Christian Science Monitor*, October 3, 1951, 1.

114. William S. White, "Senate Unit Votes to Reject Jessup as Delegate to UN," *New York Times*, October 19, 1951, 1, 6. Less than a week later Truman circumvented the Senate and used a recess appointment to make Jessup a UN delegate ("Truman Gives Jessup Recess Appointment as U.N. Delegate," *Boston Daily Globe*, October 23, 1951, 1).

115. "McCarthy's Victory Vote Trails Ticket," *Washington Post*, November 6, 1952, 7.

116. See "Letters to the Editor" section of the *Washington Post* from the first five days of November 1952.

117. Roy Cohn, as quoted in Zion, 81.

CHAPTER 6

1. President Eisenhower himself was invited, but he and Mamie sent their regrets because they were hosting the president of Panama that weekend.

2. This account of McCarthy's wedding is based on a Universal Newsreel report ("Wedding of Senator Joe McCarthy"), a BBC newsreel, Oshinsky, 328–329; and "M'Carthy Marries Former Staff Aide" *New York Times*, September 30, 1953, 15.

3. Anthony Leviero, "1,456 Ousted by U.S. as Security Risks in 4-Month Period," *New York Times*, October 24, 1953, 1. Executive Order 10450 updated a Truman-era regulation designed to improve government security. It declared that government employees could be dismissed for being "security risks"—no proof of disloyal action was necessary. The *New York Times* article noted that only 863 of the 1,456 government employees had actually been dismissed; "the remaining 593 resigned when they were made aware the Government had adverse information on them." This promotion of self-policing—the ending of a career without due process—was arguably where McCarthyist policies made their most damaging impact.

4. Like the majority of McCarthy's charges, those about Fort Monmouth proved to be less significant than the senator promised. Though approximately forty-two employees were dismissed as "security risks," an organized spy ring was never uncovered, most of the fired employees were ultimately reinstated, and McCarthy's charges were revealed to be retreads of earlier ones that had been proven false.

5. David A. Nichols, *Ike and McCarthy: Dwight Eisenhower's Secret Campaign against Joseph McCarthy* (New York: Simon & Schuster, 2017).

6. Zion, 81–84. There are numerous, conflicting stories about how McCarthy and Cohn first met—one congressman claimed that J. Edgar Hoover had originally introduced the pair. See Tye, 241.

7. McCarthy's prejudice can be seen in his attack on the Fulbright international cultural exchange program as "the half-bright program," whose continued existence he attributed to "a group of the old Acheson braintrusters." See Reeves, 491.

8. Murrey Marder, "Red Inquiry Draws Fire on McCarthy," *Washington Post*, March 25, 1953, 1.

9. Reeves, 465. Charges of anti-Semitism among anticommunists gained plausibility because the left had attracted high numbers of immigrant Jews with Eastern European roots.

On McCarthy's use of Cohn as a shield, see Drew Pearson, "The Washington Merry-Go-Round: McCarthy, Cohn Visit Baruch," *Washington Post and Times-Herald*, March 27, 1954, 47.

10. "McCarthy to Sokolsky, August 29, 1951," box 83, folder 3, George Sokolsky Papers, Hoover Institution, Stanford University.

11. Alan Betrock, *The Personality Index: To Hollywood Scandal Magazines, 1952–1966* (Brooklyn: Shake Books, 1988).

12. Schrecker, *Many Are the Crimes*, 256; Zion, 83. Sokolsky was such an important figure in Cohn's life that Cohn dedicated his 1968 biography of McCarthy "To my mother and father, Dora Marcus Cohn and Albert Cohn; and to George E. Sokolsky, who often served *in loco parentis*." Roy Cohn, *McCarthy* (New York: New American Library, 1968), v.

13. Evan Thomas, *Robert Kennedy: His Life* (New York: Simon and Schuster, 2000), 58–66.

14. Zion, 87; Reeves, 442. Robert Kennedy did end up securing the (lesser) position of assistant counsel. This episode began a shared, life-long hatred between Kennedy and Cohn. Cohn claimed that Flip Flanagan, general counsel to the committee, told him that Kennedy didn't like Cohn because, "First of all, [Kennedy] isn't crazy about Jews. Second, you're not exactly a member of the Palm Beach polo set. And thirdly, you've got the job he wanted." Cohn, as quoted in Zion, 88. Kennedy left McCarthy's staff in July 1953, only to return to help represent the committee itself during the Army-McCarthy hearings.

15. Reeves, 464, per an interview with J. Edgar Hoover's assistant Lou Nichols.

16. Fred J. Cook, *The Nightmare Decade: The Life and Times of Senator Joe McCarthy* (New York: Random House, 1971), 398.

17. Joe McCarthy, as quoted in Schrecker, *Many Are the Crimes*, 256.

18. Drew Pearson, "The Washington Merry-Go-Round: Roy Will Be Missed," *Washington Post and Times-Herald*, July 24, 1954, 35; Drew Pearson, "The Washington Merry-Go-Round: Quiz Shows Joe's Need for Roy," *Washington Post and Times-Herald*, July 25, 1954, B5.

19. The story of exactly how Cohn and Schine first met is unclear, but the duo probably met through shared political and social connections in New York or Washington. Cook, 409; Reeves, 465; von Hoffman, 142.

20. Piper Laurie, *Learning to Live Out Loud: A Memoir* (New York: Crown Archetype, 2011), 106.

21. Nat McKitterick, "Covered Like an Election: Mr. Cohn and Mr. Schine Needed No Press Agent," *Washington Post*, April 26, 1953, B3.

22. Drew Pearson, "The Washington Merry-Go-Round: Schine 'Studied' Via Secretary," *Washington Post and Times-Herald*, May 4, 1954, 39; von Hoffman, 146.

23. Richard Rovere, as quoted in Cook, 409.

24. For an account of Schine's entitled behavior, see "Schine at Harvard: Boy with the Baton," *Harvard Crimson*, May 7, 1954, http://www.thecrimson.com/article/1954/5/7/schine-at-harvard-boy-with-the/.

25. On the debate over a Cohn-Schine romantic relationship, see von Hoffman, 188–190, 202, 226, 230–231. Despite the opinion of most historians that Cohn and Schine did not engage in a physical relationship, rumors of such a coupling were strong enough to queer both men in the public imagination and firmly ground the relationship in popular culture. In Tony Kushner's 1996 one-act play "G. David Schine in Hell," Roy Cohn refers to Schine as a modern-day Helen of Troy, calling his visage "the face that launched a thousand slips." See Tony Kushner, "G. David Schine in Hell," in *Death & Taxes: Hydrioptaphia & Other Plays* (New York: Theatre Communications Group, 2000), 234.

26. Though the subcommittee's executive sessions were confidential, transcripts of them were finally released in 2003. Executive Sessions of the Senate Permanent Subcommittee on Investigations of the Committee on Government Operations, 83rd Congress, First Session, 1953 (Washington, DC: Government Printing Office, 2003), vol. 1, 143.

27. Willard Edwards, "Tell Cover-Up of State Dept. Homosexuals," *Chicago Daily Tribune,* February 6, 1953, 9.

28. McCarthy, as quoted in Roger D. Greene, "McCarthy Demands Penalties in Missing Files 'Reprisals,'" *Washington Post,* February 17, 1953, 2. McCarthy's hyperbolic claims seemed to work; when Matson was demoted in an apparent reprisal for his critical testimony, McCarthy went to the press and forced Secretary of State John Foster Dulles to direct that Matson be returned to his old job.

29. Dean, 127.

30. Charles, *Hoover's War on Gays,* 130–131.

31. Von Hoffman, 148.

32. "Samuel Reber to Retire," *New York Times,* May 30, 1953, 13; "Ex-Envoy Reber Refuses to Enter McCarthy Row," *Chicago Daily Tribune,* April 23, 1954, 9.

33. Schlesinger to Stevenson on May 26, 1953, as quoted in Dean, 140–141.

34. "Charles Thayer, Soviet Expert, 59," *New York Times,* August 29, 1969, 29.

35. Charles, *Hoover's War on Gays,* 122–123.

36. "Thayer Quits As Consul in New Inquiry," *Washington Post,* March 27, 1953, 3. Another theory to explain Thayer's resignation holds that Cohn blackmailed Thayer about another dalliance, when he apparently impregnated the daughter of a "good family" while in Mexico City. Cohn's threats to raise the issue during Chip Bohlen's confirmation hearing frightened Thayer because he worried about his mother learning of the pregnancy, marriage, and speedy divorce. See von Hoffman, 169–170.

37. Reeves, 480.

38. "2 M'Carthy Aids Queried Sharply," *New York Times,* April 20, 1953, 7; "McCarthy Counsel in Europe to Study U.S. Information," *Washington Post,* April 6, 1953, 2.

39. "2 M'Carthy Aids Queried Sharply," *New York Times,* April 20, 1953, 7.

40. In order, they went to Paris, Bonn, Berlin, Munich, Vienna, Belgrade, Athens, Rome, Paris (again), and London.

41. Nat McKitterick, "Covered Like an Election: Mr. Cohn and Mr. Schine Needed No Press Agent," *Washington Post,* April 26, 1953, B3.

42. J. Edgar Hoover, "Radiogram to Rolland O. L'Allier," April 3, 1953, Joseph McCarthy FBI File, part 4 of 56 (part 3 of 28).

43. July 8, 1953, entry from anonymous diary in Stevenson, Adlai (folder 2), box 32, Names Series, Ann Whitman File, DDE Library.

44. July 13, 1953, entry from anonymous diary in Stevenson, Adlai (folder 2), box 32, Names Series, Ann Whitman File, DDE Library.

45. July 9, 1953, entry from anonymous diary in Stevenson, Adlai (folder 2), box 32, Names Series, Ann Whitman File, DDE Library. The diary had been passed to Eisenhower to give insight into Stevenson's strategy should he again earn the Democratic presidential nomination and challenge Eisenhower in 1956 (as he ultimately did). It is unclear whether the unnamed reporter was aware that Eisenhower had gained access to this copy of the diary. From the perspective of the 1956 election, the diary's most important entry was from June 20, 1953: "It seems to us that this world tour has given [Stevenson] a good opportunity to approach McCarthyism from a new angle, namely, the crippling effect it has had on our foreign service, our propaganda effort and our relations with our Allies. Stevenson confessed that he had been genuinely shocked by what he has seen abroad and heard from home, and I think he has made up his mind to try and grab the ball away from Eisenhower on this issue and perhaps thereby to win back a lot of disillusioned liberal Republicans." The fear that Stevenson would adopt that strategy undoubtedly influenced Eisenhower's decision to attack McCarthy somewhat more directly beginning in late 1953.

46. June 22, 1953, entry from anonymous diary in Stevenson, Adlai (folder 2), box 32, Names Series, Ann Whitman File, DDE Library.

47. Drew Pearson, "The Washington Merry-Go-Round: McCarthy's Men Get Attention," *The Washington Post*, April 22, 1953, 41; "McCarthy Men Depart England amid Laughter," *Washington Post*, April 26, 1953, B3.

48. *Manchester Guardian*, as quoted in Reeves, 489.

49. "McCarthy Men Depart England Amid Laughter," *Washington Post*, April 26, 1953, B3.

50. Reeves, 491.

51. Johnson, 131–134. Despite these "successes," Cohn referred to the trip as one of his major regrets, ostensibly because of the impact it had on his and Schine's image in the United States. See Zion, 90–91.

52. Report from the *Abendpost*, as quoted in Drew Pearson, "The Washington Merry-Go-Round: McCarthy's Men Get Attention," *Washington Post*, April 22, 1953, 41.

53. Clipping from folder "26. McCarthy—(Schine)," box G222 (2 of 3), Pearson Papers.

54. Roy Cohn and G. David Schine, as quoted in Cook, 412.

55. Von Hoffman, 151.

56. Laurie, 123.

57. Drew Pearson., "Washington Merry-Go Round," *Madera Tribune* (Madera, California), July 17, 1953, 12.

58. Oshinsky, 363.

59. *Point of Order!*, directed by Emile de Antonio (1964; New York: New Yorker Video, 2005), DVD.

60. Schrecker, *Many Are the Crimes*, 263.

61. "Text of Army Report Charging Threats by McCarthy and Cohn in Interceding for Schine," *New York Times*, March 12, 1954, A9.

62. Drew Pearson. "The McCarthy-Go-Round," *Washington Post and Times-Herald*, March 19, 1954, 63.

63. "Army Charges McCarthy and Cohn Threatened It in Trying to Obtain Preferred Treatment for Schine," *New York Times* March 12, 1954, 1.

64. W. H. Lawrence. "Stevens a Target," *New York Times*, March 12, 1954, 1.

65. W. H. Lawrence. "M'Carthy Charges Army 'Blackmail,' Says Stevens Sought Deal with Him; 'Utterly Untrue,' Secretary Replies," *New York Times*, March 13, 1954, 1.

66. Reeves, 575–577.

67. Clayton Knowles, "Cohn Again Denies He Asked Favors and Accuses Army," *New York Times*, March 15 1954, 1.

68. W. H. Lawrence, "Mundt Will Direct Senate Unit Study of McCarthy Fight," *New York Times*, March 17, 1954, 1.

69. Andrea Friedman, "The Smearing of Joe McCarthy: The Lavender Scare, Gossip, and Cold War Politics," *American Quarterly* 57, no. 4 (December 2005): 1110.

70. FB, "Memo for DP," June 28, 1950, folder "McCarthy et al.—Law Suit I," box G221 (2 of 3), Pearson Papers.

71. Oliver Pilat and William V. Shannon, "Smear, Inc.: The One-Man Mob of Joe Mc-Carthy, Part 12: Joe Changes the Subject to Sex," *New York Post*, September 17, 1951, 2.

72. W. O. Berry, "Letter to Jacob R. McCarthy" enclosed in "Letter to Drew Pearson," May 14, 1950, box F41, folder Anti-McCarthy #2 (1 of 2), Pearson Papers.

73. William Evjue, "Letter to Drew Pearson," May 15, 1950, folder 33. McCarthy General II (folder 3 of 3), box G222 (3 of 3), Pearson Papers.

74. "Letter from 'A University Student' to William Evjue," May 11, 1950, folder 33. Mc-Carthy General II (folder 3 of 3), box G222 (3 of 3), Pearson Papers.

75. "Statement of R. Garth McMahon—'I swear to the following facts . . . ,'" Confidential Memos Folder, box G44 (3 of 3), Pearson Papers.

76. "Memo from Anderson to Pearson," November 15, 1954, folder 33 McCarthy General II (folder 2 of 3), box G 222 (3 of 3), Pearson Papers.

77. "Memo from Anderson to Pearson," October 20, 1951, folder "McCarthy et al.—Law Suit I," box G221 (2 of 3), Pearson Papers.

78. Jack Anderson, "Memo to DP," December 16, 1950, folder "IV. McCarthy (Background Info)," box G221 (2 of 3), Pearson Papers.

79. Anonymous, "Letter to William Benton," December 29, 1951, folder "6. McCarthy—Sen. Benton," box G221 (2 of 3), Pearson Papers.

80. Edwin Bayley elaborates on the *Journal's* reaction to receiving such information: "One person at the *Journal* who did advocate publication was Murray Reed, a former city editor . . . He proposed that a political reporter call every person known to be closely associated with McCarthy and ask whether the senator was a homosexual. If all of them said he was not, Reed said, the paper could run a story beginning, 'Thirty-five of McCarthy's closest friends deny that he is a homosexual,' or, if some of them refused to answer, the story could say, 'Twenty-eight out of 35 of McCarthy's closest friends deny. . . .' Reed's suggestion was rejected." Bayley, 134.

81. J. Edgar Hoover, "Memorandum for Mr. Tolson, Mr. Ladd, Mr. Nichols, 10:51," January 17, 1952, Joseph McCarthy FBI File, part 3 of 56 (part 2 of 28).

82. J. Edgar Hoover, "Memorandum for Mr. Tolson, Mr. Ladd, Mr. Nichols, 5:12," January 16, 1952, Joseph McCarthy FBI File, part 3 of 56 (part 2 of 28).

83. J. Edgar Hoover, "Memorandum for Mr. Tolson, Mr. Ladd, Mr. Nichols, 5:06," January 16, 1952, Joseph McCarthy FBI File, part 3 of 56 (part 2 of 28).

84. J. Edgar Hoover, "Memorandum for Mr. Tolson, Mr. Ladd, Mr. Nichols, [time unclear]," January 17, 1952, Joseph McCarthy FBI File, part 3 of 56 (part 2 of 28).

85. J. Edgar Hoover, "Memorandum for Mr. Tolson, Mr. Ladd, Mr. Nichols, 12:06," January 18, 1952, Joseph McCarthy FBI File, part 3 of 56 (part 2 of 28). One result of the investigation was that the Army lieutenant whose name was on the original letter admitted that he had engaged in homosexual relationships. General Alexander R. Bolling assured Hoover that the man would be dismissed from the military as a result.

86. Adam Hats soon dropped its sponsorship of Pearson. McCarthy claimed victory, but Adam countered that the change had preceded McCarthy's call, and Senator Styles Bridges noted that he believed that McCarthy knew of the impending change before initiating the boycott. See Oshinsky, 181–182. On the other hand, Anti-Defamation League executive director Arnold Forster claimed that the intent was to renew the sponsorship agreement and "it was McCarthy's boycott *alone* that changed his sponsor's mind." Herman Klurfeld, *Winchell: His Life and Times* (New York: Praeger Publishers, 1976), 146, emphasis in original.

87. FB, "Memo for DP," June 28, 1950, folder "McCarthy et al.—Law Suit I," box G221 (2 of 3), Pearson Papers.

88. Drew Pearson, "Letter to Col. William A. Roberts," February 16, 1951, folder "McCarthy et al.—Law Suit I," box G221 (2 of 3), Pearson Papers.

89. Hank Greenspun, "Where I Stand: 8/1/52," archives of the *Las Vegas Sun.*

90. McCarthy had likely intended to say "a former convict" instead of "former communist" and misspoke; Greenspun had been convicted of violating the Neutrality Act after he shipped guns, ammunition, and airplane parts to the Israeli paramilitary organization Haganah in 1947.

91. *Where I Stand: The Hank Greenspun Story,* dir. Scott Goldstein. (New York: SGP Media, 2008). Author interview with Brian Greenspun, January 2014. See also "McCarthy Clashes with Editor Also Backing Eisenhower," *New York Herald Tribune,* October 15, 1952, 21, especially the photograph and caption attached to the article. Given his passionate Zionism, Greenspun may have also been wary of McCarthy due to the senator's reported anti-Semitism.

92. Hank Greenspun, "Where I Stand: 10/25/52," in *A Few Columns on Joe McCarthy by Hank Greenspun* (1977 reprint in the archives of the *Las Vegas Sun*).

93. Hank Greenspun, copy of 10/25/52 "Where I Stand" column forwarded to Pearson, folder 12. McCarthy—(Hank Greenspun), box G221 (3 of 3), Pearson Papers.

94. Oshinsky, 310.

95. Bayley, 74.

96. At its height, Pearson's column "The Washington Merry-Go-Round" appeared in over 650 newspapers. *Time* magazine's obituary for Pearson notes that he was America's best-known columnist at the time of his death. He was also the first columnist to report the infamous "slapping" incident involving General George S. Patton in 1943. "Columnists: The Tenacious Muckraker," *Time*, September 23, 1969, content.time.com/time/magazine/article/0,9171,901423,00.html.

97. Justus Lawrence, "Letter to Drew Pearson," April 15, 1953, folder "8. McCarthy—(Cohn) see Schine," box G221 (3 of 3), Pearson Papers.

98. Drew Pearson, "Merry-Go-Round: Cohn, Schine Also Disturb Senate GOP," *Washington Post*, July 17, 1953, 51.

99. Drew Pearson, "Merry-Go-Round: Wilson Out on Limb on Manpower," *Washington Post*, July 29, 1953, 35.

100. Drew Pearson, "Merry-Go-Round: Backstage Factors in Schine Case," *Washington Post*, March 17, 1954, B.

101. Richard Gehman, "Letter to Drew Pearson," June 2, 1954, folder "33. McCarthy General II (folder 1 of 3)," box G222 (3 of 3), Pearson Papers.

102. Phillip H. Bagby, "Letter to Drew Pearson," July 30, 1954, folder "26. McCarthy—(Schine)," box G222 (2 of 3), Pearson Papers.

103. Frank J. Weber, "Letter to Drew Pearson," undated. folder "26. McCarthy—(Schine)," box G222 (2 of 3), Pearson Papers.

104. Murrey Marder, as quoted in von Hoffman, 187.

105. Joseph and Stewart Alsop, "Matter of Fact: The Tale Half Told," *New York Herald Tribune*, March 15, 1954, 14.

106. Undated note, folder 3 (McCarthy), box 4, Eyes Only Series, Fred A. Seaton Papers, DDE Library, emphasis in original.

107. Hank Greenspun, *A Few Columns on Joe McCarthy by Hank Greenspun*, April 2, 1954 (1977 reprint in the archives of the *Las Vegas Sun*). Greenspun further opined that McCarthy might be a secret communist because his actions did more to help the communist cause than hinder it. He also dedicated a column to tracing the similarities between McCarthy and Adolf Hitler.

108. Hank Greenspun, "Secret Lives of Joe McCarthy," *Rave Magazine*, June 1954, 58–73. Like *Confidential*, *Rave* seemed to have an obsession with homosexuality. The magazine's August 1954 issue featured a cover story outing Liberace and an article in the April 1954 issue asked of the male members of the British royal family, "Why [do] these juicy fruits prefer Boy Scouts to gorgeous women?"

109. "The Men in McCarthy's Life," *Celebrity Magazine*, August 1954, 4–8. The magazine only published twenty-one issues, from April 1954 to January 1956. *Celebrity* was very similar to *Confidential* in content, although it seems intended for a more male audience given the pinup models adorning its covers. It also seemed to mirror *Confidential* and *Rave's* interest in homosexuality, with the July 1954 issue featuring an article asking, "Are You a SECRET HOMOSEXUAL?" The article began with the acknowledgment that "all men, according to psychologists, fear they are not manly enough—at some time in their life. This is especially true of men in America, where social customs demand that men be strong and virile." It also claimed that "contrary to popular belief . . . true homosexuals seldom look effeminate. They usually are muscular and athletic and act very much like normal males. According to Kinsey, 6 million 'hard-core' homosexuals fit this picture." The article presented these "hard-core homosexuals" as predators "continually on the search for 'secret' homosexuals" that they can lure into "the third sex." "Are You a SECRET HOMOSEXUAL?," *Celebrity Magazine*, July 1954, 8–9.

110. Betrock, *The Personality Index*; Orval Hopkins, "Magazine Rack," *Washington Post*, February 8, 1953, B5.

111. Joe Hyams, "Hollywood," *New York Herald Tribune*, June 29, 1955, 23; "The James Masons' Suit Settled," *New York Times*, July 20, 1955, 19; "Terry Moore Sues Magazine for 2 Million," *Los Angeles Times*, November 16, 1955, 4.

112. Wilbert Martin, "Letter to Arthur V. Watkins," August 7, 1954, folder 2: "Responses from Watkins to neutral correspondence concerning McCarthy, 16 March–18 August 1954," box 47, series VI: Joseph McCarthy, Pamphlets and articles about Joseph McCarthy, Watkins Papers.

113. Arthur V. Watkins, "Letter to Wilbert Martin," August 12, 1954, folder 2: "Responses from Watkins to neutral correspondence concerning McCarthy, 16 March–18 August 1954," box 47, Watkins Papers.

114. Charles A. Francis, "Letter to Arthur V. Watkins," November 8, 1954, folder 15: "A-I, Correspondence from citizens with literature expressing anti-McCarthy views concerning the activities of McCarthy to the Senate Select Committee," box 80, Watkins Papers.

115. Thomas Doherty, *Cold War, Cool Medium: Television, McCarthyism, and American Culture* (New York: Columbia University Press, 2003), 189–190.

116. CBS and NBC wanted to carry the hearings live and asked Senator Mundt whether they could have commercial partners sponsor the broadcast, but Mundt replied that "because of the unusual nature of these hearings, it would be highly inappropriate for us to permit either direct or indirect sponsorship for the hearings of any kind." Karl Mundt, "Letter to Frank M. Russell, Vice-Pres. National Broadcasting Company, Inc.," April 22, 1954, Karl Mundt Papers, Dakota State University, box 558, folder 3.

117. Robert Shogan, *No Sense of Decency* (Chicago: Ivan R. Dee, 2009), 12, 264–265.

118. "Inquiry's Audience on TV Is Believed One of Largest," *New York Herald Tribune*, April 23, 1954, 9.

119. Rufus King, "Letter to the Editor," *Washington Post*, November 2, 1952, B4.

120. See folders 13–16 of box 54 and folders 1–4 of box 55, series VI—Joseph McCarthy, Watkins Papers. There are seven folders of correspondence protesting the decision not to air the hearings, and one folder of letters praising the decision.

121. "Mrs. E. S. Hersh to Arthur V. Watkins," undated. folder 2, box 55, series VI—Joseph McCarthy, Watkins Papers.

122. See folder 3, box 55, series VI—Joseph McCarthy, Watkins Papers.

123. "*The News* Prints the Facts," *New York Daily News*, undated, probably August 1954, newsclipping in box 47, series VI—Joseph McCarthy, Watkins Papers.

124. "N.B.C. Halts Live TV on Army, McCarthy," *New York Times*, April 25, 1954, 1.

125. Army-McCarthy Hearings, part 2, p. 83, April 22, 1954.

126. Bethan Benwell, "Language and Masculinity," in *The Handbook of Language, Gender, and Sexuality*, ed. Susan Ehrlich, Miriam Meyerhoff, and Janet Holmes (Malden, MA: Wiley-Blackwell, 2014), 240–259; Maureen C. McHugh and Jennifer Hambaugh, "She Said, He Said: Gender, Language, and Power," in *Handbook of Gender Research in Psychology*, vol. 1, *Gender Research in General Experimental Psychology*, ed. Joan C. Chrisler and Donald R. McCreary (New York: Springer Publishing, 2009), 379–410.

127. Bethan Benwell, "Male Gossip and Language Play in the Letters Pages of Men's Lifestyle Magazines," *Journal of Popular Culture* 34, no. 4 (Spring, 2001), 24. Benwell is citing a connection made by Geoffrey Hughes, *Swearing: A Social History of Foul Language, Oaths and Profanity in English* (Oxford, UK: Blackwell, 1991).

128. Robert Griffith, *The Politics of Fear: Joseph McCarthy and the Senate* (Lexington: University Press of Kentucky, 1970), 257.

129. Cook, 513.

130. "Testimony at Hearing," *New York Herald Tribune*, May 6, 1954, 14.

131. Cook, 498. Army-McCarthy Hearings, part 11, p. 437, April 29, 1954.

132. Army-McCarthy Hearings, part 2, p. 70, April 22, 1954.

133. Army-McCarthy Hearings, part 1, p. 44, April 22, 1954.

134. Army-McCarthy Hearings, part 3, p. 131, April 23, 1954. Note that the "girl friends" comment was originally made by McCarthy, perhaps in an attempt to find common ground with Stevens based on a shared masculinity.

135. *Point of Order*, DVD, 18:30–19:10.

136. "Anonymous to Arthur Watkins," August 12, 1954, folder 15, box 54, series VI—Joseph McCarthy, Watkins Papers. The word "man" is underlined twice in the original.

137. "Anonymous to Arthur Watkins," August 14, 1954, folder 15, box 54, series VI—Joseph McCarthy, Watkins Papers.

138. "G. D. Gurley to Arthur Watkins," September 4, 1954, folder 9, box 56, series VI—Joseph McCarthy, Watkins Papers; "Gerald M. Galvin to Arthur Watkins," September 29, 1954, folder 9, box 56, series VI—Joseph McCarthy, Watkins Papers.

139. "G. H. Stubblefield to Arthur Watkins," November 12, 1954, folder 10, box 55, series VI—Joseph McCarthy, Watkins Papers.

140. "George A. DeMontrond to Arthur Watkins," November 19, 1954, folder 7, box 56, series VI—Joseph McCarthy, Watkins Papers.

141. "John H. Widdowson to Arthur Watkins," September 30, 1954, folder 10, box 55, series VI—Joseph McCarthy, Watkins Papers.

142. "F. H. Mulcahy to Arthur Watkins," undated, folder 13, box 56, series VI—Joseph McCarthy, Watkins Papers.

143. "John T. Kelly to Arthur Watkins," September. 1, 1954, folder 11, box 56, series VI—Joseph McCarthy, Watkins Papers.

144. "Ralph W. Slate to Arthur Watkins," November 17, 1954, folder 15, box 73, series VI—Joseph McCarthy, Watkins Papers.

145. "Lee R. Atkins to Arthur Watkins," December 1, 1954, folder 1, box 74, series VI—Joseph McCarthy, Watkins Papers.

146. "Anonymous to Arthur Watkins," undated. folder 15, box 77, series VI—Joseph McCarthy, Watkins Papers, emphasis in original.

147. "Anonymous to Arthur Watkins," September 30, 1954, folder 8, box 74, series VI—Joseph McCarthy, Watkins Papers; "Anonymous to Arthur Watkins," November 16, 1954, folder 21, box 74, series VI—Joseph McCarthy, Watkins Papers; "Albert Horowitz to Arthur Watkins," undated. folder 14, box 76, series VI—Joseph McCarthy, Watkins Papers.

148. "Fred G. Wolverton to Arthur Watkins," November 15, 1954, folder 10, box 80, series VI—Joseph McCarthy, Watkins Papers.

149. Army-McCarthy Hearings, part 7, p. 293, April 27, 1954.

150. "What Every Boy Knows: 'Sic 'Em'{?~make sure the character before "Em" is an apostrophe, not an open single quote} Means Chase," *New York Times*, June 10, 1954, 17. Welch would later parlay his telegenic turn into a handful of onscreen roles, including as a judge in Otto Preminger's 1959 *Anatomy of a Murder*.

151. Cohn, 208.

152. James Reston, "Washington: Unintended Achievements of Senator McCarthy," *New York Times*, May 30, 1954, E6.

153. Army-McCarthy Hearings, part 3, p. 99, April 22, 1954.

154. Murrey Marder, "McCarthy and Aides Perverted Power to Force Promotion of David Schine, Stevens Testifies in Army Inquiry," *Washington Post and Times-Herald*, April 22, 1954, 1. For a smaller paper, see "Joe vs. Army: Stevens Charges McCarthy and Cohn Perverted Power in Pvt. Schine Case," *Stanford Daily*, April 23, 1954, 1.

155. Army-McCarthy Hearings, part 9, p. 355, April 28, 1954. Video footage also included in *Point of Order* DVD, 19:10–19:25.

156. Cohn later admitted that the cropped photo was his doing. See Cook, 497.

157. Army-McCarthy Hearings, part 14, p. 543, April 30, 1954.

158. Army-McCarthy Hearings, part 13, p. 15, April 30, 1954. Another meaning of "pixie" is possible. From approximately 1947 to 1951, the William R. Whittaker Company of Los Angeles manufactured and sold a tiny, fixed-focus camera called the "Pixie." It was small enough that it could be worn on the wrist, like a watch. Retailing for $4.95, the Pixie could take fourteen exposures. See "Thrifty Cut Rate Drug Store advertisement," *Los Angeles*

Times, March 26, 1950, 28, and "May Company advertisement," *Los Angeles Times*, May 1, 1949, A2.

159. "Fairy," *Green's Dictionary of Slang* (London: Chambers Harrap Publishers, 2010), ebook.

160. "Appendix: The Production Code," in Thomas Doherty, *Hollywood's Censor: Joseph I. Breen and the Production Code Administration* (New York: Columbia University Press, 2009), 353. Though the Production Code that Doherty reprints is from 1956, other citations note that "fairy" had been included since 1930.

161. "Pixie," *Green's Dictionary of Slang*.

162. Army-McCarthy Hearings, part 44, pp. 1664–1665, May 28, 1954.

163. *Point of Order*, DVD, 11:30–12:04.

164. Army-McCarthy Hearings, part 57, p. 2300, June 8, 1954.

165. Robert V. Bienvenu II, "The Development of Sadomasochism as a Cultural Style in the Twentieth-Century United States" (doctoral dissertation, Indiana University, 1998).

166. The discussion about West happened on June 8, the day before Welch's famous "decency" comment, and suggests another possible explanation for the hearings' most famous moment. Historians have long accepted that Welch was driven to his outburst by McCarthy going back on a gentlemen's agreement: McCarthy would not bring up the fact that a member of Welch's staff, Fred Fisher, had belonged to a communist-affiliated organization as a law student, if Welch agreed to not introduce evidence that Cohn had dodged the draft during World War II. But Welch's June 8 threat to call West (and thus embarrass Cohn) may have sparked McCarthy to attack Fisher on June 9, with McCarthy believing that Welch had broken their agreement.

167. Walter Winchell, "Tales of Two Cities," *Washington Post and Times-Herald*, May, 6, 1954, 59; Walter Winchell. "Man about Town," *Washington Post and Times-Herald*, June 10, 1954, 47; Walter Winchell. "Manhattan after Midnight," *Washington Post and Times-Herald*, June 24, 1954, 47; "See It Through," *Washington Post and Times-Herald*, June 10, 1954, 14.

168. Von Hoffman, 206. Marder was not a columnist but a beat reporter. The fact that Winchell resorted to threatening a beat reporter demonstrates just how ubiquitous Cohn felt the negative coverage of him and McCarthy had become.

169. Ellen Schrecker, *The Age of McCarthyism: A Brief History with Documents* (Boston: Bedford Books of St. Martin's Press, 1994), 65. Andrea Friedman argues that Murrow's *See It Now* report includes a sequence that can be read as "queering" McCarthy. She points to the report's footage of a 1951 speech by retired congressman Frank Keefe at a banquet honoring McCarthy, in which Keefe quotes from an obscure romantic poem by Jennie Earngey Hill as a means of praising McCarthy and defending him from "the vilest smears I have ever heard." *See It Now* suggested that the poem moved McCarthy to tears and rendered him unable to make his planned speech. Yet this depiction of poetry, flowers, odes of love, and crying seems to feminize McCarthy more than it queers him—though gender identity and sexual preference were irrevocably intertwined during that era. Murrow seems more focused on breaking down McCarthy's tough-guy persona than suggesting a sexual attraction to men. See Friedman, "The Smearing of Joe McCarthy," 1115–1117.

170. Drew Pearson. "The Washington Merry-Go-Round: Schine Ducks Talk of Draft," *Washington Post and Times-Herald*, May 1, 1954, 47; Drew Pearson. "McCarthy-Go-Round," *Washington Post and Times-Herald*, March 19, 1954, 63.

171. Drew Pearson. "The Washington Merry-Go-Round: Schine 'Studied' via Secretary," *Washington Post*, May 4, 1954, 39.

172. Drew Pearson, "The Washington Merry-Go-Round: More on Cohn-Schine Jaunt," *Washington Post*, June 5, 1954, 13. In 1969, Pearson again used coded language to suggest that the McCarthy-Cohn-Schine relationship was queer, if not fully homosexual. An interviewer asked Pearson, "Do you think that [McCarthy's] relationship with Roy Cohn and the Schine fellow was, shall we say, sinister?" To which Pearson replied, "Yes, it was sinister." The suggestion behind "shall we say" is fairly clear in context. See Transcript, Drew Pearson Oral History Interview I, 4/10/69, by Joe B. Frantz, Internet Copy, Pearson Papers.

173. Charles, *Hoover's War on Gays*, 91.

174. "Francis Patton Twinem to Arthur Watkins," October 7, 1954, folder 13, box 55, series VI—Joseph McCarthy, Watkins Papers.

175. "F. W. Brunner to Arthur Watkins," November 22, 1954, folder 11, box 74, series VI—Joseph McCarthy, Watkins Papers.

176. John Harris, "Alleged Letter from Hoover Stirs Wrangle at Hearing," *Boston Daily Globe*, May 5, 1954, 1.

177. Homer Bigart, "McCarthy on Stand, Admits 'Letter' Was Not from F.B.I. Head to Army, Calls It Summary of a Memorandum," *New York Herald Tribune*, May 6, 1954, 1.

178. Oshinsky, 432.

179. Ralph Flanders, "Colossal Innocence in the Senate of the United States," *Congressional Record*, June 1, 1954, 7390. Flanders's reference to "Dennis" was a nod to the nickname he had bestowed on McCarthy, "Dennis the Menace."

180. Vito Marcantonio, as quoted in von Hoffman, 241.

181. Senate Resolution 301, 83rd Congress, December 2, 1954, SEN 83A-B4, Records of the United States Senate, Record Group 46, National Archives.

182. "I have been very patient with the Senator from Vermont as he has engaged in his diatribes over the past number of weeks. I have felt that he is a nice, kind, old gentleman. I wondered whether this has been a result of senility or viciousness. In any case, we can't let him continue to intimate that he does have information, without calling him. Mr. Chairman, I may say that in this statement on the Senate floor he does more than any man I have ever heard to inflame racial and religious bigotry. It is a vicious thing. It is a dishonest thing. He brings in the question of Jewish people, Protestant people, Catholic people. May I say, Mr. Chairman, that of the three top people of our committee, the chief counsel, the chief of staff, and myself, one happens to be Jewish, one happens to be Protestant, and one happens to be Catholic. All of us are very active in our particular faiths. This has interfered not even in the slightest in this exposure of Communists. I think that it is dishonest beyond words for a Senator to take the Senate floor and try to inject religious and racial bigotry into this effort to expose communism." Army-McCarthy Hearings, part 47, p. 1827.

1. Joseph McCarthy, "Statement on the Cohn Resignation," *New York Times*, July 21, 1954, 10. Both McCarthy and Cohn sent their open letters about Cohn's resignation to George Sokolsky, apparently independently. Marked-up drafts of both are in box 37, folder 7 (Cohn), and box 83, folder 3 (McCarthy), Sokolsky Papers, Hoover Institution, Stanford University.

2. Following Alfred Kohlberg's tenure, the American Jewish League Against Communism was headed by George Sokolsky. When Sokolsky died in 1972, leadership of the dying organization passed to Cohn.

3. Cook, 535.

4. Russell Porter, "2,000 Honor Cohn at a Dinner Here," *New York Times*, July 29, 1954, 9.

5. Mary Hornaday, "Backers Fete Cohn; McCarthyism Cited," *Christian Science Monitor*, July 30, 1954, 10.

6. Gallup poll numbers as cited in Nelson W. Polsby, "Toward an Explanation of McCarthyism," *Political Studies* 8, no. 3 (October 1960): 250–271.

7. "Editors Express Views on World, US Affairs," *Detroit Free Press*, May 31, 1955, G222, 3 of 3, folder "34. McCarthy, Jos. (continued) General (folder 1 of 2)," Pearson Papers.

8. Oshinsky, 503.

9. "Sen. McCarthy Lauded at Rites," *Washington Post and Times-Herald*, May 7, 1957, B2.

10. Tim Weiner, *Enemies: A History of the FBI* (New York: Random House, 2012), 191.

11. Anthony Summers, *Official and Confidential: The Secret Life of J. Edgar Hoover* (New York: Open Road Media, 2012).

12. Summers, *Official and Confidential.*

13. Athan G. Theoharis, *J. Edgar Hoover, Sex, and Crime: An Historical Antidote* (Chicago: Ivan R. Dee, 1995), 39–43.

14. Coworker of Roy Cohn, as quoted in von Hoffman, 283.

15. Von Hoffman, 333–334.

16. Albin Krebs, "Roy Cohn, Aide to McCarthy and Fiery Lawyer, Dies at 59," *New York Times*, August 3, 1986, 1. Cohn was notoriously terrible with money and was continually securing loans from friends (loans that he rarely—if ever—paid back). In the late 1950s he purchased the Lionel model train company from an uncle and a cousin, promptly ran it into the ground, and was forced to resign his position on the board of directors.

17. Wayne Barrett, as quoted in Michael Kruse, "'He Brutalized for You': How Joseph McCarthy Henchman Roy Cohn Became Donald Trump's Mentor," *Politico Magazine*, April 8, 2016.

18. Michael Kruse, "'He Brutalized for You': How Joseph McCarthy Henchman Roy Cohn Became Donald Trump's Mentor," *Politico Magazine*, April 8, 2016.

19. Kruse, "'He Brutalized for You.'" Presciently, Sidney Zion wrote in the conclusion to *The Autobiography of Roy Cohn* that Trump would have ditched Cohn had the latter's homosexuality ever been widely reported or publicly confirmed. See Zion, 242.

20. Jeffrey Toobin, "The Dirty Trickster," *New Yorker*, June 2, 2008, https://www.newyorker.com/magazine/2008/06/02/the-dirty-trickster.

21. During the presidency of Barack Obama, it appeared that security state masculinity may have finally met its end. In spite of his bellicose posturing surrounding the death of Osama bin Laden and his expanded use of drone warfare, Obama proved to be more embracing of "soft power" than any prior president. Obama was the first president to embrace the "feminist" label, and for much of the 2016 presidential campaign it appeared that his successor would be the nation's first female president. But Trump's victory has proven that security state masculinity remains a potent political force.

22. Gregory Krieg, "Donald Trump Defends Size of His Penis," CNN.com, March 4, 2016, http://www.cnn.com/2016/03/03/politics/donald-trump-small-hands-marco-rubio/.

23. Glenn Kessler, "President Trump Has Made More Than 10,000 False or Misleading Claims," *Washington Post*, April 29, 2019, https://www.washingtonpost.com/politics/2019/04/29/president-trump-has-made-more-than-false-or-misleading-claims/.

24. David Smith, "Trump Shows Fake Hurricane Map in Apparent Bid to Validate Incorrect Tweet," *Guardian*, September 4, 2019, https://www.theguardian.com/world/2019/sep/04/trump-hurricane-dorian-alabama-sharpie-map.

25. Nicole Hemmer, as quoted in Jane Mayer, "The Making of the Fox News White House," *New Yorker*, March 4, 2019, https://www.newyorker.com/magazine/2019/03/11/the-making-of-the-fox-news-white-house https://www.newyorker.com/magazine/2019/03/11/the-making-of-the-fox-news-white-house.

26. Callum Borchers, "The Very Cozy Relationship between Donald Trump and the National Enquirer," *Washington Post*, March 28, 2016, https://www.washingtonpost.com/news/the-fix/wp/2016/03/28/the-very-cozy-relationship-between-donald-trump-and-the-national-enquirer/.

27. Joe Palazzolo, Michael Rothfeld, and Lukas I. Alpert, "National Enquirer Shielded Donald Trump from Playboy Model's Affair Allegation," *Wall Street Journal*, November 4, 2016, https://www.wsj.com/articles/national-enquirer-shielded-donald-trump-from-playboy-models-affair-allegation-1478309380.

28. John Connolly, "The Secret History of the *National Enquirer*," *DuJour*, http://dujour.com/news/national-enquirer-history-scandal/.

BIBLIOGRAPHY

Ackerman, Kenneth D. *Young J. Edgar: Hoover and the Red Scare, 1919–20.* Falls Church, VA: Viral History Press, 2011.

Adelman, Bob. *Tijuana Bibles: Art and Wit in America's Forbidden Funnies, 1930s–1950s.* New York: Simon and Schuster, 1997.

Anderson, Jack. *Confessions of a Muckraker: The Inside Story of Life in Washington during the Truman, Eisenhower, Kennedy and Johnson Years.* New York: Random House, 1979.

Anderson, Jack, with George Clifford. *The Anderson Papers: From the Files of America's Most Famous Investigative Reporter.* New York: Random House, 1973.

Anderson, Jack, and Daryl Gibson. *Peace, War, and Politics: An Eyewitness Account.* New York: Forge, 1999.

Anderson, Jack, and Ronald W. May. *McCarthy: The Man, the Senator, the "Ism."* New York: Beacon Press, 1952.

Aron, Cindy Sondik. *Ladies and Gentlemen of the Civil Service: Middle-Class Workers in Victorian America.* New York: Oxford University Press, 1987.

Axelrod, Alan. *Selling the Great War: The Making of American Propaganda.* New York: Macmillan, 2009.

Bai, Matt. *All the Truth Is Out: The Week Politics Went Tabloid.* New York: Alfred A. Knopf, 2014.

Baldwin, Davarian L. *Chicago's New Negroes: Modernity, the Great Migration, and Black Urban Life.* Chapel Hill: University of North Carolina Press, 2007.

Barbas, Samantha. *Confidential Confidential: The Inside Story of Hollywood's Notorious Scandal Magazine.* Chicago: Chicago Review Press, 2018.

Barros, James. *Trygve Lie and the Cold War: The UN Secretary-General Pursues Peace, 1946–53.* DeKalb: Northern Illinois University Press, 1989.

Basso, Matthew, Laura McCall, and Dee Garceau. *Across the Great Divide: Cultures of Manhood in the American West.* New York: Routledge, 2001.

Bates, Anna. *Weeder in the Garden of the Lord: Anthony Comstock's Life and Career.* Lanham, MD: University Press of America, 1995.

Baxandall, Roslyn, and Elizabeth Ewen. *Picture Windows: How the Suburbs Happened.* New York: Basic Books, 2000.

Bayley, Edwin R. *Joe McCarthy and the Press.* Madison: University of Wisconsin Press, 1981.

Barbas, Samantha. *Confidential Confidential: The Inside Story of Hollywood's Notorious Scandal Magazine.* Chicago: Chicago Review Press, 2018.

Beck, Frank Orman. *Marching Manward: A Study of the Boy.* New York: Eaton & Mains, 1913.

Bederman, Gail. *Manliness and Civilization: A Cultural History of Gender and Race in the United States, 1880–1917.* Chicago: University of Chicago Press, 1996.

Beisel, Nicola. *Imperiled Innocents: Anthony Comstock and Family Reproduction in Victorian America.* Princeton: Princeton University Press, 1997.

Bell, Daniel. "Interpretations of American Politics—1955." In *The Radical Right,* edited by Daniel Bell, 47–74. Garden City, NY: Doubleday & Company, 1963.

Benwell, Bethan. "Language and Masculinity." In *The Handbook of Language, Gender, and Sexuality.* Edited by Susan Ehrlich, Miriam Meyerhoff, and Janet Holmes, 240–259. Malden, MA: Wiley-Blackwell, 2014.

———. "Male Gossip and Language Play in the Letters Pages of Men's Lifestyle Magazines." *Journal of Popular Culture* 34, no. 4 (Spring 2001): 19–33.

Berinsky, Adam J., and Gabriel S. Lenz. "Red Scare?: Revisiting Joe McCarthy's Influence on 1950s Elections." *Public Opinion Quarterly* 78, no. 2 (January 2014): 369–391.

Bernstein, Samuel. *Mr. Confidential: The Man, His Magazine & the Movieland Massacre That Changed Hollywood Forever.* West Hollywood, CA: Walford Press, 2006.

Bérubé, Alan. *Coming Out Under Fire: The History of Gay Men and Women in World War II.* New York: Free Press, 1990.

Besnier, Niko. *Gossip and the Everyday Production of Politics.* Honolulu: University of Hawaii Press, 2009.

Bessie, Simon Michael. *Jazz Journalism: The Story of the Tabloid Newspapers*. New York: E. P. Dutton, 1938.

Betrock, Alan. *The Personality Index: To Hollywood Scandal Magazines, 1952–1966*. Brooklyn: Shake Books, 1988.

———. *Pin-Up Mania: The Golden Age of Men's Magazines*. Brooklyn: Shake Books, 1993.

———. *Unseen America: The Greatest Cult Exploitation Magazines, 1950–1966*. Brooklyn: Shake Books, 1990.

Bienvenu, Robert V., II "The Development of Sadomasochism as a Cultural Style in the Twentieth-Century United States." Doctoral dissertation, Indiana University, 1998.

Bird, S. Elizabeth. *For Enquiring Minds: A Cultural Study of Supermarket Tabloids*. Knoxville: University of Tennessee Press, 1992.

Blake, David Haven. *Liking Ike: Eisenhower, Advertising, and the Rise of Celebrity Politics*. New York: Oxford University Press, 2016.

Blumenthal, Ralph. *The Stork Club: America's Most Famous Nightspot and the Lost World of Café Society*. Boston: Little, Brown, 2000.

Boyer, Paul S. *By the Bomb's Early Light: American Thought and Culture at the Dawn of the Atomic Age*. Chapel Hill: University of North Carolina Press, 1985.

———. *Purity in Print: Book Censorship in American from the Gilded Age to the Computer Age*. 2nd ed. Madison: University of Wisconsin Press, 2002.Brod, Harry. *The Making of Masculinities: The New Men's Studies*. Abingdon-on-Thames: Routledge, 1987.

Brower, Sue. "Inside Stories: Gossip and Television Audiences." In "Culture and Communication: Language, Performance, Technology, and Media," edited by Sari Thomas and William A. Evans. Special issue, *Studies in Communication 4* (1990): 225–235.

Burrough, Brian. *Public Enemies*. New York: Penguin Press, 2004.

Butler, Judith. *Gender Trouble: Feminism and the Subversion of Identity*. New York: Routledge, 1990.

Caldwell, Mark. *A Short History of Rudeness: Manners, Morals, and Misbehavior in Modern America*. New York: Picador, 1999.

Canaday, Margot. *The Straight State: Sexuality and Citizenship in Twentieth-Century America*. Princeton: Princeton University Press, 2009.

Canwell, Bruce. "Craft and Tradecraft." In *Secret Agent X-9: The Complete 1930s Comic Strip*, 5–13. San Diego: IDW Publishing, 2015.

Carnes, Mark C., and Clyde Griffen. *Meanings for Manhood*. Chicago: University of Chicago Press, 1990.

Charles, Douglas M. *The FBI's Obscene File: J. Edgar Hoover and the Bureau's Crusade against Smut*. Lawrence: University Press of Kansas, 2012.

———. *Hoover's War on Gays: Exposing the FBI's "Sex Deviates Program."* Lawrence: University Press of Kansas, 2015.

Chauncey, George. *Gay New York: Gender, Urban Culture, and the Making of the Gay Male World.* New York: Basic Books, 1994.

Childs, Marquis. *Witness to Power.* New York: McGraw-Hill, 1975.

Chudacoff, Howard P. *The Age of the Bachelor.* Princeton: Princeton University Press, 1999.

Claridge, Laura. *Emily Post: Daughter of the Gilded Age, Mistress of American Manners.* New York: Random House, 2008.

Clark, Daniel A. *Creating the College Man: American Mass Magazines and Middle-Class Manhood, 1890–1915.* Madison: University of Wisconsin Press, 2010.

Clark, Kate Upson. *Bringing Up Boys: A Study.* New York: Thomas H. Crowell, 1899.

Clatterbaugh, Kenneth C. *Contemporary Perspectives on Masculinity: Men, Women, and Politics in Modern Society.* Boulder, CO: Westview Press, 1997.

Cobble, Dorothy Sue. *The Other Women's Movement: Workplace Justice and Social Rights in Modern America.* Princeton: Princeton University Press, 2004.

Cohan, Steven. *Masked Men Masculinity and the Movies in the Fifties.* Bloomington: Indiana University Press, 1997.

Cohen, Lizabeth. *A Consumer's Republic: The Politics of Mass Consumption in Postwar America.* New York: Alfred A. Knopf, 2003.

Cohn, Roy M. *McCarthy.* New York: New American Library, 1968.

Collins, Gail. *Scorpion Tongues: Gossip, Celebrity, and American Politics.* New York: Morrow, 1998.

Conant, Robert Warren. *The Virility of Christ: A New View.* Chicago: the author, 1915.

Conboy, Martin. *Tabloid Britain: Constructing a Community through Language.* New York: Routledge, 2005.

Connell, R. W. *Gender and Power.* Stanford, CA: Stanford University Press, 1987.

Connell, R. W., and James W. Messerschmidt. "Hegemonic Masculinity: Rethinking the Concept." *Gender and Society* 19, no. 6 (December 2005): 829–859.

Cook, Blanche Wiesen. *Eleanor Roosevelt.* Vol. 2, *The Defining Years, 1933–1938.* New York: Viking Press, 1999.

Cook, Fred J. *The Nightmare Decade: The Life and Times of Senator Joe McCarthy.* New York: Random House, 1971.

Cook, Susan L,. and Karen Krupar, "Defining the Twentieth Century and Impacting the Twenty-First: Semantic Habits Created through Radio and Song: A Review of General Semantics." *Et Cetera* 67, no. 4 (October 2010): 412–434.

Cuordileone, K. A. *Manhood and American Political Culture in the Cold War.* New York: Routledge, 2005.

Dallek, Robert. *Flawed Giant: Lyndon Johnson and His Times, 1961–1973*. New York: Oxford University Press, 1999.

Davies, Richard O. *Housing Reform during the Truman Administration*. Columbia: University of Missouri Press, 1966.

Dawson, Graham. *Soldier Heroes: British Adventure, Empire, and the Imagining of Masculinities*. London: Routledge, 1994.

Dean, Robert D. *Imperial Brotherhood: Gender and the Making of Cold War Foreign Policy*. Amherst: University of Massachusetts Press, 2001.

Demaris, Ovid. *The Director: An Oral Biography of J. Edgar Hoover*. New York: Harper's Magazine Press, 1975.

D'Emilio, John, and Estelle B. Freedman. *Intimate Matters: A History of Sexuality in America*. 2nd ed. Chicago: University of Chicago Press, 1997.

Demos, John. *Entertaining Satan: Witchcraft and the Culture of Early New England*. New York: Oxford University Press, 1982.

Desjardins, Mary. "Systemizing Scandal: *Confidential* Magazine, Stardom, and the State of California." In *Headline Hollywood: A Century of Film Scandal*, edited by Adrienne McClean and David A. Cook, 206–231. New Brunswick, NJ: Rutgers University Press, 2001.

Doherty, Thomas. *Cold War, Cool Medium: Television, McCarthyism, and American Culture*. New York: Columbia University Press, 2003.

———. *Hollywood's Censor: Joseph I. Breen and the Production Code Administration*. New York: Columbia University Press, 2009.

Douglas, Paul H. *In the Fullness of Time: The Memoirs of Paul H. Douglas*. New York: Harcourt Brace Jovanovich, 1972.

Dubbert, Joe L. *A Man's Place: Masculinity in Transition*. Englewood Cliffs, NJ: Prentice-Hall, 1979.

Dunne, Matthew W. *A Cold War State of Mind: Brainwashing and Postwar American Society*. Amherst: University of Massachusetts Press, 2013.

Ehrenreich, Barbara. *The Hearts of Men: American Dreams and the Flight from Commitment*. New York: Doubleday, 1983.

Ehrenstein, David. *Open Secret: Gay Hollywood, 1928–2000*. New York: Perennial, 2000.

English, Daylanne K. *Unnatural Selections: Eugenics in American Modernism and the Harlem Renaissance*. Chapel Hill: University of North Carolina Press, 2004.

Epstein, Joseph. *Gossip: An Untrivial Pursuit*. Boston: Houghton Mifflin, 2011.

Erenberg, Lewis A. *Steppin' Out: New York Nightlife and the Transformation of American Culture*. Chicago: University of Chicago Press, 1984.

Estes, Steve. *I Am a Man!: Race, Manhood, and the Civil Rights Movement*. Chapel Hill: University of North Carolina Press, 2005.

Evans, M. Stanton. *Blacklisted by History: The Untold Story of Senator Joe McCarthy and His Fight against America's Enemies.* New York: Three Rivers Press, 2009.

Ewald, William Bragg. *Who Killed Joe McCarthy?* New York: Simon and Schuster, 1984.

Ewen, Elizabeth. *Picture Windows: How the Suburbs Happened.* New York: Basic Books, 2001.

Ewen, Stuart. *PR!: A Social History of Spin.* New York: Basic Books, 1996.

Farr, Finis. *Fair Enough: The Life of Westbrook Pegler.* New Rochelle, NY: Arlington House Publishers, 1975.

Feeley, Kathleen A. "Gossip as News: On Modern U.S. Celebrity Culture and Journalism." *History Compass* 10, no. 6 (2012): 467–482.

Feeley, Kathleen A., and Jennifer Frost, eds. *When Private Talk Goes Public: Gossip in American History.* New York: Palgrave Macmillan, 2014.

Ferguson, Kathy E. "Discourses of Danger: Locating Emma Goldman," *Political Theory* 6, no. 5 (October 2008): 735–761.

Filene, Peter. *Him/Her/Self: Gender Identities in Modern America.* 3rd ed. Baltimore: Johns Hopkins University Press, 1998.

Foote, Stephanie. "Little Brothers of the Rich: Queer Families in the Gilded Age." *American Literature* 79, no. 4 (December 2007): 701–724.

Forbush, William Byron. *The Boy Problem in the Home.* Boston: Pilgrim Press, 1915).

Foster, Eric K. "Gossip." In *Encyclopedia of Human Relationships.* Edited by Harry T. Reis and Susan Sprecher, 768–770. Los Angeles: SAGE Publications, 2009.

Foster, Eugene C. *The Boy and the Church.* Philadelphia: Sunday School Times Company, 1909.

Fraser, John. *America and the Patterns of Chivalry.* New York: Cambridge University Press, 2009.

Fried, Albert. *McCarthyism: The Great American Red Scare, a Documentary History.* New York: Oxford University Press, 1997.

Fried, Richard M. *Nightmare in Red: The McCarthy Era in Perspective.* New York: Oxford University Press, 1990.

Friedberg, Aaron L. *In the Shadow of the Garrison State: America's Anti-statism and Its Cold War Grand Strategy.* Princeton: Princeton University Press, 2000.

Friedman, Andrea. *Citizenship in Cold War America: The National Security State and the Possibilities of Dissent.* Amherst: University of Massachusetts Press, 2014.

———. "The Smearing of Joe McCarthy: The Lavender Scare, Gossip, and Cold War Politics." *American Quarterly* 57, no. 4 (December 1, 2005): 1105–1129.

Friend, Craig Thompson, ed. *Southern Masculinity: Perspectives on Manhood in the South since Reconstruction.* Athens: University of Georgia Press, 2009.

Gabler, Neal. *Winchell: Gossip, Power and the Culture of Celebrity.* New York: Knopf, 1994.

Gentry, Curt. *J. Edgar Hoover: The Man and the Secrets*. New York: W. W. Norton, 2001.

Gertzman, Jay A. "John Saxton Sumner of the New York Society for the Suppression of Vice: A Chief Smut-Eradicator of the Interwar Period." *Journal of American Culture* 17, no. 2 (June 1994): 41–47.

Gilbert, James. *Men in the Middle: Searching for Masculinity in the 1950s*. Chicago: University of Chicago Press, 2005.

Gilmore, David D. *Manhood in the Making: Cultural Concepts of Masculinity*. New Haven: Yale University Press, 1990.

Grahn, Judy. *Another Mother Tongue: Gay Words, Gay Worlds*. Boston: Beacon Press, 1984.

Grant, Julia. "A 'Real Boy' and Not a Sissy: Gender, Childhood, and Masculinity, 1890–1940." *Journal of Social History* 37, no. 4 (Summer 2004): 829–851.

Greene, Theodore P. *America's Heroes: The Changing Models of Success in American Magazines*. Oxford University Press, 1970.

Greenstein, Fred I. *The Hidden-Hand Presidency: Eisenhower as Leader*. Baltimore: Johns Hopkins University Press, 1994.

Griffith, Robert. *The Politics of Fear: Joseph McCarthy and the Senate*. Lexington: University Press of Kentucky, 1970.

Griswold, Robert L. *Fatherhood in America: A History*. New York: Basic Books, 1993.

Halberstam, David. *The Powers That Be*. Urbana: University of Illinois Press, 2000.

Hallas, James H. *Doughboy War: The American Expeditionary Force in World War I*. Boulder, CO: Lynne Rienner Publishers, 2000.

Hantover, Jeffrey P. "The Boy Scouts and the Validation of Masculinity." In *The American Man*, edited by Elizabeth Hafkin Pleck and Joseph H. Pleck, 285–301. Englewood Cliffs, NJ: Prentice Hall, 1980.

Heale, M. J. *McCarthy's Americans: Red Scare Politics in State and Nation, 1935–1965*. Athens: University of Georgia Press, 1998.

Heap, Chad. *Slumming: Sexual and Racial Encounters in American Nightlife, 1885–1940*. Chicago: University of Chicago Press, 2010.

Hegarty, Marilyn E. *Victory Girls, Khaki-Wackies, and Patriotutes: The Regulation of Female Sexuality during World War II*. New York: NYU Press, 2007.

Herman, Arthur. *Joseph McCarthy: Re-examining the Senator's Life and Legacy*. New York: Free Press, 2000.

Hermes, Joke. *Reading Women's Magazines: An Analysis of Everyday Media Use*. Cambridge, UK: Polity Press, 1995.

Hoben, Allan. *The Minister and the Boy: A Handbook for Churchmen Engaged in Boys' Work*. Chicago: University of Chicago Press, 1912.

Hogan, Michael J. *A Cross of Iron: Harry S. Truman and the Origins of the National Security State, 1945–1954*. New York: Cambridge University Press, 1998.

Hoganson, Kristin L. *Fighting for American Manhood: How Gender Politics Provoked the Spanish-American and Philippine-American Wars*. New Haven: Yale University Press, 2000.

Hoover, John Edgar. *The Story of the FBI: The Official Picture History of the Federal Bureau of Investigation*. New York: E. P. Dutton, 1947.

Horowitz, Daniel. *The Morality of Spending: Attitudes toward the Consumer Society in America, 1875–1940*. New York: Ivan R. Dee, 1992.

Horrocks, Roger. *Masculinity in Crisis*. New York: Palgrave Macmillan, 1994.

Hughes, Geoffrey. *Swearing: A Social History of Foul Language, Oaths and Profanity in English*. Oxford, UK: Blackwell, 1991.

Hulbert, Ann. *Raising America: Experts, Parents, and a Century of Advice about Children*. New York: Vintage, 2004.

Hunt, William R. *Body Love: The Amazing Career of Bernarr Macfadden*. Bowling Green, OH: Bowling Green State University Popular Press, 1989.

Izenberg, Gerald N. *Modernism and Masculinity: Mann, Wedekind, Kandinsky through World War I*. Chicago: University of Chicago Press, 2000.

Jarvis, Christina S. *The Male Body at War: American Masculinity during World War II*. DeKalb: Northern Illinois University Press, 2004.

Jeffreys-Jones, Rhodri. *The FBI: A History*. New Haven: Yale University Press, 2007.

Jenkins, Philip. *Moral Panic: Changing Concepts of the Child Molester in Modern America*. New Haven: Yale University Press, 1998.

Johnson, David K. *The Lavender Scare: The Cold War Persecution of Gays and Lesbians in the Federal Government*. Chicago: University of Chicago Press, 2006.

Jonathan, Norton Hughes. *Gentlemen Aren't Sissies*. Chicago: John C. Winston Company, 1938.

Kantrowitz, Stephen. *Ben Tillman and the Reconstruction of White Supremacy*. Chapel Hill: University of North Carolina Press, 2000.

Karpis, Alvin, and Bill Treat. *The Alvin Karpis Story*. New York: Ishi Press, 2011.

Kim, Townsend. *Manhood at Harvard: William James and Others*. New York: W. W. Norton, 1996.

Kimmel, Michael S. *Manhood in America: A Cultural History*. New York: Oxford University Press, 2012.

Kinsler, Jeffrey S. "Joseph McCarthy, The Law Student." *Marquette Law Review* 85, no. 2 (Winter 2001): 466–477.

Klay, Phil. *Redeployment*. New York: Penguin, 2014.

Klurfeld, Herman. *Winchell: His Life and Times*. New York: Praeger Publishers, 1976.

Kushner, Tony. "G. David Schine in Hell." In *Death & Taxes: Hydrioptaphia & Other Plays*, 227–240. New York: Theatre Communications Group, 2000.

Kwolek-Folland, Angel. *Engendering Business: Men and Women in the Corporate Office, 1870–1930*. Baltimore: Johns Hopkins University Press, 1998.

Lait, Jack. *U.S.A. Confidential*. New York: Crown Publishers, 1952.

Lait, Jack, and Lee Mortimer. *Chicago Confidential*. New York: Crown Publishers, 1950.

———. *New York Confidential*. New York: Crown Publishers, 1948.

———. *Washington Confidential*. New York: Crown Publishers, 1951.

Landis, Mark. *Joseph McCarthy: The Politics of Chaos*. Cranbury, NJ: Susquehanna University Press, 1987.

Langum, David J. *Crossing over the Line: Legislating Morality and the Mann Act*. Chicago: University of Chicago Press, 1994.

Laurie, Piper. *Learning to Live Out Loud: A Memoir*. New York: Crown Archetype, 2011.

Lears, Jackson. *Fables of Abundance: A Cultural History of Advertising in America*. Boston: Basic Books, 1995.

———. *Rebirth of a Nation: The Making of Modern America, 1877–1920*. New York: Harper, 2009.

Legman, Gershon. "The Language of Homosexuality." In *The Gay/Lesbian Almanac: A New Documentary*. Edited by Johnathan Ned Katz, 571–584. New York: Harper & Row, 1983.

Lewis, Carolyn Herbst. *Prescription for Heterosexuality Sexual Citizenship in the Cold War Era*. Chapel Hill: University of North Carolina Press, 2010.

Lindsey, Rachel McBride. "'The Mirror of All Perfection': Jesus and the Strongman in America, 1893–1920." *American Quarterly* 68, no. 1 (March 2016): 23–47.

Lipsitz, George. *Rainbow at Midnight: Labor and Culture in the 1940s*. Urbana: University of Illinois Press, 1994.

Logan, Andy. *The Man Who Robbed the Robber Barons*. New York: W. W. Norton, 1965.

Lui, Mary Ting Yi. *The Chinatown Trunk Mystery: Murder, Miscegenation, and Other Dangerous Encounters in Turn-of-the-Century New York*. Princeton: Princeton University Press, 2004.

Lynd, Robert S., and Helen Merrell Lynd. *Middletown: A Study in Modern American Culture*. New York: Harcourt, Brace and Company, 1929.

Macleod, David. "Act Your Age: Boyhood, Adolescence, and the Rise of the Boy Scouts of America." *Journal of Social History* 16, no. 2 (Winter 1982): 3–20.

———. *Building Character in the American Boy: The Boy Scouts, YMCA, and Their Forerunners, 1870–1920*. Madison: University of Wisconsin Press, 2004.

Mallen, Frank. *Sauce for the Gander*. White Plains, NY: Baldwin Books, 1954.

Maney, Patrick J. *"Young Bob" La Follette: A Biography of Robert M. La Follette, Jr., 1895–1953*. Columbia: University of Missouri Press, 1978.

Mangan, James A., and James Walvin. *Manliness and Morality: Middle Class Masculinity in Britain and America, 1800–1940*. Manchester, UK: Manchester University Press, 1987.

Matusow, Harvey. *False Witness*. New York: Cameron & Kahn, 1955.

May, Gary. *Un-American Activities: The Trials of William Remington*. New York: Oxford University Press, 1994.

McAuliffe, Mary S. "Liberals and the Communist Control Act of 1954." *Journal of American History* 63, no. 2 (September 1, 1976): 351–367.

McCarthy, Joseph. *McCarthyism: The Fight for America*. New York: Devin-Adair, 1952.

McCoy, Alfred W. *Policing America's Empire: The United States, the Philippines, and the Rise of the Surveillance State*. Madison: University of Wisconsin Press, 2010.

———. "Surveillance Blowback: The Making of the U.S. Surveillance State, 1898–2020." *TomDispatch.com*. Last modified July 14, 2013. http://www.tomdispatch.com/blog/175724/alfred_mccoy_surveillance_blowback.

McCullough, David. *Truman*. New York: Simon & Schuster, 1992.

McHugh, Maureen C., and Jennifer Hambaugh. "She Said, He Said: Gender, Language, and Power." In *Handbook of Gender Research in Psychology*. Vol. 1, *Gender Research in General Experimental Psychology*. Edited by Joan C. Chrisler and Donald R. McCreary, 379–410. New York: Springer Publishing, 2009.

McLean, Adrienne, and David A. Cook. *Headline Hollywood: A Century of Film Scandal*. New Brunswick, NJ: Rutgers University Press, 2001.

McDaniel, Rodger E. *Dying for Joe McCarthy's Sins: The Suicide of Wyoming Senator Lester Hunt*. Cheyenne, WY: WordsWorth, 2013.

McLaren, Angus. *Sexual Blackmail: A Modern History*. Cambridge, MA: Harvard University Press, 2002.

———. *The Trials of Masculinity: Policing Sexual Boundaries, 1870–1930*. Chicago: University of Chicago Press, 1997.

Medsger, Betty. *The Burglary: The Discovery of J. Edgar Hoover's Secret FBI*. New York: Vintage, 2014.

Merry, Robert W. *Taking on the World: Joseph and Stewart Alsop—Guardians of the American Century*. New York: Viking, 2012.

Meyerowitz, Joanne J. *Not June Cleaver: Women and Gender in Postwar America, 1945–1960*. Philadelphia: Temple University Press, 1994.

Micale, Mark S. *Hysterical Men: The Hidden History of Male Nervous Illness*. Cambridge, MA: Harvard University Press, 2008.

Miller, Neil. *Banned in Boston: The Watch and Ward Society's Crusade against Books, Burlesque, and the Social Evil.* Boston: Beacon Press, 2010.

Mills, C. Wright. *The Power Elite.* New York: Oxford University Press, 1956.

Mitchell, Michelle. "A 'Corrupting Influence': Idleness and Sexuality during the Great Depression." In *Interconnections: Gender and Race in American History,* edited by Carol Faulkner and Alison M. Parker, 187–228. Rochester, NY: University of Rochester Press, 2012.

Morton, Paula E. *Tabloid Valley: Supermarket News and American Culture.* Gainesville: University Press of Florida, 2009.

Mosse, George L. *The Image of Man: The Creation of Modern Masculinity.* New York: Oxford University Press, 1996.

Mulloy, D. J. *The World of the John Birch Society: Conspiracy, Conservatism, and the Cold War.* Nashville, TN: Vanderbilt University Press, 2014.

Nadel, Alan. *Containment Culture: American Narratives, Postmodernism, and the Atomic Age.* Durham, NC: Duke University Press, 1995.

Nadler, Joel T., and Tiffany Edwards. "The 'Big Lie' Technique." In *The Encyclopedia of Deception,* edited by Timothy R. Levine, 77–79. New York: SAGE Publications, 2014.

Navasky, Victor S. *Naming Names.* New York: Viking Press, 1980.

Nichols, David A. *Ike and McCarthy: Dwight Eisenhower's Secret Campaign against Joseph McCarthy.* New York: Simon & Schuster, 2017.

Nixon, Sean. *Hard Looks: Masculinities, Spectatorship and Contemporary Consumption.* New York: St. Martin's Press, 1996.

Norton, Mary Beth. *In the Devil's Snare: The Salem Witchcraft Crisis of 1692.* New York: Vintage, 2003.

Nye, Robert A. "Western Masculinities in War and Peace." *American Historical Review* 112, no. 2 (April 2007): 417–438.

O'Brien, Michael. *McCarthy and McCarthyism in Wisconsin.* Columbia: University of Missouri Press, 1981.

O'Neill, William L. *A Better World: The Great Schism: Stalinism and the American Intellectuals.* New York: Simon and Schuster, 1982.

Osgerby, Bill. *Playboys in Paradise: Masculinity, Youth and Leisure-Style in Modern America.* Oxford: Berg, 2001.

Oshinsky, David M. *A Conspiracy So Immense: The World of Joe McCarthy.* New York: Oxford University Press, 2005.

Pearson, Drew, and Abell, Tyler. *Drew Pearson Diaries 1949–1959.* New York: Holt, Rinehart and Winston, 1974.

Peiss, Kathy. *Zoot Suit: The Enigmatic Career of an Extreme Style.* Philadelphia: University of Pennsylvania Press, 2011.

Pendergast, Tom. *Creating the Modern Man: American Magazines and Consumer Culture, 1900–1950*. Columbia: University of Missouri Press, 2000.

Peterson, Theodore. *Magazines in the Twentieth Century*. Urbana: University of Illinois Press, 1956.

Pettegrew, John. *Brutes in Suits: Male Sensibility in America, 1890–1920*. Baltimore: Johns Hopkins University Press, 2007.

Pierce, Jason Noble. *The Masculine Power of Christ: Or, Christ Measured as a Man*. Boston: Pilgrim Press, 1912.

Pleck, Elizabeth Hafkin, and Joseph H. Pleck, eds. *The American Man*. New York: Prentice-Hall, 1980.

Pliley, Jessica R. *Policing Sexuality: The Mann Act and the Making of the FBI*. Cambridge, MA: Harvard University Press, 2014.

Polsby, Nelson W. "Toward an Explanation of McCarthyism." *Political Studies* 8, no. 3 (October 1960): 250–271.

Ponce de Leon, Charles L. *Self-Exposure: Human-Interest Journalism and the Emergence of Celebrity in America, 1890–1940*. Chapel Hill: University of North Carolina Press, 2002.

Post, Edwin. *Truly Emily Post*. New York: Funk & Wagnalls Company, 1961.

Potter, Claire Bond. *War on Crime: Bandits, G-Men, and the Politics of Mass Culture*. New Brunswick, NJ: Rutgers University Press, 1998.

———. "Queer Hoover: Sex, Lies, and Political History." *Journal of the History of Sexuality* 15, no. 3 (September 2006): 355–381.

Poveda, Tony, Richard G. Powers, Susan Rosenfeld, and Athan G. Theoharis. *The FBI: A Comprehensive Reference Guide*. Phoenix, AZ: Greenwood, 1998.

Powers, Richard Gid. *G-Men: Hoover's FBI in American Popular Culture*. Carbondale: Southern Illinois University Press, 1983.

———. *Secrecy and Power: The Life of J. Edgar Hoover*. New York: Free Press, 1987.

Quartermain, Peter. *Disjunctive Poetics: From Gertrude Stein and Louis Zukofsky to Susan Howe*. Cambridge, UK: Cambridge University Press, 1992.

Radosh, Ronald, and Joyce Milton. *The Rosenberg File*. 2nd ed. New Haven: Yale University Press, 1997.

Rainey, Buck. *Serials and Series: A World Filmography, 1912–1956*. Jefferson, NC: McFarland Books, 2010.

Reeves, Thomas C. *The Life and Times of Joe McCarthy*. New York: Stein and Day, 1982.

Remy, Steven P. *The Malmedy Massacre: The War Crimes Trial Controversy*. Cambridge, MA: Harvard University Press, 2017.

Richter, Irving. *Labor's Struggles, 1945–1950: A Participant's View*. Cambridge, UK: Cambridge University Press, 2003.

Shogan, Robert. *No Sense of Decency*. Chicago: Ivan R. Dee, 2009.

Roberts, Sam. *The Brother: The Untold Story of Atomic Spy David Greenglass and How He Sent His Sister, Ethel Rosenberg, to the Electric Chair*. New York: Random House, 2001.

Robinson, Sally. *Marked Men: White Masculinity in Crisis*. New York: Columbia University Press, 2005.

Rotundo, E. Anthony. *American Manhood: Transformations in Masculinity from the Revolution to the Modern Era*. New York: Basic Books, 1993.

Rovere, Richard H. *Senator Joe McCarthy*. New York: Harcourt, Brace, 1959.

Ryan, Erica J. *Red War on the Family: Sex, Gender, and Americanism in the First Red Scare*. Philadelphia: Temple University Press, 2015.

Salvatore, Nick. *Eugene V. Debs: Citizen and Socialist*. Urbana: University of Illinois Press, 1982.

Savran, David. *Taking It Like a Man: White Masculinity, Masochism, and Contemporary American Culture*. Princeton: Princeton University Press, 1998.

Schlesinger, Arthur M., Jr. *The Letters of Arthur Schlesinger, Jr.* Edited by Andrew Schlesinger and Stephen C. Schlesinger. New York: Random House, 2013.

———. *Robert Kennedy and His Times*. Boston: Mariner Books, 2002.

———. *The Vital Center: The Politics of Freedom*. New York: Da Capo Press, 1949.

Schneir, Walter. *Final Verdict: What Really Happened in the Rosenberg Case*. Brooklyn: Melville House, 2010.

Schrecker, Ellen. *The Age of McCarthyism: A Brief History with Documents*. Boston: Bedford Books of St. Martin's Press, 1994.

———. *Many Are the Crimes: McCarthyism in America*. Boston: Little, Brown and Company, 1998.

Schultz, Brad. *Sports Media: Planning, Production, and Reporting*. Vol. 1. New York: Taylor & Francis, 2005.

Scott, Henry E. *Shocking True Story: The Rise and Fall of Confidential, "America's Most Scandalous Scandal Magazine."* New York: Pantheon Books, 2010.

Scott, Joan W. "Gender: A Useful Category of Historical Analysis." *American Historical Review* 91, no. 5 (December 1986): 1053–1075.

Sears, Clare. *Arresting Dress: Cross-dressing, Law, and Fascination in Nineteenth-Century San Francisco*. Durham: Duke University Press Books, 2014.

Serlin, David. *Replaceable You: Engineering the Body in Postwar America*. Chicago: University of Chicago Press, 2004.

Shaw, Tony, and Denise J. Youngblood. *Cinematic Cold War: The American and Soviet Struggle for Hearts and Minds*. Lawrence: University Press of Kansas, 2010.

Shibusawa, Naoko. "The Lavender Scare and Empire: Rethinking Cold War Antigay Politics." *Diplomatic History* 36, no. 4 (September 2012): 723–752.

Shogan, Robert. *No Sense of Decency: The Army-McCarthy Hearings: A Demagogue Falls and Television Takes Charge of American Politics*. Chicago: Ivan R. Dee, 2009.

Smith-Pryor, Elizabeth M. *Property Rites: The Rhinelander Trial, Passing, and the Protection of Whiteness*. Chapel Hill: University of North Carolina Press, 2009.

Snyder, Terri L. *Brabbling Women: Disorderly Speech and the Law in Early Virginia*. Ithaca, NY: Cornell University Press, 2013.

Spacks, Patricia Ann Meyer. *Gossip*. New York: Knopf, 1985.

Steakley, James D. "Iconography of a Scandal: Political Cartoons and the Eulenburg Affair." In *History of Homosexuality in Europe & America*, edited by Wayne R. Dynes and Stephen Donaldson, 323–386. New York: Garland, 1992.

Stearns, Peter N. *Be a Man!: Males in Modern Society*. Teaneck, NJ: Holmes & Meier, 1990.

Stockley, Julian L. "'Red Purge': The 1946–47 Strike at Allis-Chalmers," *Wisconsin Academy of Sciences, Arts, and Letters* 76 (1988): 17–31.

Stone, I. F. *The Haunted Fifties*. New York: Vintage, 1969.

Storrs, Landon R. Y. *The Second Red Scare and the Unmaking of the New Deal Left*. Princeton: Princeton University Press, 2012.

Straight, Michael. *Trial by Television and Other Encounters*. New York: Devon Press, 1979.

Strasser, Susan. *Satisfaction Guaranteed: The Making of the American Mass Market*. New York: Pantheon Books, 1989.

Straw, William. *Cyanide and Sin: Visualizing Crime in 50s America*. New York: Andrew Roth, 2006.

———. "Traffic in Scandal: The Story of *Broadway Brevities*." *University of Toronto Quarterly* 73, no. 4 (Fall 2004): 947–971.

Strunk, Mary Elizabeth. *Wanted Women: An American Obsession in the Reign of J. Edgar Hoover*. Lawrence: University Press of Kansas, 2010.

Stuart, Douglas. *Creating the National Security State: A History of the Law That Transformed America*. Princeton: Princeton University Press, 2008.

Summers, Anthony. *Official and Confidential: The Secret Life of J. Edgar Hoover*. New York: Putnam, 1993.

Summers, Martin Anthony. *Manliness and Its Discontents: The Black Middle Class and the Transformation of Masculinity, 1900–1930*. Chapel Hill: University of North Carolina Press, 2004.

Susman, Warren. *Culture as History: The Transformation of American Society in the Twentieth Century*. New York: Pantheon, 1984.

Tebbutt, Melanie. *Women's Talk: A Social History of "Gossip" in Working-Class Neighbourhoods, 1880–1960*. Aldershot, England: Scolar Press, 1995.

Theoharis, Athan G. *The FBI: A Comprehensive Reference Guide*. Phoenix, AZ: Oryx Press, 1999.

———. *From the Secret Files of J. Edgar Hoover*. Chicago: Ivan R. Dee, 1993.

———. *J. Edgar Hoover, Sex, and Crime: An Historical Antidote*. Chicago: Ivan R. Dee, 1995.

Theoharis, Athan G., and John Stuart Cox. *The Boss: J. Edgar Hoover and the Great American Inquisition*. Philadelphia: Temple University Press, 1988.

Theweleit, Klaus, and Anson Rabinbach. *Male Fantasies*. Vol. 2. *Male Bodies: Psycho-analyzing the White Terror*. Translated by Erica Carter and Chris Turner. Minneapolis: University of Minnesota Press, 1989.

Thomas, Calvin. *Male Matters: Masculinity, Anxiety, and the Male Body on the Line*. Urbana: University of Illinois Press, 1996.

Thomas, Evan. *Robert Kennedy: His Life*. New York: Simon and Schuster, 2000.

Thomas, Lately. *When Even Angels Wept: The Senator Joseph McCarthy Affair— a Story without a Hero*. New York: Morrow, 1973.

Trachtenberg, Alan. *The Incorporation of America: Culture and Society in the Gilded Age*. New York: Hill and Wang, 1982.

Traister, Bryce. "Academic Viagra: The Rise of American Masculinity Studies." *American Quarterly* 52, no. 2 (June 2000): 274–304.

Turner, Graeme. *Understanding Celebrity*, 2nd ed. London: SAGE Publications, 2014.

Tye, Larry. *Demagogue: The Life and Long Shadow of Senator Joe McCarthy*. Boston: Houghton Mifflin Harcourt, 2020.

Von Hoffman, Nicholas. *Citizen Cohn*. New York: Doubleday, 1988.

Walls, Jeannette. *Dish: How Gossip Became the News and the News Became Just Another Show*. New York: Spike, 2001.

Walters, Barbara. *Audition: A Memoir*. New York: Knopf, 2008.

Wannall, Ray. *The Real J. Edgar Hoover: For the Record*. Paducah, KY: Turner, 2000.

Warshow, Robert, Stanley Cavell, and Lionel Trilling. *The Immediate Experience: Movies, Comics, Theatre, and Other Aspects of Popular Culture*. Cambridge, MA: Harvard University Press, 2002.

Weiner, Tim. *Enemies: A History of the FBI*. New York: Random House, 2012.

Weingartner, James. *A Peculiar Crusade: Willis M. Everett & The Malmedy Massacre Trial*. New York: NYU Press, 2000.

Weinstein, Allen. *Perjury: The Hiss-Chambers Case*. New York: Random House, 1997.

Wernick, Robert, and Arnold Roth. "When It Comes to Gossip, We're All-Ears Listeners." *Smithsonian* 23, no. 11 (February 1993): 76–83.

Wexley, John. *The Judgment of Julius and Ethel Rosenberg*. Revd. and updated ed. New York: Ballantine Books, 1977.

Whitehead, Don. *The FBI Story: A Report to the People*. New York: Random House, 1956.

Whitfield, Stephen J. *The Culture of the Cold War*. Baltimore: Johns Hopkins University Press, 1991.

Wickberg, Daniel. "Heterosexual White Male: Some Recent Interventions in Cultural History." *Journal of American History* 92, no. 1 (June 2005): 136–157.

Wicker, Tom. *Shooting Star: The Brief Arc of Joe McCarthy*. Orlando: Harcourt, 2006.

Wiebe, Robert. *The Search for Order: 1877–1920*. New York: Macmillan, 1967.

Wilkes, Roger. *Scandal!: A Scurrilous History of Gossip, 1700–2000*. London: Atlantic Books, 2002.

Williams, Timothy J. *Intellectual Manhood: University, Self, and Society in the Antebellum South*. Chapel Hill: University of North Carolina Press, 2015.

Wood, Molly M. "Diplomacy and Gossip: Information Gathering in the US Foreign Service, 1900–1940." In *When Private Talk Goes Public: Gossip in American History*, edited by Kathleen A. Feeley and Jennifer Frost, 139–160. New York: Palgrave Macmillan, 2014.

Wylie, Philip. *Generation of Vipers*. With new annotations by author. New York: Reinhart, 1955 [1942].Zegart, Amy. *Flawed by Design: The Evolution of the CIA, JCS, and NSC*. Stanford, CA: Stanford University Press, 1999.

Zimmer, Kenyon. *Immigrants against the State: Yiddish and Italian Anarchism in America*. Urbana: University of Illinois Press, 2015.

Zion, Sidney. *The Autobiography of Roy Cohn*. Secaucus, NJ: Lyle Stuart, 1988.

NEWSPAPERS

Atlanta Journal-Constitution

Bakersfield Californian

Baltimore Sun

Boston American

Boston Daily Globe

Boston Post

Bronx Home News

Chicago Defender

Chicago Sun

Chicago Daily Tribune

Christian Science Monitor

Cincinnati Enquirer

Door County Advocate

Los Angeles Times

Las Vegas Sun

London Evening News

Madera Tribune

Madison Capitol Times

Manchester Guardian

Milwaukee Journal

Milwaukee Sentinel

Mobile Register

St. Petersburg Times

Stanford Daily

New York Daily Mirror

New York Daily News

New York Evening Graphic

New York Herald-Tribune

New York Post

New York Times

New York World-Telegram

USA Today

Washington Herald

Washington Post

Washington Star

Washington Times-Herald

Zanesville Signal

OTHER PERIODICALS

American Mercury
Broadway Brevities and Society Gossip
Celebrity
Collier's
Confidential
Liberty
Maclean's
Newsweek
The New Yorker
The Progressive
Rave
The Saturday Evening Post
Spy
Time
Town Topics
Woman's Day

INDEX

Page numbers in italics refer to illustrations.

INDEX

conspiracies, 152, 156, 162, 168–69; anti-Semitic, 111–12; communist, 102, 153–54, 186, 190; public paranoia, 154

consumerism, 8–10

Cook, Fred J., 164

corporatization, 36

Costello, Frank, 212, 248n41

Counihan, Maybelle, 239n30

Cox, John Stuart, 224–25n8

criminality, 5

crisis theory, 222n30

Crucible, The (Miller), 223n41

Cruz, Ted, 211–12

Cummings, Homer, 61

Cuordileone, K. A., 220n9

Curran, Charles, 82

Czolgosz, Leon, 73–74

Dailey, Dan, 139

Damaged Goods (Brieux), 34

Daughters of the American Revolution (DAR), 71, 76

Davies, Joseph E., 156

Davies, Richard, 106

Davis, Charles, 178

Dean, James, 10

Dean, Robert D., 220n9

Debs, Eugene V., 73

DeGroot, Margaret Mary, 84

D'Emilio, John, 98, 256n65

Dempsey, Jack, 161, 190

Department of Defense, 7, 71, 156–57, 171, 181

DeWeese, Cornelius, 228n71

Dewey, Thomas, 137–38

Dick Tracy (comic), 62

Dick Tracy's G-Men (serial), 61

Dietrich, Marlene, 139

Dillinger, John, 46, 55, 60, 62

dime novels, 26

Doherty, Thomas, 184–85, 269n160

Door County Young Republicans, 90

Douglas, Paul H., 105

Dulles, Allen, 161

Dulles, John Foster, 100, 261n28

Dunne, Matthew, 143

Durfee, James, 85–86

Dvorak, Ann, 60

Earp, Wyatt, 45–46, 58

Eberlein, Mike, 83, 238n17

economic panics, 26–27

Egan, Pierce, 78

Eighteenth Amendment, 67

Eisenhower, Dwight D., 159, 162–63, 165, 169, 181, 205, 259n1, 262n45

Eisenhower, Mamie, 259n1

Eliot, Charles William, 29

elitism: attack on, 91, 163; Eastern establishment, 149; Midwestern and Western states, 149–50; power elite, 107–8, 127; power elite, as term, 248n40

England, 32, 169; royal family, 265n108

Equitable Life Insurance Society, 61–62

espionage, 56–57, 75–76, 137, 141–42, 162, 202, 206, 259n4

Espionage Act, 73

Europe, 50, 97, 104, 168, 170, 179, 198–99

Everett, Willis M., 103

Evers, Walter A., 86

Evjue, Bill, 176, 178, 241n64

Ewen, Elizabeth, 103

Fairchild, Thomas E., 159

Faithfull, Starr, 138, 254n29

fascism, 70–71, 74, 128, 146

FBI in Peace and War, The (radio program), 61

Federal Bureau of Investigation (FBI), 11, 25, 44–46, 65, 70, 121–22, 127, 138, 140, 150–51, 155–56, 162, 167, 177, 183–84, 199, 209, 226n41, 230n13, 230n17, 232n34, 234n69, 234n75; agents, as action heroes, 47, 62; basketball team, 232n42; code of conduct, 55; code of ethics, 52; COINTELPRO, 205–6; counter-surveillance programs, 76; cultural depictions of, 72; domestic surveillance program, 74–75; as force for good, 62–63; gendered policies of, 77; and G-Men, 47, 60, 62; hiring practices, redesign of, 54–55; ideological warfare, as specialty of, 71; information, weaponizing of, 74; manliness, 57; masculine ideal, embodiment of, 52; masculinity, 57–58, 134–35; as modern policing unit, 51; moral character, 56; national security apparatus, central pillar of, 63; Obscene File, 49–51; obscenity, combatting of, 224–25n8; paternalistic role of, 63; Police Training School, 232n40; rebranding of, 52, 54–57; Sex Deviates File, 166; sexual morality, policing of, 51; subversives, investigating of, 205; White Slave Division, 73; wiretaps, use of, 51, 76–77, 205. *See also* Bureau of Investigation (BOI); G-Men

Feller, Abraham, 250n73

First Presbyterian Church of Washington, 34

First Red Scare, 183–84, 206. *See also* Red Scare; Second Red Scare

Fisher, Fred, 269n166

Flanagan, Flip, 260n14

Flanders, Ralph, 101, 201–2, 204, 244n101, 270n179

Fleischmann, Julius, 41–42

Floyd, "Pretty Boy," 46, 55, 60

Flynn, Edward J., 109–10, 248n41

flyting, 187

Folliard, Edward T., 118

football, 27, 32–33

Forbush, William Byron, 30

Foresman, Shirley, 92

Fort Monmouth investigations, 161–62, 172, 189, 199, 202, 259n4

Foster, Eric K., 144

Foster, Eugene C., 30

Founding Fathers, 59

Fox and Friends (news show), 211

Fox News, 211

Franklin, Benjamin, 27

Freedman, Estelle B., 98, 256n65

Freedom of Information Act, 252n11

Friedman, Andrea, 269n169

Friendly, Alfred, 155–56

From the Record (campaign mailer), 155–56; composograph, use of, 157–59

Front Page, The (Hecht and MacArthur), 121

Fuchs, Klaus, 131, 252n5

Fulbright, J. William, 159

Fulton, William, 147

Gabler, Neal, 13–14

Galante, Carmine, 209

Galleani, Luigi, 73

Gang Busters (radio serial), 61–62

Gannett, Betty, 121

Garrett, Pat, 58

Garrison, William Lloyd, 27

Gauvreau, Emile, 120

"G. David Schine in Hell" (Kushner), 261n25

gender, 4, 14, 39, 51, 58, 64, 128, 136, 174; American security state, 220n9; business management, gendered understanding of, 232n35; gendered boundaries, of newspaper industry, 121; gendered imagery, 71; gendered language, use of, 132, 190–91; gendered performance, 11; gender identity, 9, 11, 25, 47, 52, 77, 107–8, 113, 116–17, 122, 144, 183–84, 202, 219–20n6, 221n11, 269n169; gender inversion, 139; gender performativity, 222n27; gender politics, 134, 220n9; gender relations, 28, 31; gender roles, shifting of, 5, 8–9, 11, 29, 36, 41, 98, 116; gender segregation, 98; political culture, gendered valences of, 5; public percep-

tions of, 46; sexual identities, 15, 17; sexual politics, 7, 41; as socially constructed, 9

General Federation of Women's Clubs, 29, 58

Gentleman Prefer Blondes (film), 181

Gentry, Curt, 67, 237n125

Germany, 47–48, 148, 167, 257n89. See also West Germany

Gilbert, James, 222n30

Giles, Roscoe C., 123

Gillette, Guy, 159

girlie magazines, 134–35

G-Men, 47, 65, 69, 72, 137, 179, 192; creation of, 52–53, 206; as cultural icons, 60, 63, 77; as family men, 62–63; frontier lawmen, as modern incarnations of, 58; home, protecting of, 62; masculinity, as central to identity, 63; as moral figures, 77; myth, perpetuation of, 67; preparedness of, 57; in public imagination, 53; white-collar masculinity, personification of, 51, 56. See also Federal Bureau of Investigation (FBI)

G-Men (film), 60–61, 234n70

G-Men (radio program), 234n76

Goebbels, Joseph, 153

Goldman, Emma, 73–74

Goldwater, Barry, 161

Goodland, Walter S., 100

Goodman, Bill, 124

gossip, 4–5, 7, 12, 39, 65, 119, 153, 174, 180, 208, 210; celebrity, birth of, 6; circulating information, means of, 14; Cold War, effect on, 141; Cold War and Red Scare, fueled by, 6; columns, 66, 120, 127, 136, 162, 202; distilled malice, 13, 15, 17; domesticity, guardians of, 58; forms of, 12–13; impact of, 15; as industry, 6, 36, 120, 132; and innuendo, 6; journalism, 120–21, 253n25; and modernity, 14; in national security, 6; as perennial presence, 141; political intrigue, as source of, 184, 204; positive rumors, 13; power of, 13–14; rumor, difference from, 13; in shadow worlds, 14–15; surveillance, as form of, 15; as term, 12. See also gossip magazines

gossip magazines, 15, 41, 136, 163, 173, 195, 202, 208, 212; acceptable behavior, defining and policing of, 144; blind item, 38; flourishing of, 134; golden age of, 135; guilt by association, 211; hyperbole, 211; imitators of, 141; insinuation, 211; libel charges, avoiding of, 143; origins of, 36–37; photography, 26, 120; popularity of, 144, 184; tactics of, 132, 144, 211. See also individual magazines

Gotti, John, 209

Great Depression, 11, 63, 101, 121
Green, T. F., 161
Greenglass, David, 125, 250n80
Greenspun, Harold, 178–79, 181, *182*, 195,
265n107
Gregory, Thomas, 230n12
guilt by association, 16, 105, 132, 134, 143–44, 159,
174, 211

Hall, G. Stanley, 27
Hamilton, Alexander, 14
Hammett, Dashiell, 121, 234n75
Hanes, John W., 100
Hannity, Sean, 211
Hanson, Haldore, 152–53
Hantover, Jeffrey, 27–28
Harding, Warren G., 48, 52
Harriman, W. Averell, 41–42
Harris, Field, 92–93
Harrison, Robert, 135–36, 138–40, 185, 252n15
Hart, Ed, 83
Harvard University, 139
Hayden, Carl, 177
Hearst, William Randolph, 120, 212
Hefner, Hugh, 10
Heil, Julius P., 239n36
Hemmer, Nicole, 211
Herblock (cartoonist), 153, *200*
Hill, Jennie Earngey, 269n169
Hiss, Alger, 122–23, 131, 154, 204, 240n54, 247–
48n39, 249n59, 249n61
Hiss-Chambers trial, 122–23, 148
Hitler, Adolf, 153, 257n89, 265n107
Hitz, William, 230n12
Hoben, Allan, 30, 32–33
Hoey, Clyde, 150, 256n77
Hollywood (California), 137
Hollywood Production Code, 195, 269n160
Hollywood Ten, 141–42
homosexuality, 115, 209, 256n65, 256n77; attacks
on, 146–47, 150; blackmail, susceptibility to,
145, 148; Cohn, rumors of, 162, 170, 174, 179–
81, 184, 193, 195–202, 261n251, 270n172;
communism, link with, 122–23, 132, 147–48,
183–84; as dangerous, 148; fairy, usage of,
195; Hoover, rumors of, 64–65, 162, 207–8,
235n81; masculinity, as threat to, 108, 113;
McCarthy, rumors of, 87, 146, 162–63, 173–82,
182, 183–84, 193, 195–98, 200–202, 270n172;
obsession with, 265n108, 266n109; pixie,
usage of, 195; queer, as term, 219–20n6; sadomasochism, association with, 197; Schine,
rumors of, 170, 174, 179–81, 184, 193, 195–99,

261n25, 270n172; security risk, 144–45, 166;
sissy, as term, 219–20n6; slang terms, 139,
195, 240n54; in State Department, rumors of,
122–23, 144–50, 165–68, 198–99; Stevenson,
rumors of, 139–41, *142*
Hoover, Annie, 34, 36
Hoover, Dickerson, Jr., 21, 36
Hoover, Dickerson, Sr., 21–22, 35–36, 228n71
Hoover, J. Edgar, 5–8, 12, 20, 27, 44, 46, 49, 60,
68, 75, 79–80, 87–89, 100, 107–8, 118, 120, 127,
132–33, 137–38, 145–48, 153–56, 164, 166–67,
177, 183–84, 192, 199–200, *200*, 204, 206, 209,
211, 226n41, 230n13, 232n34, 232n38, 233n47,
234n70, 236n98, 255n53, 259n6; American
home, as defender of, 70; Americanism,
conception of, 58–59, 72; anticommunism,
embrace of, 139; authoritarianism of, 224–
25n8; as bachelor, 66, 68, 236n100; celebrity
status, 68, 236n100; character of, 24–25;
Christian manhood, 29, 33–36; class valedictorian, 23; cult of personality, fostering
of, 66, 206; as debater, 23–24; desanctification of, 206; distilled malice, target of, 17;
as domestic guardian, 70; domestic surveillance, 205–6; drill team, 23–24; effeminacy
of, 63–64; "Eleanor blue" wardrobe of, 64,
235n83; FBI, personification of, 25, 52; FBI,
rebranding of, 52, 54–57; foreign isms, as
threat to national security, 70–72, 206;
G-Man, creation of, 52–53, 206; G-Man,
as example of, 63, 69; and gossip, 15–16, 65,
208; height of, 23, 225n16; homogeneity, 23;
homosexuality, rumors of, 64–65, 162, 207–8,
235n81; Hooverism, 252n11; as household
name, 62; machismo of, 11, 47; manliness,
debate over, 63; manliness, definition of, 59;
martial discipline, belief in, 25; masculinity,
25, 52, 54, 64–66, 69–70, 139, 206, 208;
masculinity, as vehicle, 4; mass media, use
of, 77; McCarthy, association with, 150–51;
"mincing step," 64, 235n81; moral character,
and self-restraint, 56; muscular manhood,
adoption of, 11; myth, perpetuation of, 67;
national security apparatus, central pillar of,
63, 72, 74, 76–77; national security state and
masculinity, as link between, 77; newspapers
and magazines, contributions to, 56–57; nickname of, 22, 225n15; as nineteenth-century
relic, 21; Official and Confidential file on, 65;
the other, distrust of, 23; paternalistic role of,
63; public persona of, 208; public relations
push of, 45; queering of, 65, 207; rapid ascent
of, 48; as respected, 151; scientific policing

Milwaukee (Wisconsin), 81–82, 93, 176, 178–79, 181

Milwaukee County Young Republicans, 176

modernity, 36; and celebrity, 14; and gossip, 14

modernization, 11, 19–21, 30, 40; and individualism, 53

momism, 114–15; and McCarthyism, 246–47n29

Monroe, James, 34

Monroe, Marilyn, 181

Moore, Terry, 182–83

Morgan, J. P., 228n84

Morris, Robert J., 204

Mortimer, Lee, 135

Motion Picture (magazine), 136

Motion Picture Association (MPA), 60

Muncie (Indiana), 19

Mundt, Karl E., 172, 187, 189, 197, 266n116

Murphy, Audie, 94

Murrow, Edward R., 198, 269n169

muscular Christianity, 29, 31; origins of, 32

Naked and the Dead, The (Mailer), 195

Napoleon, 31, 227n46

National Enquirer (tabloid), 211–12. See also *New York Evening Enquirer* (newspaper)

National Police Academy, 50

National Purity Congress, 29

national security, 5; gender identity, 183

National Security Act, 7, 72–73

National Security Agency (NSA), 73, 137

National Security Council, 7, 205

national security state, 77, 128–29, 200, 206; advent of, 7; surveillance states, 72–73. *See also* security states

national surveillance, 4, 7; security state, and masculinity, 206

National Vigilance Association, 29

Nation of Islam, 205

Native Americans, 26

Nazism, 67, 71, 128, 186

Nebraska, 149

Nelson, "Baby Face," 46, 60

neurasthenia, 228n71

Nevada, 149

New Deal, 11–12, 62–63, 74, 83, 90, 95–97, 99, 103; and communism, 256n66; perversion, association with, 148

New England, 14

New England Watch and Ward Society, 28, 226n39

Newhouse, Si, 246n10

New York City, 29, 67, 73, 137, 167, 209; Jewish community, 111; nightlife circuit, 165

New York Daily Mirror (newspaper), 120

New York Daily News (newspaper), 120

New York Evening Enquirer (newspaper), 212. See also *National Enquirer* (tabloid)

New York Evening Graphic (magazine), 134, 144, 157, 212; composographs, pioneering of, 120–21; morally questionable tactics of, 121

New York Post (newspaper), 119

New York Society for the Suppression of Vice (NYSSV), 29, 226n41; Clean Books Crusade, 231n20

Nichols, Louis, 65, 151, 155

Nimitz, Chester W., 92–93

Nixon, Richard M., 133, 146, 149, 161, 164, 205, 210

North Dakota, 100

Obama, Barack, embracing of soft power, 272n21

O'Brian, John Lord, 85

O'Brien, Jack, 248n46

O'Donnell, Jack, 145

O'Dwyer, William, 110, 136–37

Ohio County Republican Women's Club, 130

old boys' network, 105

Old First Presbyterian, 52

On the Q.T. (magazine), 136, 143

Operation Whitewash, 132

Oppenheimer, J. Robert, 204

organization man, need for belonging, 251n92

Orton, Peter, 139

Oshinsky, David, 179, 204, 241n59, 252n2

Oswald, Lee Harvey, 212

Pacific Islands, 26

Palmer, A. Mitchell, 48, 73

Palmer Raids, 73–74

Parker, Bonnie, 46

Patton, George S., 265n96

Pearl Harbor, 57

Pearson, Drew, 125, 146, 171, 180–81, 198, 235n81, 254n39, 255n54, 265n96; coded language, use of, 270n172; McCarthy, homosexuality rumors, 174–78, 198, 270n172; McCarthy, as nemesis of, 174–75

Pecker, David J., 212

Pegler, Westbrook, 41, 120, 162

Peiper, Joachim, 103–4

Pendergast, Tom, 109

People (magazine), 224n47

Pepsi-Cola, 175

Peters, Andrew J., 138, 254n29

Pettegrew, John, 53, 222n26

Peurifoy, John, 144–45